AMBASSADORS OF
THE WORKING CLASS

ERNESTO SEMÁN

AMBASSADORS OF THE WORKING CLASS

Argentina's International Labor Activists
and Cold War Democracy in the Americas

Duke University Press—Durham and London—2017

Cover designed by Matthew Tauch
Interior designed by Courtney Leigh Baker
Typeset in Minion Pro and Din by Westchester Publishing Services

Library of Congress Cataloging-in-Publication Data
Names: Semán, Ernesto, [date] author.
Title: Ambassadors of the working class : Argentina's international labor activists and Cold War democracy in the Americas / Ernesto Semán.
Description: Durham : Duke University Press, 2017. | Includes bibliographical references and index.
Identifiers: LCCN 2017006738 (print) | LCCN 2017008444 (ebook) |
ISBN 9780822363859 (hardcover : alk. paper)
ISBN 9780822369059 (pbk. : alk. paper)
ISBN 9780822372950 (ebook)
Subjects: LCSH: International labor activities—Argentina. | Labor union members—Argentina. | Diplomatic and consular service—Argentina. | Peronism.
Classification: LCC HD6475.A1 S46 2017 (print)
LCC HD6475.A1 (ebook) | DDC 322/.20982—dc23
LC record available at https://lccn.loc.gov/2017006738

COVER ART: Illustration of a worker attaché from Luis Guillermo Bähler's *La nación Argentina: Justa, libre, soberana*. Buenos Aires: Peuser, 1950.

para Marambio, mi Castro,
y para Clarita

CONTENTS

ACKNOWLEDGMENTS

The acknowledgments section of a book is a space to affirm the reality of common ownership, a truth obscured under the alienated emphasis on one individual, "the author." We (the author and everybody mentioned below) have been working together on this study for many years, before we knew it, before it became a project.

One day, while working as a journalist during the 1999 presidential campaign in Argentina, I met Leopoldo Bravo, the long-time caudillo of the province of San Juan, who was offering the support of his powerful provincial political structure to the future president. We were at his office, and he sat in an armchair, brown, comfortable, nondescript. Bravo searched in one of his pockets and pulled out a pen.

"A gift from Stalin," he said.

Bravo had been part of the team that opened the first Argentine embassy in the Soviet Union, in 1947. In 1953, as ambassador, he was among the last foreigners to meet Stalin before he fell ill and died. The pen, it turned out, was not a gift from Stalin, but one more myth Bravo had built around his days in the Soviet Union. The day we met, Bravo also told me stories about the group of Argentines that represented the country in Moscow, including very colorful tales about the worker attachés, labor activists sent by President Juan Perón who joined the Argentine delegation in Moscow and throughout the world. In the Soviet Union, Bravo told me, the attachés had tried to smuggle Spanish refugees out of the country, but were discovered by Soviet agents on their way to Prague—one of the most extraordinary incidents Bravo experienced in his time there.

The conversation (along with the presidential campaign and my own life) took a different path, but I remained captivated by those labor activists, spread across the world, who nobody seemed to remember. Many years and several projects later, this book is the final result of that original spark.

Before that meeting with Bravo, I was fortunate to join conversations about populism and democracy under the guidance of a generous and brilliant group of Argentine intellectuals, who can collectively be represented by a reference to three institutions—the School of Sociology at the University of Buenos Aires, circa the late 1980s; the Club de Cultura Socialista; and the political journal *La Ciudad Futura*—and to the names José Aricó, Juan Carlos Portantiero, and Jorge Tula.

This book is, to a great extent, part of ongoing conversations with friends, two of them in particular: Greg Grandin and Mark Healey. I met Mark Healey in February 2001. We sat at Rocco in the Village and started to discuss politics, literature, and history. We have not stopped since then. Mark gently induced me to become a historian, and helped me to make the most of that step, including countless revisions and edits for this book. With him, I thought about the unique relation between Perón and labor activism, and the schism between them that is central for this study. I benefit from Mark's unwavering intellectual curiosity and even more so from his enormous friendship, as well as that of the entire Healey-Parera family. This book is one of the many adventures we plan to share.

Greg Grandin knew what I wanted to say better and earlier than I did. That was partly because of the patience with which he read hundreds of pages of my drafts, persisting until he found the version that could be interesting. But more important, he is able to absorb an almost infinite range of ideas and stories, and then draw them out of his mind in the form of an intellectual project. He has been a most generous mentor since we first met in 2007. The "feedback effect" of Peronism in U.S. domestic politics discussed in this book owes much to his insights and our conversations. His friendship, his welcoming home, and his family have made these years of work a pleasant journey.

Over these years, Barbara Weinstein has inspired me at every step of the way, personally and intellectually. Her subtle reflections about Latin American populism have enriched my understanding of the region's modern history and improved this work in many ways. To Barbara I also owe, among other things, the title of this book. Sinclair Thomson has opened for me more worlds than he can imagine. Years ago, he asked his students if we wanted to start a seminar on Latin American history by discussing the 1,299 pages of Trotksy's *History of the Russian Revolution*—a suggestion that shows the degree of dedication and creativity that he puts into training future scholars. As a whole, the history department at New York University is an island of intellectual commitment within an institution that otherwise seeks to prioritize profit and influence to the detriment of critical thinking. On such an island, I benefited immensely from the work of Ada Ferrer, Linda Gordon, Manu Goswami, Molly Nolan, Marilyn Young, and Danny Walkowitz.

I worked all these years side by side with Carmen Soliz. We talked about every single page of our works, and then we talked about everything else. My daughter carries a broad smile on her face each time she sees her. I believe that my daughter's smile expresses, too, the love I feel for mi amiga. For many years, Jennifer Adair and I worked together in our individual projects. We learned a lot, and we enjoyed it. I benefited immensely from our conversations and her insights on Latin American and U.S. history. Dylan Yeats, his reports from the belly of the beast, his boundless love, and our interminable walks are a not-so-hidden force of this project.

Throughout the years, I discussed parts of this work with several colleagues. Javier Auyero's insights were immensely helpful in the last stage of writing this book; his suggestions improved crucial arguments. His work and our friendship over the decades, as well as the friendship of his father and his family, are a source of calm and inspiration. This book has also benefited from readings, suggestions, and comments from Barry Carr, Michelle Chase, Martín Sivak, Josh Frens-String, Max Paul Friedman, Margaret Power, Jorge Nállim, Patrick Iber, Christine Mathias, Leandro Morgenfeld, Aldo Marchesi, Christy Thornton, and Miguel Winograd.

Endless conversations about Peronism are a national sport in Argentina. Those that I have had in Buenos Aires with Gerardo Aboy Carlés, Carlos Altamirano, Gastón Chillier, Alberto D'Alotto, Martín Granovsky, Jorge Taiana, and Mario Wainfeld have materially informed this book.

Colleagues and officials at the Argentine Ministry of Foreign Affairs have also made this project possible. Héctor Timerman has been enormously generous all these years, providing all kinds of support and granting me access to very valuable sources and documents. Some of the most revealing sources about the history of the worker attachés came from uncatalogued copies of reports found on the premises of Argentine embassies, in bookshelves, lockers, and desks that had not been touched in decades. Copies of dispatches describing six vibrant years of history in Bolivia, for example, were lost in a desk in the basement of the Argentine embassy. A retired worker approached the Argentine ambassador to Cuba in a small town far from Havana to give her a brochure that a worker attaché had distributed there more than half a century before. It would have been impossible to rescue these documents without the generosity and cooperation of the following people: Counsellor

Silvina Montenegro, in Bolivia; Ambassador Darío Alessandro and his wife, Marta Cichero, in Perú; Ambassador Juliana Marino, in Cuba; Ambassador Ernesto López, in Guatemala; and Ambassador María Cristina Perceval, with whom I worked for two years at the United Nations.

Several people provided me with invaluable help during the editing of this book. Rachel Nolan edited an early version of the manuscript. Her perceptive reading detected problems in arguments and sources throughout the book; always, she generously offered me a solution. Elizabeth DeBusk-Maslanka edited one version of the text, improving it throughout. This is a better book thanks to Isis Sadek, who did a wonderful job with the final revision of the manuscript. She detected problems, spotted "hispanismos," and suggested ways to refine the arguments. My special thanks to Gisela Fosado, at Duke University Press, for her trust in this project and for the kindness with which she guided me along the way. Also at Duke, Lydia Rappoport-Hankins and Danielle Houtz provided valuable editorial assistance.

I counted on the help and dedication of the people working at the following archives and libraries: in Argentina, CeDinCI, Archivo de la Cancillería Argentina, Archivo Internmedio del Archivo General de la Nación, and Archivo del Sindicalismo Argentino at Universidad Torcuato Di Tella; in the United States, the Tamiment and Bobst Libraries at New York University, the Rare Books and Manuscripts Library at Columbia University, the Kheel Center at the Catherwood Library at Cornell University, the Hoover Institution at Stanford University, the Boatwright Library at the University of Richmond, the U.S. National Archives, the Mudd Manuscript Library at Princeton University, and the Eisenhower Presidential Library; in Colombia, the Archivo General de la Nación.

I am thankful to the many public libraries (and their workers) in which I wrote this book. In particular, the Biblioteca Nacional in Argentina and the Biblioteca Nacional in Chile, the Carroll Gardens branch of the Brooklyn Public Library, the New York Public Library, the Cambridge Public Library, and the Henrico County Public Library, where I am writing these lines.

During the last two years, I have been working at the University of Richmond's Jepson School of Leadership Studies. I cannot think of a better place to finish this book. Jepson, the university and, above all, my colleagues here, have been enormously generous. They provided me with the time and resources and friendship to make my life and work easier and more exciting.

Relatives of the attachés and protagonists of this study scattered around the world offered their time to share memories (and reports and pictures and mementos): Hugo Soriani (my infinite gratitude), Carlos Tomasini, Irene

Segovia, the Antueno family, Torcuato Di Tella, Pedro Conde Magdaleno (son) and Pedro Conde Magdaleno (grandson), Edelberto Torres Rivas, and Silvia Maestro.

Several people provided all kinds of support during these years, including friendship, advice, ideas, food, loans, housing, babysitting, a drink, encouragement: Mariano Siskind, Analía Ivanier and the two *galanes*, Valentín and Bruno, Claudio Benzecry, Daniel Fridman, Manuel Trancón, Jane Folpe, Michael Staunton, Susan Schneider, Gabriel Puricelli Yañez, Beatriz Taber (for being always there), Sylvia Molloy, Martín Plot (our conversations opened for me the appetite for analyzing U.S. politics through Latin American lenses that is central for this book), Diego Armus, Sergio Chejfec, Graciela Montaldo, Claudia Prado, Diego Panich, Guillermo Bodner, Pablo Semán (my brother, a guiding example of intellectual commitment), Charlotte Gartenberg, Hernán Iglesias Illa, Bat Ami Klejner (and Leo, Kayla, and Luca), Mariela Méndez and her family in Richmond, Jenny Pribble and her family in Richmond, María Esperanza Casullo and her family in Richmond, Felipe Muller (and the incredible Christmas of 2010), Tommy (for being there only when I needed it), Andrea Oñate, Eduardo Porretti, Eduardo Valdes, Guadalupe Gallo, and Alejandro Bonvechi.

I am fortunate to have Mariluz and Sime, my *suegros*, in my life. They have provided warmth and food and love during our stays in Chile. Their house feels like ours, only with the best *sopaipillas* in Latin America. And they have become the best *abuelos* that we could have wished for our daughter.

Elias Semán, my father, disappeared in 1978 during the military dictatorship in Argentina. According to witnesses, he spent his last days at the concentration camp El Vesubio wondering about his sons—and about the notes he was taking for a book on Argentine history. My mother, Susana Bodner, took care of both, sons and notes, and for the rest of her life sought the truth in a future of hope. I learned from them in the most courageous and joyful ways that history is about people's collective struggle for a better life and what we make out of what happened with those struggles.

Above all, Soledad Marambio, mi Castro—her life has changed mine. She deserves more than I can express in a few lines. We've built a family of books and people and love that I could not have even imagined before we met. And this is only the beginning. This work is dedicated to her and to our daughter, Clarita, history in the making, whose first toy was an Ikea doll with a hard hat we attached to it, christened "Monsieur Attaché."

INTRODUCTION. **FROM THE FRINGES OF THE NATION TO THE WORLD**

In 2009, as the United States entered the seventeenth month of its Great Recession, some 15 million American workers were jobless. With the burst of the housing bubble, the economy shrank by 3 percent in its fifth consecutive year of decline. People bought fewer cars, computers, and furniture. Factories were closing across the country. Comparisons to the Great Depression and the New Deal abounded, but there were a few more recent references by which people and policymakers could make sense of the crisis and possible ways out of it.[1] Then, on 30 April, the government announced the takeover of General Motors and Chrysler as part of an effort to protect them from shutdown and to prevent the cascade effect that such closures would have on economic activity and employment. That morning, the conservative radio host Rush Limbaugh presented this news to his audience with the following declaration: "In a few short minutes, the president of the United States, Barack Perón, will announce his Argentinean-like takeover of Chrysler."[2]

Most likely, Limbaugh's American audience were not familiar with Juan Perón or with what he did in Argentina in the 1940s. But in 2009, the name "Perón" still could stand for something liable to enrage Limbaugh's listeners about Obama's approach to the crisis. If Limbaugh's invocation made sense at least to him and his followers, it was largely because Perón's name conveyed a set of meanings and images: power for unions, industrial workers, wealth redistribution, and government intervention in the economy, with the threat it posed to private property in the name of the common good.

Fast forward seven years. Against all odds, Donald Trump succeeded in challenging political elites during the presidential campaign. He had not yet won the election, but commentators already struggled to find historical examples to explain the appeal of his vociferous movement. On 11 August, the *Financial Times* ran an article titled: "Donald Trump Evokes Latin America's Old Style Strongmen." The article was illustrated with cartoons of Trump, Venezuelan leader Hugo Chávez, and, yes, Perón. Many followed. "Is Donald Trump a Peronist?" "It's What Perón Sounded Like." This time, analysts' emphasis was not only placed on government intervention in the economy, but on the supposed political irrationality of the lower classes: under economic duress, blue-collar workers—allegedly unlike bankers or dentists—are prone to support demagogues who trick them into believing that there are easy shortcuts to their daily hardships.[3]

Where did those images associated with Perón come from? How did they arrive in the United States in 2009 or 2016? Many of them were born in the mid-1940s in remote places like León Segovia's house in the Chaco territory, a region in northern Argentina, eight hundred miles from Buenos Aires. On 9 December 1946, Segovia received a letter with a presidential seal and the signature of President Juan Perón. Segovia was a welder at Las Palmas, a sugar mill that belonged to an Irish couple until a traditional Argentine family bought both it and the entire town. Housing, food, drink, currency—everything was provided by the mill. Of criollo descent and indigenous features, Segovia did not even use the official Spanish language at home.[4] Although fluent in Spanish, he spoke mostly Guaraní—a language spoken by native inhabitants of the Chaco Forest—with his parents and friends. Three aspects of Segovia's life were deeply entangled with the larger national community: he was a member of his union, he had had run-ins with the National Gendarmerie, and he had voted for Colonel Juan Perón in the presidential elections. His decision to vote for Perón seemed an unlikely one, given that his socialist union had supported the republic in the Spanish Civil War and the Allies in World War II, while Perón was a nationalist who revered Spanish Falangism and belonged to a group of officers with Nazi sympathies.

In the official letter, President Perón notified Segovia that he had been selected as a student in the training course for diplomatic worker attachés.[5] It was a new position within the Argentine foreign service that Perón created a few weeks after taking office. Along with Segovia, approximately one hundred rank-and-file union members received similar letters. The General Confederation of Labor (CGT) had selected its most valued activists to represent Argentina abroad. A few months later, leaving the country for the first time in their lives, Segovia and forty other labor activists traveled to embassies worldwide with the mission of spreading Perón's gospel of social revolution. Originating from the small towns of the countryside and the crowded working-class suburbs of Buenos Aires, the attachés were stationed in Washington, São Paulo, Moscow, Bogotá, and Paris, "as [Perón's] personal representatives beyond the national borders."[6] Over the following decade, five hundred labor activists became members of the Argentine foreign service.[7] Self-described as Perón's proud foot soldiers, they represent the largest presence of blue-collar workers in the foreign service of any country in history.[8]

Once abroad, the attachés wielded their own diplomatic position as proof of the swift changes occurring in Argentina under Perón. Nowhere else had workers accomplished so much, reaching positions in a realm usually reserved for elites. As part of their mission, they described the Argentine reality: hundreds of factories—many of them state-owned—were producing everything from steel to canned food. Unions held unprecedented bargaining power. They managed hotels for their workers at the most scenic vacation resorts. And hospitals and schools were free to all. The attachés showed that the daily caloric intake of an Argentine worker was among the highest in the world. And they emphatically attributed these advances to Perón and his wife, Eva Perón. In diplomatic dispatches, personal letters, and news articles, they reported back to Argentina about a European continent ravaged by the war. From Latin America, they described with ethnographic precision the meager wages of workers at an oil refinery in Peru and the kilometers that Guatemalan peasants at a plantation had to walk between their shacks and the first source of running water. From the United States, they chronicled layoffs at telephone companies, the end of rent regulation, which had benefited low-income workers during the New Deal, and the massive strikes in the automaker sector. The attachés made sure that the setbacks of unions and the efforts of the business sector to reverse workers' gains in the United States were widely publicized in Argentina and the rest of Latin America.

The attachés joined the democratic spring that swept Latin America after 1945. The contrast in the achievements of organized labor at home and the difficulties of workers abroad reinforced their belief in the exceptionality of the Peronist recipe. And this, in turn, provided a class ethos to a long-standing sense of predestination and to ambitions for regional leadership that ran deep in Argentine nationalism. They promoted Peronism as a path for the expansion of social citizenship for the emerging working class and denounced

U.S. foreign policy as an ally of local elites in obstructing that mission. With this basic toolkit of ideas, they allied with the leftist leader Jorge Eliécer Gaitán in 1948 in Colombia and made sure that indigenous people in Peru had a copy of Perón's Declaration of the Rights of Workers, which had been translated into Quechua by 1950. They funded an early venture abroad of a young Cuban law student, Fidel Castro, and befriended an equally young Argentine doctor, Ernesto Guevara. In 1954, a Peronist attaché sheltered members of the future leadership of the Guatemalan guerrilla in the Argentine embassy during the CIA-backed military coup.

The attachés confronted U.S. labor diplomats of the American Federation of Labor and Congress of Industrial Organizations (AFL-CIO), who had deployed representatives throughout the world since the end of World War II. Particularly in Latin America, they had worked closely with the U.S. government, the State Department, the Central Intelligence Agency (CIA), and the business sector. Labor diplomats became part of the larger U.S. efforts to contain communism by gaining the support of workers in the region for the strengthening of liberal democracy.[9] The U.S. labor diplomats saw Peronism as a fascist threat and worked with U.S. officials in containing Perón's transnational aims. They shared with Peronism the idea that inequality was a major problem in Latin America. They also argued that democracy could not be achieved without social reform. But they claimed that workers should gain their rights without violent upheavals of social order, which could be used by demagogues (i.e., Perón) to create a totalitarian government that would curtail citizens' freedoms.[10] The Peronist specter captured the concerns of officials and elites in the Americas. By 1946, Argentina was already mentioned as one of the main threats to democratic liberalism in the document that became the blueprint for Cold War containment.[11] And two years later, a U.S. official stationed in Europe reflected, "The threat which gives us the worst case of cold shivers is that of a southern bloc dominated by Argentina."[12] Attachés like Segovia came to represent this menace to the extent that their actions were eventually described by Robert Alexander, the scholar with the greatest influence on U.S. officials working with organized labor in Latin America, as part of "the whole *Peronista* propaganda apparatus . . . against the United States [that] outdid even that of the Communists."[13] By the onset of the Cold War, the image of Peronism as a symbol of social change gone awry was engraved in such a powerful way that it survived the Cold War itself. Seven decades and five thousand miles later, the specter reemerged in the voice of a swooning Limbaugh during the first major social crisis of the twenty-first century.

Ambassadors of the Working Class is a transnational history of the hopes and fears stirred by populist politics in the Americas and of the competition between Peronist and U.S. labor diplomats for the conquest of the region's labor movement. At the core of the study is the question of how organized labor became crucial in defining democracy in the postwar Americas. It explores the way in which debates about the "labor question" influenced contemporary perceptions of social rights, individual freedom, national sovereignty, and the common good across the Americas. This study centrally shows how, against the background of the growth of urban working classes in Latin America, U.S. labor diplomats and promoters of economic and political liberalism placed emphasis on the primacy of private-property rights, individual free-dom, negligible government intervention in the economy, and free trade, in-evitably clashing with populist and nationalistic labor leaders who located social rights and a moral economy at the center of their democratic agenda. From this competition between liberal and populist projects emerged chang-ing visions of democracy, which defined Latin American politics during the first years of the Cold War.[14]

This book tells the history of the Peronist worker attachés from their emergence in 1946 until a military dictatorship ousted Perón (and expelled the attachés from government) in 1955. During those years, the attachés joined a wide range of movements in the region, promoting social reform and pre-senting the centrality of workers' rights as the distinctive quality of Argentine democracy. The narrative ends toward 1959 with the triumph of the Cuban Revolution, the year in which we can locate the exhaustion of this form of populist politics. This book analyzes three different but connected aspects of the attachés' story: the domestic transformations in Peronist Argentina that they helped to set in motion; their efforts to create a regional movement in Latin America inspired by the Peronist success; and, finally, the confronta-tion of U.S. officials, labor diplomats, and elites against Peronism and its regional ambitions.

Fashioning an Identity for the Argentine Working Class

The backdrop of *Ambassadors of the Working Class* is the growing presence of workers in Argentine society during the first half of the twentieth century and the changes this presence produced after 1945 with the rise of Peronism. Few things were more disruptive of the national cultural milieu than the ac-cess of labor activists, most of them from anarchist and socialist background and with no formal education, to the most aristocratic realm of public administration. Perón created the program of worker attachés only six weeks after taking office. With a stroke of a pen, workers invaded the Ministry of Foreign Affairs, the area dominated by patrician families who had used their diplomatic position to build the idea of exceptionality of the "Argentine race," as Argentine society was presented to the rest of the world.[15] In the diplomatic world, labor was a worldwide focus of attention since the 1910s, when the foreign offices of many European countries started to report on workers' living conditions overseas. But the program of worker attachés not only described workers lives and aimed to promote Peronism abroad; it also reshuffled domestic power relations. One need only compare the picture of the first cohort of worker attachés to any portrait of diplomats of the time to get a sense of the revulsive effects of Peronism in established ideas of power, hierarchies, and rights (see figure Intro.1). Dark-skinned faces, suits that did not fit them elegantly, lack of hats, an abundance of short dark moustaches in lieu of polished white beards, their youth—every detail indicated the ascent of a new class. Notably, the presence of only one woman (the unnamed administrative secretary of the program) suggested some continuity with old institutional traditions. Workers' access to greater economic resources and their growing participation in political power provided clear evidence of their arrival to a more inclusive society. The story of these attachés exposes the inextricable link between economic redistribution and the myriad of symbolic and institutional transformations that lay at the center of the democratization of Peronist Argentina.[16] The restricted role of women in the program also highlights the limits of that democratization. No more than twenty women received a worker attaché diploma, and just three of them went abroad as diplomats. The fact that Eva Perón took the program under her wing could have suggested a wider opportunity for Peronist women to engage in labor diplomacy. But as was also the case with the creation of the Partido Peronista Femenino, gendered power relations under Peronism exhibit the ambivalences of populist political dynamics. The movement led by Perón and Evita opened up new spaces for the political participation of women, while recreating patriarchal hierarchies that often demanded women be subordinate to the leading role of men.[17]

At the center of this history is labor activism. Rank-and-file union members and labor activists have been a fruitful area of study in the history of Peronism. The study of their actions has shifted the understanding of populist politics away from top-down approaches (with their emphasis on state control of labor, indoctrination, and personalism) and from bottom-up ones

FIGURE I.1. The first cohort of worker attachés at the public school in Buenos Aires where the training courses took place during the first year of the program, October 1946. The distinguishable features and clothing of Argentine workers contrasts with the usual pictures of members of the Foreign Service, who were drawn from the national elites. Only one woman appears among the attachés—the administrative secretary of the program. Source: Personal papers of Eduardo de Antueno.

(with their emphasis on workers' agency and workers' lively productivity in public life).[18] Yet few studies have focused on workers' new roles in foreign affairs, even at a moment when the country's position in the postwar global order has been a main domestic concern.[19] This book examines the crucial function of these activists in the creation of a political identity among workers, taking "identity" as a less essentialist notion than "class consciousness," but stressing the construction of a shared subjectivity among workers as central to the existence of a working class.

Labor activism in Argentina, of course, predates 1945. But as a working-class political identity, Peronism has been the most powerful, effective, and lasting in history. Scholarly focus on labor activism tries to answer the simple questions of how workers came to present their individual grievances as a collective cause and how that collective cause took a specific Peronist shape. As the labor historian David Montgomery put it in relation to the labor movement in the United States, a basic and very political step is workers' realization that while others in society could wield power and influence as individuals, workers' could obtain what they wanted only through collective action.[20] Conceiving of individual complaints, deprivations, and demands as part of a collective project is not the unmediated product of workers' material condition (nor is it, I should add, the simple effect of indoctrination). It is a project built by activists seeking to "foster a sense of unity and purposiveness among their fellow workers through the spoken and printed word, strikes, meetings . . . and to promote through those activities widely shared analyses of society and of paths to the 'emancipation of labor.'"[21] This realization, which has formed the heart of social history since the 1960s, is the key to this story, decentering an international history from its narrower narrative of diplomatic relations, restoring the realm of human experience in the study of working-class politics and of this rare space of labor history.[22]

Ambassadors of the Working Class focuses on these labor activists to analyze how the first years of Peronism were produced, lived, and decoded as a cultural conflict. Scholars have employed the term *cultural* to downplay the significance of those conflicts against "real" changes that would entail, in this case, the expropriation of means of production. On the contrary, the present reframing of this historical object as a cultural one is an effort to interpret the wider inputs that constitute it or to analyze it, as would have been said decades ago under the influence of Gramsci, within the historical bloc of a socioeconomic formation.[23] The analysis therefore comprises the economic transformations that affected Argentina, the relation between institutions and citizens and between government and organized labor, and domestic and international economic policies and constraints. Above all, it focuses on the traditions and cultures that informed (and were reimagined by) the supporters of and the opposition to Peronism. The opening to workers of spaces of power like the Cancillería, as the Foreign Ministry is known, is sufficient to understand the support that Peronism garnered. Yet considering how elites were able to preserve their space and privileges and, to a large extent, to contain the advance of the worker attachés, the vitriolic reaction against them can be understood as a concern about shattered hierarchies. Elites reacted to the arrival of Peronism by deploying a battery of characterizations that emphasized the cultural differences rather than the material interests affected. The detractors of Peronism described Perón's followers as *cabecitas negras* and the arrival of the movement they created as a *zoological flood*; in the case of the attachés, they questioned the workers' ability to assume positions of power in society beyond the bounds of organized labor and their ability to acquire skills beyond the world of laborers. The fears that the presence of a worker with diplomatic status at an Argentine embassy triggered among elites should not be analyzed in relation to the actual impact of workers actions but to a new culture that this presence imposed. To understand these reactions as part of the cultural historical phenomenon implies a crucial assertion about the period: Peronism came to power at a moment of deep political crisis in the Americas. Raising the labor question after World War II challenged not only the distribution of wealth but also the very idea of the social order and hierarchies from which the distribution of wealth derives.[24]

Within this approach, *Ambassadors of the Working Class* explores the investment of labor activists, policymakers, and leaders within Peronism in creating a vision that made sense of the changes it was producing. The lack of a preceding ideological corpus, the efforts of indoctrination, the centrality of the leader, and the florid loquacity of Perón have led to an underestimation of any ideological corpus in Peronism. Nothing could be further from the reality of those early years. The case of the attachés shows that the realm of foreign affairs became a suitable venue to work out the contradictions among the competing worldviews gathered under Perón's leadership and to synthesize them into a relatively coherent whole. This worldview was not lacking conflicts as Perón's foreign policy evolved from a class-based nationalism with anti-imperialist tones to a conservative nationalism that joined the U.S. crusade against communism. But even those changes required extensive debates, were interpreted in conflicting ways, and were translated into different actions. This function of foreign affairs as a realm that absorbed contested ideas and produced a new synthesis was clearly expressed in the training courses for attachés.

This space was a unique laboratory in which attachés like Segovia—most of them former communist, socialist, and anarchist activists with international experience in the support of labor in the Spanish Republic—met a group of professors selected by Perón from his cohort of Argentine nationalists, Spanish Falangists, and Catholic *integralistas*. For weeks, leftist activists, rightist intellectuals, and Perón himself debated how Marxism and the teachings of the Church could coalesce into a new political vision. Later, attaché reports that contrasted the prosperity of Argentina with the labor setbacks in the United States and the daily deprivations under Stalin in the Soviet Union contributed to the domestic legitimacy of a Third Position as an alternative to liberalism and communism. Finally, their actions in Latin America to seek a rapprochement with democratic and revolutionary movements pushing for social reform and their denunciation of U.S. foreign policy outlined a version of Peronism different from the one their leader promoted.[25]

The Leader, Revisited

One crucial aspect of Peronism revealed by the study of the attachés is the divergent strategies, ideas, and actions of Perón and of the labor activists who followed him, manifested in their notions of how to push for social change. *Ambassadors of the Working Class* reveals how activists configured spaces of action alternative both to their subordination to Perón and to a frontal rebellion against him. Within the constraints of nationalism, the attachés downplayed Perón's instructions and developed strategies that were different from, or plainly against, Perón's foreign policy; yet they always acted in the name of Perón, without questioning his authority. Their background in international labor solidarity, the relations they built with other activists, their own idea of Peronism, what they witnessed abroad, the forms of political affect built over time—all these factors contributed to mold their identity. By establishing alliances with communist forces, supporting labor struggles against regimes supported by Perón, or sheltering leftist activists from military repression backed by Argentina, they produced a form of Peronism different from that of their leader. The story of the attachés opens a window into the lively reality of those early years that goes beyond straight subordination of activists to Perón or their outspoken rebellion. The book proposes an alternative reading of Peronism as the history of the perpetual and always imperfect attempt by Perón to put the proverbial working-class genie back into the bottle. It shows not only that Perón might have been the first victim of the plebeian spirit of the movement he created, but also that the failure to entirely contain the "heretical challenge" of labor activists was, paradoxically, a central part of Peronism's long-term survival.[26]

Most studies devote their attention to the consequences of Perón's efforts to subordinate the labor movement, its dependency on the state, and how unions' blind loyalty to Perón limited their autonomy. While acknowledging the relevance of these elements in Peronism's demobilizing effects on organized labor, I rearrange these elements by also showing Perón's frustrated efforts to discipline its labor base. The book shows the activists efforts to pull their leader and the movement, against all odds, back to the inclusive policies of the early years, to its emancipatory rhetoric, to its symbology of hope.

In order to understand the potential and limitations of this strategy, it is important to note that this happened during a period in Argentine history when Peronism was perceived not only as the best option for labor, but as the only one. For unions in many Latin American countries (including Brazil, Uruguay, Chile, and Bolivia), nationalism was one more program in a menu of competing options for advancing workers' rights. Liberal, leftist, or ethnic identities were all means of expressing realistic alternatives of power, separately or in various combinations.[27] In Argentina, competition for the heart of the working class was limited at best. The rise of Peronism shattered the Left's base, and it would neither recover its strength nor present a viable alternative to Peronism for decades.[28] In order to confront Peronism, liberal and moderate parties opted for alliances with conservative sectors and economic elites, all groups that became increasingly reactionary in their social views as the Cold War settled in. By the early 1950s, when Perón showed a manifest interest in social containment, he managed to foreclose other political options on the Left. So, lacking any other available options, it seemed reasonable for workers and activists to try to make the best out of the movement they had already helped to create.

Within these constraints, Peronist nationalism provided a very productive "language of contention" for the fashioning of an Argentine working-class identity.[29] As such, it would be absurd not to see its enormous (and at times tragic) shortcomings. Perón's actions also reoriented labor activism onto demobilizing paths. Activists did not act in a historical vacuum, and the program of worker attachés suffered the consequences of Perón's conservative policies in terms of decreasing resources, conflicting signals, and plain rejection by their leader. There is no spoiler to this story if we anticipate that the main goal of the attachés, the creation of a regional labor movement inspired by Peronism, never materialized. The focus on the agency of labor activism does not disregard these factors. Instead, it seeks to illuminate crucial aspects of mass politics that explain Peronism's appeal during the postwar and its enduring legacies in Latin America. Over the last decade, scholars have focused on cases studies about Peronism, providing very precise reflections on aspects such as public policies, geographical differences, identity formation and policies in the rural sector, relation with local elites from the interior, and broader social transformations in leisure and consumption. The result is a complex and multifaceted picture of the movement and a very nuanced assessment of the impact of the first decade of Peronism. Yet the prevailing impression still is that the rise of Perón was a watershed in Argentine history. The transformations that it set in motion could be perceived in daily life as well as in the country's social structure and political institutions. This book joins the work of these scholars by providing an account of the still unexplored case of the worker attachés.[30]

In this respect, the approach of *Ambassadors of the Working Class* to the relation between leader and followers is informed by two important scholarly interventions of the last two decades. One involves debates in the fields of sociology and anthropology about twentieth-century patron-client networks and clientelism. A growing body of works has illuminated the potential and limits of those exchanges, bringing to light the agency of clients in the face of patrons and powerbrokers, the vast symbolic economy involved in those exchanges, and the reproduction of hierarchies and inequalities within the egalitarian projects and practices.[31] The second is the recent historiography about Latin American *caudillismo* during the period of state formation in nineteenth-century Latin America. Earlier works about mass politics developed under the shadows of modernizing theories stressed how "strongmen" in Latin America were in a position to divert people's rational choices by offering paternalistic protection during their transition from traditional to modern, abstract social relations.[32] These approaches often obscured those leaderships' democratizing undercurrents. The renewed scholarly interest in *caudillista* politics has not taken for granted the motivations of followers, exploring instead symbolic and material exchanges, as well as the wide range of onsite opportunities that this relationship with the leaders offered for followers.[33]

Inevitably, questions about the depth of the changes operated by Peronism, the conflicts between state policies and labor activism, and the tensions between the expansion of social citizenship and Perón's conservative authoritarianism remit to the protean attributes of the category of "populism." Partly because it is not a "native category" that the protagonists themselves assumed as an identity, "populism," or more exactly "Latin American populism," has eluded concrete definition. Political changes in Europe and the United States such as the vote in the United Kingdom to leave the European Union and the triumph of Trump in the U.S. presidential elections, both in 2016, precipitated extensive reflections about the appeal of populist discourses. This defective origin and its later expanded usage have also produced a rather taxing test in academic debates for the exact meaning of "populism" that few other categories would pass. Problematic notions such as "citizenship," "civil society," or "liberalism" are frequently employed with fewer qualms.[34] Yet, elusive as its meaning might be, "populism" has been nonetheless applied to define Peronism as a historical object, a radical expression of the "classic" cases of populism that include also Varguismo in Brazil and Cardenismo in Mexico.[35] The historian Tulio Halperín Donghi never used the category "populism," yet he provided the clearest description of a populism from below, in tension with its cultural attributes and the limits of its transformations. Analyzing the changes triggered since 1945, he did not hesitate to describe the rise of Peronism as a revolution: "Only those who believe that it was a blasphemy to doubt the existence of only one social revolution . . . could argue against the idea that Peronism was in fact one [social revolution]: under the aegis of the Peronist regime, all the relations between social groups were suddenly redefined, and one needed only to walk the streets or ride a streetcar to notice this."[36]

For the purpose of this work, I will use the term *populism* in three different and related forms. The first is as a *historical phenomenon* in relation to the movements that swept Latin American status quo in the 1930s and 1940s with the arrival of mass politics. Characterized by strong personalist leadership, authoritarian and yet highly effective in expanding economic and political citizenship for the working class, these movements produced what can be called a form of authoritarian democratization. They are usually exemplified with the national cases of Cardenismo in Mexico, Varguismo in Brazil, and Peronism in Argentina. Not surprisingly, they are named after the leaders who created them and present substantial differences between themselves. The second use of the term *populism* follows the *political language* of U.S. officials, journalists, and labor diplomats during the postwar in relation to Peronism in particular and to their concern about the dominant role of the leader and the perceived subjection of the labor movement to the government. The third is as a *category of analysis* of Cold War social sciences. Intellectuals throughout the Americas focused on these movements to reflect on the relationship between mass politics, modernization theories, and the individual. They contended that collective action and its expression in working-class politics in the form of unions posed a threat to freedom and rational political choice. Most contemporary uses of the term "populism" carry reverberations of these ideas.

Turning Transnational

The rallying cry "Workers of the World, Unite!" is an unmistakable sign of the transnational roots of the labor movement from its inception. This signal is even clearer in the case of labor activists who were also diplomats. The worker attachés offer a unique opportunity for a novel transnational history of Peronism. *Ambassadors of the Working Class* examines the actions and ideas of the Argentine attachés, as well as those of Latin American and U.S. labor and political movements, that mutually shaped crucial notions about the place of workers in society. In particular, it discusses how answers to the question of labor and to the emergence of mass societies traveled beyond national borders. This movement of ideas fashioned a new hemispheric order, which manifested itself not only in national political bodies and the emerging inter-American system, but also in cultural preferences and notions of social rights as much as in individual, racial, and gendered hierarchies. It also contributed to a fluid understanding of common good and of how a democratic society should look. The attachés sought to expand a particular "Peronist" answer to these questions. While they promoted populist ideas and the figures of Perón and Evita, they were ultimately engaged in a much wider world of contested projects that informed their vision of what Peronism was. Thus, this book offers a history of the Western Hemisphere after 1945 that relocates populism as a central protagonist of the Cold War, a conflict that in the region is primarily defined by competing answers to the rise of labor.[37]

As a transnational history of Peronism, *Ambassadors of the Working Class* examines this movement beyond the constraints of its own nationalist rhetoric.[38] And in doing so, it unveils the hemispheric changes in which Peronism was involved. As Thomas Bender argues, "Nationalism and national identity are founded largely on a sense of shared memories." In advocating for a transnational approach to U.S. history in particular, he writes, "Thinking of the global dimensions of a national history, historians must step outside the national box—and return with new and richer explanations for national development."[39] I take this approach in order to understand not only the history of Argentine Peronism but also the inner dynamics of the Cold War, and to provide new arguments for an analysis of the swift transformations in postwar United States.

The first transnational dimension of this history is the fashioning of Peronist nationalism. This book shows how the class-based nationalism embraced by Argentine workers was, as a historical construct, a singular expression that captured various ideas, traveled across borders, and processed these ideas into a national form. The scope of these ideas is broader than what is usually considered, ranging from the social doctrine of the Church that informed social policies throughout the world to the relation between democracy and workers' rights in the U.S. New Deal and including modernizing theories prevalent in Latin America that adopted a racialized language to envision a way out of the perceived regional backwardness. The confrontation with the United States was a central component of Peronist labor activism, of its strength at home, and of its potential abroad. Therefore, it is crucial to know what the attachés observed and reacted to when they talked about the United States. We should not assume that we can collapse the manifold rhetorics of criticism of the United States throughout history, or even across different political movements, into one thing without rigorous distinctions. It would imply that we believe that all historical protagonists have meant the same thing. It would suggest also that the "United States" they confronted has always been the same.

In exploring the actions of Argentine labor activism in Latin America, what emerges is a specific form of anti-Americanism. Peronism emulated the social reform and nationalism of the New Deal in order to denounce the imperialism of U.S. foreign policy and to criticize the inconsistency between the legacy of Franklin D. Roosevelt and postwar foreign and domestic realities. Perón and the attachés developed a form of class-based, anti-U.S. rhetoric aimed at producing an intermittent but scrupulous differentiation and periodization of U.S. history.

Perón and the attachés appropriated certain elements of the New Deal and stressed both the backlash of conservative and business sectors against the power of organized labor and the complicity of union leaders and the government after 1945. In doing so, Peronists repeatedly positioned themselves as the legitimate heirs to the New Deal. Scholars have long analyzed how U.S. liberalism became a source of inspiration for progressive movements in Latin America, yet they have been noticeably shy in studying the strong connections between Peronism and the New Deal. In his fundamental work about Peronist labor activists, Daniel James briefly mentions this relation, yet there is no further elaboration about the connections between the two political visions.[40] This might have to do, to some extent, with the fact that the strength of Argentine nationalistic discourse, the anticommunist jargon of Peronism, and Perón's actual fascist inspiration made other factors less immediately visible.

The study of the activists' engagement in conjunction with what was happening abroad helps us to recast some basic notions about domestic transformation in Argentina. One of these ideas is the assumption that Perón's conservative shift toward a marked anticommunism and an emphasis on social order was a consequence of the obstacles to economic expansion that he faced on the domestic front.[41] A closer look at Argentina's engagement with hemispheric politics shows that the Peronist shift long preceded the economic downturn that became visible in 1949. It shows that Perón and Argentine officials started a visible move toward anticommunism and social contention by early 1948, in connection with U.S. pressures across the region to sign on to a Cold War agenda. The hemispheric episode that catalyzed these transformations was the 1948 Pan-American Conference, which gave birth to the Organization of American States amid the popular riots for the killing of the leftist Colombian leader Jorge Eliécer Gaitán.

Another theory about the evolution of Peronist identity, prevalent among diplomatic historians, claims that Perón radicalized the anti-American rhetoric of his movement as a domestic distraction to make up for economic constraints.[42] The actions of the attachés sometimes seemed to justify this idea. A comprehensive view of Peronism within a regional context, though, offers a very different picture. The most salient feature of that picture is the asynchrony between beliefs, international constrains, domestic policies, and institutional changes. Perón created the program of the attachés in 1946 as an aggressive form of international labor activism with the purpose of consolidating an Argentine stance in the region by creating a regional anti-imperialist movement. Such an original program took time to materialize. The process of selection, training, deployment, and the minimal experience needed to be more assertive in their new diplomatic role meant that it was around 1948 before the attachés were ready to act. Only by this time, Perón was more than eager to dismantle the program. In 1948 and even more so in the following years, the attachés expressed an anti-Americanism that no longer corresponded to Perón's strategy and often ran against his specific orders and those of the Foreign Ministry. What happened between 1948 and 1955 was largely a permanent confrontation between the materialization of Perón's early creation and Argentina's realignment in the Cold War.

The second transnational dimension of *Ambassadors of the Working Class* refers, precisely, to the Cold War in Latin America. This book relocates Peronism, the disputes around the expansion of social rights, and the opposition to its labor-based policies and regional ambitions as crucial features of the conflict in the region. In the decade in which the Cold War took shape, Peronism animated one of the most robust forms yet of anti-Pan-Americanism at the sensitive moment when U.S. efforts at regional dominance were taking new and concrete forms in the consolidation of the postwar interstate system. Argentina's role as the main contender against a U.S.-inspired Pan-Americanism, which it had held since the late nineteenth century, loomed on the horizon in the form of a worldview that advanced the notion that a region's sovereignty was tied to a critique to materialism and individualism.[43] In 1945, this vision was much more than a diffuse historical specter. The Argentine economy emerged from World War II as the most powerful and modern one in Latin America. The country exerted an enormous influence in the region, particularly among its Southern Cone neighbors. Perón aggressively sought bilateral agreements that reinforced Argentina's presence and obstructed the free-trade deal under which the United States sought to expand into Latin American markets. Talks about a Marshall Plan for Latin America funded with Argentine capital and Argentine agricultural production seemed realistic for many in the region.[44]

Peronist anti-Pan-Americanism also served as a powerful source of inspiration for social reform. And at the same time, Argentina's economic performance served as a platform for political expansion. When Perón launched his most forceful attempts at regional leadership in 1948, the Argentine working class enjoyed one of the best living standards in the world by most accounts. An extended net of public institutions provided housing, education, and healthcare for millions of workers. The state strongly enforced progressive labor regulations, some of which had been sanctioned decades earlier but were never fully enforced. In the hands of the Argentine government, which relied on large-scale and often repetitive, hyperbolic, and embellished propaganda, tales about these domestic changes were powerful weapons abroad.

But the fireworks and clichés of Peronist propaganda should not preclude us from seeing the deep connections it established with Latin American traditions at a special historical juncture. Movements and leaders from every corner of Latin America connected Peronism with rhetoric and policies. Workers and peasants had access to a Peronist version of the region's shortcomings and the responsibility that U.S. foreign policy bore for them. Activists and leaders often built contacts with Buenos Aires and explored common political strategies through the worker attachés. It is not surprising that most of the movements that expressed some forms of anti-Americanism in Latin America during the twentieth century related in different ways to Peronism. The attachés were instrumental in producing those encounters. In the emergence of the inter-American system in 1948, we can see both the extent of regional affinities around the expansion of populist projects and the mighty reaction of the United States and of local elites in Latin America to contain any form of social unrest.

The most important and contested idea of this period was that of social rights. The notion that rights did not apply exclusively to individual citizens was disruptive of long-standing beliefs in liberal democracy. For populist movements, some groups in economic disadvantage, such as "workers," had been historically marginalized and were entitled to specific benefits and protections as a class, so that its members could achieve collectively the same influence in society that others were able to forge individually. In a region that was experiencing a broadly similar (if extremely uneven) postwar industrialization boom, Peronism gave new energy to a notion of national sovereignty that promoted the common good over an individualistic notion of citizenship. For decades, Argentine elites had grounded their anti-Pan-American rhetoric in the idea of national sovereignty, a tenet shared in Latin America since the emergence of nation states in the nineteenth century and within which the government's legitimacy was based on fulfilling certain social obligations. Peronist anti-Pan-Americanism was something else. Perón seemed to have turned the ideal into a reality at a moment in which many Latin American nations were experiencing the same postwar boom of industrialization and in which workers' mobilization in favor of a rapid expansion of their rights had produced cracks in the kind of dominating relation between elites and the rest of the society. For many in the region, the Peronist self-aggrandizing slogan of the Third Position was much more than propaganda. It also emerged as a robust attempt to finally overcome the fissures and contradictions of post-independence Latin America.[45]

Finally, the third transnational dimension of this history broaches the transformations in the United States during the postwar. *Ambassadors of the Working Class* argues that the rise of Peronism, its labor-based policy, and its mobilizational style were not only the target of the U.S. foreign policy but also the source of crucial inputs in a hemispheric cultural exchange. The images Peronism produced became part of a hemispheric cultural milieu in which U.S. intellectuals, scholars, and policymakers looked to the experiences of mass politics in Latin America to include them in domestic debates about the legacies of the New Deal and the rise of Cold War liberalism and conservative thinking. Of course, this argument is not an attempt to explain the many changes occurring in postwar United States through the rise of Peronism, a temptation that in this case would indicate the influence of our object of study on our own views. I seek to contribute to the understanding of these changes through a different light, joining the new historical writing that challenges the drastic separation between the United States and Latin America. This book disputes the idea that a transnational history of the Americas should focus only on the influence of the United States in Latin America and argue that there is a very productive field to explore in the opposite direction.

Scholars, U.S. diplomats, and union leaders portrayed Peronism as an extreme form of a Latin American take on the relation between individual freedom and workers' rights, between citizenship and equality, and between democracy and change. By 1946, U.S. labor diplomats liberally referred to

Peronism as "one brand of totalitarianism," along with fascism and communism. They did so while social scientists elaborated on similar concepts, and they did so in debates that overlapped with heated discussions about how domestic legacies of the New Deal threatened postwar democracy. Government intervention in the economy, the place of organized labor, and workers' rights were insistently singled out in these discussions. U.S. labor diplomats described these domestic legacies in a way that was remarkably similar to the "totalitarian" features that they assigned to Peronism. Critics feared that a strong labor movement could destroy free institutions by forcing increasingly violent struggles against other elements of society in order to obtain unsustainable benefits in the name of equality. Rejection of unions was conceived not as a bigoted stance but as a positive action in defense of workers. As Henry Ford had said a few decades earlier, "The safety of the people today . . . is that they are unorganized and therefore cannot be trapped."[46]

Scholars were crucial in producing this conceptualization of the totalitarian threat of Latin American nationalism. Diplomats and democratic allies of the United States in the region explained how Perón had blinded the uneducated masses by offering them immediate benefits from the state at the cost of political submission, comparing Peronism with similar projects in the rest of Latin America and in the United States.

The parallel evolution of the concern of U.S. officials about the dominance of organized labor in Argentina and the development of the conceptual toolkit of Cold War social sciences is remarkable. With different approaches, authors, such as Seymour Martin Lipset and Kenneth Organsky, and scholars working on early theories of modernization came to view Peronism alternately as a species of fascism or as a form of communist politics. Peronism offered them a platform for portraying communism and Nazism as two variants of the same problem, totalitarianism, based on how claims for equality and the advance of a collective identity suppressed individual freedom. Even as the decades passed, the study of Peronism was like an exercise in time travel that allowed the observer to see in it the genesis of these movements as an escape from personal responsibilities or as a longing for a traditional kinship lost in the transition from patriarchal social relations to industrial societies. "Extremist movements," Lipset wrote in reference to Peronism, "appeal to the disgruntled and the psychologically homeless," as well as to "the socially isolated" and "the economically insecure."[47] Once this framework was established, the threat of a too-powerful labor movement became apparent in its demands for immediate action, its acceptance of simplistic explanations, its escape from personal responsibilities, its favor of collective claims, its support for authoritarian leaders. As a category of analysis, "Peronism" came to represent for scholars and policymakers a form of mass politics with a dangerous edge. It was joined with communism and fascism in debates about the dangers that would linger in the United States if the New Deal legacies of strong organized labor and an interventionist government were not revised. Peronism offered for social scientists what Eldon Kenworthy argued any global theory requires: "the little known case which, bent to the requirements of theory, imparts an aura of universality" to some very locally grounded concerns.[48]

The roots of events that occurred during this period are the need for social reforms associated with the rise of the new urban working classes, the inability of elites to either contain or repress the democratic expansion coming from below, and the consequent need of a new ruling class in an age of mass politics. Most U.S. officials and labor diplomats shared the concerns about the need for social reforms in the region and were harsh critics of local elites. Yet they tried to square the circle by demanding a new social order without a violent rearrangement of the positions in society. U.S. diplomats who questioned the rise of Perón reaffirmed that the country urgently needed social change, but lamented that it took the form of populist politics. This quandary trapped U.S. liberals in an impossible situation. Divested of the ideological connotations of communism and its frontal attack on private property and of the tragic features of ethnic cleaning and massive repression that connoted the totalitarian experiences of Nazism and Stalinism, Peronism offered the naked truth of social reform and its violent impact on the status quo. Discussions about Peronism advanced the questions that guided U.S. liberalism in its domestic and foreign policies in the following decades: how to redistribute resources without exerting some form of coercion over those who possess those resources, and how to incorporate massive groups of workers in politics without affecting established hierarchies. If people like Segovia will now have a say in foreign affairs, how do we maintain the status quo that preceded and prevented his arrival?

In parallel, social reform came under a more frontal attack from an alternative point of view as scholars developed an assault against the very idea of social reform. By the time of Peronism's ascent, the Austrian philosopher Friedrich A. Hayek developed an incipient criticism to the notion of "social justice," precisely the main slogan that identified organized labor in Argentina under Perón, and about which Hayek would later expand in the 1960s and 1970s. The Road to Serfdom was published in 1944. In it Hayek warned about the advocacy for "community consumption" and a "planned economy" exemplified in the case of the Labor Party in the United Kingdom. He stressed the lack of any real single social goal: a strongman with the blank mandate to decide in the name of the common good what that goal is would only hurt the freedom of the individual and start the society's slide into authoritarianism.[49] The influence of Hayek's work was vast in Latin America—*The Road to Serfdom* was widely discussed in Argentina at the time of its publication—and it also informed the views of U.S. policymakers dealing with Peronism. By 1947, Spruille Braden, the U.S. ambassador who introduced Peronism to American audiences, declared that liberals should declare a fight "against all forms of statism, among which I include socialism of such governments as that of the Labor Party" and complained about U.S. "government interference and participation in what should be the exclusive field of private enterprise."[50]

This book shows the direct ways in which the confrontation of Peronism and the perceived excessive power of labor informed these two alternatives in U.S. politics. Cold War liberals argued in favor of social reforms as a way to prevent the rise of movements like Peronism. A few years later, during the early 1960s, U.S. officials involved in the early relation with Peronism became promoters of the War on Poverty in the United States and of the Alliance for Progress in Latin America, the two major U.S. attempts at development and reform in the region and at home. At the same time, early reflections about Peronism informed those who actively sought to suppress any challenge to the social order. Even by the 1960s, some scholars and policymakers involved in the containment of Peronism or in its conceptualization joined the incipient forms of the neoconservative movement. With Peronism as a specter, they warned U.S. audiences about the risks that changes such as those derived from urban poverty or those promoted by the civil-rights movement posed for the final outcome of the Cold War.

FINALLY, THIS BOOK IS not the history that Segovia and the worker attachés wanted to make. The dream of an international Peronist movement never became a reality. Perón was ousted in 1955, and in general, populist projects in Latin America were exhausted by the end of the decade, even if they lived a generous afterlife. The attachés fought against an array of forces that ranged from their own leader to the fearsome deployments of the United States during the Cold War. By 1952, the Agrupación de Trabajadores Latinoamericanos Sindicalizados (ATLAS), the labor-based regional organization they had envisioned, was a weak bureaucratic instrument with no impact on workers' lives, a testament more to the attachés' project's shortcoming than to its achievements. Yet to simply assess their defeat would be to miss the opportunity that their history offers as an access to the inception of the Cold War in the region. In their rise and fall, the attachés offer a testimony that helps us to understand the strength and resilience of one of the most powerful political identities in twentieth-century Latin America. Within their defeat, the attachés' history offers a singular, panoramic view of the Cold War from below, of how the conflict was lived and produced. Activists who did not make it to the big history, whose lives have been mostly forgotten and their actions dismissed, contributed to the fashioning of a political process that affected daily lives, neighborhoods, salaries, songs, books, and life and death decisions across the entire hemisphere. In many cases, the attachés' contributions also set in place broader connections between leaders, movements, and policies that later symbolized Latin American changes during the postwar. When seen from that perspective, the Cold War, including its history of Peronism, evolves in nonlinear ways, contradicting in thousands of ordinary events the grand narratives that the regional periodizations take for granted. Here, too, as Walter Benjamin puts it, the "street insurgence of the anecdote" that the attachés epitomized from the fringes of politics conspired against "the spirit of the period" expressed by the United States' growing intervention in the region and by Perón's foreign policy in ways that would have a long-term impact in Latin America.[51] Against the current and beyond defeat, the attachés' lives expose the meaningful connection of Peronism with the political movements that shaped the region's life in the decades to come.

CHAPTER ONE

IN SEARCH OF SOCIAL REFORM

The most influential study published in Argentina in 1945 was a book few people read. Written by the nationalistic journalist José Luis Torres, it described the country's history from 1930 to 1943 as a period of fraudulent elections, social injustice, and capitulation to foreign economic powers. The distinctive label for the regime was *oligarchy*, a term that nationalists, leftists, and U.S. observers used to characterize both an unfair system and a backward society in which no modern sense of universal rights prevailed over wealth.[1] The argument was appealing but not particularly original to the country. From then on, what reverberated as a symbol of the historical transition between a sordid past and a bright future were the three words of the title: *La Década Infame* (The Infamous Decade).[2]

The book's title conveyed the sense of national purification that Colonel Juan Perón wanted to ascribe to the 1943 Revolution. Torres, an acquaintance of Perón, had put in writing the feeling of a rupture with the immediate past that nationalism conveyed. On 4 June of that year, a group of army officers overthrew President Ramón Castillo, putting an end to a period of electoral fraud that had started in 1930, after the military coup against the elected president Hipólito Yrigoyen. That day, Perón, an ascending but by no means powerless figure of the revolution, started the construction of a new relationship between the state, politics, and the massive working classes that became the single most important event in Argentine history.

In the nationalistic narrative, the past of simple exclusion and oligarchic domination had finally been left behind. Yet infamous as it was—"a thinly veiled conservative dictatorship," in the words of American scholar Robert Alexander at the time—the preceding decade had been much more complex than the blighted era against which Peronism fashioned its disruptive identity.[3] Conservative governments, facing the effects of the Great Depression, had experimented with interventionist policies that helped Argentina's economic recovery. Agricultural exports to British markets made Argentina one of the richest countries on earth. In order to defend this relationship from the rising dominance of the United States, elites developed a set of cutting-edge arguments against the primacy of economic power over political sovereignty. The oligarchic landowners who benefited from trade with the United Kingdom were prominent, but in their shadows flourished a group of industrialists. In parallel, a modern working class emerged in the main urban centers. The state was as repressive as it was acquiescent to union demands. Many among the elites who controlled the country were aware of the fact that society was changing beneath their feet, and they explored, however ineffectually, the improbable gamble of integrating these new sectors without sacrificing their own power. As much as Peronism inaugurated a new era in 1945, it did so by recasting into a new vision the trends that preceded its arrival.

Argentina's relationship with the rest of the world was a central realm in which elites worked out their views of change. Argentine nationalists, liberal intellectuals, and the Church established their positions in domestic affairs by situating the country in a global context. They produced ideas of race, class, and nation through which they explained the country's enormous economic prosperity, Argentina's modern economy in relation to Latin America, the threat that the expansion of the U.S. economy posed for traditional values in the region, and the social formation of which they were the leading force.

This chapter examines ideas about Argentina's place in the world during the 1930s and early 1940s, and look at the Ministry of Foreign Affairs as the favored venue in which these debates coalesced into a dominant, fluid worldview. As a privileged space in which global debates took place, the Ministry of Foreign Affairs was an "institution of hegemony" for a narrow elite. This body was perhaps so narrow that the arsenal of rhetorical, political, and juridical tools of modern politics that it produced was easily appropriated by sectors then left out of power, which came to overthrow this elite years later. In particular, it shows the tensions within dominant groups concerning democracy, modernization, and reform. It examines how government officials tried to create a coherent world-view by discussing social rights and political citizenship as central to the country's foreign policy.[4] While liberal and nationalistic sectors of the administration were unable to translate these principles into a domestic agenda, the study of the Infamous Decade's foreign policy demonstrates how elites were more attuned to the need for these changes than the later Peronist rhetoric suggested. Moreover, this chapter examines the ground that these elites shared with the sectors that overthrew them, ultimately revealing a productive space that connected domestic and foreign concerns. It shows how the regional competition with the United States was conceived—in legal, political, and philosophical realms—in terms of a challenge to the primacy of property rights, believed to be the driving force in the emergence of the inter-American system as promoted by the United States. This "Argentine challenge" predated the arrival of Perón and persisted, while he was in office, in a different and more threatening form.

A Modest Industrial Revolution

Latin America reacted to the effects of the Great Depression of the 1930s in large part by using import substitution to deepen the industrialization process that other countries had started in previous decades.[5] The three largest economies in the region—Argentina, Brazil, and Mexico—bounced back stronger than before and, in some aspects, sooner than the United States. In Brazil and Mexico, this process was accompanied by an at least partial adaptation of political institutions to lingering "social questions," such as those regarding the inclusion of disenfranchised masses into politics and the expansion of economic and social rights for the growing urban workers and peasants. However, in Argentina, this was not the case. In Mexico, President Lázaro Cárdenas (1934–1940) expanded the revolution by enacting agrarian reform, passing a progressive labor code, and expropriating U.S. oil companies. In Brazil, Getúlio Vargas led a military coup, in 1930, that put an end to the liberal republic and set in motion authoritarian and controlled social reform. Argentina went in the opposite direction. In September 1930, a military coup overthrew the populist government of Hipólito Yrigoyen, starting a thirteen-year political period in which, as the historian Barbara Weinstein says in relation to the last years of the liberal republic in Brazil, "regional oligarchies monopolized political power, [by] manipulating elections and minimizing popular participation."[6]

The crash of 1929 badly hurt Argentina. It disrupted the basic functions of an economy grounded in its external sector by dependency on the exports of raw materials to Europe and the import of manufacturing and capital from Europe and the United States. Even if the GDP did not fall in Argetina as far as it did in most of the Western Hemisphere ("only" 13.2 percent between 1929 and 1932), exports dropped from one billion dollars in 1928 to $335 million four years later. The social impact was evident in an unemployment rate that soared above 25 percent.[7] In 1933, the conservative government made a crucial step toward reestablishing exports by signing the Roca-Runciman Pact with the United Kingdom (named after the two signatories, Argentine Vice President Julio Roca Jr. and the president of the British Trade Council, Walter Runciman). Argentina resumed its pre-1929 status as privileged provider of beef for Britain. In exchange, Argentina exported 85 percent of its beef through British meatpacking firms, removed all tariffs for British manufactures, and gave priority to British products for purchases abroad, to be bought with pounds obtained from its exports to British markets. Historians have characterized this agreement as a form of neocolonialism, albeit one that provided a comfortable position for Argentina in the world economy at a critical moment.[8]

Some critics of the Roca-Runciman Pact exaggerated the domestic limitations it imposed. But they rightly made the treaty a symbol of Argentine dependency by associating the imbalance of the foreign trade with the domestic inequality in income distribution.[9] This accusation foresaw the basics of economic discourse in the decades to come. Since the late 1950s, developmentalist theories centered on terms of trade, in particular the relation of export prices to import prices, to understand the domestic dynamics of Latin American dependency.

Yet in the shadow of the policies that Roca epitomized, the economy evolved in ways that the government did not necessarily promote and that its critics did not expect. The pact implied an early reopening of the country's foreign trade and underpinned a recovery that was already under way. In the following years, the government made a series of decisions that appeared to be integral parts of an early Keynesian program. In reality, Keynes's ideas of public spending as a way to expand domestic demand had not yet been published, and the conservative administrations did not share their embryonic versions anyway. As free trade crashed again with the 1937 recession, Argentina made other bilateral agreements in addition to the one with the United Kingdom, which represented some 60 percent of its exports. In search of revenues, the administration built a large barrier against imports through high tariffs, protecting a frail industrialization and helping to rebuild the country's exports. By addressing infrastructural bottlenecks and the demands of local caudillos and by trying to absorb the available labor force to avoid unemployment, the government expanded its presence and fueled domestic demand. Against the laissez-faire that it promoted, the government spent more than it collected during the worst years of the Depression. By the mid-1930s, the country had the second-largest industrial sector in Latin America, only after Brazil. Unlike its neighbor, Argentina had no steel industry, as observers noted. But Argentina's economic landscape had changed drastically. In 1936, the *Economist* estimated that "Argentina is still far from exporting manufactures ... but ... its dependence from imports has considerably decreased," which it explained by an "industrial revival of the last years." It was a surprising compliment for a country governed by an oligarchy of landowners and ranchers.[10] Rather than an adherence to Keynes's ideas, the actions of Argentine elites amounted to what Pablo Gerchunoff and Lucas Llach playfully called a "passive Keynesianism."[11] It showed how notions of modern industrialization, economic nationalism, and social inclusion had permeated the thinking of dominant groups and took those groups' political view farther than the term *oligarchy* suggested.

Only in 1940 did the government present an economic plan that advanced interventionist aims, a proposal that came to be known as Plan Pinedo, after the minister who wrote it. But even then, the proposals were transitory exceptions in light of a coming global conflict.[12] The plan was never implemented as such, but it offers a picture of how ideas about anticyclical public intervention pervaded economic debates in Argentina (and the rest of Latin America) by the early 1940s.[13]

Social Reform

FACTORIES PLUS CITIES EQUALS WORKERS

At first glance, the elites' realization of how much the country had changed under its rule did not affect its old habits. Electoral fraud and limited political participation for workers continued. Doubtless, the most outstanding feature of this large reconfiguration of the Argentine economy was the emergence of an industrial sector and a modern working class, which occurred mostly but not only in the expanding urban centers. Vast textile factories, symbolic of the industries that British imports had suffocated, appeared in Buenos Aires and its main industrial suburbs. British and U.S. meatpacking factories grew and diversified. Imports that had once defined Argentine dependence on the

British empire were increasingly supplanted by local production. In 1929, Argentina produced just 7.7 percent of the cotton textiles it consumed. A decade later, that number had climbed to 57.6 percent.[14] Some national factories produced capital and intermediate goods. The factory funded by Torcuato Di Tella Sr. came to symbolize national industrialization. The closest representative of an Argentine national bourgeoisie, Di Tella found a way to obtain protective tariffs from the government and to supply the domestic market with goods that were either more expensive or unavailable abroad before and after 1929.[15] As his son, the renowned sociologist Torcuato Di Tella Jr., demonstrated decades later, the 1930s witnessed a notable growth of the textile industry, metallurgy, and the steel industry.[16]

These transformations brought along others. Even if elites preferred European fashion, most people wore nationally produced clothing. The expanded domestic market consumed food produced in national factories and harvested in national fields and, in some cases, with national machines. Workers, consumers, and products traveled throughout the country in a transportation system more extensive than those of countries three times the size of Argentina. But the most visible changes could be seen in the streets of Buenos Aires, in the expansion of factories in the main industrial suburbs of the country, in the frantic activity at the ports of Rosario and Buenos Aires, in the wineries of Mendoza, in the wheat fields of Lincoln in Buenos Aires Province, and even in the sugar mills of the remote Chaco territory.

The industrial economy became increasingly diversified but remained grounded in processing raw materials. It was in this setting that the future worker attachés found their first jobs as young industrial workers. Before Pedro Otero became a city employee, in 1937, and well before becoming a Peronist labor diplomat, he carried two-hundred-pound bags as a worker on the Buenos Aires docks in the 1930s.[17] In 1936, a decade before Agustín Merlo became the representative of Peronism in Washington, he worked at the U.S. meatpacker Swift, in the industrial suburb of Berisso, later known as the birthplace of Peronism.[18] In Las Palmas, a company town in the Chaco territory, León Segovia, the future attaché in Paraguay, was hired as a welder in the local Ingenio, the largest sugar factory in the northeast in the 1930s.[19] In the Province of Buenos Aires, the railroad worker Modesto Alvarez was transferred to a post in a small, countryside town that, like other such municipalities, depended on both the country's export performance and the trains' reliability. While there, he joined the Socialist Party, an involvement that informed his political future as attaché in Bolivia.[20] In the late 1930s, César Tronconi, who would later

FIGURE 1.1. Céscar Tronconi, a future worker attaché in Cuba who contacted a young Fidel Castro on behalf of Perón, speaking at a meeting at the meatpacking workers' union, 1945. Like Tronconi, most attachés joined Peronism during the 1943–1946 period, after years of activism in socialist, communist, and radical unions. Source: Personal papers of César Tronconi.

become an attaché for Perón in Cuba, led a series of food-industry strikes in Entre Ríos Province. By 1941, Tronconi migrated to the Buenos Aires working-class neighborhood of Pompeya and found work at Tronconi Sausages and Cold Cuts, an expansive meatpacking factory owned by a distant relative.[21]

More and more diversified jobs appeared. But the social costs of that economic reconfiguration were similar to those of any period of original accumulation since the Industrial Revolution. During the Depression, unemployment reached some 25 percent, and even though that number dropped after a decade, salaries remained stagnant at 1929 levels or below as inflation eroded purchasing power. Workers had grown as a percentage of the total population, yet their share of the national wealth had shrunk.[22] In the mid-1930s, migrants from the interior arrived in the city of Buenos Aires. The city's working-class suburbs and poor villages grew. Decades later, the social writer Bernardo Verbitsky called them *villas miserias*.[23] These shantytowns, similar to Hoovervilles, emerged on a massive scale. In the meantime, electoral fraud guaranteed that the workers' and peasants' votes hardly mattered. To a large extent, government and politics still functioned mostly as a club of notables that included wealthy landowners, liberal educated professionals, nationalistic military groups, and the Church.

NATIONALISM

In this context, unions increasingly demanded a new view of the relationship between government and society, one that would include workers' interests. But they were not alone in this demand. Since the turn of the twentieth century, nationalistic scholars, policymakers, and members of the army, as well as Catholic intellectuals and members of the Church, had reflected on the emergence of mass society and had considered corporatist ideas for integrating the working class into an organic whole so as to avoid the rise of leftist radicalism. All of these groups shared an anti-liberal emphasis and took inspiration from corporatist views of society, which included but were not limited to fascism.[24]

Loris Zanatta has persuasively argued that the decline of the liberal and anticlerical state, which had been consolidated in the 1860s, gave way to a "re-Catholicization" of the country. In this process, an alliance between the Church and the army refurbished Argentine nationalism between 1930 and 1943 with a corporatist worldview and an authoritarian form of access to political life for the masses. For Zanatta, these nationalists were in line with totalitarian movements in Europe: they blamed liberal institutions for failing to incorporate "the social question" and advanced hierarchical forms of integrating the working class into politics as a way of avoiding the spread of communism and radicalized leftist activism. "Social peace," as opposed to "class conflict," was at the core of their ideology.[25]

The debates around the rise of the working class laid the groundwork for the emergence of Peronism after 1943. In 1930, nationalist sectors of the army (including the young Captain Juan Perón) ousted democratically elected President Yrigoyen. This action put an end to fifty years of democratic stability, the last sixteen of which were under extended popular suffrage, though women were still excluded. The nationalist sectors installed José Félix Uriburu, a Germanophile general who exalted the fascistic roots of his administration. Through its intellectuals and institutions, the Catholic Church supported the "anti-liberal and prestigious government" as an expression of the reenergized and widely spread nationalism that sought the salvation of the country in a return to a mythical race of Hispanic origin.[26] Two years later, Uriburu was replaced by another general, Agustín P. Justo. Like Uriburu, Justo did not relinquish this understanding of nationalism; however, Justo located the nation within liberal inspirations and further away from univocal fascist ties. By 1935, most of the Church was disillusioned with the process started five years earlier. Military revolts and palace coups were not enough; rather, what was needed was a radical transformation, "a new Christian order." This new order would destroy liberalism, reinforce traditional hierarchies, and prevent the rise of communism by focusing on a concept that had permeated the Church in the previous decades: social justice. The nationalist Federico Ibarguren noted in his diary: "This intervention of the Church in the social struggles of this century . . . is the most important event in contemporary history."[27] As Zanatta argues, the centrality of the social question put an end to an era in which social conflicts were attributed only to external factors (radical ideas, antisocial behavior), establishing a theoretical differentiation from the ideas long held by local upper classes.[28] The idea of social justice was also nurtured by the 1891 papal encyclical *Rerum Novarum*. During the 1920s and 1930s, this encyclical's message had become a transnational discourse that permeated social reform in Latin America, providing an argument in favor of restraining the excesses of labor and capital as the means for a peaceful social and economic modernization.[29]

The growing presence of the "social question" in nationalist groups was aided by institutions such as the Cursos de Cultura Católica. Since the early 1930s, the Cursos had concentrated the ideological exchange of Catholicism within nationalistic cadres in the military, governmental, and scholarly sectors. In a few years, Catholic nationalism and its *impronta* of social justice, order, and national salvation went from being one strand of rightist nationalism to constituting its dominant force.[30] In 1935, the Vatican's consecration of Argentine Monsignor Santiago Luis Copello as cardinal provided grounds for including the idea of a social transformation as part of the nationalist sense of a broader regional mission. Copello was the first cardinal from Hispanic America in the history of the Catholic Church (a fact widely celebrated within and outside of the Church). His consecration contributed to the Church's self-image as the driving force of a crusade that ran deep in Argentina: the Christianization of Hispanic America.[31]

But it was a more relevant world event that helped define ideas and programs that later coalesced into Perón's vision: the Spanish Civil War. The adherence of the Argentine church to fascist ideas was so dogged that when Jacques Maritain, the world-eminent philosopher who had led a movement to frame the social question within the teachings of Thomism, announced his support of the Republic in 1936, the Argentine church abandoned him.

When Maritain visited Argentina that same year, his conferences generated heated debates, at a time when the government was deploying an ambivalent and contradictory policy toward Spain. Despite its anticommunist rhetoric, the conservative Argentine administration always recognized the legitimacy of the Republican government. Perceiving Falangism as one more expression of the growing ascendance of fascism, Foreign Minister Carlos Saavedra Lamas aligned not only with many opposition leaders but also with conservative landowners. While these landowners might have feared the rise of communism, they were particularly sensitive to the foreign policy of the United Kingdom. Nationalistic sectors in the government, including those aligned with Vice President Ramón Castillo, instead offered wide support to Franquismo and warned that the Republican government could pave the way for the rise of leftist extremism worldwide.[32]

The nationalists who felt betrayed by Maritain were strong supporters of Francisco Franco. Not all of them remained with Perón after 1945. Among those who did were the Curso de Cultura Católica students, who became the professors of the courses to train the worker attachés.[33] Labor activists, many of them future attachés, volunteered with the Republican side during the Spanish Civil War, as part of the intense international activity developed by unions.[34] Finally, Perón himself had already been to Italy and admired fascist corporatism as a superior form of social order that allowed for the advancement of the working class while preserving social peace. Appointed at the military school in Mendoza, Perón was far from the turbulence generated by Maritain in Buenos Aires. Despite his fascist sympathies, Perón took from the French philosopher (who later grew further from fascism and closer to the Christian Democratic and Liberal Parties) not only the Thomist take on social conflict but also the very expression "Third Position" as a political order that would control the excesses of labor and capital.[35]

THE ELITES

Rightist nationalists and leftist labor activists decried the Justo administration as the political front for the old Argentine oligarchy of ranchers and landowners and their British counterparts. Yet this bold, and to some extent truthful, characterization veils the same elites' intense, if ineffectual, attention to the problems that defined the country during the period, namely industrialization, government intervention, and the expansion of economic and political citizenship to the emerging working classes.

Few people embodied this prismatic configuration of the elites' worldview better than Saavedra Lamas, the most prestigious and popular member of the administration. Lamas was a descendant of one of the Argentine founding families and was hailed as "the dandy ambassador of London chic in Buenos

Aires." An advocate of liberal progress and reader of Herbert Spencer and Karl Marx, Lamas was the minister of foreign affairs during the entire Justo administration and personified the Década Infame.[36] Despite (and partly because of) the European overtones and the markedly pro-British policies of Argentina, he led a government that was an institution of privilege, having been coopted by the gentry since the nineteenth century, and turned it into a powerful and effective tool for containment of the United States in the region. He was not alone in the desire to curb the influence of the United States in the Americas. Early on, Argentine intellectuals connected with their Latin American counterparts and with commercial and political partners in Europe and the United States to turn the realm of foreign affairs into a space for the fashioning of a nascent Argentine identity.[37] From the late nineteenth century onward, Argentine diplomats shared with most of their Latin American associates the spirit of *Ariel*, an influential essay by the Uruguayan José Enrique Rodó that claimed an exceptional place for the region as a reservoir of moral values against the materialism expressed in U.S. expansion.[38] Partly influenced by European positivism and crafted around a regional reinvention of *hispanismo*, ideologues of Latin American liberalism embraced miscegenation and racial progress as founding principles of the consolidation of national states and the modernization of its societies. Argentine foreign policy connected with a broad romanticist spirit in the region well beyond the narrow space of the oligarchy of landowners that captured the country's wealth. The region's cultural production sought symbols to represent (and create) its traditional values in a modern world. As the Nicaraguan poet Rubén Darío said, artists and intellectuals from all over the world found "in Argentina the counterweight to Yankee power, that will save the spirit of our race and put a stop to imperialist projects undoubtedly already approved."[39] Argentine criticism of the United States was not merely an idealist stance of resistance; it appealed to others in Latin America because it represented a viable chance to make traditional self-perceptions of order and equality compatible with the realities of a rapidly changing social formation.

Argentine elites conceived this mission as both inwardly civilizing and outwardly emancipatory, envisaging the consolidation of the national state as intimately tied to its role abroad. Around the same time of the publication of *Ariel*, José Ingenieros crafted for Argentina a notion of a *raza neolatina*, called to lead a new type of "pacific imperialism." This argument's undertones of indigenous extermination are partly, but certainly not exclusively, what made it powerfully attractive to diplomats. "Argentine hegemony depends on its economic expansion," Ingenieros said. "It only needs to let some years pass until its distance from the rest [of the region] is impossible to diminish."[40] This message encouraged a more aggressive push for regional leadership among Argentine diplomats. They contrasted the "Anglo" and "Latin" Americas in terms of opposing views of rights and sovereignty—one being too limited to the preservation of individualistic gains and the other built around a more open sense of community. These elites devised their own idea of a Pax Latinoamericana, and under this umbrella, they justified a creative (and daring) foreign policy in which Argentina moved forward to intervene in remote events on the grounds of expanding or preserving that peace. During the 1912 "Little Race War" in Cuba, in which the Cuban army massacred thousands of Afro-Americans, Argentine diplomats extensively discussed the possibility of an Argentine intervention with a multinational peace mission in order both to compensate for the U.S. presence on the island and to protect property rights in the hemisphere, "preventing the attack on private property by the *negrada*."[41] Four years later, these ambitions became a reality on a larger scale when Argentina promoted a joint mediation with Brazil and Chile (the ABC Group) in response to the crisis triggered in Mexico when U.S. President Woodrow Wilson ordered the military occupation of Veracruz. The ABC Group considered the occupation illegitimate and contrary to the principle of non-intervention. The multilateral efforts of the group led to the Niagara Falls peace conference, which helped to settle the dispute peacefully and resulted in U.S. withdrawal. The ABC Group's influence on this final result varied considerably depending on whether the story was told by Argentine officials, who considered it fundamental, by the Mexican government, which considered it incidental, or by the American government, which judged it counterproductive.[42] But the event revealed the ambitions of Argentine diplomats and the tensions that those ambitions spurred vis-à-vis the United States.

Anti-Pan-Americanism was a complex ideological stance on foreign policy. Deployed since the 1880s as an answer to the expansion of U.S. power in the region, it opposed various U.S.-sponsored initiatives of political, commercial, juridical, and military alignment on the basis of the primacy of national sovereignty of the states over any form of hemispheric integration. Those U.S. initiatives (first presented in a coherent way in the 1823 Monroe Doctrine) revolved around the perceived need to rationalize Latin American markets in order to suit U.S. exports and investment priorities, and favored political and military interventions in defense of property rights. The Argentine view denounced U.S. materialism and emphasized the need to sever the link between foreign capital and foreign state powers. In practical terms, the Argentine position presented property rights as subordinated to ideas of international peace, national sovereignty, and common good. Over time, these robust (and effective) efforts carved "enduring rhetorical patterns," which imposed discursive constraints not only on the rise of the United States but also on Argentine foreign policy.[43]

Symbolically and practically, the most successful expression of this international stance occurred in 1936, when Argentina led the mediation in the Chaco War between Bolivia and Paraguay, the largest and bloodiest interstate military conflict in the Americas during the twentieth century. The conflict over a disputed border in the Chaco Forest was also a proxy war between U.S. and British economic interests about the region's natural resources.[44] Argentina had large interests in Paraguay and opposed the U.S. stance, which favored Bolivia. Argentine mediation displaced the United States from a position of political leadership in the Southern Cone, realizing the general principles of non-intervention and arbitration advanced by Latin American countries.[45] And it confirmed Argentina as the most powerful expression of those general principles.

To round off the success, the mediation also garnered the Nobel Peace Prize to Saavedra Lamas, the first Latin American Nobel Laureate.[46] Argentina's intervention angered U.S. diplomats. Reinforced by their perception of Argentina as a threat, U.S. officials' irritation with Saavedra Lamas's dominance at that time was so deep that Spruille Braden, then the U.S. mediator in the conflict, described his achievement in bitter (though not entirely inaccurate) terms: "The best way to win the Nobel Prize is to start a war and then to help settle it."[47]

At a moment in which Argentina was successfully avoiding the worst effects of the Great Depression, achievements like this one confirmed among elites the perception of a country uniquely suited for regional leadership. When Copello's consecration as cardinal was hailed by rightist Catholics as a sign of Argentine hemispheric leadership, it was none other than Saavedra Lamas who congratulated the Church on behalf of the government, arguing, in prose of unequivocal reverberations, that Buenos Aires had become an "unabating beacon shining over the entire continent."[48]

Concerns about "the social question" had permeated the debates and practices held by these elites since the beginning of the twentieth century. Professionally trained as a lawyer in the preparation of the first labor code in Argentina, Saavedra Lamas started his political career before his diplomatic one. Under the umbrella of progressive groups, Lamas began in politics by advancing the notion that fulfilling social rights was part of state obligations. As a young official of the conservative administration of the city of Buenos Aires in 1907, he could be seen inaugurating the working-class housing project Butteler Neighborhood, the first housing project in Argentina built under the Affordable Housing Act of 1905. The picture of that inauguration opens a window into dynamic ideological exchanges: we see neither communists nor anarchists, two groups singled out by the administration as national threats (the very reason for the housing project was to prevent the rise of extremism). But liberal Saavedra Lamas shared the stage with Carlos Thays, the French landscape architect who had designed parks and plazas for some of the most important cities in Argentina; Ramón Falcón, the nationalistic military chief of the federal police who later led the bloodiest repressions against organized labor and early social movements; and Alfredo Palacios, the socialist congressman who for decades pushed for socially progressive legislation in the country, most of which was enacted by Perón after 1945.[49]

Saavedra Lamas was also the visionary official who, in the early 1920s, envisioned a Secretariat of Labor, which was the first government agency focused on labor and served as a blueprint for the one Perón created two decades later. And it was Saavedra Lamas the diplomat who, in 1928, serving as president of the International Labour Organization (ILO), proposed that organized labor join states in representing countries' foreign relations, an idea that Perón carried through almost two decades later with the appointment of worker attachés as one more component of the foreign service.[50] The Argentine diplomat participated in the 1919 creation of the ILO, and in 1928, as president of the ILO conference in Geneva, he established the basis for making Buenos Aires the location for the Ibero-American Workers Federation.[51]

The End of Infamy

The modernizing features of Argentine elites and the role of government in the economic recovery from the Great Depression complicate the caricature of the Infamous Decade as shaped by an oligarchy blind to changes, against which Peronism later fashioned its drastic rupture with the national past. As in most of Latin America, elites appeared receptive to the changes occurring in society and absorbed the impact of the Great Depression by adopting, if mildly, forms of state intervention, protectionism, and industrialization. Peronism was effective at dismissing this immediate history, strengthening its power by denouncing in toto the defeated old regime.[52]

This inconsistency has provided grounds for many scholars to contradict the familiar Peronist narrative and assert that Argentina was on its way to modernizing its society and political system before Perón came to power. This argument is informed in important ways by theories of modernization coming from Marxist and structural-functionalist approaches. From this perspective, Perón disrupted the process of modernization by taking advantage of a favorable conjuncture in order to offer a distorted idea of social democratization, one in which Argentine workers enjoyed a centrality in the polity that not even the Left had imagined, followed by strong state control of the labor movement's autonomy. One of the most lucid scholars of Peronism, Juan Carlos Torre, went even further and wrote an essay that imagined an alternative history, in which Perón loses the 1946 elections, and the elites split into a progressive liberal sector and a conservative nationalistic one, in line with the political divisions of Western European countries during the postwar.[53] In narratives like this one, Justo emerges both as an enigma and a lost opportunity, and Perón appears as an ill-timed obstacle on the Argentine path to modernization.[54]

These appraisals were right to explore the continuities that cross the historical border of 1945 and to call into question Peronist claims of an ex nihilo revolutionary movement. But they also overstate the transformative prospects of old elites. Opening the gates to social inclusion and expansion of citizenship, they argued, could easily give rise to a movement that would challenge the economic and political dominance of their closed group. During the 1930s and 1940s, this anxiety was better conveyed under the notion of the totalitarian threat.[55]

By the time Justo and Saavedra Lamas left government, in 1938, the world was heading toward war, a military conflict that further accelerated the process of import substitution. From 1938 to 1943, and despite pressures from both sides, Argentina maintained its neutrality. The volatility of the moment precluded the introduction of any substantial political opening. The utmost (and last) expression of estrangement from elite-ruled society came in 1943, with the unpopular designation of Robustiano Patrón Costas as the government candidate to succeed President Castillo. Patrón Costas, a conservative landowner from the interior who embodied the very idea of an oligarch, was not the best representative of a project for industrial modernization. Quite the contrary. By that moment, the government had become the very caricature that nationalistic sectors had made it out to be. This was the image the army needed in order to gain popular support.

The war was influential in determining the fate of the conservative government. Yet it would be misleading to assume that this influence was uniformly felt in Latin America or that domestic struggles were not central in determining how that influence played out in each country. In the case of Argentina, the global conflict helped end the Década Infame by galvanizing two growing and very different groups among the armed forces, political forces, and public opinion: a liberal opposition that sided with the Allies in denouncing neutrality as synonymous with Nazi sympathies; and nationalistic groups that tied Argentine neutrality to a socially inclusive idea of national sovereignty and condemned traditional elites.[56]

The Rise of the Masses

On 4 June 1943, the revolution, led by a group of nationalistic and pro-Axis army-officer members of United Officials Group (GOU) firmly supported by the Church, put an end to the decade-long controlled experiment of fraudulent democracy and set the grounds for dynamic transformations ahead. The war helps to explain why that conservative era ended with a coup by nationalistic officers with Nazi sympathies. But it also clarifies why unions and workers shaped politically by the struggle against fascism found plausible the construction of a common ground with the revolution.

As a member of the GOU, Perón quickly started to build a political project. Based on the blueprint of the fascist regime he had witnessed as a military attaché in Italy, Perón conceived of a multiclass coalition of business elites, labor leaders, the Church, the military, and some traditional parties, and developed a vision of a corporatist society in which the state would guarantee some social and political rights to the working classes, preventing the rise of extremism.[57] But those whom he considered his potential allies reacted to his offer to contain radical extremism with disdain, fear, or plain rejection. One by one, between 1943 and 1946, the traditional parties, his military colleagues, the Catholic Church, and economic elites distanced themselves from Perón. Correspondingly, his relation with (and dependence on) the labor movement grew. By 1945, the man who conceived of himself as an instrument for the containment of social unrest had become the leader of a labor movement that embodied many of the radical visions and goals that he had originally aimed to prevent.[58] Rejected by elites and supported by powerful unions, he was almost pulled to create a radical form of populism that, without questioning the basic capitalist forms of production, went further than any of its homologous movements in challenging the social order.

At first sight, the 1943 Revolution seemed to amount to the kind of change championed by rightist Catholic nationalists. It was a national revolution that questioned the constraints of liberal democracy and proclaimed the end of the old oligarchy. At its heart, the new nation addressed the social question through the government regulation of labor and capital, following the strongly hierarchical model of European corporatist societies. Perón took special interest in social policies and particularly in their relations with organized labor. The 1944 earthquake in the province of San Juan offered him the opportunity to introduce and to perform for the first time in Argentina the national government's obligation to tend to those in need during an emergency. This act expressed a direct relationship between the government and the common good and appeared to be a continuation of Depression-era debates around the government's duties. These choices made Perón popular. By the end of 1944, he had risen from being assistant to the secretary of war to being the head of that office, in addition to being vice president and head of the then insignificant Department of Labor. He turned this department into a secretariat and quickly built a solid relationship with the labor movement, correspondingly losing the support of most of the right-wing Catholic nationalists who had inspired him.

Perón built his epoch-making career on this shifting but powerful political platform.[59] Many factors turned Peronism into something drastically different not only from European fascism but also from other Latin American populist projects. The new reality was created by various protagonists—intellectuals, political elites, the military, organized labor, the business sector, U.S. officials, Catholic nationalists, and Latinoamericanist thinkers and policymakers in the region—as well as by the very different social structures of Argentina and Europe, the interactions between fascist intellectuals, and the singular historical moment at the end of the war, after the defeat of the Axis powers and the rise of the United States as a global hegemonic power.

On the one hand, these early years defined the unique centrality of organized labor in Argentina for the rest of the century. Economic elites and traditional parties had not felt the pressure of workers' radical demands and the corresponding need for a corporatist project to contain them. Organized labor had a conciliatory approach to the state, and at the time, its practices did not present a challenge to the property rights on which wealth was accumulated and transformed into political power.[60]

The paradoxical outcome of the closure of the path for a broad social alliance in Perón's imagined terms was—in the now famous words of Juan Carlos Torre—the corresponding "sobrerepresentación del movimiento obrero organizado."[61] Perón soon realized that the labor movement, which he had considered a subordinate part of a large multiclass alliance, was going to constitute the only reliable support he could obtain. From the Secretariat of Labor and in the favorable economic conjuncture of the period, he was able to do what his military peers did not see as relevant and what progressive and liberal elites had been incapable of accomplishing: Perón swiftly reorganized labor by offering concrete and immediate benefits to the working class in order to sweep away the old guard who resisted him, doing so by enacting a vast set of new rights for workers and enforcing existing ones, and by privileging the unions that supported his policies while repressing those that did not. If elites had not felt Perón's need to stop workers from challenging the status quo, they now had in him the leader who represented that very same challenge.

This process reflects the pragmatic nature of the radicalization of Peronism. Studying the relation between elites and radical demands from the country's interior, Mark Healey argues that the centrality of workers (mostly from the industrial centers) to Peronism was, rather than a goal pursued by Perón, "closely related to the abandonment of the more comprehensive and ambitious goals on the periphery."[62] This reckoning applies more broadly. The radicalism of organized labor emerges not as the outcome of a uniform ideology previously designed, but as the byproduct of the previous decades' historical developments, condensed in the three years from 1943 to 1946. The lack of ideological firmness made Peronism different from organized labor grounded in the traditional Left. But its radicalism also set it apart from other populist experiences in the region. Barbara Weinstein rightly describes the relation between Varguismo and the business sector in Brazil in the late 1930s: "Despite the turbulence associated with . . . the proto-populist discourse articulated by Vargas, industrialists soon acknowledged the government's commitment to maintenance of order and protection of property."[63] This was a certitude never fully reached by Argentine economic elites who faced the emergence of Perón. As a political culture, best expressed in the 1949 Constitution, which established the social function of property, Peronism became a living challenge to the unrestrained primacy of individual property rights without ever unleashing a radical attack on capital. The upper classes, which had not perceived the need for a fascist leader, given the lack of a radicalized threat, had now helped to produce a somewhat different version of it.

The way in which the future labor attaché León Segovia came to join Peronism in the Chaco territory illustrates the multiple social, political, and ideological factors that converged in the rise of Peronism and its particular combination of radicalism and social order. As a socialist activist at the Sindicato Unión Obrero Fabriles de Barranqueras during the 1930s, Segovia led a struggle against the Ingenio Las Palmas, demanding that workers stop living in crowded company barracks and that the Ingenio allow them to acquire portions of land on which to build their own houses. The owners had rejected similar petitions for over a decade. In many instances, local police had helped the company repress worker demonstrations. After the 1943 Revolution, Segovia and other socialist members of the union traveled to Buenos Aires and asked for help from the national government. Perón received them and promised the government's support. The administration—in charge of the Chaco territory until it became a province under the name of Provincia Presidente Perón, in 1951—ordered the company to resume negotiation with workers. The company refused, so the government expropriated part of their land in order to build a new *barrio obrero*, or workers' quarters. The company resisted, so this time, Perón sent the National Gendarmerie not to defend the company and its property, but to make the Ingenio comply with the government's resolution. At the head of the force sent to Chaco to defend the socialist union was Guillermo Solveyra Casares, a military man with Axis sympathies who went on to organize the most brutal aspects of Peronist repression against labor and progressive activists during the following decade. He enforced the national decree and also repressed the activists (some of them foreigners working at the Ingenio) who advanced more radical demands. The unlikely confluence of Segovia and Solveyra allowed for the construction of the new houses. The national government made sure that several other regulations and labor rights at the company were respected. Once workers obtained these victories, Perón revised the terms of the expropriation, offering the company more money for less-valuable land than originally claimed. In less than a year, Perón also managed to displace the union's old guard, allowing for the rise of Segovia, now a resolved member of his rising movement.[64]

Conclusion

The profound transformations that occurred in Argentina during the 1930s were more complex than the indictment of Infamous Decade suggests. The relationship between Argentina and the outside world and the actions of the Ministry of Foreign Affairs were distinctive realms in which elites tried to make sense of that complexity. As liberal elites located Argentina in a regional and global context, they debated over competing views of social order in relation to the transformations occurring in Europe and the United States. Emerging from fraudulent elections, the administrations faced the challenges of the Great Depression by looking to ideas of government intervention in the economy that moderated the impact of the crisis. These policies also helped to ignite a process of national industrialization that diversified economic elites and expanded the working classes. Even if this was still a nation ruled by landowner oligarchs, the country of 1943 had little resemblance with the one over which they had taken control in 1930.

Liberal and nationalistic sectors, as well as the Catholic Church, recognized the need to change the political system and make it more inclusive. They also acknowledged that this democratization would have an impact on wealth redistribution. Events like the Spanish Civil War and the Second World War became venues in which these changes were discussed across traditional lines. Unions and labor activists, coming mostly from the Left in support of the Spanish Republic first and the Allies later, were active participants in these debates, opening spaces for workers' voices in national and foreign policy. Liberal elites were more open to supporting the republic abroad than to exercising democracy at home. At the same time, they were more capable of embracing neutrality during World War II because this position embodied the national principles that were at the center of the confrontation with the United States.

Ideologically, Peronism fashioned its identity as a movement of social reform that reinvented national debates about the need for a new social order. To a large extent, it conceived of the incorporation of the urban working classes into the benefits of capitalist industrialization as an answer to workers' pressure. Perón initially envisioned this incorporation as part of a corporatist project in which the extension of economic benefits and political rights, granted in a hierarchical order, could achieve what liberal democracies had failed to do in Europe: avoid the rise of radicalism.

As the domestic and international events following 1943 unfolded with the end of both the Década Infame and World War II, the Peronist project relied more than originally expected on the centrality of organized labor and less on a solid alliance with economic elites. This configuration provided Peronism with an aggressive radicalism, which set it apart from other populist experiences and provided the cultural tenets for an enduring anti-elite impulse. Benefiting from the economic bonanza of Argentina, Peronism absorbed and processed a wide set of experiences, including the fascist hierarchical notion of social order and the New Deal, into a new worldview. It was, in this sense, both a continuation of a variety of experiences and a totally new one.

The hypothetical question about what would have happened if the old elites had led the transition to mass politics will remain an open one, as must all questions of counterhistory. The patrician diplomat Saavedra Lamas, in his formidable vision of a nationalism that incorporated a modern state with the social question at its core, was the best expression of this hope and of its limitations. For Saavedra Lamas, in the end, class emerged as a more important concern than nation. The Nobel Laureate retired from the Ministry of Foreign Affairs without having fulfilled his ideas of progressive democratic liberalism. In the mediation of the Chaco War, he constructed the most formidable and successful challenge to U.S. dominance in the region, much to the exasperation of the U.S. representative, Spruille Braden, who saw in him the embodiment of all the vices of Argentine nationalism. In August 1945, as Perón was about to rise to power and carry out most of the initiatives for which Saavedra Lamas had advocated for decades, including the very program of worker attachés, the patrician diplomat was in a place that nobody would have imagined for him years earlier: he was sitting next to Braden, his most recalcitrant adversary and now a leader of a crusade against Perón across the world, during his farewell dinner as U.S. ambassador to Buenos Aires. While a social revolution led by Perón was taking place in the factories and plazas of Argentina, one U.S. official caustically described the dinner presided by Braden and Saavedra Lamas as "the most extraordinary thing that could be: 800 *gente bien* [hoity-toity people] congregated in the various ballrooms of the Plaza Hotel. . . . All these sedate people were deliberately getting up and dancing on the tables to hear their own government denounced."[65]

date In April 1945, the U.S. State Department wrote the first official document to call for an end to the Good Neighbor Policy (GNP). The report, written about Argentina, focused on the new kind of danger that Argentine politics represented to hemispheric security. The title was self-explanatory: "Policy Re: Dictatorships and Disreputable Governments." Demanding a revision of the GNP, it called for the suspension of its basic tenet of non-interference in other sovereign states. It justified the change by claiming that "our future self-preservation is . . . endangered" by "a careless tolerance of evil institutions," which had flourished under U.S. self-imposed limitations during World War II. "The principal example of those limitations," the report concluded, "is our non-intervention commitment." The author of the report was Spruille Braden.[1]

The State Department deemed the argument "a most interesting discussion of a problem which deserves careful consideration."[2] The department circulated the cable widely and asked all embassies in Latin America to send feedback. This feedback was then compiled and shared with officials in Washington and with those posted in Europe and Asia. The document informed the general language and content of U.S. officials and their actions for the following years. But in Latin America in particular, it provided the rationale for the United States's aggressive forms of indirect pressures and direct military and political interventions. Even before the conclusion of World War II, "Disreputable Governments" had laid the ground for the Cold War in the region.

Braden was probably the person best-suited to prepare the send-off speech for the Good Neighbor Policy. As U.S. ambassador to Cuba, Braden had notoriously clashed with Argentina at the 1933 Pan-American Conference in which the GNP had been proclaimed. Later, he led the United States to one of the major setbacks in its hemispheric policy during the multilateral mediation of the Chaco War. A few weeks after writing his dispatch about disreputable governments, Braden landed in Buenos Aires in his new role of ambassador to Argentina with the goal of bringing down the meteoric rise to power of Colonel Perón. It was 27 May 1945.

Braden was born in 1894 in Elkhorn, Montana, a small mining town that was experiencing a period of brief and unexpected prosperity triggered by a silver boom. His father, William, was a mining engineer who made a fortune early in his career as a technical witness in lawsuits involving some of the largest mining companies in the United States. By his late twenties, William had acquired some copper companies and had real-estate investments on the East Coast. Politically identified as extremely conservative, William used the expansion of the U.S. empire and the routes it traced to try to avoid first the hit of the crisis at the turn of the century and then to escape his family's fall. Spruille's first contact with Latin America was in 1902 in Velardeña, Mexico, where William bought his first nondomestic silver mining and smelting company. Spruille remembered the "odd mixture of Catholic and Indian" cultures, voicing an enduring obsession among U.S. businessmen for whom the legacies of Spanish Catholicism and miscegenation were the sources of Latin American backwardness. As his father expanded his companies to include copper mines in Chile and Bolivia—where "Spaniards had treated those poor Indians so badly that not even actual cash could still their fear that they would be cheated if they dealt with us"—Braden studied at Yale and married María Humeres Solar, a Chilean woman from a renowned family but with no financial resources.[3]

The 1929 crash put a drastic end to the Bradens' affluence. Spruille, who had become a Democrat in the late 1920s, was forced to leverage his father's personal relationship with William H. Woodin, secretary of the treasury under Franklin D. Roosevelt, to secure a role in the new administration. His father resented the incoming government but saw no other chance for the family's future. Braden aimed for the U.S. embassy in Chile. "I did the best I could," Woodin wrote a few months after taking office in 1933, announcing to Spruille that the post had gone to another person. "Maybe something will come to pass in the future where I can be of some help to you." This offer panned out late in the same year, when Woodin was able to add Braden to the U.S. delegation to the 1933 Pan-American Conference, in Montevideo.[4]

The Montevideo conference shaped Braden's views of hemispheric politics. At the conference, Argentina and the United States advanced opposing views of hemispheric integration. Argentina not only pushed for the now famous "nonintervention" resolution, but also tried to locate labor and social issues at the center of the debate.[5] Following the conference, Braden went on to become the U.S. representative in the mediation during the Chaco War, then ambassador to Colombia, in 1939, and to Cuba, three years later. Braden's career flourished within the Roosevelt administration, but his political views also grew out of exchanges with his conservative father and his business associates. William had resigned himself to seeing his son serve in the public service; he considered the New Deal an attack on freedom in the United States, which had developed "matters such as the labor, wage and hours and Social Security and taxation acts that cry to high heaven for intelligent revisions," and FDR as a president who had "perpetrated evils on this country which will take decades to eradicate." William engaged in political conversations with his son but was dismissive of his opinions. He called Spruille's moderate support of the New Deal nonsense. "Apparently, you have inherited a certain yankee stubbornness of your mother, without her intellectual integrity," he wrote at one point.[6] Never belligerent with his father, Spruille oscillated between conciliatory and didactic replies. William's aggressive disapproval and Spruille's submissive reaction framed the political conversation. This fundamental element of Spruille's political education ended abruptly, interrupting a heated exchange of letters between father and son. On 17 July 1942, William died after having "swallowed a small chicken bone which lodged in his throat."[7] Braden acknowledged a feeling of guilt, and the precarious balance in his own political opinion was irretrievably broken. From that time, he increasingly incorporated his father's criticism into his own political worldview.

Braden's political evolution and personal life laid the framework for his approach to Peronism. The mid-1940s was a moment preceded by more than a decade of Argentine obstruction to U.S. Pan-Americanism and with the rise of Perón in its future. Braden saw this period as arising from the same years of the birth of the Good Neighbor Policy: "The current Nazi trend in Argentina, as is so generally believed, [is not in fact] a new development . . . but a sturdy growth, the seeds of which were planted by the Uriburu-Justo Revolution of 1930." He wrote that the threat of Argentine nationalism was "so strong that [it] could not easily be plucked out by the adoption of a few high-sounding resolutions at an Inter-American conference."[8]

FIGURE 2.1. Spruille Braden, U.S. ambassador to Argentina and later undersecretary of state for Hemispheric Affairs, 1946. Braden introduced Peronism to American audiences. He also wrote one of the first diplomatic dispatches that called for an end to the Good Neighbor Policy, precisely in order to confront Peronism more directly. Source: Spruille Braden Papers, box 59, Rare Book and Manuscript Library, Columbia University Library.

Braden's view of Peronism anticipated a central theme of the Cold War: the interpretation that pitted old forms of cultural romanticism against forces of modernization, and blamed that clash for the emergence of regimes that were capable of dissolving individual rationality under mass manipulation. U.S. diplomats saw in Latin America an atavistic, obscure imagery. It revived glitches in the region's path to modernization, which U.S. scholars and diplomats traced to the Spanish Conquest.[9] As Braden put it, "By reasons of history, language and spiritual similarities which link Spain to the Latin American nations, we should likewise give special attention to the Falangist movement as it evolves into Hispanism or other isms such as for instance what may be called *Argentinism*."[10] This totalitarian experiment was, for Braden, a form of "excessive nationalism" that "has assumed such proportions that it is not purely economic, but a trend that may destroy the whole peace structure we are so laboriously trying to build" in Latin America.[11] It was different from mere dictators, who dotted the region's history, in most cases with the sponsorship of the United States. "We do not have to deal with a stereotyped Latin American dictator or military oligarchy, but are faced with a much more fundamental problem," Braden wrote to a friend: "Right here in America we have the tumor of Fascism."[12]

This mindset shaped the way that Braden introduced Peronism to American audiences. Shared among policymakers, diplomats, journalists, intellectuals, and those in a position to shape the American worldview, this imagery was far-reaching. Discussions about Peronism found reverberations in domestic debates about the role of organized labor and in Cold War containment abroad. In a Western Hemisphere immersed in debates about the emerging postwar system of interstate relations, the rise of Peronism became a crucial point in hemispheric debates about democracy. By 1945, Perón already had the rare privilege of leading the only country in the region to which the U.S. State Department had dedicated a task force with an eloquent name: "The Argentine Problem."[13]

This chapter discusses three ways in which the rise of Peronism informed hemispheric debates about democracy. The first involves the history of Argentine efforts to undermine U.S. ideas of Pan-Americanism by questioning the primacy of property rights over national sovereignty. The second way is how Peronism put a crucial twist on this long-standing anti-Americanism, doing so, as Braden aptly perceived, by injecting nationalism with a new class ethos. Peronist rhetoric was informed by a language that tied nationalism to social reform and that was not alien to what the New Deal had propagated in Latin America. And in its antagonism to the United States, this rhetoric offered a realistic vision for the expansion of citizenship for the region's emerging working class. The third way is the combustive encounter between the rising force of Peronism and a climactic moment in the history of U.S. liberalism. In this encounter, many of the ideas and practices advanced in Argentina—centrality of organized labor in politics, intervention of the government in the economy, and primacy of common good over individual freedom—came to be discussed domestically in the United States. Common to the analysis of the three ways in which Peronism influenced the public discourse on democracy is an attempt to show the critical role of Latin America, and Peronism in particular, in what the historian Mark L. Kleinman describes as the transformation of the U.S. perspective from a "world of hope," with emphasis on social rights and domestic reform, to a "world of fear," with emphasis on domestic and foreign containment that connected the "liberal fear of potential domestic fascism" with the related "fears of a Latin American revolution."[14] As the attachés reported to their posts at the beginning of 1947, their actions became an intrinsic part of that transformation.

The Threat

PAN-AMERICAN EMPIRE

Argentina had disrupted U.S. efforts to establish a Pan-American interstate system since the 1880s, and it continued to do so until the creation of the Organization of American States, in 1948.[15] Pan-Americanism originally reflected the dispute between the British economic empire and the multiple forms of expansion of the United States in the region. Worldwide, it was a period of emergence of movements and systems that encouraged and regulated the relations among the recently consolidated national states. In the case of the Western Hemisphere, the United States conceived Pan-Americanism as the interstate system of political diplomacy, military force, and international law that could open up Latin American economies under the rationality of free markets in order to absorb the accelerated expansion of international lending and investment.[16]

The wealthiest country in Latin America, Argentina benefited from sustained agricultural exports that flooded British ports and had sufficient resources to confront the liberalization of the region's economies. Argentine elites conceived of the region's integration as the product of a shared cultural, political, and racial background. This integration was, in fact, presented as resistant to economic materialism. During the time between the First and Sixth Pan-American Conferences, held in 1889 and 1928 respectively, Argentine diplomats developed an extensive corpus of philosophical, juridical, and political arguments that systematically opposed the use of state resources (diplomatic pressure or military force) for the safeguarding of economic rights beyond national borders. The international doctrines of Luis María Drago and Carlos Calvo became fundamental tenets of this kind of internationalism, in which the higher principles of national sovereignty and political integration were placed above notions of private-property rights.

The friction with the United States increased in the 1930s despite the establishment of the Good Neighbor Policy in 1933. The GNP was a transformative element in U.S. foreign policy and was generated, to a large extent, as a response to the pressures of Argentina (and of Mexico after the 1910 Revolution). It proclaimed the principle of non-intervention in other countries in the region and the respect of other countries' sovereignty. It was launched at the Seventh Pan-American Conference, in Montevideo. During that conference, the Argentine delegation clashed with the United States over two issues that defined the shape of Pan-American relations.

The first was the antiwar pact (known as the "Argentine pact"), which prevented state member countries from recognizing sovereignty over annexed territories if their incorporation had not gone through regional forms of arbitration. Foreign Minister Saavedra Lamas pursued Article II, which established that "territorial questions must not be settled by resort to violence," so state members "shall recognize no territorial arrangement not obtained through pacific means, nor the validity of an occupation or acquisition of territory brought about by armed forces." The U.S. State Department opposed the initiative, arguing that it overlapped with existing signed protocols. Behind closed doors, it advised the U.S. delegates that the reference to "a non-recognition of 'occupation' of territory by armed forces is much broader than the provision in the Pact of Paris," and warned, rightly: "Unless an appropriate safe-guarding reservation were made, it might conceivably raise questions as to our rights under certain existing treaties (e.g., those with Cuba, Panama, Haiti, and the Dominican Republic)."[17]

The second issue also reveals how Argentine elites were quite attuned to the social changes triggered by the Great Depression. Along with Mexico and Chile, Argentina promoted the creation of an Inter-American Bureau of Labor. It was conceived as the regional expression of the International Labour Organization (ILO), which was created in 1919 and over which Saavedra Lamas had presided in 1928. Mexico's involvement was part of a broader push for the creation of international social and financial institutions, something that Argentina supported, though with less enthusiasm.[18] For the Argentine delegation, the regional labor agency would focus not only on the collection of regional data, but also on the recommendation and elaboration of public policies for state members regarding issues such as the "improvement of the conditions of living workingmen," the "promotion of safety in industry," and "improved housing conditions." It also advanced one of the first attempts to generate "practical forms of unemployment insurance." Across the board, U.S. delegates resisted the proposal. The U.S. delegation "welcomed" the discussion of housing conditions but found "no adequate reasons for international action in this field"; they considered any U.S. action related to unemployment insurance "impracticable" since "the competence of the U.S. Federal Government is very limited." Finally, they considered the creation of such a regional body to be too expensive and argued that "the United States Federal Government could hardly expect to receive a return adequate to the expense in which it would be involved."[19]

After the conference, these two differing ambitions met again during mediation in the Chaco War. Conflict remained contained and relations cordial, even if the United States viewed with suspicion any step Argentina took in the peace process. In the 1938 Pan-American Conference, held in Lima—the last conference before World War II—Argentina insisted on the idea that the coming war was not a Pan-American issue but a U.S. concern. The head of the Argentine delegation, Foreign Minister José María Cantilo, stated that the "US must face certain world problems that are not ours. It works out world relations according to its own ideas . . . but then brings those positions here to us in Latin America and says, 'Let us adopt this as a Pan American policy.' We do not like this."[20]

The end of World War II opened debates about the consolidation of a new interstate system and the rise of multiple demands for new social and political rights postponed during the conflict. This period offered a new stage for the confrontation of opposing Argentine and U.S. views. In the context of Argentina's growing regional presence, the Peronist ambassador in Washington announced in 1947 that Perón had his own smaller "Marshall Plan" for Latin America.[21] The overstatement had its rationale. During his first years in office, Perón had sought two ambitious objectives: to partner with the United States in the European recovery program that was later called the Marshall Plan and to develop his own plan for Latin America, thereby eroding U.S. dominance in the region. Each objective was significant on its own. Together, they were more than difficult to achieve. Yet this did not prevent protagonists of the time from taking Perón's goals seriously, as a blessing, a puzzle, or a threat.

The immediately propagandistic aims of those promises align them with other populist leaderships before and after Perón (most notably the examples of Venezuelan foreign policy under Hugo Chávez). But Perón's vision was also an expression of the economic and political ascendancy of Argentina in the region at the end of World War II.[22] Peronism envisioned South America as Argentina's main sphere of influence, but the rest of Latin America and the Caribbean were also a territory for political action. Perón pushed for broad bilateral trade agreements with Chile and Bolivia, promoted specific economic pacts with Peru, Paraguay, and Venezuela, and used Argentina's economic muscle in an attempt to influence domestic politics in Uruguay or Ecuador. The pursuit of bilateral agreements ran against the principles of free trade advocated by the United States. They also hindered U.S.-specific plans in Chile and Bolivia, both producers of strategically important metals, and contradicted the broader idea of a hemispheric free trade zone under American ascendancy.[23]

AN ARGENTINE NEW DEAL

Peronism reinvigorated the social question as part of Argentine nationalism. It was not only a rhetorical point. As the worker-attaché program revealed, it expressed the larger role of organized labor in domestic politics and the space that workers had achieved in the construction of domestic and hemispheric institutions. As workers became dominant in fashioning postwar Argentine nationalism, its leaders and activists incorporated a variety of sources into their language of social reform. The New Deal is probably one of the most crucial—and certainly one of the least studied—sources in the configuration of the Peronist identity.[24] At times, this element has been dismissed as evidence of Perón's opportunism, with some arguing that the Argentine leader would claim any identity that he considered politically profitable at the time. This claim misses the larger historical point of how a movement of fascist inspiration was so efficient—certainly much more so than its liberal opposition—in incorporating central aspects of the New Deal, a policy developed in and funded by the United States. References to the New Deal in early Peronist rhetoric were more ubiquitous than is usually acknowledged. In analyzing the press from 1930 to 1945, Laura Ruiz Jiménez has shown how "the widespread admiration [in Argentina] for Roosevelt's work stands in stark contrast with the image given by historians who, almost without exception, presented the society of the period as holding anti-US beliefs."[25] In this context, a subtle but clear distinction emerged between a working-class-based anti-Americanism and a vindication of the New Deal as a specific way to understand freedom, government intervention, and some forms of subordination of property rights that were important in Peronist identity. Even the nationalistic book that gave the name Década Infame to the previous period abounded in FDR's characterization of "private economic monopolies as a form of Fascism."[26]

This rhetorical operation had vast consequences. It differentiated Perón's position from earlier forms of anti-Americanism. Also, it helped to render meaningless the accusations of fascism that the Unión Democrática launched against Perón—not because the charges were not true, but because they were insufficient to describe the varied experiences of workers' incorporation into Peronism and the worldview they developed along the way. As the Unión Democrática closed its campaign in 1946 under a sign with the inscription

"No Al Fascismo," Perón closed his with a subtler narrative. In a now memorable speech, he stated that the option for workers was to choose between "Perón or Braden," the U.S. ambassador to Buenos Aires. But a few paragraphs later, he claimed to be the legitimate bearer of the New Deal legacy, praising "the Great American democrat, Franklin D. Roosevelt" who "had begun to bring private autocratic powers into their proper subordination to the public's government." Perón, the nationalist candidate with fascist roots running against a candidate publicly sponsored by the United States, ended his campaign by quoting an extended paragraph of FDR's Second Inaugural Address: "The legend that [autocrats] were invincible has been shattered. They have been challenged and beaten."[27] In this and other speeches, flyers, and statements, Peronists carefully reconstructed an image of the U.S. president (with abundant material to do so) that helped to cement Peronist identity. Peronism underscored the domestic impact of the New Deal in the United States and its "political and social opposition as a denial of the dominant elite's power, symbols, and values."[28]

While Perón's reference to Braden is among the most frequently mentioned pieces of oratory in works about the origins of Peronism, the second part of the speech has been surprisingly absent in these studies. With this absence, fascism becomes an obvious reference for the period, obscuring the elements that are more singular and powerful expressions of Peronism as it was historically lived. Considering this particular rhetorical relation between Peronism and the legacies of the New Deal illuminates the emergence of a worldview composed of different ideological legacies, social interests, domestic struggles, political practices, and global conflicts. All of these shaped the stance both of the labor movement and of Argentine liberal elites. And it was with this toolkit of ideas that the Peronist attachés launched a frontal assault on liberalism's claims of advancing democracy in Latin America, a dispute that defined crucial aspects of postwar democracy and of the emergence of the interstate system.

The Stakes of Peronism

Most studies in the field of diplomatic and economic history explain the U.S. aversion to Perón by stressing fears regarding Argentina's relationship with Nazi Germany, the possibility that Peronism could become a dictatorship and lead other countries in the same direction, or a combination of these concerns and the country's economic rivalry with the United States.[29] While recognizing the importance of these factors, I want to shift the investigation of the fundamental spirit of the United States's virulent hostility into a different sphere: U.S. elites were challenged not only by Peronism's alien nature, but also, paradoxically, by its similarities to the New Deal at a time when some of its most important legacies were being discussed, rolled back, or dismantled in the United States. For many U.S. diplomats, labor leaders, intellectuals, and policymakers, Peronist Argentina raised the specter of the more radical elements of New Deal liberalism, which the United States had managed to suppress at home.

Four aspects of the U.S. reaction should be studied under a new light. The first aspect is the change in U.S. foreign policy, which moved from understanding Argentina as a traditional society in which the search for social reform was a positive aspect of a broader modernization of social and economic relations, to expressing a virulent hostility toward that reform. The second is the centrality of the labor question in shaping the view of Peronism as a totalitarian threat that, from the U.S. perspective, was particularly effective at suppressing individual freedom. The third is the wide circulation of this characterization of Peronism among diplomats and how this dissemination informed various aspects of U.S. foreign policy beyond Latin America. And the fourth is the vigorous efforts made by the U.S. government and elites to bring this image of Peronism home and to implant it in domestic debates.

In this sense, a better understanding of Peronism should illuminate the particular area in which the identity of postwar U.S. liberalism took shape. At the very least, it should contribute to the study of one aspect of identity formation in the United States: the way in which reflections about Latin American populism became an important input in, and were a relevant product of, the constitution of the U.S. postwar cultural milieu, which had Cold War social sciences at its center.

IN NEED OF SOCIAL REFORM

The United States immediately opposed the 1943 Revolution. After recognizing the new government, it conditioned the total normalization of bilateral relations to Argentina's declaration of war against the Axis powers. Argentina remained neutral during most of the conflict, and it (along with Chile) declared war only in March 1945 (the last two countries in Latin America to do so) after signing the Chapultepec Act, which paved the way for joining the United Nations later that year.

But Americans following the events in Argentina (including many of the same diplomats) seemed to develop a different perception of the revolution. They described the nationalist revolution in sympathetic terms. In many cases, their characterizations were grounded in a perception of the revolution as a reaction against both traditional social relations and direct forms of exertion of economic power without any intermediate sphere of universal rights. Above all, they appreciated the need for social change in Argentina. Reactions to the revolution like the one by Clara Applegate, for example, were not unusual. A young and relatively wealthy American woman, she traveled to Argentina for a long vacation and ended up working for the U.S. Board of Economic Warfare. Three days after the revolution, she wrote in her diary, "Most Argentine people have been pleasantly surprised by some of the very good things done by decrees under the present regime, i.e., reduction of rents, ceilings on certain goods, economies in the government, etc."[30] A few days later, she reiterated these feelings with a personal story, highlighting the recent changes as well as the country's constraints: "We had an amusing example of how the new government affects us, when last night the doorbell rang while Joan and I were having dinner, and in came the building porter. He stood in the middle of the floor, feet planted firmly together, and recited in Spanish 'I am here to put into force, by order of the Executive government, Decree # _____ relative to the reduction of rents,' and then, with a broad smile on his face he refunded us thirty pesos (about eight U.S. dollars) on the rent we paid a few days ago. I laughed and said I liked that law, to which he replied, 'Oh, but you won't like this one,' and proceeded to intone that, because of the fuel shortage, we would have hot water only for one hour in the morning, half-hour at noon, and an hour at night!"[31]

As the revolution evolved, many U.S. officials also developed an understanding of the negative impact of oligarchies that, in their view, were not able to express any interest other than their own. In this narrative, the rise of Perón appeared as an atavistic reaction to premodern rulers. A U.S. diplomat stationed in Buenos Aires analyzed the local class relations in 1945, and reached the dim assessment that the upper class was incapable of leading a process of integration: "The old families here make New York bankers sound like [the secretary general of the Communist Party of the United States] William Z. Foster," he wrote.[32] He witnessed the long-feared events of 17 October 1945, when, for the first time, Perón spoke from the balcony of the government house to a multitude of Argentine workers, launching his epic political career. And upon that scene, he reflected: "Peron's rising is likely to result in a fairly long step forward toward social revolution in Argentina.... With extremes of wealth and poverty, this in itself is perhaps proper; the tragedy is that a Fascist dictator is leading it."[33] Visions of modernity permeated the opinions of all the players involved. Peronist modernizing discourse had simplified the history of the prior decade as a prepolitical form of power. With the rise of

Perón, many Americans came to understand the need for change in Latin America under the same lenses, albeit guided by different strategies.

The word of U.S. labor experts and labor diplomats was central to the construction of these views about the backwardness of Argentina and the dangers of the Peronist answer. Argentina emerged as posing a different dilemma from the rest of the region, as, in this case, political backwardness combined with modern ideas of social rights and economic industrialization. Robert Alexander was a central figure in molding this notion of the Argentine transition from tradition to modernity as a historical construct, introducing a scientific analysis of labor relations in the perceptions of U.S. diplomats and union leaders. As a young scholar specializing in labor relations, he had been in touch with Argentine labor unions and reformist socialist leaders, with whom he collaborated in the early 1940s as a U.S. correspondent for their magazine in Buenos Aires. Late in 1946, Alexander went to the industrial belts of Buenos Aires, Rosario, and Córdoba as an unofficial envoy of the American Federation of Labor (AFL), sharing his views with both unions and the U.S. State Department. Alexander translated for his American audience the perplexity of his local friends, now furious anti-Peronists. He described how a labor movement of leftist ideology and strong antimilitarist tradition had allied with a rightist military leader and how they had plotted together to remove the old guard of reformist, moderate union activists, creating the most powerful experience of labor politics in the region.[34] For U.S. labor diplomats like Serafino Romualdi, the AFL's representative to Latin America, this analysis, which attributed the disruptive role of Peronism to the reimagined traditionalism of the national past, laid the ground for the characterization of labor activism in Argentina. It recuperated liberal criticism against conservative regimes and warned about the need for urgent liberal reforms across the region. Even in 1947, the AFL reaffirmed that the explosion of social demands made palpable by the rise of Perón was the product of a country that had been "ruled for decades by an oligarchy of *Estancieros*, meat packers, and other powerful economic groups which dominated the political life of the country and held in check the aspirations of the working people."[35]

FROM REVOLUTION TO REFORM

U.S. labor diplomats were on the front line of a constant redefinition of notions of social change, progress, and totalitarianism.[36] Cases like Romualdi's show the tight connections between U.S. labor, government, and elites in advancing these reflections. Born in Italy in 1900, Romualdi had escaped fascism and migrated to the United States in the 1920s. After working in different unions, joining the staff of the International Ladies' Garment Workers' Union, and traveling extensively to Latin America, Romualdi worked for the U.S. government during the war. In 1943, he joined the Office of the Coordination of Inter-American Affairs (OCIAA) led by Nelson Rockefeller, leading the Allies' publicity and propaganda efforts among unions.[37] Less than a year later, he joined the Office of Strategic Services (OSS), the immediate predecessor of the modern Central Intelligence Agency (CIA), initially working at the Italian branch. Once the war ended, he returned to the United States to establish relations between the OSS and the AFL and between them and union organizations in Latin America.[38]

For labor leaders and U.S. officials, "modernization" and "social change" became essential to their efforts to define the role of unions in postwar democracy. In discussions that echoed and overlapped with U.S. domestic debates, the AFL perceived in Peronism a distortion of a beneficial strategy to defend workers' rights. Paradoxically, the emphasis that Argentine labor placed on wealth redistribution and the immediate benefits that they obtained from subordination to the state engendered this characterization, serving as the most visible evidence of the labor base's lack of "democratic consciousness" and of the risks that this condition entailed.[39]

Curiosity, interest, and the simple perception of the enormous appeal that Peronism could have abroad moved U.S. unions to develop an intense relationship with Argentine organized labor in the mid-1940s. These contacts constituted a productive field not only in the characterization of Peronism but also in the latter's relation with the U.S. government, cementing the space in which they would act during the Cold War. A few weeks before Perón took office, representatives of the General Confederation of Labour (CGT) sent a letter to AFL president William Green, criticizing an article about Perón published in the AFL magazine and inviting him to visit Buenos Aires.[40] Two months later, in what was described as a cordial meeting, George Meany, a future president of the AFL, met in Mexico with the soon-to-be director of the worker attachés training courses, Anselmo Malvicini, and received an invitation from Perón to visit Argentina.[41] The AFL had rejected the legitimacy of the Peronist CGT in international meetings, but decided to invite its leaders along with others from Latin America to its 65th Convention, to be held in Chicago in October 1946.[42]

The AFL presented the idea to the U.S. State Department as part of a hemispheric strategy to speed up the creation of an Inter-American Trade Union. The answer from the government was cautious. "There are good reasons which compel me to ask that further actions on the project be delayed," wrote Spruille Braden, now assistant secretary for hemispheric affairs at the State Department. "Whereas I am in complete agreement with the principle of inter-American exchange of labor leaders, one reason [for the delay] involves the current industrial upset in the United States,"[43] Braden added, in reference to the largest strike wave in the country's history. Later, the end of a 119-day strike at General Motors, led by the Congress of Industrial Organizations (CIO) and carried out by 320,000 members of the United Automobile Workers (UAW) union, made even more evident the domestic implications of labor diplomacy.[44]

– Most scholars of U.S. labor history agree that a variety of domestic factors transformed the General Motors strike of 1945–1946 into a watershed in the history of U.S. liberalism. The struggle led by the UAW produced regional transformations in the Democratic Party's electoral base, in race relations, in the status of unionized workers, and in the overall dispute between the CIO and the AFL. As the historian Nelson Lichtenstein has argued, an overarching factor that catalyzed these changes was the redefinition of the relation between organized labor and politics, "the turning point" in U.S. liberalism that took place "between 1946 and 1948, when a still powerful trade union movement found its efforts to bargain over the shape of the postwar political economy decisively blocked by a powerful remobilization of business and conservative forces. Labor's ambitions were thereafter sharply curbed, and its economic program was reduced to a sort of militant interest group politics."[45]

After arguing at length with the government, U.S. labor leaders finally invited three members of the CGT to Chicago, overturning the State Department's warnings.[46] It would be one of the last times they did so. Along with delegates from other countries, the Argentine activists took the stage in Chicago during "Pan-American Day" to join the United States in urging the creation of an inter-American labor organization.[47] One of the Peronist delegates congratulated Romualdi because "our brothers of the Great Republic of the North have now given the correct interpretation to the historical climate in which the labor movement of my country lives and operates."[48]

They had not. The AFL's actions quickly developed into a dual effort to contain the expansion of communist unions in the region (as led by the Mexican Vicente Lombardo Toledano) and to undermine the perceived ambitions of a Peronist-style social revolution. The AFL viewed this battle as part of its struggle against fascism. Romualdi landed in Buenos Aires for his first "informal" visit accompanied by two international antifascist leaders. The visitors reaffirmed the need for an independent labor movement. When the U.S. labor diplomats expressed doubts about the *personería gremial*, or legal recognition, of unions (which the Argentine government had used to bolster some and weaken others since 1944), the Peronist hosts told them that the system was similar to that used in the United States. When the labor diplomats returned to Washington, they sent a mixed report about the visit to William Green.[49] A copy of the report was forwarded to the U.S. State Department.[50]

Romualdi led a larger official delegation of U.S. labor diplomats during a second visit to Buenos Aires, to help clarify the opposing projects of the two labor movements.[51] In 1947, as the first worker attachés were leaving Buenos Aires for their new destinations, a dozen U.S. labor officials landed for a visit that started with a confrontation and ended with a rupture. The purpose of the visit devolved, starting as an intended evaluation of organized labor in Argentina and ending with its denunciation. Perón led a set of public arguments and discussions with Romualdi and quickly turned Romualdi into a public icon of U.S. pressure on Peronism.[52]

In the confrontation against Peronism, the AFL presented the problems that the conception of organized labor in Latin America posed for the democratic regulation of social conflict. In an article for *Foreign Affairs* published right after his trip to Argentina, Romualdi argued for a marked contrast between liberal and populist views of economic rights.[53] For Romualdi, what made the gains of the Argentine working class unsustainable was the fact that they derived from the distribution of wealth from capital to labor, rather than from an increase in workers' productivity. Government's vast regulation of economic activity, the basis of the welfare state, was the main problem in Argentina, where "a high degree of governmental intervention in labor conflicts under the Perón regime" had resulted in "laws raising the minimum wage and prescribing paid vacations and yearly bonuses."[54] Perón was attuned to a corporatist idea that permeated labor relations in Latin America, Romualdi argued. Across the region, other similar measures, such as "severance pay up to the amount of several months' wage required by law," presented a social legislation that seemed an "enlightened attitude toward workers" but that had "not resulted in an appreciable betterment of their standard of living."[55] This was, Romualdi went on, "in sharp contrast to the program of trade unions in the United States, where workers aimed first for a high level of wages—a 'saving wage' [basically a version of the living wage or universal minimum wage that was expanded in the United States through the 1920s]—and *then* sought social security and welfare legislation to supplement it."[56] "Then" was the central argument, as Romualdi thought that the deferment of further rights gave the economy time to produce more wealth without hurting capital's profit. Borrowing from the Peruvian leader Víctor Raúl Haya de la Torre, himself a populist until he signed on with the U.S. diplomatic efforts in the region in 1945, Romualdi summarized: "We do not need to take away wealth from those who have it; we must rather produce wealth for those who don't have it."[57] In this view, then, a core aim of trade unions in the United States was to *avoid* class conflict over wealth distribution, in opposition to a prevalent conception in Latin America whereby workers obtained benefits at the expense of capital.

Romualdi's view was informed by the modernization theories of the time. The views of Peronist Argentina, which he brought from Buenos Aires to the United States, also provided scholars and public opinion with fresh evidence of the threats that a deviation from that path could pose. From union magazines to the *Chicago Daily News* and other major newspapers, the ample coverage of Romualdi's visit to Argentina and its aftermaths was populated in the following months by images of Hitler, Mussolini, and Stalin.[58] According to the labor diplomats, Argentina had laid the ground for a strongman who could manipulate the working class by promising gains that would ultimately prove unsustainable. This specter resignified Argentina's achievements in expanding social and political rights for the working class.

Romualdi probably made the clearest exposition of this pessimistic take on populist politics in an academic setting, where he presented the conflict between workers' benefits and liberal democracy in its most paradoxical form. After one of Romualdi's visits to Argentina, Robert Alexander organized an event at Rutgers University in which Romualdi could share his view of Peronism with labor experts, policymakers, and scholars. Romualdi stated,

> The claims of Perón and his government that the workers of Argentina are no longer exploited—that wages have been increased—that working conditions are better—that good social security legislation has been enacted—that organization of workers has not only been encouraged but actually promoted under government guidance and sponsorship—that a large proportion of legislators are from the ranks of organized labor—that labor tribunals have been instituted to supplement the defense of organized labor in those fields where unions do not operate—that to all intents and purposes government and labor are the same things—all this and even more may be true. . . . But the fact remained that democracy, as understood here in the United States, does not exist in Argentina.[59]

As a *labor* diplomat, Romualdi itemized most of the demands of postwar working classes in the Americas and presented them as having been fulfilled by the regime he was trying to vilify. The timing of his ambiguity is particularly revealing in its larger implications for the United States. He delivered his speech at Rutgers on 9 June 1947, only thirteen days before the U.S. Senate passed the Taft-Hartley Act into law by overriding President Truman's veto. The act precisely circumscribed organized labor's political and bargaining power by outlawing the closed shop, the use of union funds in political campaigns, and strikes by government employees, ushering in the roll back the labor rights secured during the New Deal.[60]

With the large wave of strikes as a backdrop, the debate about the role of unions in democracy was relevant not only in conservative circles but also for progressive liberal mass audiences, where powerful voices insisted on the need to restrain workers' rights in order to preserve liberal democracy. Debates like those held on the influential radio program *America's Town Meeting of the Air* provide hints about this shift in the public conversation, increasingly focused on how to guarantee social peace and restrain unions' power. The radio show, perceived as a space for progressive liberalism and reaching an audience of three million people, had already dedicated one episode, in 1944, to "What to Do with Argentina?," in addition to making abundant references to the emergence of Peronism. In the months before Romualdi's speech, the radio program addressed questions such as "Should There Be Stricter Regulations of Labor Unions?"; during this particular discussion, labor leaders defended unions' power against accusations of privilege levied by both Democratic and Republican representatives. The program that aired on 29 January 1946 was a solid indicator of the contrasting conjunctures of the two labor movements in Argentina and the United States: airing in New York only five days after Perón's first electoral victory in Argentina, the episode was eloquently titled "Can We Find a Substitute for Strikes?"[61]

THE RISKS OF EXPORTING PERONISM

The deployment of the Argentine worker attachés increased alarm over the possibility that the kind of mobilized labor created by Perón could penetrate Latin American countries experiencing similar processes of industrialization. Just a few weeks after the Argentine government created the program, the U.S. State Department sent a dispatch assigning a new task to all its embassies and consulates in Latin America: they now had not only to report anti-United States and communist activity, but also to provide periodic updates about the actions of the Peronist attachés in particular.[62] American officials called attention to the nature of the worker-attaché program and to how it reflected on the preeminence of organized labor in Peronist Argentina. A U.S. diplomat in Mexico wondered "whether by calling their Labor Attaché 'Agregado Obrero,' which strictly translated means Worker Attaché, rather than Labor Attaché (Agregado del Trabajo), the Argentines are attempting to call attention to the fact that their attachés come from workingmen's ranks is, on the basis of the information available to this Embassy, a matter for speculation."[63]

This form of international labor activism made more visible the danger of Peronist ambitions for expansion, which U.S. officials had perceived from the beginning. This U.S. concern started well before Perón appeared on the horizon, with Braden's claims about Argentina's strong influence over the entire Southern Cone. And it grew with Braden's characterization of "Disreputable Governments," which viewed the rise of Perón as a beachhead for fascism in the Americas. The attachés provided one more element for U.S. diplomats' conceptualization of social unrest and expansionism. U.S. officials' perception of the actions of Argentine activists abroad had reverberations in early stages of the Cold War, setting the stage for a struggle against totalitarianism, understood as something broader and more diffuse than communism.

A close reading of the Long Telegram, for example, offers a hint of how U.S. debates spurred by the rise of Perón echoed abroad. The U.S. diplomat George F. Kennan wrote the 8,000-word text, which became the blueprint for Cold War containment, in the dawn hours of 22 February 1946, from the bedroom of his residence in Moscow, where he was an official at the U.S. embassy. Bedridden with a high fever, sinusitis, and a severe toothache that anticipated the need for a root canal, the diplomat was exasperated at the stubborn difficulty of his superiors at the State Department in understanding the Soviet Union. In the telegram, Kennan famously described communism as an alien ideology, which was imposed upon rather passive people and which was ripe to be spread throughout the world. "All persons with grievances, whether economic or racial, will be urged to spelt redress not in mediation and compromise, but in defiant violent struggle for destruction of other elements of society," he wrote, well before the Cold War even existed as a category. Kennan believed that the Soviet Union would try to reinforce its relations with countries that had "strong possibilities of opposition to Western centers of power." He concluded: "This applies to such widely separated points as Germany, Argentina, Middle Eastern countries, etc."[64]

The diplomat's enumeration is casual but not random. Why did Kennan mention Argentina among his few specific examples? The references to Germany and the Middle Eastern countries are self-explanatory; however, no scholar has interrogated Kennan's reasons for singling out Argentina in what is among the most studied documents of Cold War history.[65] Kennan was an obsessive observer with a fierce intellectual appetite and a sense of exacting scrutiny in his writing. Argentina was not even close to the geopolitical center of the postwar world; communism was not a significant force there (in fact, the Communist Party had joined the U.S.-sponsored liberal alliance against Perón); and neither Argentina nor Latin America were included in the diplomat's vast areas of interest, something that would change in the 1950s.[66]

In the year before the Long Telegram, the Soviet Union had made a decisive push for admitting Argentina to the United Nations (UN). But the Soviet authorities' argument was related to a broader negotiation with the United States about other countries in the Soviet sphere of influence and did not reflect a strategic alliance with Argentina. The Soviet Union advocated for Argentina's admission into the UN with the certainty that Argentina would try to restrain the power of the United States in the Western Hemisphere. The mention of Argentina in the Long Telegram seems to have been influenced by the wide circulation of Braden's "Disreputable Governments." Kennan corresponded with Ellis Briggs, a U.S. diplomat stationed in the Dominican Republic. As Braden's closest colleague at the State Department, Briggs had commented extensively on early drafts of "Disreputable Governments." Unlike Kennan, Braden was not an intellectual: his knowledge of world politics was limited; his writing artless; his ideas propelled by a primeval anticommunism. Yet the writings of Braden and Kennan were circulated among U.S. officials and mutually reinforced one another's perception of the need for global containment and the emergence of threats in the Western Hemisphere. In Washington, the dispatch of the Long Telegram inspired one official to "strongly recommend it to Mr. Braden's attention."[67] Kennan thanked Briggs and, in response, acknowledged his limited knowledge of the region: "I wish I could give you more from here on Soviet relations with Central and South America. We have been working under great limitations of staff and housing and have not been able to do nearly the specializing we would have liked to."[68] Though there is no conclusive evidence explaining Kennan's reasons for including Argentina in his text, the specific context suggests an early understanding of Latin America as a locus in which conflicts over economic and social rights in an industrialized society could engender a threat to liberal procedures. In postwar Latin America, the populist threat to democracy was an ideological construct, but one that was paradoxically scaffolded by concerns about the democratizing dynamics of populist politics and the destabilizing effects that those dynamics entailed. The timing of political developments in the region seemed to confirm the menace: less than forty-eight hours after the Long Telegram arrived in Washington, Colonel Juan Perón was winning his first presidential election.

DON'T BRING PERONISM BACK HOME

Toward 1945 and in the early years of the postwar, Argentina became increasingly relevant both for the agenda of U.S. policymakers and for the general public back in the United States. This centrality was anything but unplanned. The U.S. deployed government and government-related resources to monitor how Peronism was portrayed at home, encouraging an increasing attention to Argentina. Labor leaders and policymakers brought home their concerns about the risks that Peronism posed for hemispheric security. The government, in turn, reciprocated with incentives and sanctions. The mobilization of government resources and the actions of a broad array of individuals with the power to influence or shape public opinion became crucial in order to call attention to Peronism and to the risks posed by its model of labor relations.

Journalists who favored the United States and attacked Peronism were explicitly considered assets to the national interest. Among them was Arnaldo Cortesi, who covered the rise of Perón for the *New York Times*. His writings were in complete alignment with the State Department's position, and he was given special privileges by the officials about whom he was writing. Cortesi was born in Italy; his father, also a journalist, had covered the rise of Mussolini, a legacy that shaped Cortesi's reporting on Argentina. Cortesi applied for U.S. citizenship as he was writing from Buenos Aires. During the application process, Braden described Cortesi as an ally whose work justified special treatment. The ambassador "urged on the Department that a special exception be made," so Cortesi did not have to leave Argentina to obtain his U.S. papers. Braden stated, "Aside from our personal friendship for Mr. Cortesi, I feel we should go all-out in helping him as a matter of fundamental policy here. The work he is doing is of tremendous importance to our Argentine policy and, for that matter, for our entire Latin American policy."[69] This proximity with the government did not damage Cortesi's career; on the contrary, his worked garnered accolades, and Cortesi eventually won a Pulitzer Prize, in 1946, for his coverage of Perón's rise to power. Herbert Matthews, the legendary journalist who covered Fascist Italy for the *New York Times* and "introduced" Fidel Castro to U.S. audiences a few years before the Cuban Revolution, cast Cortesi's work in a very different light. Matthews, himself a vitriolic anti-Peronist, described Cortesi's award as "an example of the *New York Times* tolerance and ignorance," and Cortesi's work about Perón as a product of "inordinate laziness. He spent all his time between his hotel and The Times Office, with side-trips to the nearby American Embassy." Given the tragic reporting on the European recovery from World War II and the harsh judgment of Cortesi by his colleagues, Cortesi's Pulitzer appears to have resulted from pressure brought by Arthur Krock, an all-powerful *Times* member of the Pulitzer Committee and a staunchly conservative southern Democrat close to President Truman.[70]

American unions also actively promoted an increase in the attention paid to Peronism. Victor Riesel, a labor journalist with a column syndicated in more than three hundred newspapers in the United States, corresponded extensively with Romualdi. Riesel's columns repeated, almost verbatim, the AFL's claims that Perón and the Soviet Union had "secret agents whispering to Latin Americans about what to do—Listen to the Perón agents tear down the US and you'd think you were hearing a stump speaker on a state-owned soapbox in Red Square."[71] Romualdi encouraged, sometimes bluntly, U.S.-funded activists who were in Argentina to dedicate part of their time to the general public in the United States. In 1951, for example, he contacted Alfredo Fidanza, an Argentine labor activist in exile in Uruguay, where the AFL had particular hopes of building a relation with local unions. Romualdi wrote to Fidanza, telling him that Jay Lovestone, from the Free Trade Union Committee of the AFL, had sent Fidanza "a $250.00 check as a first contribution," adding that "Brother Lovestone also needs you to write an article of 1,200 words about unions in Argentina (*with special mention of the tortures to prisoners*) in order to publish at the *Free Trade Union News*."[72]

As the discourse of functionalist social sciences became prevalent, the U.S. government's use of statistics and polls to gauge public opinion became a crucial component of the decision-making process. Correspondingly, the State Department also monitored how Peronism was perceived in the United States by ordering periodic surveys. Polls were conducted by Paul B. Sheatsley, the legendary founder of the National Opinion Research Center (NORC), located at the University of Denver, who had aided the U.S. government during the war. By 1946, when Perón had been in office for just a few months, an extensive poll found that 50 percent of those Americans interviewed had some "interest" in the evolution of Argentina, that around 70 percent of this group believed Perón was a dictator, and that, expectedly, most disagreed with the idea of "sending arms to South American countries" in order to strengthen hemispheric military defenses.[73]

These episodes reveal an important aspect of how the public sphere was created. This is not to say that U.S. domestic debates are simply a manufactured product of elites. But it does suggest that U.S. political and economic groups of influence actively—and not always in coordination—generated and highlighted Peronism's particular relevance for the domestic agenda, bringing Latin America to the United States through debates over the risks posed by personalist leadership, government intervention in the economy, and the rising role of organized labor.

Conclusion

Peronism was one facet of U.S. concerns abroad. It was certainly only one of many components in a much more diverse domestic conversation around social unrest and totalitarianism. The purpose of this chapter has been to historicize the perception of Peronism as a threat by contextualizing it within the long-term confrontation between Argentina and the United States. Argentina's arguments against the centrality of property rights in the emergence of Pan-Americanism during the first half of the twentieth century acquired a new dimension under Peronism. Perón's strong reliance on organized labor and the related expansion of workers' benefits turned the original association between national sovereignty and social rights, which Argentine elites had proclaimed in the past, into a political program. Embraced by Argentine workers, Peronism's specific form of class-based democratic nationalism emerged on the global stage at a moment when U.S. liberalism was immersed in debates about the domestic legacies of the New Deal. These debates, in turn, had a dual focus: on the one hand they were concerned with the extent to which the government could intervene in the economy for the sake of creating a more just society without damaging individual liberties and property rights; on the other hand, they were concerned with how to define the place of organized labor in democracy and to characterize the risks that the power achieved by organized labor in its defense of workers' rights could pose for the stability of liberal forms of negotiation. Argentina was, in this context, a relevant and much-discussed example of what many in the United States saw as excessive state intervention in the economy and as the exaggerated influence of unions in politics.

This account does not exclude the many other factors that influenced the confrontation between Argentina and the United States, nor does it try to explain the many transformations brought about in postwar U.S. liberalism by its opposition to Perón. But it demonstrates the relevance of the labor question in the heightened tension between the two countries in the aftermath of World War II. It also illuminates the way in which anxieties about the foundation of what will be later called Latin American populism reflected on, and contributed to, domestic debates about the nature of the New Deal. A direct byproduct of these debates was the configuration of a form of liberalism with stronger emphasis on preventing social conflict. The analysis of the tensions with Peronism and their influence in U.S. foreign policy sheds light on the early features of the Cold War's driving forces in the region.

CHAPTER THREE. **APOSTLES OF SOCIAL REVOLUTION**

Early in August 1946, an official letter from President Juan Perón arrived at Manuel Lobato's small office. Lobato was director of parties and celebrations for the tailors union in Tucumán, a thousand miles north of Buenos Aires. The president informed Lobato that the General Confederation of Labour had chosen him as a "pre-candidate" for the worker-attaché training course. This letter was among a hundred identical notes sent across the country to labor organizations, ranging from powerful unions in the working-class suburbs of Buenos Aires to small branches in remote provinces. Four months later, the training was finished. Lobato then received a new note on presidential letter-head. This time, Perón praised him for completing the course and appointed him as worker attaché to the Pan-American Union in Washington, D.C. "Your action abroad will do more than justify the incorporation of workers into the diplomatic activity of the State," the president said. The new leader hoped that Lobato and the others would "take abroad a popular and truthful representation of the proletariat."[1]

Worker access to government—a noticeable departure from the recent political past—was a symbol of the changes Peronism had produced. During the presidential campaign, Perón promised to incorporate workers and unions into the new political order. Once in office, he quickly delivered. Overcoming the resistance of other Peronist factions, union members filled the lists of *Laborista* candidates to national congress, provincial legislatures, and city councils.[2] Perón's most loyal union supporters also won key positions in his cabinet. Whether measured by numbers or influence, worker and union participation in the decision-making process had never been so high. Workers and union members did not exactly constitute an elite, for no group in Argentina seemed able to be so, as José Luis De Imaz had claimed. But for the first time workers were to be counted fully and officially, following De Imaz's characterization, among "Those Who Rule."[3]

Created only one month after Perón took office, the *agregados obreros* program expressed a new vision of the relationship between social and political rights. It showed how the furthering of social rights—the notion that groups economically marginalized in society were entitled to some benefits as a group *in addition* to the inalienable rights of its individual members—had turned political rights into a new platform for workers' empowerment. The program's significance went beyond other policy steps that had been taken since the 1943 Revolution. It was not about giving power to the seasoned union leaders who had helped Perón create his powerful political structure since 1943. The attachés were rank-and-file union members, many of them young, with little or no political experience outside their unions. They represented the entry of Perón's "new Argentina" into the Cancillería. Finally, the attachés' mission was as innovative as it was vital to Perón's worldview. The attachés aimed to promote among governments and political and social organizations the populist notion of the intrinsic relation between social justice, political citizenship, and national sovereignty, and to create a regional labor movement fashioned around this credo. In Latin America, the attachés acted as the third leg of an ambitious view of regional leadership, as their role complemented efforts to create bilateral economic agreements with neighboring countries and to strengthen diplomatic relations with governments close to Peronism.[4]

Two general themes run through the next three chapters. First, these chapters illustrate how the incursion of workers abroad was part of a vast reconfiguration of nationalism as the dynamic core of Peronism. Under Perón, workers recovered long-standing ideas of national exceptionalism, yet they did so under a radically new class ethos that made sense of domestic transformations and located them in a historical and global perspective. Second, they show the distinctive appeal of this form of "populist nationalism" in postwar Latin America. In their actions, the attachés conceived the rise of organized labor, the radicalization of popular politics, and the expansion of the welfare state as moves that *confronted*, rather than *embraced*, an aggressive internationalization, which was identified in the region with the expansion of the U.S. interests in the Western Hemisphere. This worldview produced a powerful critique of liberal democracy, which Peronist activists presented as the ideological edifice of the domestic and regional status quo under U.S. dominance. This nationalistic view and the rising tide of labor activism became central factors in the creation of the interstate system in the Americas and its founding principles. They also offer insight into the fundamental motivations of the forces that later led the fierce reaction against the postwar democratic spring in Latin America.

This chapter examine the creation and launch of the worker-attaché program as part of a vast revamping of social and political relations, characterized by the new and unfamiliar presence of organized labor in all aspects of Argentine life. The incorporation of blue-collar workers into the foreign office was part of both a massive social uplifting and an effort to overhaul government personnel (an effort incomplete, in part, due to the limited removal of the old guard). Though labor diplomacy was not a Peronist invention, the worker-attaché program was pioneering in its aggressive international mobilization of labor activists whose explicit mission was to promote a Peronist form of social revolution abroad in the name of the Argentine government. The foundations of the singular spirit that the attachés promoted came to light during their training courses, which became the realm of intense sessions of ideological debate between Falangist intellectuals and leftist labor activists. In the courses, anti-liberal ideologies drawn from Spain and Portugal, usually associated with the most conservative moments of Peronism, encountered Marxism and other ideas from the Left and coalesced into a new and compelling political vision during its most progressive years.

Peronism was more than a byproduct of Argentine nationalism and leftist union ideologies. It shared concerns with local elites about the integration of the working class into national politics, the politics of cultural nationalism, and the postwar social dynamic in the region. Old ambitions of regional leadership gave the attachés fresh impetus, but in addition, the early success of domestic social reform and the rise of organized labor turned Peronism into something different from other populist expressions in the region. Peronism possessed broader potential than other populist expressions. In the version of Peronism that the attachés embraced and presented, the potential for change situated it in line with (rather than in opposition to) the regional spring of the immediate postwar, which Leslie Bethell and Ian Roxborough describe as the combined surge of organized labor, democracy, and the Left.[5]

This vision also spoke to major themes in Latin American political thinking across a region that had historically posed the preeminence of social rights as a central tenet of democratic politics.[6]

The Foreign Policy of Uneven Development

As president, Perón saw the strengthening of the country's position in Latin America partly as a means of obtaining a larger degree of autonomy in relation to the United States. This delicate equilibrium between rapprochement and confrontation with the United States called for adjustments in Argentine foreign policy. These changes, which were not without contradictions, pragmatic rearrangements, and unforced errors, included the pursuit of external funds to deepen the policy of Import Substitution Industrialization (ISI), the consequent revision of the country's relation with the United States and Great Britain, and the attempt to solidify political and economic dominance in Latin America in competition with the United States. The need to limit the power of the foreign service's old guard by increasing the presence of new officials devoted to the cause was a component of this view.

As soon as Perón took office, he made every possible effort to dispel the justified suspicions of Argentine sympathy for the Axis powers during World War II. In August 1946, he submitted for ratification by Congress the Treaty of Chapultepec (which forced its signatory countries to dismantle Nazi economic, political, and military infrastructure in the hemisphere) and the country's membership in the United Nations. Perón's foreign minister, Juan Atilio Bramuglia, advanced the more pragmatic and strategic arguments for integrating with the global economy against the nationalistic arguments of the opposition and even of Perón's own Partido Laborista. "Are we going to live again in isolation? Are we not going to join the other nations of the world?" asked Bramuglia. The former socialist lawyer answered the question himself by placing Peronist achievements and aspirations in a measured perspective: "The country lacks capital. We have wheat, we have beef, but we don't have machinery, and we need to be in contact with the rest of the world in order to exchange its production."[7]

This realistic approach did not necessarily soften the nationalistic rhetoric of Peronism, but Argentine officials understood it as a slow-paced offensive. As Perón put it in a handwritten, private letter to Bramuglia, "Since we are not strong enough, let's apply 'the tactic of the microorganism,' which is also strong: to gain access, and to gnaw, gnaw, and gnaw, until we perforate the intestine and see the colossus fall. . . . Then the field is open. Might God inspire us, the Motherland is waiting."[8]

But in public, Peronism reinvigorated nationalism as a "language of contention." Within this framework, the president and labor activists explored the prospects and limitations of anti-Americanism as a foreign policy and a source of legitimacy for social reform at home.[9] The results of this exploration varied over time and led them to different arrival points. Perón soon ran up against the limits of confronting the United States. As he faced U.S. pressure for an unwavering allegiance to the Cold War struggle against communism, his nationalism increasingly became a vertical call to sacrifice gains and social struggles in the name of the nation. Labor activists continued to present anti-Americanism as intrinsically tied to the expansion of social rights. They denounced liberal democracy as a U.S.-sponsored obstacle to workers' participation in the fruits of industrialization. Domestically and abroad, they forced Perón's increasingly narrow interpretation of nationalism without confronting the limits of Peronist identity.

Perón did not invent the idea of involving organized labor in a foreign policy of regional expansion as a means of touting increases in worker benefits and the dilution of class conflict at home. As William Appleman Williams and Charles Bergquist have observed, the engagement of unions in U.S. foreign policy had been a central characteristic of the relationship between imperialist projects and the American working class at both the weakest and strongest moments of organized labor during the twentieth century.[10] In fact, Perón's general formula of a state that guaranteed a link between capitalist expansion abroad and social peace at home parallels the fundamentals of the corporatist view that guided the U.S. Good Neighbor Policy toward Latin America during the 1930s and 1940s.[11]

Politically, if the attachés were the channel for the crucial task of building a transnational labor movement akin to Peronism, Argentine foreign policy also needed a diplomatic corps attuned to this new project. Although Perón appointed a large number of political allies and Peronist officials as ambassadors, he did not eliminate an old guard, which far from believing in his project, was explicitly hostile to it. Patrician surnames like Bunge, Serrano Redonnet, Labougle, Victorica Rocca, Portela Oneto Stegno, or Güiraldes remained prominent at the Cancillería.[12] But most patricians did not go abroad. Some opted for a low profile in Buenos Aires as a passive form of resistance to the new administration. Others had been abroad during the war and learned that diplomatic life had become much less glamorous than people believed.

Anti-Peronists to the bone, they nonetheless acknowledged a fact that would be especially meaningful in the experience of the attachés abroad: living conditions were much better in Peronist Argentina than almost anywhere else in the world.[13]

Origins of the Worker Attachés: International Precedents and the Domestic Legacy of Progressive Labor Activism

The presence of labor leaders and activists in Perón's inner circle became dominant during 1945 and as the 1946 presidential election drew closer. Most of them were seasoned activist on the Left. Their political background was strikingly different from the ideas of those closer to Perón, who until then had primarily come from the military, the Church, and nationalist political groups. This legacy of leftist labor activists' traditions and ideas is particularly evident in the creation of the worker-attaché program. Evidence suggests that the program was the initiative of Foreign Minister Bramuglia and the union activists who worked with him. Pedro Otero, a former socialist worker who had been an activist in several unions before becoming a worker attaché, recalled, "I think that [the program of worker attachés] came up during a conversation with Bramuglia, it was his idea. If there were international meetings and organizations, we had to be there, we said."[14] Another possibility is that the idea was brought to Bramuglia's men by the Mexican Luis Morones, a powerful leader of the Confederación Regional Obrera Mexicana (CROM). Morones was close to Peronist labor diplomats from the time they were socialist activists, and had participated in a similar experience in Mexico a few decades earlier. Otero recalled the relationship that both unions and the Argentine Socialist Party had established with other labor organizations abroad: "We already had a relationship with the Unión General de Trabajadores from Spain through Lázaro Peña, we had a good relationship with British unions through the Labour Party, and with the Italian workers, through the cooperatives and the Italian Workers Federation. We could go abroad to tell them the truth about what was happening in Argentina and explain to them what Perón was doing."[15]

Outside of unions, none of the people working with Perón on labor issues had any prior experience in international labor activism.[16] At that time, large parts of the labor movement were engaged in international organizations and were active in world affairs. In addition to socialist unions, both anarchist and communist unions also were historically engaged in initiatives beyond national borders before joining Perón. Since the beginning of the twentieth century, Argentine unions had been lively protagonists of international labor organizations, particularly those across Latin America, and had been engaged in gathering workers' support for crucial Argentine initiatives in foreign affairs, including the country's neutrality in World War I.[17]

At the same time throughout Latin America and particularly in Argentina, union support of the Spanish Republic during the Civil War galvanized labor activists' commitment to their unions and to events beyond national borders. Bramuglia, as well as the future Argentine attachés Otero, Antonio Ferrari, Enrique Reznik, and Cirilo Liendo, participated in solidarity work for the republic and mentioned it as their main, if not only, experience of international activism. During his time as a worker attaché for a government that fervently supported the Falangist Spanish government, Pedro Conde Magdaleno dissented from that stance, as he remembered with pride his offer "to go to fight for the ideals of the Republic and of the left."[18]

THE LONG SHORT STORY OF WORKERS PARTICIPATION
IN GOVERNMENT

The involvement of this group of progressive labor activists differentiated the worker-attaché project from other initiatives for labor diplomacy. Governments around the world had long debated the need for their foreign services to address the labor movement, but in almost all cases, these discussions did not include incorporating representatives of the working class into diplomatic activity. The American Revolutionary War in the eighteenth century and the wave of democratic revolutions across Europe in the following century had prompted a gradual expansion of workforce enfranchisement. As most economic activity in the United States relied on slave labor, "workers" there defined a much narrower group of white farmers and artisans who owned a minimum amount of land. It was not until the U.S. Civil War that property qualifications (for white voters) were reduced. In most cases, this meant the slow enfranchisement of rural and urban workers. The very idea that the social identity of "worker" could be a legitimate platform for political power began to be presented as a possibility by communist and socialist forces only late in the nineteenth century.[19] As for worker participation in the foreign service, political elites debated seriously the relationship between labor movements and global affairs only toward the end of World War I, with the eruption of the Soviet Union in 1917, the revolutionary wave in Europe, and the growing strength of communist parties among the working classes. Only then did the visible impact of the labor movement on the economy, political stability, and foreign policy of the industrialized world become a key component of the international agenda. In 1919, the same year in which the International Labour Organization (ILO) was created, the British foreign service made the first suggestion to appoint labor attachés (not workers) as part of a wide reform of its consular service. "The events of the present war have shown how great is the importance of possessing real knowledge of labour conditions, so far as they affected the political situation," it reported. "Moreover, specific problems are likely to arise, which involve labour questions, as for example, the special tariff treatment of the products of sweated labour, or concurrent labour legislation." The foreign office proposed the appointment of members of the foreign service, many of them formerly commercial attachés, as labor attachés in Paris, Berlin, "Moscow or Petrograd," Rome, Tokyo, and Washington.[20]

The first explicit proposal to allow blue-collar workers to join the foreign service (as opposed to government officials specialized in labor affairs) emerged during the early 1920s as part of the interaction between U.S. unions and the Mexican revolutionary government. Mexico was determined to project its novel revolution abroad. In 1921, at the third conference of the Pan-American Federation of Labor, celebrated in Mexico City, the U.S. leader Samuel Gompers proposed that governments appoint workers across the Western Hemisphere as attachés to their embassies so they could research living conditions abroad. The host of the conference, the powerful CROM, which had been created in 1918, embraced the idea as part of the expansion of the revolutionary experience abroad. During the conference, Gompers and other union leaders were received by the Mexican secretary of interior, General Plutarco Elías Calles, who encouraged the administration of President Alvaro Obregón to consider the idea. From Washington, Roberto Haberman, an American who had become an important member of the Mexican labor movement, insisted on the idea. He shared it with some U.S. congressmen, including the progressive senator Robert La Follete Jr., of Wisconsin. Writing to General Calles, Haberman suggested that an attaché to the United States "should be familiar with the American labor movement, speak English, and be able to become popular among workers' leaders and the press."[21]

With the rise to power of Calles in 1924, the CROM became tightly aligned with the Mexican government. Morones became the all-powerful minister of industry, commerce, and labor, and more generally, the government increasingly privileged its relation with CROM when it came to expressing ideas of national economic development, industrialization, and modernization. A few months after taking office, Calles created the program of worker attachés, the first of its kind in the history of foreign relations. The foundations and purposes of the program anticipated many of the ideas that Perón put in practice in Argentina two decades later. The 1910 Mexican Revolution was the first political experiment in modern Latin America that actively sought to expand its message regionally, to promote and propagandize its social achievements, and to recover the tradition of a regional diplomacy, which would dispute U.S. ascendancy in Latin America by advancing notions of national development and equality as opposed to the strict materialism and free market of American diplomats.

In 1925, President Calles announced that the mission of the Mexican attachés would be "to study social development in other countries" and to produce "reports on social and labor legislation, social security systems and the labor movement at large."[22] But beyond the written law, the attachés took the message of CROM abroad. Equipped with plenty of resources, magazines, and movies, they presented the story of a revolution that had put an end to injustice, uplifted the lower classes, and benefited peasants and workers.

To Buenos Aires, Calles sent the typographer Carlos Gracidas. During his three years in Buenos Aires, Gracidas worked with socialist labor leaders (who would later oppose Perón), traveled throughout the country explaining the Mexican Revolution, opened small libraries that offered information and publications about workers in Latin America, established links between the Mexican political process and the cause of Sandino in Nicaragua, and consequently denounced the U.S. misrepresentation of popular politics in the region. He would refer to Rubén Darío and other Latin American writers as the Mexican political project's source of legitimacy. Thanks to Gracidas, movies (an unusual and expensive propaganda means at the time) about Mexico's revolution reached peasants in Santa Fe and workers at the wineries of Mendoza. After this extensive work, Gracidas saw, during travels to Tucumán, graffiti, apparently written by a local union, with an unequivocal inscription: "Imitemos a México."[23]

But the experience was limited in every sense. There were only six attachés worldwide. Selected by CROM and the government, they went to the United States, Germany, the Soviet Union, Italy, France, and Argentina. With the exception of Gracidas, the attachés did not achieve significant impact in their posts, which could partly explain why the program was never expanded. With the decline of *Callismo* and the swift readjustments in the relation between government and CROM after Calles, the government lost interest in labor diplomacy. The last attachés returned home in 1928, three years after they had started their missions.[24]

Toward the end of World War II, the United States also finally considered the need to include labor issues in its foreign affairs. But the U.S. labor-attaché program was entirely different from the Argentine one; it was not conceived as a means for the incorporation of blue-collar workers into the foreign service or for direct connection between American unions with labor movements abroad.[25] In 1941, the U.S. Foreign Service created the Foreign Service Auxiliary in order to incorporate qualified personnel from outside the department. The goal of the global reform was to reinforce "the economic defense and cultural relations programs in Latin America."[26] There would be two kind of auxiliary—specialists and junior officers. Labor specialists belonged to the first category. After years of deliberation among officials, diplomats, and academics about the need to gather information about (and gain influence over) labor movements outside the United States, the State Department created the position of labor attaché in 1944. The attachés were appointed to U.S. embassies in the United Kingdom, Chile, and, not surprisingly, Argentina. While the initiative for U.S. labor attachés in the United Kingdom and in Argentina responded to the requests of the same embassies, the appointment of the U.S. labor attaché in Chile was an organic decision by the U.S. government, which made it the first official appointment of a U.S. labor attaché abroad.[27] In a pilot exercise, the State Department sent Daniel Horowitz to Santiago. A Harvard and New York University graduate in political sciences and labor economics, Horowitz had worked at the research division of the National Labor Relations Board. From Chile, his reports focused mostly on unions and communism.[28] The program expanded gradually over the next three years. Most of the attachés were diplomats from the State Department, officials from the Department of Labor, and academics. Meanwhile, unions, organized around the AFL and the CIO, started to establish their sizable group of representatives abroad, working with the U.S. government's official and covert support.[29] Although the State Department started to incorporate union members as attachés during the 1950s, most of them were not blue-collar workers, but professionals employed by unions; even then, this group never comprised more than a small percentage of the total number of attachés.[30] In foreign relations, as well as in the rest of the administration, the United States maintained separation between government and unions. By contrast, in Perón's more classical populist approach, workers came to symbolize the nation, gaining unprecedented political power at the cost of enforced subordination to the political leader and of subsuming working-class demands to a general "national interest."[31]

Perón was sworn in on 6 June 1946, and on 23 August, the new president signed Executive Order 7976, which created the position of the worker attaché within the Ministry of Foreign Affairs; the decree also stipulated training courses for the future diplomats, but did not specify their duties. A week later, another executive order created the Instituto de Capacitación. Located close to Perón at the Legal Secretary of the Presidency, the institute's mission was to design and conduct training courses. At the same time, the General Confederation of Labour had already organized a rapid selection of union candidates. On 3 September, less than three months after taking office, Perón, along with most of his ministers, arrived at a public school in downtown Buenos Aires, the provisional location of the institute, to launch the training course in front of union activists from all over the country. The president gave the first official presentation of the program, though it was still an incipient and intricate institutional arrangement between the presidency, the Foreign Ministry, and the General Confederation of Labour (CGT), and moreover lacked an official description of the activists' future duties.[32]

Changes arrived earlier than technicalities, as the early days of the new administration were impregnated with an extraordinary sense of hopeful urgency. The Peronist revolution had actually started well before Perón won the presidential elections. In fact, what we call Peronism can be reconstructed in the thousands of executive decrees issued by the military government between the 1943 coup and Perón's 1946 election. These decrees included measures that guaranteed a minimum wage, universal annual bonuses (*aguinaldo*), paid vacations, and severance pay, and that created the Institute of Social Security and Labor Courts, as well as the institute that established the state monopoly over foreign sales.[33]

Along with these changes came a dramatic increase in the presence of workers in Argentine daily life. Clothing, sports, and movies reflecting the experience of the new urban working classes, and recent migrants from the countryside became the cultural core of a renewed form of nationalism. New themes, new authors, new sounds—like the voice of the folk singer Antonio Tormo—steadily invaded the airwaves, independent from commercial campaigns or the strategies of record companies. "The singer of our things," as Tormo was known, was unheard on national radio and rejected by record companies in Buenos Aires until 1945. His fame grew despite such indifference; his records played in houses, clubs, and parties organized by migrants who had come from the interior to live in the new industrial suburbs of Buenos Aires. Five years later, in 1950, record companies finally agreed to release his hit "El rancho e' la Cambicha" (Cambicha's Ranch), which described life in the destitute interior. The song was an immediate hit. The record sold an astounding five million copies (in a country of sixteen million inhabitants), breaking the all-time record for national music sales.[34]

The many changes that permeated the country's daily life reaffirmed the certitude that this time the working-class experience, "historically presented as the opposite to culture, had its own value and cultural worth."[35] These transformations were more than the mechanical reflection of changes in Argentine economic structure as part of the larger impact of industrialization. The year 1943 was the first one in which industrial production exceeded agriculture in the national GDP. Workers in the industrial and service sectors grew from 64 to 74 percent of the total employed population between 1930 and 1949. But during the same period, unionization grew at a much more energetic pace. Membership increased from 200,000 to 4 million. Fostered by the state after 1943, this growth accelerated through the following decade.[36] What emerged from this reconfiguration of the Argentine social fabric was a defining feature of Peronism, one that transcended the realm of the material transformations, one that was capable of molding political identities and collective actions. Javier Auyero describes it "as an affirmation of workers' rights . . . and a collective claim for dignity that was ready to call into question certain social and cultural hierarchies."[37] With Perón's rise to power, this social transformation affected even traditional political institutions, such as the Cancillería. In the heavily loaded, racist catchphrase of an opposition congressman, Argentina was experiencing an *aluvión zoológico*—literally, a "zoological flood," a barbarian invasion.[38]

"Let the Working Masses Know"

With the launching of the worker-attaché program, the president proclaimed the arrival of Peronism to an area of government known at the time as the "tearoom" of the Argentine aristocracy. For unions, the appointment of the attachés was an opportunity for workers to represent their own interests and a chance for organized labor to shape the country's foreign policy. "The Argentine oligarchy was so abusive that it was accepted as a fact that half a dozen families would distribute among their members rather capriciously the totality of the destinations of the Foreign Service," said a 1948 brochure from the bank-workers unions about the attaché program.[39] The opposition reacted against this change within the same social polarization; they upheld the traditions of the foreign service and said that attachés would degrade its quality. Since there had been no professional training for diplomats, this often amounted to nothing more than a defense of the elites' cultural capital. Opposition congressmen gave voice to the diplomats' complaints about the arrival of political appointees.[40] While at times the attachés were seen as a minor Peronist eccentricity, most coverage was openly hostile to the program's class component, understanding foreign affairs to be a matter that only the upper classes could handle properly. "The whole idea of the attachés is that they are *obreros*, who lack the intellectual training required for high diplomatic posts," said the conservative paper *La Nación*.[41] For the labor movements, the stakes were equally clear: loyalty to a new idea of workers' power and national interest, and not to professional training in particular. "The revolution [of 1943] dignified workers by making them custodians of our own interests, within and outside the country.... Some thought that 'the worker attachés don't know how to wear a tuxedo,' but the truth is that they know how to wear their pants."[42]

The government encouraged this view and presented the attaché program as a new form of democratic politics. An official publicity poster showed a young man wearing overalls. The headline, written in the handwriting of a child, said, "True Democracy: Argentine Workers Participate in Public Administration." Four different paths led the young man to childishly illustrated professional destinations: senators and congressmen, worker attachés, ambassadors, and ministers. Yet the design of the same poster also suggested the limits of such conquests. For a movement that had drawn from Mexican muralists and fascist publicists to depict workers' strength, the use of a childlike aesthetic to represent the Argentine labor movement's ultimate goals also revealed an unusual timidity (by Peronist standards) about how to represent workers in power, a fundamental friction in populist politics.[43]

The first cohort of attachés left the country for their new destinations in early 1947. Before that, they had completed the training courses, during which they met with Perón and Evita, and they had received their diplomas at a massive ceremony at the Teatro Colón, the aristocratic *porteña* opera house now used for sacrilegious political celebrations. Banners with the face of Perón and the names of hundreds of unions and towns from across the country hung from the balcony boxes usually occupied by the most prestigious families.[44] Workers and leaders sang the national anthem in the style of soccer fans, and the folklorist Angelita Vargas performed popular dances from the interior with the Pérez Cardozo Quartet.[45] On the same stage, the president and his wife performed the miracle of turning workers into diplo-

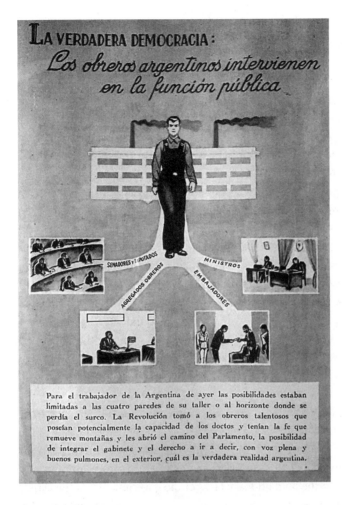

FIGURE 3.1. Government and unions hailed the worker-attaché program as an expression of the new place of the working class in Peronist Argentina. This official poster from 1950 illustrates potential professional destinations for blue-collar workers: senators and congressmen, worker attachés, ambassadors, and ministers. Source: Juan Atilio Bramuglia Papers, box 29, Hoover Institution Archives, Stanford University.

mats. They spoke briefly with each of the attachés, wishing them well, emphasizing the importance that their mission in particular had for Argentina, and answering personal needs, job requests, and even demands for the political freedom of some of the attachés' friends and relatives.

The attachés' departure from Argentina strayed from the usual farewell of officials traveling to diplomatic destinations. Relatives flooded ports and train stations, bringing furniture, clothes, and paper-wrapped food for the trip. Pictures of those events reveal the particular circumstances of their journey. One family picture of León Segovia, a metal turner at a sugar mill, shows him with his wife and two daughters not in Buenos Aires but on the shores of Las Palmas, the small forest town in Chaco where he had lived all his life and where he boarded the *Setiembre* to travel to his new appointment in Paraguay.[46]

Initially, Perón had thought of sending Segovia to the Soviet Union, but he opted for Paraguay after learning that Segovia was fluent in Guaraní, the native language of the indigenous population that lives in an area spanning Paraguay and parts of Argentina, Brazil, and Bolivia.

Others did not board ships. Jaime César Tronconi, a former socialist worker in the meatpacking industry, appears in family pictures at the Retiro railway station, preparing to leave for his new post in Havana, Cuba; he is surrounded by relatives, friends, and coworkers, who had brought all sorts of packages for his journey. Like other attachés, he took advantage of his excursion abroad to first visit other places. With his wife, he crossed the Andes to Chile, caught a ship on the Pacific, and crossed the Panama Canal to the Atlantic in order to reach the Caribbean port.[47]

Unions and media extolled the opportunity the worker-attaché program offered to explain and publicize Peronism abroad. Most flyers and news stressed the unique opportunity that the presence of workers presented for Peronist foreign policy. An article in the magazine of the powerful Metalworkers Union (UOM)—this magazine, like many others, published individual photos of the first forty-nine attachés—stated, "Our workers are going to the wellspring of work, in a loyal mission with workers from all over the world. From that encounter, a new brotherly and peaceful union among people of good will shall emerge."[48]

Perón opened the training courses on 2 September 1946. In his speech, he surprised skeptics by announcing that he would supervise the training of the new corps by regularly visiting the training courses. He was doing this for two reasons, he said: "First, in order to mark students with the original seal [*sello primitivo*] of the revolutionary task [of the government], so the classes can inculcate in students the indispensable enthusiasm for the mission that they will fulfill abroad after training. And second, in order to personally assume the real responsibility of setting in motion, for the first time in the world, this drastic change in diplomatic rules."[49]

Even though the government had not prepared a job description, and the executive orders did not specify the mission of the attachés, Perón's speech about the activists' duties abroad was eloquent. In his view, their mission oscillated between regular diplomacy, propaganda, and intervention in other countries' domestic politics. They had to "let the working masses know, particularly in the Americas, the truth about the Argentine revolution." Perón seemed to limit the scope of their actions abroad by saying that the attachés should work "as missionaries of an apostolate and not as soldiers of conquest."

Yet, at the same time, he placed the attachés' goal in a much larger frame: Argentina had to "expand the revolution abroad" by "asserting [*imponer*] its truth to the world through representatives of the working class." Somewhat hyperbolically, Perón likened the social transformations occurring in Argentina to the French Revolution in terms of their humanism and universalism, adding: "Revolutions that do not transcend their domestic borders die in time and space; they have to survive in the ideas they create."[50]

The worker-attaché program started operating well before the position itself was officially ratified by law during a general reform of the foreign service. In fact, the first official instruction from the Foreign Ministry to the attachés was sent on December 1948, almost two years after the program was created.[51] While the mission, functions, and regulations of the attachés evolved over time, the attachés always worked within the notion of spreading Peronism abroad, particularly in Latin America. Beyond what they learned in the training courses, they also received official and unofficial instructions, advice, and suggestions about what they should and should not do in their new destinations. These instructions came from Perón himself, CGT leaders, individual union members, diplomats, and officials of the newly created Dirección de Organización Internacional del Trabajo at the Foreign Ministry.[52]

Instructions and orders also came from Eva Perón, who rapidly took a personal interest in the initiative as part of a larger parallel diplomacy effort deployed during the first years of Peronism and which famously included her 1947 visit to Europe, where she met the Spanish dictator Francisco Franco. Her dominant role in the development of the program did not translate, however, into a larger presence of women in the new corps, even as women's empowerment became an important domestic aspect of Peronism. Eva Perón started the public campaign to establish women's right to vote just ten days after her husband took office, in 1946 (passed by Congress a year later.) The creation of the Partido Peronista Femenino in 1949 offered a vehicle for women's participation, both for workers and for wives working at home. Women occupied more positions in unions, and Peronism was widely perceived as improving women's situation on the shop floor.[53] Yet there were no women in the first cohort of attachés, and the program never had a section or an agenda related to women. Over the decade, approximately twenty women received the attaché diploma, and just four of them were appointed abroad.[54] The very limited participation of *mujeres peronistas* in a program in which Eva Perón played an important role exemplifies the contradictory gender dynamics within Peronism, in which women's increasing presence in politics

FIGURE 3.2. President Perón and Eva Perón hosting a dinner for worker attachés and labor activists, 1947. Source: Personal Papers of César Tronconi.

often remained subordinated to traditional gender hierarchies that Perón and his wife also reinforced.[55]

The first cohort of attachés arrived abroad with no institutional memory from which they could draw examples. The attachés' mission, which synthesized the multiple and often contradictory orders issued during the first year of the program, appears to have involved five primary tasks. First, the attachés were to establish contact with host country labor leaders and union activists in order to organize an international labor movement, which would be different from those promoted by the United States and the Soviet Union. Second, they were to contact political leaders and activists who were potentially sympathetic to Peronism and invite them to visit Argentina. Third, they were to organize information campaigns and events about Argentina, Peronism, and recent social changes in order to counteract the campaigns against Peronism led by the U.S. government and labor diplomats. Fourth, they were charged with disseminating Peronist influence abroad by promoting the social work of the recently founded Fundación Eva Perón. Each attaché was assigned the specific goal of immediately reaching five hundred families in his area of influence with the offer of food and clothing from the Fundación. (Officials estimated they could directly reach a quarter of a million people every year, thus producing additional media coverage in each country.)[56] Fifth, attachés were to travel throughout the host country to gain a deeper knowledge of the place and report back on labor conditions.[57] With Perón's launch of the program in September and the presidential commitment to send the first corps of worker attachés abroad by the beginning of 1947, the government had barely four months to turn a group of labor activists into revolutionary labor diplomats.

The Training Courses

THE SETTING

The carved wooden chairs at Public School No. 9 in downtown Buenos Aires hardly accommodated the worker-students' robust bodies. But aside from that singular group of adult workers, who in most cases had arrived from the provinces, the classroom looked exactly like any other in the public-education system: a glass and wood door on one side, wide windows on the other, a map of Argentina and portrait of General San Martín hanging in the back, a large blackboard and teacher's desk at the front.[58] The main singularity was not the classroom, but the content of the lessons. The syllabus included topics such as the achievements of the 1943 Revolution, Argentine international relations, the role of the Fundación Eva Perón in the social uplifting of the Argentine working class, and Perón's political thought and concept of social justice in Latin America.[59] Rapidly but not hastily prepared, the first training courses for worker attachés required a vast mobilization of political and economic resources. The structure, design, and even location of the courses would undergo significant modifications over the following years due to changes in Peronist views of workers' education, Argentine foreign policy, and the program itself. But the class of 1946 offers a unique insight into a formative moment of Peronist foreign and domestic policies, and into the ideas that gave them meaning.[60]

Training labor activists to become diplomats was a disruptive move in at least two ways. First, it was one of the many instances in which Perón's administration took ownership of the liberal notion of education as an instrument for social mobility. It considered *educación obrera* to be a way of promoting workers' progress and their assimilation into society. Peronism, in addition, also devised the training of labor activists as a means of inculcating new citizens with the values expressed by Perón and Evita.[61] Second, it was an original step toward the professionalization of political personnel. Despite the

Foreign Ministry's importance for liberal elites since the nineteenth century, there was no specific training for diplomats, nor any clear, universal, and publicly shared set of principles for what members of the foreign service should do abroad. This was the first effort at the professionalization of workers, and it stands in contrast to the stereotype, at times nurtured by Peronism itself, of a lowbrow movement that displaced an elite of instructed decision-makers. The courses for agregados obreros were the first formal training that the state provided for Argentine diplomats, and it preceded the foundation of the Instituto del Servicio Exterior de la Nación, which trained all diplomats and was also created under Perón.[62]

The future attachés arrived in Buenos Aires for their classes, most without their families, only two weeks after the CGT and the unions had finished the selection process and sent them the official invitations. The attachés were divided into two groups, A and B, with the first starting on 2 September, and the second on 2 October.[63] On their arrival, the attachés were immersed in a four-month intensive course. Classes ran six days a week, Monday to Saturday, beginning at four o'clock in the afternoon and ending at eight o'clock in the evening. Although there was no extra homework, most areas covered in class were new to the students and required further reading during the day.[64] The courses also included many extracurricular activities, even during weekends, leaving little free time for the attachés and making the training a truly full-time activity.

In order to make the process politically and economically sustainable, the CGT and the government agreed on two important points. One was that the legal secretary was going to create a specific fellowship for the courses. Students were granted a stipend equivalent to the salary that they received at their unions (or their regular jobs, if they were not unions' employees). Students were also required to fulfill regular tasks at their unions. The second decision, crucial in order to expedite the selection process, was that all students must retain (at least formally) their union posts during the courses and during their terms as attachés, reinforcing their double political and institutional insertion in both government and the labor movement.[65]

THE STUDENTS

In light of the positive reception of the initiative among unions, the government decided to double the number of candidates in the first cohort. However, not every activist invited to the first course became an attaché. Of the first one hundred candidates, some seventy activists arrived in Buenos Aires for the courses, with fifty-seven actually attending classes and receiving diplomas. Forty-nine were immediately deployed abroad at the end of the courses, with three more sent out six months later. Almost everyone in the first and second cohort of attachés was assigned a post abroad after receiving a diploma.[66]

Who were they? What did they do? Where had they come from? The biographies of the future diplomats themselves give substantial evidence of the transformative effects of the program, as people from historically marginalized social, political, and geographical segments were becoming part of a new political class. The first attachés were a sample of the social bases that had brought Perón to power and of the ensuing social transformations. Yet there was only one woman in the first cohort. The extremely limited participation of female labor activists remained characteristic of the program. It is true that women's participation in unions was not as extended during the early years of Peronism as it would later come to be. But not only were women already union members, but their actions in the factories were important signs of the challenge to traditional hierarchies at home and on the shop floor. Moreover, the almost total exclusion of women from the program did not change when women expanded their presence in public and political life. Again, those few who were incorporated as attachés representing Peronism abroad emphasized a role for women under Peronism that simultaneously challenged established notions while promoting basic gender and family roles in society.[67]

With some variations, the social and geographical composition of the successive cohorts of the five hundred union activists who received diplomas as worker attachés remained relatively unchanged. Many came from the industrial suburbs of Greater Buenos Aires, a stronghold of Peronism; around half came from the interior. Some were from the incipient industrial belts of Córdoba. Others, like Agustín Viale, a worker in the prosperous wine industry, had been born in Gualeguaychú, a small town in the Province of Entre Ríos. León Segovia arrived from the Chaco national territory (population 225,000), an area without full political rights until it became a province, in 1951. The first cohort of attachés belonged to thirty unions; thirty-five of the fifty-two attachés deployed abroad came from the industrial sector. A look at their occupations highlights the crafts (and unions) that prevailed in the economy developed since the mid-1930s under Import Substitution Industrialization (ISI). This economy was dominated by the steel, textile, port, transportation, and food sectors.[68] It was from these areas that many of the future worker attachés originated, including Diego Pisera, a metal turner from the UOM; Francisco Costantino, a crane operator affiliated with one of the railway workers unions; Carlos Quinto Monza, a die maker at the UOM; and Luis

Badano, a weaver from the textile workers organization. While many were already working within their unions when they started the courses, others went straight from their jobs in the factories to the new diplomatic school.[69]

Only three activists came from the public sector: a teacher, a Buenos Aires municipal worker, and a national government employee. The rest belonged to the private sector (commerce, sports institutions, hotels and restaurants, banks). These two groups included members of unions that had been crucial to the rise of Peronism. The cases of the municipal and commerce workers are the most notable examples: some of these union leaders had switched allegiance to Perón during the 1943–1946 period and had fought bitter struggles with their former comrades for control of their unions. They won these battles with the undisguised support of the secretary of labor.[70]

These not-so-old disputes underscore another crucial aspect of the program. Almost all of the attachés had been members of communist, socialist, and anarchist unions until at least 1943, when a fracture in the labor movement brought together the majority of those who would support Perón in the following decade in the "CGT1."[71] For elites who had witnessed the first steps of the new government with trepidation, the political background of the attachés was now as threatening as (if not more so than) their social class. But it also posed a challenge for Perón and the heterogeneous coalition that supported him.

Perón had successfully used government resources and his personal intuition to navigate the fractious world of the Argentine labor movement. From the secretary of labor, he had designed a new leadership, exacerbating the conflict between different sectors. He had won activists and leaders to his side by officially supporting their positions, giving them more standing than their employers, and providing unprecedented legal and economic rights for their constituencies. Meanwhile, he had violently dismantled the organizations that resisted his advances—most of them affiliated with the Communist Party.[72]

By 1946, the problem of popular support had been solved in unequivocal terms, as evidenced by the impressive machine of labor and political activists who had brought Perón to power. But the question of what ideas would guide this new government either remained largely unanswered or had as many answers as there were factions of the Partido Laborista. For some of the attachés, their leftist backgrounds overlapped with the beginning of their lives as workers. Modesto Alvarez, a future attaché in Bolivia, had been a member of the Socialist Party for twenty years. He had pursued a transfer at his railway job from the city to the interior in order to organize the Socialist Party deep in the heartland of Buenos Aires Province.[73] Others, like Pedro Conde Magdaleno, had felt inspired by the 1917 Bolshevik Revolution as a young worker.[74] Like most of Perón's followers, both Alvarez and Magdaleno had left those experiences behind by 1945. But others were like Roberto Federico Ferrari, who embraced Perón after more than two decades of activism within the Socialist Party. Far from severing ties with his former comrades, Ferrari continued his communication with them even while living abroad as a Peronist diplomat, corresponding with Nicolás Repetto, the socialist leader with whom he had worked and who was now harassed (and frequently jailed) by his own government.[75]

The attachés' background in leftist unions did not, however, have a univocal meaning. The leaders and activists who approached Perón after 1944 brought with them a variety of ideological and political traditions, which ranged from the forceful confrontation of the anarchosyndicalism of the 1910s to the more reformist strategy of an already bureaucratized union structure in the 1930s.[76] Under both progressive democratic governments or conservative fraudulent ones, unions had found ways to negotiate with the state and obtain benefits and rights for their bases. This "legalism" tamed the radicalism of leftist activists.[77] Once this relationship with the state changed, after 1944, and proved immensely more productive than in the past, unions encouraged a renewed radicalism, nurtured this time in the perceived empowerment that came from the rapid realization of long-postponed demands. If one common ground remained constant despite all the differences among these activists during the decade preceding the arrival of Peronism, it was, paradoxically, the commitment to fight against the same European fascism that had inspired the leader they now joined.

THE PROFESSORS

The executive order that created the courses also established the Consejo Superior, which assumed political responsibility for the project but wasn't directly involved in designing the syllabus or teaching the classes. Perón appointed Anselmo Malvicini as the head of this body. Malvicini was an activist from the railway union who had represented the working-class neighborhood of Liniers at the CGT during the foundational events of 17 October 1945. The decree placed the school of worker attachés in the hands of a Dirección Técnica, subordinated to the Consejo Superior and led by Juan Carlos Juárez, who was aided by Luis Cerrutti Costa, Rodolfo Tecera del Franco, and Jorge A. Dávalos. Four more people would join them in teaching the courses. If the names were not immediately recognizable, the institution from which they came was already well known in official circles: the Ateneo de Estudios Sociales, a right-wing think tank that had been working with Perón from the very beginning of his political career.

Even if this institution had had a great deal of experience in workers' education, its ideological origin could hardly have been more distant from the one embraced by the attachés. The members of the Ateneo had specialized in unions and labor relations since the early 1930s. But what became immediately clear was that, for Perón, the courses were not only about diplomatic training; they were, above all else, an opportunity to galvanize ideas that he had proclaimed during the campaign among supporters of very diverse backgrounds. The members of the Ateneo might have lacked the knowledge of foreign relations or diplomatic etiquette that the attachés needed, but few could call themselves *Peronistas de la primera hora* (the first Peronists) with more authority.

Toward the end of 1942, a growing number of nationalist militants and intellectuals had started to visit a charming but still obscure Juan Perón. Their conversations circled around a patriotic revolution that would put an end to the liberal democracy that had delivered a decade of fraudulent conservative governments and an economy tied to the ailing British empire. Reflecting the historical norm, conversations in these circles mainly consisted in conspiring within the military, the Church, and the elites while devising pro-German international strategies.[78] To many, the mere suggestion of expanding the scope of their project to incorporate representatives of the working class was risible at best and suspicious at worst.[79]

Yet not all of Perón's early allies ignored the importance of labor. José Miguel Francisco Luis Figuerola y Tresols was a Catalan lawyer who had worked for Primo de Rivera's military government in 1923. Working at the Spanish Ministry of Labor and Social Welfare, Figuerola had helped to create a corporatist labor apparatus, had served intensively on the state-run arbitration boards, had represented Spain to the International Labour Organization in Geneva, and had been sent by Primo de Rivera to Italy to examine the organization of Mussolini's labor programs.[80] He had extensively studied social and legal issues related to the Spanish working class. Once he immigrated to Argentina in 1930, he started to publish detailed articles, informed by corporatist ideas of the time, about changes in modern societies and the necessity that the government integrate the working class into its project to stem the surge of labor radicalism. Equally inspired by Italian fascism, Figuerola's works used the force of numerical evidence to unveil an unquestionable fact: aristocratic Argentine society was being corroded from below by the surge of the working class and the spread of radical ideologies. Figuerola and Perón were immediately drawn to each other in 1942. This attraction arose "with the magnetism of reciprocal necessities," as the historian Joseph Page puts it. The Spanish intellectual saw in Perón the man who could finally put his words into action. The Argentine colonel appreciated Figuerola as the erudite professional who could buttress his own intuition with modern language and precise statistics that were solidly backed by the quintessential intellectual cliché embodied in the hours of solitude Figuerola had dedicated to mastering Greek and Roman classics.[81]

As Figuerola grew close to Perón, he recruited an active group of Argentine nationalists, Spanish Falangists, and Catholic *integralistas*, and quickly established relations with the members of the Ateneo. The Ateneo's members represented a broad range of nationalists of the time, including conservatives, anti-British admirers of Primo de Rivera, long-standing Germanophiles who remained so during Nazism, and positivists who advocated for the superiority of an Argentine race in a region predestined to become a moral reservoir against materialism and communism. They were almost all professionals, mostly lawyers, and had begun to gain political experience in the Unión Nacionalista de Estudiantes Secundarios, (UNES) and the Asociación Nacional de Estudiantes Secundarios (ANDES), right-wing student organizations that had flourished since the late 1920s against the democratically elected government of Hipólito Yrigoyen (although some members of the Ateneo also came from the *Yrigoyenista* ranks). Some had participated as a young supporters in the nationalistic coup d'état of 1930 (their motto: "José Félix Uriburu, presentes estamos ya, y te gritamos ¡presente!, José Félix General"). One was the son of the director of the newspaper *Crisol* and the Catholic magazine *Criterio*, two rightist publications that received financial support from the German embassy during the 1930s and 1940s. Almost all had been active members of the Cursos de Cultura Católica, which were developed during the second half of the 1930s.[82]

But it was their interest in labor issues that distinguished the Ateneo's members from the rest of the nationalist crowd and brought them close to Figuerola. This interest was partly inspired by their study of Mussolini's Italy, but also derived from their interactions with officials and academics who had turned their attention to the social changes occurring in Argentina with the steady industrialization of the late 1930s. They aimed big. The Ateneo was one of the first political organizations to understand the importance of radio in reaching mass audiences and one of the first think tanks outside the Left to develop training courses for unions, a tradition among anarchist, socialist, and communist organizations. The courses included classes and discussions on economics, labor regulations, sociology, politics, and oratory. The slogan for their radio courses on labor relations was simple and anticipated core components of the hierarchical populist rhetoric on workers and education: "To learn from he who knows more; to teach he who knows less" (Aprender del que sabe más, enseñarle al que sabe menos).[83]

By the 1940s, the discourse of the members of the Ateneo had departed from conventional Argentine nationalism. It remained deeply anticommunist, but now its anti-imperialism was directed at the United States rather than Great Britain. Above all, the members of the Ateneo now linked any revolutionary project to a strong proletarian leadership. In their opinion, the potential for proletarian-led unrest permeated the social atmosphere in Europe during the 1920s and until the "plutocratic bourgeoisie . . . suppressed the rise of a revolutionary proletariat that was ready to inaugurate a new social order." Fascism, Nazism, and Falangism were defined as "a trinity that is the legitimate daughter of the same bourgeoisie that no longer acknowledges."[84]

One member of the Ateneo remembered his first contact with Perón. In May 1943, Jorge Ochoa de Eguileor received an invitation to meet at a traditional *confitería* in downtown Buenos Aires with Héctor Bernardo, a boss within Catholic nationalist circles who had met Perón in Italy during the early 1930s. In the main room, Perón sat at the head of the table. They talked about politics for hours. At the end of the conversation, the colonel invited the new guest to join them for future "and promising" endeavors. At the table, Perón did not disclose that he was already organizing the military coup of 4 June of that year as part of the Grupo de Oficiales Unidos (GOU).[85]

With the revolutionary government in place, the members of the Ateneo immediately started to work with Figuerola and Bernardo to forge the ideological link between nationalism and labor, a core feature of the future movement, and to organize a powerful Secretariat of Labor that would spearhead a massive expansion of social and political citizenship. Figuerola provided Perón with a discourse of the scientific organization of labor relations and social order, and established initial ties with the labor base. The members of the Ateneo joined the new secretariat and provided some ideas about the need for new labor relations. But they also supplied Perón with something much more important by using their position from within the state to create a powerful labor movement and displace the old guard who distrusted him; they wrote the statutes for the new unions, provided houses so these unions could operate, joined unions during strikes, and offered lawyers and aid during the unions' negotiations with employers.[86] When an earthquake reduced the city of San

FIGURE 3.3. Worker attachés attending class during a training course at a public school in Buenos Aires, 1946. Source: Personal Papers of César Tronconi.

Juan to rubble on the evening of 15 January 1944, several members of the Ateneo were immediately sent to the city, either as part of the federal intervention or to work with the new minister of public works, a Catholic integralist who had been notoriously photographed giving a Nazi salute during a public event during World War II. These aid efforts marked the public launch of Perón's epic political career, connecting his nationalist program to the symbolic and material demands of those in need and against a social order in ruins. The members of the Ateneo were among his closest allies.[87] Two years later, Juárez and Cerrutti Costa were among the propaganda aides who disseminated the effective slogan "Perón o Braden" among workers days before the presidential election of February 1946. When the new government was in place, the Ateneo was in charge of various propaganda activities, including a vast information program designed to explain the Five Year Plan in unions throughout the country.[88] And when Perón delegated the task of training his diplomatic emissaries, he chose them. The move was at odds with the possibility of finding an ideological common ground between students and professors, but it was absolutely in line with the recent and brief history of Peronism.

For Malvicini and the members of the Ateneo, the scarcest resource was time. A few days after taking office, "Perón called us and told us: I need these courses right away."[89] The professors rushed to prepare a draft of the program, which was to be personally approved by Perón. It partly drew from the training courses that they taught at unions, but a large component was specifically modeled for the occasion.[90] Courses included general introductory classes that would have been pertinent for any official in the foreign service. But some courses combined the specific demand to explain the social accomplishments of Peronism to foreigners with the urgent need to establish some sort of common language among Peronists themselves.

The fourteen classes stressed the usual themes of Peronism: industrialization, nationalism, the working class, and social forms of property rights. Half of the classes were about the arrival of Peronism and its implications, and provided the attachés with the early elements of Peronist ideology: "Economic Argentina," "Industrial Argentina," "Cultural Argentina," "The Work of the Revolutionary Government and Economic Reconstruction," and "The Revolutionary Work Fulfilled by the Secretary of Labor and Welfare." Other classes described alternative forms of property and social organization, such as seminars on "Cooperativism" and "Mutualism." Another course, taught by Pedro Wiurnos, was called "Argentina Advocates for Public Health," naming one central theme in the rhetoric and expansion of the welfare state.[91] The program also had notable deficits. Surprisingly, for an initiative that was going to deploy most of its resources in Latin America, the courses offered no classes on or references to indigenous peoples. This omission was amended two years later when the Ateneo included one class titled "Indigenous Studies," but even that addition was the result of the solitary insistence of a folklore singer sympathetic to Peronism, who eventually taught the class.[92]

Another original aspect of the program involved its extracurricular activities. Visits to factories, movie theaters, and radio and TV stations, as well as interviews with Argentine artists, sportsmen, and singers, were among the mandatory activities that the activists pursued in their free time.[93] Newspapers and labor publications particularly highlighted the attachés' incursions into the Teatro Colón (Buenos Aires Opera House) and the National Museum of Fine Arts more as a social gain than as part of a professional training.[94]

The professors also adapted some of the techniques used during their previous union courses. Convinced, not without reason, of the powerful effect of Perón's rhetoric among workers, the courses tried to inculcate his skills in the attachés. Oratory classes, taught by Ochoa de Eguileor, became an important element of their training. Students were asked to prepare five-minute speeches based on a topic previously discussed in class. Instructors emphasized the ability to condense large ideas into a few sound bites. The professors had studied Perón's speeches in detail and tried to teach the leader's approach: "Perón had a technique with which he compelled people to say 'yes' and to scream. He said only two or three words, but ended them with an emphasis that made the plaza explode. If you analyze those speeches, you will see that there are only two or three *verdades* that he wants to put in people's mind, nothing else." The attachés would later use this background in their appearances at public rallies much more often than they would use their diplomatic knowledge.[95]

Fulfilling his original promise, Perón participated in the courses, appearing once or twice a week during the first year. The president would arrive with a few members of his government (usually Bramuglia and Interior Minister Angel Borlenghi, formerly a socialist leader at the Commerce Workers Union). He would often show up with Evita.[96] He would shake hands with each student at the beginning and at the end of the class, "plain and friendly, filling the classroom with emotions," in the words of one union magazine.[97] Pictures show Perón during the class either behind the desk or drawing figures on the blackboard, dressed in civilian clothing, closely watched by his military detail and by the attachés.[98] The fact that the president took the time to participate in the courses during the hectic early days of his administration indicated (to the enthusiastic attachés but also to the reluctant diplomats) the importance of the initiative. For labor activists themselves, it was also an unexpected opportunity to talk face-to-face with the leader they had to represent. Although classes adopted more protocol during the presidential visits, the participants in the courses remembered the atmosphere as being relaxed, allowing for a rather open exchange among professors, students, and Perón. But the interactions with the all-powerful president were also indicative of the importance Perón gave to these discussions and to the inevitably controlled environment in which they occurred. Perón's participation lent relevance to the initiative, but it is plausible that his imposing presence also left much less room for disagreement.[99]

Perón had shown his specific concern for the ideological formation of the new cadres long before classes started. The president combined the military's vertical conception of command with the intellectual ambitions of nineteenth-century statesmen. He believed that by leading this process, he imbued it with meaning—through something close to indoctrination—and helped those who were producing (and were a product of) those changes to make sense of them. His experience as professor in the army undoubtedly validated these conceptions. At one point during the preparation of the courses, the president met the members of the Ateneo and gave some basic guidelines as to what his ideas were. Asked by one of the professors how they should lay the groundwork for his own class, Perón replied: "Just teach them what you find in *Quadragesimo Anno* and *Rerum Novarum*, but don't tell them where it comes from. I'll do the rest."[100] The recommendation, of course, entirely pleased the Catholic professors, prepared for a true act of evangelization of their leftist students.

Perón really meant that he would "do the rest" in the larger sense of helping to forge the attachés beliefs from a specific set of ideas, but also through the minute details of the classes. The encyclicals summarized what Perón thought of as the inner core of his movement's ideology: the need to establish rights and duties for labor and capital so as to avoid a deadly clash between the emerging working classes and elites, the notion that property rights should be limited based on their social function, and the conviction that unrestrained capitalism and totalitarian communism posed the most serious threat to human freedom.[101] In a greater sense, this set of principles guided reflections about freedom and political stability after World War I. Seeds of those ideas could be found, with different emphases, in the major political experiments of the 1930s. They were rationales that explained the need to expand the sphere of government in order to control both excessive economic inequality and political radicalism. As the historian Wolfgang Schivelbusch argues, the beginnings of the American New Deal, Fascist Italy, and Nazi Germany "all profited from the illusion of the nation as an egalitarian community" in which "people were attracted by the feeling of being treated as equals . . . and could enjoy the protection, security, and solidarity of the nation."[102]

For activists who were transitioning from established (and often anticlerical) ideological backgrounds to the new ideology they were helping to create, the implications of the social doctrine of the Church were immediately evident. In this remarkable incident remembered by Ochoa de Eguileor, Perón ordered the professors to distribute the religious texts without mentioning the sources, then got directly involved in follow-up discussion of the readings he had recommended.

FIGURE 3.4. A union magazine shows Perón teaching a class during a worker-attaché training course, 1947. Source: Personal Papers of César Tronconi.

Perón would come and tell the students: "You've studied the Peronist Doctrine. The professors here have not told you where it comes from, but I'll tell you. They're two papal encyclicals, *Rerum Novarum* and *Quadragesimo Anno*." ... And there would be a big scandal, because most of the people in these classes still were anarchosyndicalist-Peronist, socialist-Peronist; they strongly rejected the Church. So they'd say: "You want to fool us, giving us the Church through our noses." ... And Perón would answer: "But you all said that you agreed with what has been taught here, right?" "Yes. ..." "Well, I'll show you the evidence," and he would distribute the mimeos, thirty or more copies, with the encyclicals to the astonished students, saying with laughter in his voice while he was distributing them: "*This* is the Peronist Doctrine."[103]

On first reading, the story suggests that Perón is essentially tricking workers into accepting the teachings of the Church as those of Peronism. More likely, there is a dose of exaggeration in the professor's recollection of the students' beliefs, similar to the many nationalists who have tended to highlight Perón's disruptive power by embellishing the former prevalence of leftist cultural symbols and their supposed position as outsiders of national culture.[104] Yet even taking this deviation into consideration, the dialogue also suggests a dynamic scene of discussion and dispute that runs against the image of Peronism as a monolithic movement in which ideological debates are either unimportant or loose enough to peacefully contain a wide variety of opinions.[105] Rather, it shows an active concern, from the highest political figure all the way down to rank-and-file labor activists, about elaborating an ideological framework with which to make sense of the important changes occurring in Argentina. What was at stake was not only the outright end of the liberal state, but also the creation of a postliberal state with a legitimacy based on guaranteeing the egalitarian inclusion of workers in its affairs.

Conclusion

The ascent of Peronism swept up the old social order well before its leaders, activists, and supporters had a shared and defined conception of what was going to replace that order. Drawing on decades of antiliberal thinking, Perón conceived of a corporatist society, but the horizon of building it around a powerful labor movement became real only toward the end of 1945 and only when all the other, more traditional paths had failed.[106] For union activists, access to power meant abandoning years of negotiation and struggle with the state that had delivered slow but steady benefits for their constituencies and for themselves. Finally, for the millions who became Peronists around 1945, everyday life forged a shared subjectivity of empowerment and dignity that they hadn't expected to find and that was not tied to the triumph of a well-defined worldview. In the same way the working class became a political subject, Peronism rose to power in a truly accelerated state of becoming.

The program of worker attachés illustrated the intertwined evolution of democratic politics and the place of workers in the nation. Juan Carlos Torre has pointed out that what was unique about Peronism as a movement and as a regime was the political overrepresentation of organized labor.[107] The expansion of the polity allowed for the enfranchisement of millions of workers, who were now the core of a powerful movement. Also, unlike other rising labor movements in Latin America, Peronism opened the gates of almost every political institution to blue-collar workers, union leaders, and activists. Symbolically and effectively, the arrival of activists to foreign affairs was a culmination of this process. Now Argentina was embodied before other nations and labor movements by "true representatives" of the nation and its workers. A movement that did not advocate for the overthrow of the capitalist system was now lending a class ethos to its idea of the nation, and this idea was strong enough to permeate even its most aristocratic institutions.[108]

Impressive as this was at the time, the first steps taken by Peronism also exposed the conflicts and limitations of this explosive ascent of the working class. The weak institutional arrangement of the program—supported on a three-legged base comprising the Ministry of Foreign Affairs, CGT, and the presidency—did not allow the new Peronist activists to overwhelm the established organization at the Cancillería. The figure of "attaché" remained subordinated to the authority of the ambassador in each diplomatic representation. While the label "personal representatives of Perón" stressed the attachés' importance abroad, it also became a liability in an institution that still ranked ambassadors above attachés as institutional representatives of the country. In most cases, the ambassadors resisted the presence of the attachés. This particular and incomplete transformation of the Cancillería was characteristic of the Peronist approach to the state, in which its most radical projects were undermined by its more moderate efforts to reconcile programs of reform with the forces resisting them. This undermining of the worker attachés presented an obstacle that ultimately reduced their impact and limited the scope of their actions.

Creating the position of attaché was a paradigm of the expansion of workers' power under populism. As the attachés rose to express the higher national interest (now invested with class rhetoric), they simultaneously had to subordinate their representation of specific workers' interests to that of the nation, and Perón was the ultimate judge for deciding how to reconcile the two.[109] The outcome of this paradigm has always been contingent on the countries and historical moments in which it has appeared. But with the creation of the attachés program, the paradox acquired a new level. These activists had the mission of representing a nation that was openly proposing itself as an inspiring model for labor movements abroad. Thus, their actions oscillated between integrating into a vast network of workers' transnational activism and embodying a national ambition of regional leadership.[110]

Probably the most interesting element of this conjuncture is how the repudiation of an oppressive social order led these leftist labor activists to take up common cause with Perón and his cohort of reactionary intellectuals. This convergence of ideologies opposed to liberalism has been the focus of attention in several studies of Peronism. However, most analysis of the period focuses on the fascist ideas that Perón brought back from his years in Europe, a focus that almost always leads to finding similarities and analogies between Peronism and Italian fascism and European corporatist model in general.[111] The training courses for the attachés are an extraordinary scene of the early years of Peronism that adjust and rearrange that perception. The singular historical conditions of postwar Argentina allowed for these ideas to move in a very different direction. Placed in the hands of an aggressive cadre of international labor activists who were determined to lead the region's struggle to expand political participation and economic justice, Church teachings acquired a powerful thrust of progressive reform, rather than the conservative features attached to fascism. Perón's rightist intellectuals organized the Secretariat of Labor (the same that Saavedra Lamas had imagined decades earlier), helped to train the attachés (the same attachés that Saavedra Lamas had also proposed in the past), and assisted in establishing Perón's labor base. The economic prosperity and vast expansion of the urban working class along with the reformism of its unions and the fierce alignment of the elites and the middle classes against Perón made it possible for European fascism to contribute to both the most radical and, as is more broadly accepted, the most conservative aspects of Peronism.

As such, the confluence of antiliberal ideologies that had been on the fringes of power since 1944 did not always and necessarily amount to the total capitulation of union activists to rightist intellectuals' authority. Once Perón was in office, the construction of a new political worldview was, to some extent, a space for contention. In describing the beginning of Peronism and its ideology, scholars generally focus either on the political arrangements with union leaders or Perón's efforts toward mass indoctrination in the construction of a new, Peronist citizen.[112] In this view, the political education of Peronist activists seems to have been the passive result of their practical experience. The training courses show a more willful side of Perón. From assembling the team to selecting the texts that would be discussed in class, Perón's personal involvement during the busiest times of his administration evidences both the importance he assigned to this project and the strength of his desire to draw attention to the program. Yet, regardless of Perón's wishes, the attachés leftist backgrounds and international experiences could not simply be expunged. The very existence of the program revealed the imprint of the Left. The professors' perception of the attachés as "still" anarchosyndicalist-

Peronist and socialist-Peronist also suggests that the transition toward the monolithic structure they had in mind was, if not a never-ending project, at least an endeavor that could not immediately be solved by the incorporation of workers into the new movement under the monolithic leadership of Perón.

CHAPTER FOUR. **FROM THE BELLY OF THE BEASTS**

In meetings and rallies, pamphlets, local papers, and national media, labor organizations throughout the country hailed the launch of the worker-attaché program as the Peronist activists reached their destinations abroad. Organized labor showed how, between liberal claims of extending freedoms and communist declarations of imposing workers' rights against the capitalist class, there was an alternative vision for advancing democratic principles of freedom and equality—what is known as the Third Position, of which Perón considered his movement an example. This chapter focuses on the labor activists' experiences as diplomatic messengers abroad, particularly in the United States and the Soviet Union, and analyzes how the insights the activists gained from these experiences affected their understanding of changes in their homeland.

"We're living a spiritual celebration," declared the Metalworkers Union (UOM) in a four-page article in its weekly paper: "These workers will be the truest expression of the new spirit that is making progress possible in Argentina; it will be the optimistic voice of our young workers deployed in a dark world shaken by a brutal war."[1] The celebration of the initiative was not the only indication that the attachés' mission abroad was inseparable from domestic matters. Concern about what was happening beyond national borders prompted fundamental reflections about the Peronist project, domestic reforms, and nationalism. The attachés' roles as worker envoys of the Peronist revolution meant that they were uniquely suited to contribute to that debate back home.[2]

The attachés were going to expand the principles of the Third Position among workers abroad. But the idea of workers acting as diplomats to export a revolution was a new, creative initiative, and both the impact of the attachés' work in foreign lands and the real power of Peronism as a world player beyond Latin America remained to be seen. At the same, the attachés' daily reports to Argentina on the deprivation and struggles of people abroad played an equally important role in fashioning the incipient Peronist identity. In public articles and official dispatches, attachés argued that the expansion of political rights and economic benefits under Perón had left them better off than workers almost anywhere else. They confirmed with hard evidence that an alternative to capitalism and communism was not only desirable, but was a project in the making for which they were the best representatives. In this context, while the dispatches presented Peronism as a dramatic rupture with the past, they also repurposed notions of national exceptionality that ran deep throughout Argentine history. Peronist nationalism forged a worldview in which European corporatism blended with a regional understanding of liberalism that equated the nation with the defense of equality and sovereignty with social rights.

Life abroad confirmed the attachés' beliefs. Arriving in Europe and elsewhere, the attachés corroborated the deprivations that were ravaging the postwar world. These initial impressions reinforced the attachés' perception of the singularity of the Argentine experience and their sense of mission, which they deployed mostly in Latin America and which distinguished Peronism. In this context, the actions and reports of the attachés in the United States and the Soviet Union became an essential component of this emerging interpretation of the historical conjuncture. The connections traced between the reality outside Argentina and the changes within the country, along with Perón's and Evita's roles in turning abstract changes into immediately palpable transformations, allow us to explore the particular domain of identity formation in which the global intertwined with the domestic. The study of this realm partly shows how Peronists constructed their narrative and why it was convincing when staged on a global scene. A crucial asset of the Third Position was that it was new and concrete, modeled in the confluence of political ideas, daily social practices, and affective forms that transformed Peronism into an inclusive and durable form of political consciousness.

Conquering the Acropolis

Even those attachés who were dispatched to the most remote places, with which Argentina had no historical connection and of which the attachés had no particular knowledge, arrived at their destinations fully funded and with a missionary-like faith in their duty to organize workers' demands. The first group of forty-three attachés left Buenos Aires between December 1946 and March 1947. They arrived at thirty-eight different embassies and diplomatic legations (some embassies had more than one attaché). In line with the priorities of the program and of the overall Argentine foreign policy, the largest group of these labor activists went to Latin America. Nineteen attachés were based in seventeen countries in the region: Bolivia, Brazil, Colombia, Costa Rica, Cuba, Chile, the Dominican Republic, Ecuador, Guatemala, Honduras, Mexico, Nicaragua, Panama, Peru, El Salvador, Uruguay, and Venezuela. Three attachés went to North America—two to the United States and one to Canada. Two more attachés went to the international organizations established in U.S. territory: the United Nations, in New York, and the Pan-American Union, predecessor of the Organization for American States (OAS), in Washington. Attachés went also to fourteen embassies in Europe: France, Greece, Italy, the Netherlands, Norway, Poland, Portugal, Romania, Spain, Sweden, Switzerland, the United Kingdom, Yugoslavia, and the Vatican. Finally, other attachés were dispatched to three Argentine representations in Asia: Turkey, Lebanon, and the recently opened embassy in the Soviet Union.[3]

This ambitious deployment was a distinctive characteristic of Peronism that set it apart from other populist movements and their foreign policies. In the postwar years, labor movements throughout the world challenged local elites by demanding social and political rights. But only one country considered it necessary to send an envoy like Eduardo García—an electrician from the telephone workers union—endowed with diplomatic status and fifty thousand brochures with pictures of the country's leader and his wife to a remote place like the Greece of 1948.[4] By that time, Greece was in the midst of a civil war between communist guerrillas and royalist forces, which the United States had come to consider as a new frontier in the struggle for democracy. Greece was about to become the ground zero of the Cold War.[5] The attaché landed in Athens with Greek translations of the Declaration of the Rights of Workers and the Declaration of the Rights of Senior Citizens, which Perón and Evita, respectively, had proclaimed in Buenos Aires. The day after the two declarations were presented in Athens by the attaché and the Argentine ambassador, a picture of the ambassador shaking hands with his American

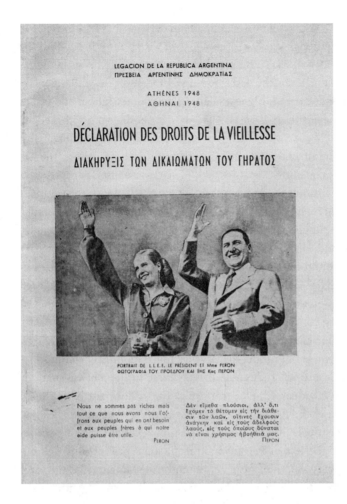

FIGURE 4.1. Greek translation of Eva Perón's Declaration of the Rights of Senior Citizens, which the worker attachés distributed in Greece in 1948. At that moment, Greece was at the peak of a civil war between royalists and communist guerrillas, and the country was about to become the ground zero of the Cold War. Source: Juan Atilio Bramuglia Papers, box 29, Hoover Institution Archives, Stanford University.

counterpart graced the front page of the local paper *Acropolis*. The reporter did not hold back on any stereotype (and offered a few gross inaccuracies) in describing the ambassador as "a descendant of the old Argentine race in which the picturesque features of Inca origins brings all its mysticism to join the enlightening intellect of the European." The article described Evita's declaration in a prose that was much closer to the attachés' newly acquired beliefs, considering the text to be "not merely a political decision . . . but a crusade for the highest and more humane principles of the Christian spirit."[6]

Elsewhere, the attachés also saw the postwar social and political crisis as an opportunity to disseminate their message, although the meaning of that message varied markedly. In France, Antonio Cornara, a boilermaker from the railway union, suggested that an alliance with the communist unions would be beneficial for his work. While witnessing the massive strikes and the split of the workers' federations in 1949, Cornara visited workplaces throughout the country. The Peronist media in Buenos Aires reprinted his stop at the mines of Ostricot, in Lille. The attaché described how miners worked under deplorable conditions and "earn the highest salary in the country (about 800 francs per day), which nevertheless is barely enough to cover their most immediate needs."[7]

In Germany, the attaché confirmed the horrors of reconstruction. The Argentine activist revealed that "vast parts of the cities are just destroyed" and that "movement within the country is severely restricted." In his report about meeting with unions in Berlin, the attaché also noted "the total ignorance about Peronism and about the reality in Argentina" among German union activists.[8] In Poland, Héctor Cerrillo, a carpenter from the powerful brewery workers union, found that, despite his protests, he needed government authorization to meet any activist or to visit any union. Diplomats also required special authorization to travel within the country. Nonetheless, he managed to visit the mining zone of Katowice to report on workers' living standards, food rationing, the black market, and the very low salaries paid.[9]

There, as in the rest of Europe, the attachés met with mostly communist-controlled unions and left thousands of brochures in French, German, or Greek with general ideas about Peronism.[10] The real extent of the local unions' attraction to the Argentine experience and the varied obstacles that the attachés had to overcome in order to turn that interest into a political asset determined the fate of Peronism's transnational project. But well before that, the reports from Europe generally confirmed for attachés the ideas they had held prior to their departure: living conditions in Argentina were superior for the population in general and for the working class in particular to those in most of Europe. They confirmed that the changes produced by Peronism were indeed part of an altogether different worldview. In this context, the comparison with the United States and the Soviet Union acquired particular importance.

The United States

THE JOURNEY

As a worker attaché to the United States, Agustín Merlo became acquainted with the obstacles to his mission even before reaching Washington. Despite (or precisely because of) the radical changes at home, Merlo found that class and status differentiation returned with a vengeance as soon as he left the native shores. On 7 February 1947, after a public rally that included officials and union leaders, Merlo left Buenos Aires on the Argentine steamer *Río Santa Cruz*. The ship carried an assorted crowd of officials and members of the Argentine Navy, Argentine businessmen, American merchants, even a European tycoon. But for the captain, Alberto Insanti, Merlo in particular stood out. A linotypist at the Swift meatpacking plant who had spent his life in Berisso, the working-class suburb and birthplace of Peronism, Merlo was now on board an exclusive cruise ship with an official mission. Despite Merlo's novel diplomatic status, the captain excluded Merlo from the lavish dinners he sponsored in his private rooms for the navy attachés and a few Americans. Merlo despised the captain in return, describing his coterie as made of foreign enemies, recalcitrant opponents of Peronism, including a businessman "to whom is attributed the blasphemy of having hummed 'La Cucaracha' [The Cockroach] during the national anthem on the steamboat *Río Jachal* on July 9th, 1945, during the reactionary campaign against the work of then-Colonel Perón."[11]

The attaché used the journey to fraternize with sailors and workers on the ship, listening to their complaints about long workdays and telling them about their new rights under Perón. The captain then summoned Merlo and forbade him to talk with the crew. Merlo rejected the instruction in the clear terms of that historical moment: "I represent the government of a free country, where the president would have never forbidden me from doing anything." The captain's reply stunned him: "On board, I am more than the president."[12] On his arrival in the United States, the attaché reported the incident to the ambassador, Oscar Ivanissevich, a political appointee and Perón's close friend. Ivanissevich took notice of the complaint but otherwise instructed him to forget the incident and get to work.[13]

ARRIVAL IN THE UNITED STATES

The unpleasantness on board the *Río Santa Cruz* was trivial compared to the challenges Merlo faced once ashore in the United States. Promoting Peronism among American workers proved much more complicated than designing a propaganda campaign and placing it in the hands of a labor activist. That was precisely the strategy of a small group of Argentine diplomats who were trying to infiltrate the entire United States and its labor movement in 1947, and it did not correspond to reality. True, their work was sustained by an Argentine propaganda apparatus that paralleled its leaders' ambitions. Perón's speech of 6 July 1947, about the Argentine Tercera Posición, was broadcast worldwide by 1,165 radio stations, some 400 of which were in the United States. But that alone was not sufficient to solve the problem of establishing a relation with a long-standing, diverse, and developed labor movement.[14]

This imbalance puts in perspective the disparity between Peronist ambitions, labor-activist ideas, and the power relations that shaped social and political forces at the onset of the Cold War.[15] The actions of the attachés in the United States and elsewhere did, however, trigger serious and extended concern among U.S. officials and labor leaders. The government and unions coordinated efforts to prevent the U.S.-based attachés from fulfilling their objectives on American soil. They discussed extensively how to react to the attachés' activities and mobilized efforts to monitor, survey, and counteract their actions among the American people. The U.S. media, on its own and in coordination with officials, presented a closed front toward the attachés, and universities offered an academic setting in which to discuss the attachés' ideas, the nature of the threat that these ideas posed, and what was to be done to resist them. This resistance to the Argentine labor activists occurred as part of a larger, unyielding opposition to Peronism in any of its iterations, which were presented as a threat to liberal forms of social change.[16]

Part of that defense implied a united opposition to the attachés' influence. The two attachés stationed in the United States, Eduardo de Antueno and Osvaldo Nani, arrived in late June 1947 and immediately contacted the U.S. Labor Department and the American Federation of Labor (AFL) to request formal introductions with American labor diplomats. Antueno was a bank teller from the city of La Plata. He was one of the few labor activists who did not come from the Left. He had been employed at the bank workers union during the 1930s and had joined the Radical Party, the populist movement that rose to power after universal suffrage was enacted in 1916 and which preceded Peronism in its direct appeal to the masses against the oligarchy. He joined Peronism with Nani in 1945; two years later, they arrived in New York.[17]

After receiving the request for formal introductions from the Argentines, U.S. union leaders and officials exchanged correspondence about the best way to proceed. The Labor Department called AFL Secretary George Meany, who in turn sent them to the International Labor Department of the AFL after considering "the inadvisability of rejecting the Argentines' request without knowing first its nature." They met on 9 July 1947. The Americans offered Antueno and Nani a rather cold reception. The meeting was led by Serafino Romualdi, then head of the AFL's International Section for Latin America. Meany and his closest collaborators on domestic matters were not present. The conversation was short, and the conclave resulted in a simple commitment on the part of the AFL to "add their names to the mailing list of its publications" that contained statistical information about the labor movement. It was the first official meeting between the worker attachés and the higher ranks of the AFL. And it would be their last.[18]

Working with local unions, rank-and-file union activists, and ordinary workers also proved difficult for the Peronists deployed in the United States. Merlo had had only two years of English instruction in school, and the initial courses in the worker-attaché program did not provide language classes, which in any case would hardly have provided the necessary training. Furthermore, Peronism was widely viewed as suspect and fascist by unions and the press, as well as by communist, Trotskyist, conservative, and liberal activists.[19] Perón had excited only modest sympathies among Republican representatives, who detected in him an early anticommunist ally, but these were not the kind of approvals that made the attachés' work easier. With the attachés' outreach efforts limited, the AFL and the U.S. government were able to coordinate an opposition to any form of effective action they might carry out.[20]

From the beginning, then, the attachés' task in the United States was downgraded to a kind of state-sponsored propaganda guerilla war, which yielded results that were dubious at best. With the exception of Mexico and the Soviet Union in the 1920s, no other country had combined state support and worker organizations in its efforts to penetrate the U.S. labor movement. The tradition of an independent international labor movement developing a campaign in the United States was limited mostly to socialist and communist organizations during the second half of the nineteenth century. Antueno, with the rest of the Argentine embassy, coordinated a way of using U.S. media to reach workers, although in most cases, their elaborate brochures and pamphlets were ignored (and in some cases blocked) by the media that they had hoped would propagate them. Almost univocally, Peronist efforts were portrayed within the same parameters as Nazi propaganda. The *Los Angeles Mirror* ran an editorial in 1951 that was illustrated with a dozen books and publications bearing pictures of Perón and Evita. The article complained about Peronist agents at large in the United States. "Six bulging manila envelopes full of blatant propaganda have reached *The Mirror* in the past 10 days—all bearing a comfy little notation where the postage stamps ought to be: 'Diplomatic Mail Free,'" the text said. Not without some naiveté about the mammoth proportions of U.S. propaganda abroad, the article asked, "Assuming this reciprocal mailing gimmick is on the level—how can the United States send its democratic propaganda to Argentine newspapers when Perón has blotted out any semblance of a free press?" Amid constant disparaging coverage of Peronism, the attachés' publicity efforts were doomed to fail. Since 1947, anti-Peronist editorials, articles, op-eds, and cartoons had appeared throughout the American press, from the *New York Daily News* to the *Chicago Tribune*.[21] Presenting a uniform and crudely hostile coverage of Peronism, American media operated within an ongoing framework of wartime coverage, which sought to preserve national interest against external threats, both in coordination with and independent of the advice of U.S. officials. In almost all the coverage, the attachés' work simply fell within that grand narrative of the fascist threat to the Western Hemisphere.[22] Language and hostility aside, the attachés did not attempt to work directly with Americans, beyond unions. They did not pursue unmediated contact with popular sectors or with segregated minorities. The attachés' reports make no reference to the situation of black workers in the United States, other than a matter-of-fact notation that once on U.S. soil, black people from other countries were under the same restrictions as domestic blacks.[23]

In one daring action, though, the attachés managed to avoid the blockade and introduce the Fundación Eva Perón into the United States while working toward the original goal of trying to reach five-hundred families within each attaché's area of influence. The plan might not have seemed particularly well-suited to the United States, which was one of the few countries that, like Argentina, had emerged from the war with some level of prosperity. But in 1947, Merlo started a relentless campaign to contact welfare and philanthropic societies across the country, particularly in Washington and New York, explaining the Fundación Eva Perón's work in Argentina and its mission abroad. Eventually, at the end of 1948, they received from the Children's Aid Society a letter asking for a personal donation (a general and rather formal request sent to hundreds of diplomats). The attachés acted immediately. Within weeks, six crates bearing the official seal of Fundación Eva Perón and containing complete outfits for five-hundred children were at the offices of the society in Washington. The Rev. Ralph E. Vawters and his wife, who ran the society, rejected the present, saying that they were seeking a personal donation, not propaganda, which, they argued, could be exploited by Russia as evidence that the United States could not care for its own needy children.[24] In the end, the State Department, fearing the possibility that the incident could escalate into a scandal, convinced the society to accept the gift. In the *New York Times* the following day, the clergyman said "the society was 'very scant' on clothing and would have to buy some clothes for the needy children if the foundation's gift had been rejected."[25] That was the end of the episode, which marked the highest propaganda achievement of the attachés on U.S. soil. A picture of Merlo and Lobato with the Fundación Eva Perón's crates in Washington was published in U.S. and Argentine newspapers.[26] In the U.S.

media, the incident was attributed, not without reason, to Merlo's background: he "was trained less as a diplomat than as a follower of President Juan Perón. As such, he is fully aware [of] how desirous Señora Perón's social welfare foundation is of favorable attention on a world-wide scale."[27] The incident quickly disappeared from newspapers; its spectacularity showed the short-lived effects and narrow impact that the attachés actions could have on daily life in the United States.

The United States also became a stage for presenting the basic ideas of the Peronist project as an alternative to the excesses of the capitalist and communist models. When U.S. intellectuals, such as the writer John Dos Passos, offered complimentary words about Argentina or Perón, the comments were immediately propagated in Europe and Latin America and disseminated throughout universities and schools.[28] When Bertrand Russell denounced Peronism as a totalitarian threat, the official refutations were also widely circulated. The *International News Bulletin* of the General Confederation of Labour (CGT), which was printed in Buenos Aires, written in English, and distributed in the United States, immediately ran an article about the British writer. The piece repeated the original Peronist view, denouncing the shift in postwar U.S. liberalism that betrayed the socially inclusive legacies of the New Deal. "Does he [Russell] know," the CGT wondered, "that his present ruler, Harry Truman, betrayed Roosevelt to become an agent of Wall Street?" The reference to Wall Street was designed not only to emphasize the unfairness of new policies but also to underscore some key themes of the Peronist Third Position, that is, how materialism eroded humanism and revealed a fraudulent anticommunism that was weaker and less sincere than the Peronist one. "Does Russell not know that Truman is not an anti-communist who is concerned with principles of civilization—but a mere agent of North American capitalist interest?" the Peronist paper asked.[29] The writing was in line with Perón's Catholic beliefs. It highlighted the shortcomings of the United States, and it conceived of Argentina as a regional moral bastion that would lead a more sincere and efficient fight against extremism. This was a belief that Perón held publicly and in private. In 1947, after Foreign Minister Juan Atilio Bramuglia failed to pass an anticommunist declaration at the Pan-American Conference in Río because of U.S. opposition, Perón sent him a note: "I knew that Marshall would react in this way against us. The U.S. is not in a position to open a new front against communism, for domestic reasons, their 1948 elections, and, finally, because they lack cojones."[30]

As with many other Argentine bulletins, magazines, and brochures, these texts were circulated widely in the United States among unions, media outlets, congressmen, and officials. The attachés deployed considerable efforts to disseminate these while, from Buenos Aires, the Foreign Ministry, Perón, and Evita emphasized in memos and correspondence that the attachés had all the funds they needed to fulfill their task.[31] The effects nevertheless remained quite limited relative to the proposed goals.

WHAT THE ATTACHÉS SAW IN THE UNITED STATES

Conversely, Merlo and other worker attachés focused their attention on the context of labor conflicts and accelerated political transformations in the United States. They described the atmosphere in detail and reported extensively back to Buenos Aires. They wrote neither with the trained eye of the ethnographer nor with the respectful curiosity of modern travelers and professional diplomats, but with the appetite of first-timers and the determination to identify what they were looking for—a weakening labor movement, a massive transformation underway, and a business sector regaining command. And they easily found such a country simply by focusing on things that fit into their preconceptions.

No matter who was observing them, strikes commanded attention. During the first month of his stay, between 19 March and 16 April 1947, Merlo sent twenty-six reports to Buenos Aires.[32] Fourteen were about strikes sweeping the country. Three of the remaining reports were about laws attempting to curb those strikes—the Taft-Hartley Act, the Condon-Wadlin Act in the state of New York, and the Disloyal Employee Law enacted by President Truman— and their effects. Another two provided related statistical information, one giving a detailed description of union leader incomes, the other reporting on workdays lost during 1946 and 1947. Four reports offered the attaché's observations about news and events: about Truman's pledge to make businessmen lower their prices; about Merlo's conversations with "ordinary workers" about their union leaders; about the mourning among miners' families after a fatal accident in Louisiana; and about U.S. legislation concerning foreigners. Finally, three reports were related to Argentina. One of these related the incidents onboard the *Santa Cruz*, and another offered a set of recommendations about how to describe the Argentine labor movement at an international conference in which the United States would likely attack Peronist leaders. The last was a thank-you note to an official in Argentina for having solved a conflict among merchant sailors in which Merlo had mediated. This conflict had arisen after Merlo's conversation with the sailors of the *Santa Cruz* on his way to the United States, justifying the captain's concern about Merlo's subversion of the ship's ancient order.

In describing the postwar social scene, the attachés' minutes framed a specifically populist critique of the United States. Their writing helped them to define the meaning of Peronist achievements at home with more complexity than could offered by the radical terms that reduced them to the rise of a mobilized labor movement. The reports supported the more social-democratic presentation of a movement that had achieved social peace in Argentina by empowering workers and redistributing wealth to balance the excesses of capital and dispel the danger of extremism. Describing accelerated changes in U.S. politics, the attachés insistently noted the private capital's aggressive attempts to curb unions' rights, reversing the gains of the New Deal, and the degree to which basic rights had been suspended or postponed during the war. Merlo reported that 1,200 workers at the Brooklyn-Battery Tunnel demanded that their workday be reduced to six hours, divided into two periods of three hours with a three-hour break instead of the current two four-hour sessions. It was a sensible demand for work that required excruciating physical effort. The strike took place less than a mile away from the Brooklyn Bridge, where a hundred years earlier doctors had discovered the "bend disease" affecting "sand hogs," as the bridge's workers were known. The bend disease was caused by long periods of immersion under forty feet of water, rapid decompression, and little rest during the construction of the bridge. "The local union did not authorize the strike," Merlo wrote in a somber and critical observation of the way U.S. unions represented workers' rights, "but the strikers' leader says that those who don't join them just don't care about surviving until the tunnel is completed."[33]

The U.S. economy was being reconfigured before their eyes, and they avidly described it. At Brown and Williamson, a tobacco company operating in the southern states of Louisiana, Virginia, and North Carolina, some 3,300 workers went on strike, demanding a 6 percent salary increase. The railway union led 125,000 workers to threaten to do the same if Congress did not accept their plan to increase pensions and social benefits. The four largest newspapers in New York City, including the *New York Times*, came out with smaller printings or were not published at all after the International Typographical Union rejected an offer for salary increases. Under a recently approved state law, three female union activists were arrested for their role in leading a strike of 20,000 workers against the long-distance service of telephone companies. A federal judge ordered the United Mine Workers to pay 3.5 million dollars for striking to demand better safety measures, claiming it was opportunistic and not justified.[34] From New York, the attaché at the United Nations reported with some alarm on the safety of working conditions in the

United States: "One American worker dies every four minutes. . . . Last year there was a record in work-related deaths and accidents of 17,000 and 2 million, respectively."[35] Their reports portrayed a violent period plagued with appalling working conditions, large strikes, crooked unions, state repression, and the business sector's counteroffensive. They described a climate of social tension marked by the rise of conservative thinking within the Democratic Party and a widespread reaction on behalf of the business sector against organized labor's bargaining power. The picture they drew is congruent with what U.S. historians have described as postwar years of social contention and of workers' reactions against the renewed power of the business sector. It confirmed that the attachés, while strongly ideological, were reliable reporters of the time they witnessed, providing Buenos Aires with information and perspectives that traditional members of the foreign service were either unable or unwilling to supply.

The attachés contrasted this dismaying landscape with the recent experiences in Argentina, stressing how Peronism, in very little time, had simultaneously modernized the economy and improved workers' lives. "One year was enough to change the course of events," the attaché at the Pan-American Union told the general assembly.[36] "Another Bastille had fallen," he proclaimed in the hyperbolic prose that Perón himself had used when he compared the rise of his movement to the French Revolution. This radical change rejected "the economics that, with sluggish immutability, had ruled the country for the previous fifty or hundred years" and fulfilled demands that "were a hundred years old . . . in matters of salaries, work hours, education, social benefits, and retirement, among other things."[37]

Peronist aspirations of modernization shaped the attachés' worldviews. They presented industrialization and social reform as signs that Argentina, after so long, had finally overhauled its social and economic outlook. Yet they never mentioned the technological gap that separated the U.S. economy from the Argentine one, nor the impact of this gap in the economic development of the two countries. Sometimes, they inadvertently recorded this in passing, such as when Merlo mentioned that Truman had given the "green light" to a new price regulation. He was then forced to explain that the green light was an analogy based on traffic lights, an invention generalized in some U.S. cities and just starting to pop up in Buenos Aires and few other urban centers in Latin America.[38] Other times, it was their personal decisions that testified to their own ambivalences. Attachés like Merlo were critical of U.S. imperialism and genuinely proud of Peronist achievements; an omnipresent example of these achievements was the development of the national automobile industry, which conveyed the sense of economic modernization with aspirations for social justice as few other activities did. In 1948, Perón launched the project to produce El Justicialista, the first automobile made entirely in Argentina, released in 1952. Yet for all the symbolism and the material connections between nationalism and modernization that Peronism set into motion, the trophy that Merlo brought back to Buenos Aires from his expedition to the United States was a brand-new 1949 Ford Mercury. Many other attachés returning from their own destinations brought this same prize home. An American symbol (both in the United States and abroad) of prestige and upward mobility, the Ford car was a luxury yet affordable item. On arriving in Argentina, it disrupted the modest scale of Merlo's working-class Peronist suburb, where a U.S.-made Ford was nonetheless a source of status. As a symbol, the Ford also exposed the uneven development of the Argentina to which Merlo returned. In order to conceal this extravagance in the neighborhood, the family built a shed in the house's front garden for the new acquisition. The shed was made with the wood of the container in which the automobile had traveled from the United States to Argentina. Only a hundred cars of the "Peronist automobile" were ever built.[39]

The attachés' anti-U.S. rhetoric was also nuanced by a populist appreciation of the government's role in regulating conflicts between capital and labor. They elaborated an almost sympathetic view of the Truman administration in its clashes with the business sector. On more than one occasion, Merlo shifted in his references to Truman from the usual hostile jargon to the more respectful phrases "the head of state" or "the president" to report, for example, that Truman had "said that if prices remain as high as today, workers will have the right to demand salary increases," a process that could only be gradual "because with the termination of price-control policies, the government has been stripped of its powers."[40]

But the attachés were also skeptical about the vitality of the labor movement in the United States. Several reports referred to the bureaucracy that had "taken" leadership and recounted in detail the salaries and benefits received by union leaders. In more than a few cases, this information was circulated by conservative politicians and the business sector. In other cases, the attachés adopted neutral language to describe the impact of labor belligerence, or reported with alarm numbers from the Bureau of Labor Statistics that illustrated the changes facing the U.S. economy with the conclusion of the war: "The United States lost 116 million workdays because of the strikes during 1946. The number tripled the time lost for the same reason during 1945."[41] Thus, when it came to describing the advantages of the Peronist experiment to the U.S. audience, workers' welfare was both an end and a means by which to reach social peace within a capitalist society. This was a limited goal for activists who claimed to represent a revolutionary government. But as their diplomatic and labor roles coalesced into a single representation, this rhetoric embodied the populist dynamic, identified by Castro Gomes, in which workers gain access to the polity by giving up their own expression (*palavra operária*) in order to become a central part of the "state voice" (*palavra do Estado*).[42]

Unsurprisingly, in this context the most common indicators used by Argentina to demonstrate the benefits brought by Perón were the index of caloric intake and the number of days "lost" in strikes. This was a very different method than the one used by U.S. unions. Both domestically and abroad, the discourse of U.S. unions was heavily invested in the modernizing symbology of economic efficiency and usually underlined indicators such as the average real income per employee or work-time buying power of American workers.[43] The attachés preferred to stress how the vast array of concrete benefits and power obtained by Argentine workers had reduced the days lost in strikes to a historic low. This signaled how a progressive social reform "eradicated" the "vices of . . . leftist extremism."[44] In an environment of food rationing and economic hardship, food consumption had become a global indicator of general well-being, and Argentina insistently displayed the extent of the prosperity reached by its workers in this realm. The embassy in Washington invited the U.S. Surgeon General to talk to Western Hemisphere diplomats about "Nutritional Conditions in Europe and the Near East," with the ultimate purpose of showing that caloric intake in Argentina was higher than in all Latin America and most of Europe.[45] Merlo, in turn, explained in his conference that "the daily per capita dietary intake in Argentina was of 3,275 per inhabitant, surpassed only by New Zealand with 3,281, and immediately above the United States with 3,249."[46]

Merlo's numbers were indeed impressive. They confirmed what U.S. sources themselves had found: that Argentine workers had full bellies was more than propaganda. But Merlo arrived at his numbers through artifice. The statistics did not express any positive impact of Peronism in Argentine society; in fact, they were taken "from the prewar period," before Perón had even considered a political career. This figure was the only available statistic according to the attaché, "but it was flattering enough for our country."[47] True, had the attaché found more up-to-date numbers, they would have been even more impressive. But the attaché's use of prewar numbers to show the achievements of the revolutionary government that came to power eight years later was more than a historical transliteration. This ambivalence was intrinsic to Peronist identity, which was built around the notion of a radical break with a supposedly dark past, yet was deeply rooted in beliefs also derived from that rejected past. Peronist nationalism, Merlo argued, did not look for inspiration in "the leftist extremism of Russia or the crude capitalism of others, but [in] old European culture, from which we received a race and civilization . . . that leads us to our goal of social justice."[48]

More precisely, this European legacy was that of the mestizos, and its influence extended beyond the issue of social justice to the notion of a country that, as the attaché Antueno put it, contributed to the region's peace by "helping to free the peoples of America, always solving its differences through international arbitration . . . a position defined by our axiom, carved in bronze: *La victoria no da derechos* [Victory does not establish rights]."[49] The attachés connected the new Argentina with the legacies of the old Argentina that they denounced. The two historical periods coalesced in the ideas through which Peronism defined itself as the bearer of a regional tradition, combining emphasis on social rights with preexisting defenses of national sovereignty and arbitration. With its focus on international arbitration, Peronism expressed Argentina's alignment with long-standing Latin American interpretations of interstate relations. The phrase quoted by Antueno symbolized one Peronist Argentina's contributions to the nascent Inter-American system. A few months after Antueno declared that "victory does not give rights" in the Pan-American Union, the Organization of American States, which succeeded the Pan-American Union, incorporated the phrase as one of its founding principles.[50] And even then, the words chosen by the attaché also revealed the complexity of relations between Peronism and Latin America. The author of the phrase "Victory does not give rights" was Mariano Varela, the Argentine minister of foreign relations during the War of the Triple Alliance, which Argentina, Brazil, and Uruguay fought against Paraguay in the 1860s. As became evident over time, Varela was trying not so much to preserve the territorial integrity of the defeated and devastated Paraguay, but to stop the victorious Brazil from advancing into the areas controlled by the also victorious Argentina.

The juxtaposition of class-based anti-imperialism and ambitions of regional leadership exposed an intrinsic tension within Peronist identity, which occurred between the rupture with the past—a rupture expressed by Peronists' own access to political power—and the continuities of that past, visible in the redefined sense of national superiority that they embraced. This tension also affected their actions toward the region in fundamental ways. As U.S.

State Department officials had observed earlier, the job of the attachés in the United States was not necessarily to convince U.S. unions (or diplomats), but to use the country as a platform to reach Latin American workers. Positioning Argentina in opposition to the U.S. domestic reality and asserting its power and ideas for the region was a central aspect of the Peronist Third Position. But the hint of "junior imperialism," which this position projected onto the region, often hindered the attachés' work with the labor movements of other countries. The equally complicated relation of the attachés with communist ideas and the Soviet Union also showed the singularity of the Peronist political intervention, as well as its weaknesses.

The Soviet Union

On 27 August 1947, Alicia Masini de Conde, the wife of the worker attaché in the Soviet Union, hosted an Argentine couple at her room in the Grand Hotel in Moscow. "Sympathizing with the regime, they left everything they had in Argentina 12 years ago and came with their little daughter to their 'fairytale country,'" she wrote in her diary. The couple lived in Odessa, she added, where the wife had secured a job at the military orphanage. After years of war and bad harvests, she saw how "many mothers, rather than seeing their sons die, took them to the asylum hoping that someone would take care of them." Things became even worse after the war, at least in this family's story. "Every morning, she would find babies' frozen bodies outside. She told me about scenes of cannibalism, including one about a family that would invite poor people to stay at their house, lock them up, wait until they froze to death, then butcher them and sell their meat as beef," the wife of the attaché wrote. Concluding the horrific description, Masini added: "This family," whose name she carefully crossed out in the letter, "no longer 'thinks' as before. They would do whatever it takes to return to Argentina, their motherland. But they made the mistake of becoming Soviet citizens, and now they won't let them leave."[51]

There possibly was some hyperbole in the family's saga. Tales about cannibalism ran through Soviet history, particularly in Ukraine after the thousands of documented cases of cannibalism that occurred during the famine of 1932–1933.[52] It is unclear whether they could have actually witnessed cannibalism after that period. But the story they told Masini summed up all the themes of redemption that laid the foundations for workers back home in Argentina to embrace their novel Peronist worldview. The couple had left Argentina in 1935, during the period of fraudulent conservative governments known as the Infamous Decade. Having lost all hope, they were deceived by extremist communism as they found only poverty and desperation in the Soviet Union. Now that Argentina was a prosperous country under Perón, the couple's cursed gesture of having renounced their Argentine citizenship was already irreversible, as they could not break through the repressive measures of Stalin's regime.

Masini's husband, the attaché Pedro Conde Magdaleno, was a former anarchist and later communist who left Argentina with a utopian expectation of seeing Stalin as a leader "mingling with clamorous young people . . . as Perón does when he joins workers' rallies." He was immediately disappointed. His illusion vanished amid beggars asking for bread and police forces beating them on the shores of Odessa.[53] These images added to a complex rejection of the Soviet Union, a dramatic political, ideological, and emotional transition undergone by Argentine labor activists, and one that fashioned crucial aspects of their new Peronist allegiance. Some of them were members of the Communist Party; others had allied themselves with communist activists in their unions through tactical deals or in native versions of the popular front.[54] Communist leaders controlled most unions in the meatpacking sector, where Peronism first flourished in 1943–1944. Workers who were ideologically committed to the struggle against totalitarianism in Europe confronted communism at home and built a relationship with Perón, a nationalist military leader who was sympathetic to the Axis powers and had a progressive social agenda. Some socialists and anarchists saw the Soviet Union not as a model but as an inspiring symbol of workers' sacrifices in the twofold struggle against European fascism and U.S. imperialism.

That was the heteroclite background that Conde Magdaleno brought to Moscow. A son of Spanish immigrants, he was born in 1914 and married a Catholic neighbor of Italian descent. As a baker in General Madariaga, a town some two-hundred miles from the French-inspired boulevards of downtown Buenos Aires, Conde Magdaleno entered the powerful bakers' union, UPPA, as a teenager, "forging my political beliefs under the influence of the leftist extremism of anarchosyndicalism and communism." In 1944, after Perón, as secretary of labor, enforced additional payment for workers doing night shifts, Conde Magdaleno used his influence and undisguised government support to turn the union away from anarchism and closer to Perón. He became a member of the Partido Laborista in 1945, and a year later his work was rewarded when a general assembly chose him as worker attaché.[55]

Yet rejection of communism was not a straightforward operation. It came along with the labor movement's embrace of Perón, a nationalistic leader influenced by fascism. These changes were not free of contradictions; they constituted a dramatic ideological and personal shift, and one that fashioned crucial aspects of populist beliefs. Perón described communism as a form of foreign extremism to be prevented through social reform, and he decried local communists for their alliance with the conservative, U.S.-backed opposition. At the same time, one of Perón's first foreign-policy decisions was to reestablish diplomatic relations with Moscow in 1947. By then, the normalization of bilateral ties offered not only the prospect of economic gains— Argentina was looking for a market for its agricultural production, which the postwar Soviet Union largely lacked—but also a way of countering the political weight of the United States in Latin America.[56] Perón appointed Federico Cantoni as Argentina's first ambassador to the Soviet Union. Cantoni was a popular caudillo from the interior with progressive inclinations. He had broken with Perón before the elections, then rejoined him. [57] Along with the ambassador and the attaché, some forty-one other people left Buenos Aires on the *Andrea Gritti* for Moscow on 17 February 1947. Conde Magdaleno traveled with his wife and three small children. They appeared in the pictures at the dock, all wearing sailors' outfits for the official portrait with Evita, who had made the personal gesture of joining them before the departure. Relatives mingled with officials at the dock while shipyard workers brought to the steamboat trunks containing Peronist propaganda, including Perón's Declaration of the Rights of Workers, fifty official portraits of President Perón, and fifty more of Eva Perón. At thirty-three years old, Conde Magdaleno was setting foot outside of the country for the first time.[58]

Conde Magdaleno got the first hint of the asymmetry between the task he was assigned and the resources given to him to fulfill it well before reaching Moscow. At the port of Genoa, where the Argentine delegation needed to obtain the visas, Soviet authorities objected only to his documentation. Conde Magdaleno was told that the worker's fatherland did not need worker-activists. Soviet authorities were not ready to make official the position of worker attaché. This clash was only solved when the Argentine delegation accepted to cross out the word *obrero* on Conde Magdaleno's diplomatic passport. The idea of building ties between the Argentine and Soviet labor movements seemed as gratifying as it was impractical. Propaganda was ruled out almost immediately. Diplomats circulated in a controlled environment, escorted by officials and interpreters from the Soviet foreign office. None of them was allowed to visit a factory or to distribute pamphlets in public places. The attaché never even suggested to local officials the idea of setting in motion any of the Fundación Eva Perón's initiatives.

Conde Magdaleno wrote to Basilio Kusnietsof, president of the Soviet Union of Professionals, hoping to be introduced to labor activists. He also sent letters to the bakers unions and other workers' institutions. He requested authorization at the foreign office to visit worker retreats, schools, hospitals, and housing in order to analyze and report on Soviet workers' living conditions. Some of these requests were denied. The rest went unanswered. The attaché had no better luck than the rest of the mission, which was plunged into a bureaucratic ordeal that stalled their initial optimism. At some point, Conde Magdaleno was invited to the Stalin automobile factory, but when the Argentine requested to talk with workers, he was told that it was not planned in the visit.[59]

As it soon became clear, reestablishing diplomatic relations was one thing on paper but a different reality existed on the ground. Argentine officers experienced not only general political restrictions, but also their share of postwar deprivation in the Soviet Union. The diplomats sent by Perón lived and worked in two different hotels with scant facilities. They had a single room per family, one bathroom per floor. Access to running water was occasional; their food was severely rationed.[60] It took them very little time to notice that diplomatic salaries did not cover half their monthly expenses and that Soviet living standards were impossibly low—not only for patrician diplomats but also for political caudillos from the interior and ordinary workers accustomed to relative abundance in Argentina.

For Conde Magdaleno, suddenly removed from his usual environment, the chances of accomplishing his goals were remote. The Peronist attaché opted for a different path in his attempts to establish contact with Soviet workers. In June 1947, he joined some Spanish Republicans who had fled Franco's dictatorship. Disguised as one of them, he entered Plane Factory Number 43 on the outskirts of Moscow. Months later, he used the same strategy to gain access to one of the two factories that produced all of the bread for the Soviet capital. With the help of people outside the embassy, he crafted an informal method of making systematic observations of workers' lives in the Soviet Union.[61] The combination of Conde Magdaleno's observations and his wife's letters and personal diary constitutes a detailed denunciation of daily life under Stalin. They add a unique perspective to the works of the foreigners and diplomats who chronicled those years in the Soviet Union, the most notable of which were the impressions that Kennan drew on for his memoirs.[62] The Argentine baker lacked the intellectual scope and ambition of the American diplomat; but his writings reveal the concerns and preoccupations of their respective societies at the time. Conde Magdaleno's observations exemplified the justifications for the ideological shift of vast parts of Argentine labor activism and the localization of the newfound belief in Peronism as a democratic, nationalistic, and successful project of social change. Unlike Kennan's reports, the Argentine attaché's dispatches did not aim to captivate a diplomatic elite (that would not have listened to a union member anyway). Conde Magdaleno's writings are the product of his class background in Argentina and of the points of view he constructed within the larger workers' milieu of unions, activists, and public opinion. His notes reveal the domestic concerns discussed among Argentine workers and the way in which they were elaborated by labor activists.

The reports from Moscow offered a detailed description of Soviet society. They noted items included in rationing cards, the infrastructure of sanitation in houses, the deficiencies of public transportation, the technology in factories, the different access to goods and services granted to Party officials, and the income for every category of worker. Workers received three different types of ration cards: one for workers in general, another for those in the military industry, and one for the privileged, a broad and subjectively defined category. The attaché estimated that 60 percent of workers received the basic ration card, covering a pound of bread per day, six pounds of rice per month, an equal amount of meat, and less than two pounds in fat products. "If he does not rob or have someone else that can support him, the regular worker is condemned to perish," Conde Magdaleno wrote.[63]

Repression and hunger hovered above all of this. Through one of his Spanish friends, Conde Magdaleno visited the house of a woman working for the Soviet train system. "I say 'house' but it really was a small bed that she shared with her mother in a 3×10 meter room where there were nine more beds with their occupants," he said. The attaché also went to a factory cafeteria to count the caloric intake of those memorable Soviet workers. He observed that "rations at the cafeteria do not cover the most essential needs . . . and there is no way that a worker could have enough rubles to afford the rest of the food."[64] He did not need exact numbers: the economic deprivations after the war were huge, hunger was everywhere in the streets. And as his wife registered in her diary, "The salary doesn't mean anything because there's no food to buy anyway."[65] She described how workers at the hotel collected and ate rotten food that she and her family had discarded weeks before. "If we had any doubt about how hunger was drowning these people, this was the last straw that confirmed it. . . . When Pedro came back, he found me crying, but admitted: 'You're right. These things break your heart.'" Repression added to the gloomy horizon: two weeks after this entry, Conde Magdaleno's wife learned that the workers' supervisor had severely punished them for "showing such a bad example of Soviet life in front of foreign visitors."[66]

The impact of those scenes of misery gained momentum. In Conde Magdaleno's notes, as in most chronicles of the time, poverty was the most ubiquitous feature of Soviet Russia. It not only corroborated the failure of communism, but also harshly contrasted with the increase in well-being Conde Magdaleno had experienced in Argentina both under Peronism and before it. "At the exit of the theater, the subway, or the church, the scene is pathetic, beggars abound," the attaché wrote. "They know who foreigners are and they harass them, for he is the best candidate. They are children, old people, crippled people. They are so many that it is impossible to help them all."[67] Comparing prices, the attaché estimated that the monthly salary of a Soviet baker could cover the family's needs for about ten days, depending on which ration card they had. "How do they make it to the end of the month?" he asked. "Simply by adjusting their stomachs."[68] The lack of a decent income was paired with the crisis in food production. In 1947, Soviet agricultural production had shrunk to the levels of a decade earlier. Empty supermarkets and rationing of "essentials such as milk or bread, even for children" are common in the attaché's descriptions.

Poverty under communism also put daily life in Argentina in perspective. Conde Magdaleno's wife wrote to her brother: "Our kids survive only because they have been fed like Argentines all their lives, they can resist." The search for food reinforced the contrast between Soviet Russia and Peronist Argentina: "All the men go shopping very early in the morning, buying everything . . . they can find. There are no potatoes, vegetables, fruits, milk. We did find white bread, but what bread! We should show what these people call 'bread' to *los delicados* in Buenos Aires." [69] For Masini, food consumption was, again, a crucial representation of Argentine prosperity. Her son was able to withstand communist hardships thanks to the Peronist diet. Her comparisons of bread quality and existing hunger exposed the shallowness of the complaints of *porteño* middle-class opposition to popular diets. Her words also foreshadowed the anti-Peronist stereotypes that emerged in Argentina after 1952, when the government authorized the domestic sale of a mix of less-processed flour and millet in order to meet the quota of flour export to Great Britain. Not exempt from racial subtleties, anti-Peronists, or "delicados" for Masini, remembered the flour as *pan negro* or *pan de perro*.[70]

Going beyond food consumption, Masini's mention of delicados, the delicate souls of Buenos Aires, was laden with gender connotations, typical of the feminization of the opposition made by Peronist sympathizers, and used in this case by a woman. Her view of gender roles encapsulated the Peronist ambivalence about women's participation in the labor force. During her first weeks in Moscow, the attaché's wife also confessed, "We are astonished to see women driving train locomotives." She herself felt "heartbroken" ("me parte el alma") by the "image of women driving train locomotives." At one train stop, she observed "a machinist, her face sullied by the mark of her craft, devouring a huge sandwich." At another one, she noted "a plow, pushed by five women (replacing the beast) and driven by a man."[71] Masini was witnessing the massive incorporation of women into an industrial economy deprived of male workers (and of animals) in the aftermath of the war. Her appreciation of Soviet Russia added one more dimension to the tensions within Peronism, reinforcing a vision in which "the self-affirmation of women, particularly those of the popular sectors, remained in constant tension with the reformulation of their subordinate status."[72] As Masini reflects during her first weeks in Moscow, "Women work with the serenity of those who had not done anything else in their lives. They work in the most thankless tasks, in construction or sweeping streets. . . . But those who suffer the most in this are actually the children: If all women work, who is left to take care of them?"[73]

Critically for the Argentines, the Soviets were alienated from the outside world and had developed a delusional perception of well-being. Alicia Masini could not resist comparing food stores in Moscow and Buenos Aires. She described in detail the time in which they "entered desperately after seeing from the sidewalk hams, sausages, beef, and vegetables hanging in its window, only to find that they were all made of wood." Her husband framed this delusion as a byproduct of political and social repression and denounced its consequences abroad. "I'm outraged by the communist hypocrisy that imposes inhumane living and labor conditions on its own people while it proclaims itself abroad as the champion of freedom," he wrote. Condemning indoctrination, he added: "The Iron Curtain is a false illusion. They eat half-pickled cucumber and a piece of bread made of sawdust and straw as their only meal, and still feel they're the best-fed workers on earth."[74]

In contrast to the descriptions from the United States, descriptions of the Soviet experience offered a dystopian perspective of the expansion of government and the "excesses" of organized labor when subject to government control. The scarcity of both freedom and food was portrayed as the twin curses of communism; the attaché revealed the truth about "the workers' paradise in which some in Argentina still believe."[75] In so doing, he highlighted the opposite of this curse in the association between freedom and food guaranteed under Peronism, underscoring the unity of social and political rights that characterized its populist ideology. Workers' ample access to food in Argentina was not only an economic indicator, but also a symbol of their central role in the emerging culture of popular consumption and of the corresponding freedom that they enjoyed under Perón. In a context in which workers spent half of their income on food, and the government developed a vast bureaucracy to guarantee the quantity and quality of what they ate, the comparison of caloric consumption in Argentina with the rest of the world was powerful evidence of the superiority of the Peronist regime.[76]

Conde Magdaleno's disenchantment with the Soviet Union opened the door to the most significant incident involving any worker attaché abroad. He had befriended the Spanish communists who were staying in the Soviet Union under political asylum granted by Stalin. In 1947, in an effort to help them, he arranged for the Argentine embassy to hire two of them, Pedro Cepeda Sánchez and José Antonio Tuñón Albertos, as translators.[77] As many of their comrades, eight years after the Spanish Civil War, they had become critical of communism and were ready to leave, but the Soviet Union had firmly closed off that possibility.

On 2 January 1948, Conde Magdaleno left Moscow for Buenos Aires via Prague. A few hours into the flight, members of the crew heard noises coming from his carry-on luggage, only to see five minutes later the face of a suffocating man emerging from one of the Peronist attaché's trunks. The attaché had tried to smuggle José Tuñón, one of the Spanish refugees, out of the Soviet Union. Since the end of 1947 and for twelve entire weeks, Tuñón and Cepeda had spent a few hours a day locked in luggage bags and practicing breathing techniques on the premises of the Argentine embassy, but the training had not prepared them for the reality of the flight. Conde Magdaleno later confessed to Tuñón's brother, a communist in Mexico, that his brother's sympathies with the Spanish Republic were long and unyielding, but after having a "close look at this antiproletarian dictatorship," he had wanted to exploit his escape with a denunciation of living conditions under communism at the United Nations. The plane landed in Kiev, where agents from the M.V.D., the infamous special forces of the Ministry of Internal Affairs, arrested the attaché and kidnapped Tuñón, who spent the following eight years in prisons and concentration camps, before being expelled to Mexico in 1956.[78]

There is a noticeable gap in Alicia Masini's diary after December 1947. The next log is dated January 15: she is with her husband in Moscow, awaiting the

FIGURE 4.2. Diplomatic passport of Pedro Conde Magdaleno, worker attaché to the Soviet Union. In Italy, before the final leg of the trip that took Conde Magdaleno to Moscow, Soviet authorities crossed out the word *worker* in his official documents. Source: Personal Papers of Pedro Conde Magdaleno.

FIGURE 4.3. Cover of the book by Pedro Conde Magdaleno, worker attaché to the Soviet Union, denouncing political repression and economic deprivation under communism, 1949.

official order that will expel them from the country. Four days later, she announced: "The visas have arrived. For all of us. The official papers say that we have 24 hours to leave Moscow, but they gave them to us 12 hours after that time started running."[79]

All along, Conde Magdaleno had acted on his own, without informing Perón or his government of his decisions. But his daring action perfectly suited the Peronist narrative of the Argentine labor activist on a liberating mission. Media throughout the world covered the incident. In Buenos Aires, the daily *Clarín* and all the Peronist media celebrated the attempt. The *New York Times* reported the incident, confirming also that another Argentine diplomat, Antonio Bazán, had helped in the smuggling operation. The Argentine Communist Party portrayed Conde Magdaleno as a puppet of the United States. But a later event—a rumored attempt by the United States to publish Conde Magdaleno's book, which the attaché presumably rejected in the strongest terms—framed his actions in Moscow as the direct outcome of Peronist beliefs.[80]

The attachés validated their belief in the Third Position by framing it against the reality of the two emerging superpowers. Peronism distanced itself from crude capitalism and communism by offering a different way of identifying the interests of workers with the national interest and the guarantee of social peace. From their authorized positions as representatives of the working class, the attachés provided a vast amount of evidence documenting the beneficial situation of Argentina under Perón. This evidence supported the beliefs shared by the rest of the attachés, labor activists in general, and public opinion at large. If the United States was portrayed as a system where unrestrained capitalism had led to labor exploitation and social unrest, the Soviet Union was depicted as an example of the risks of brutal hunger and repression that could result from further radicalism.

For activists who had been on the Left most of their lives, this was a thorough transformation. Few people conveyed this shift more persuasively than Conde Magdaleno in the weeks before the incident that ended his tenure in the Soviet Union. In one of the few unofficial contacts he had with Soviet workers at the Argentine ambassador's dacha, he offered the most succinct and eloquent lesson of Peronist conversion: "I was a member of a communist union until 1943, and I quit because it elevated political interests above workers' interests. But in 1947, I came here, leaving behind a union of happy members, satisfied, and united—workers who enjoy social justice as never before. *Comencé siendo peronista por agradecimiento; hoy lo soy por convicción* [I first became a Peronist out of gratitude; today I'm a Peronist by conviction]."[81]

Conclusion

A close look at the attachés' encounters with the postwar superpowers teases out the deep ideas underlying Peronist identity formation. While the attachés and other officials showed Argentine per capita caloric intake as evidence of Peronist superiority vis-à-vis liberalism and communism, U.S. labor diplomats stressed the productivity of American workers as proof of their better and more sustainable living standard. An AFL brochure showed that an American worker needed to work 30 hours and 44 minutes to buy a bike, while his Soviet counterpart needed 466 hours and 40 minutes. For a car, he needed to work one thousand hours in the United States, and almost four thousand hours in the Soviet Union.[82]

The use of different numbers not only stemmed from a search for data that favored ones' argument, but also revealed specific understandings of welfare and labor-capital relations in democratic politics. Obsession with food consumption was at the very foundation of Peronism: the first meeting between Perón and José Miguel Francisco Luis Figuerola y Tresols in 1943 had ended at two o'clock in the morning with the Argentine colonel and the Spanish Falangist discussing the nutritional deficiencies in the diet of workers' families. In what became his own great leap forward, Perón took home the statistics Figuerola compiled about vitamin and mineral intake and came back with the idea of strengthening the Secretariat of Labor and Welfare from which he started his epic career.[83] This spirit permeated the actions of officials and activists during Argentina's period of prosperity, a philosophy that turned out to be much more problematic after 1949, when the economy stalled and the limits of redistribution became evident. But the dynamic of these early years imprinted a worldview that did not vanish. In their speeches abroad, Peronists presented the references to caloric intake as evidence of the positive resolution to the confrontation of organized labor against capital, as evidence of strong government intervention's ability to check the excesses of laissez-faire, and, unlike in the communist utopia, as evidence of a sense of moral economy that recognized the existence of social diversity but imposed on all members the duty of guaranteeing the fulfillment of universal standards.

As Romualdi's speech and articles from 1947 made clear, U.S. labor diplomats presented increases in productivity not only as a way to ensure that workers' gains were sustainable but also as a way to *avoid* a confrontation with capital. AFL brochures proclaimed that "8.000.000 AFL members reject the blight of 'class struggle,' [and] seek only economic justice."[84] This stance also projected abroad the domestic confrontation with the Congress of Industrial Organizations (CIO), a conflict that will materialize in the AFL's increasing ideological rigidity. If the basic regional problem of Latin American economies was workers' low income, the solution was for countries as a whole to improve their productivity by modernizing capital and training workers. In what became a basic tenet of postwar liberalism, labor diplomats sought to limit the power of their own unions and restrain the activism they promoted. For workers' gains to become sustainable and compatible with political freedom, they had to stem from a more collaborative effort with capital. Thus, unions had to avoid the lure of charismatic leaders who used government to offer immediate benefits in exchange for their freedom.[85]

The Peronist approach to workers' welfare presented some obvious advantages. But the attachés' incursions into the belly of the beasts also proved that gaining sympathy among U.S. and Soviet workers was difficult at best and that the goal of building a Peronist-inspired labor movement in each of those two countries had been preposterous from the beginning. For the attachés, the asymmetry between their own powers, even as enhanced by Peronist propaganda abroad, and the vast resources of the United States and the Soviet Union to contain these efforts—as well as the long history, struggles, and power of their respective unions—was a humbling experience. The attachés confronted the obvious reality that labor movements abroad were not going to simply erase their own ideas and traditions and embrace Peronism, as had happened in Argentina. This forced the attachés to redesign their labor diplomacy. Perón quickly narrowed the role of his envoys in the United States to the task of propaganda while reducing labor diplomacy in the Soviet Union to zero. (After the incident with the attempted smugglers, Perón would have his own inconsequential revenge five years later, when he appointed Juan Otero as Argentine ambassador to Moscow. Otero was one of two worker attachés who reached the position of ambassador.)

But the way the attachés made sense of their actions abroad had much larger implications for their view of Peronism and its domestic role. It recast their own experience of building a new political identity through new lenses, in which "gratitude" and "conviction" reinforced one another as collective bonds to their leader. The social turmoil in the United States, the setbacks of its labor movement, and the bullying role of its business sector in politics confirmed the value of Argentina's achievements and the risks of unchecked capitalism. The overwhelming economic deprivation and political repression the attachés witnessed in the Soviet Union cast in a new light what they now defined as "idealized sympathies" of an ideology that undermined workers' freedom. It provided new grounds for the anticommunism that they had initially accepted more with resignation than with enthusiasm.

Conversely, the limited interaction of U.S. unions with the attachés and the visit of U.S. labor leaders to Argentina provided unique elements in the United States for reflections about a new kind of totalitarian threat. Romualdi and the AFL labor diplomats characterized Argentina before Perón as an archaic country in need of modernization and social inclusion. In their view, the delay in fulfilling these aspirations had paved the way for a three-step fall into totalitarianism: a leader gained the workers' support by offering unsustainable benefits while keeping the workers under his political control; social conflict increased as workers' living conditions improved through wealth redistribution rather than by increasing labor productivity; and those who tried to stop Peronism's abuses were consequently repressed. Crystallized in colorful descriptions of a struggle for freedom, this view was avidly consumed in the United States by scholars, officials, and labor leaders at a moment characterized by the partial rollback of New Deal labor gains and the accelerated moves to contain social conflict at home and abroad. They used the example of Peronist Argentina not only to describe the external threat of a totalitarian regime but also to contrast it with their vision for the future of the labor movement and its place within U.S. liberalism. It is this historical conjuncture that explains part of the attention (and the little sympathy) that Peronism received in the United States and helps to situate American reactions toward this foreign movement within the broader domestic transformations of U.S. liberalism.

These two confronting views clashed in Latin America. Along with the attachés' reports from Europe before and in the early years of the Marshall Plan, their dispatches from abroad provided new evidence and arguments in favor of the Third Position. It was clear that Argentina did not have the same power as the Soviet Union and the United States, but it became even clearer, in the Peronist perception, that their Third Position had allowed Argentina and its labor movement to secure a much better situation in the postwar than most of the rest of the world. Consumed domestically, their reports offered vivid accounts that reaffirmed the contrast between the crisis that ravaged the world and the prosperity achieved by the working class in Argentina under Perón. In a subtle and ongoing process, their dispatches revealed (and helped to produce) an image of Peronism that represented both a continuity with a country that had been economically prosperous and politically independent, and a rupture with that tradition, by now centering the exceptionality of Argentina in a new kind of nationalism symbolized by its working class. The information coming from each of the two poles of the Cold War complemented each other, offering a vindication of Peronist rhetoric against U.S. imperialism while, at the same time, reinforcing the need to fight extremism. These elements, in turn, proved fundamental to fashioning an enduring identity among Argentine workers during their incorporation into democratic politics.

"I feel sure that the Bogotá Conference will make history—
the kind of history we all want to see made."—SPRUILLE BRADEN,
Assistant Secretary of State for American Republic Affairs

CHAPTER FIVE. **AT THE TURN OF THE TIDE**

No Peronist movement ever flourished beyond the Argentine borders. Yet, for a few years, until the early 1950s, Peronism was everywhere, or so it appeared to Peronist activists deployed abroad and to more than a few of their foes. When a worker attaché entered the grocery shop in Casma, a small Peruvian town located 2,700 miles from Buenos Aires, in early September 1947, he was more thrilled than surprised to find a portrait of General Perón hanging on the wall. "We asked the owner what he knew about our President," the attaché reported. "He said he knew Perón through the news published in the Peruvian media—he felt true admiration for his work on social justice." It was a quick stop, but long enough for the attaché to hand out some brochures, including ones that covered the Declaration of the Rights of Workers and the Peronist doctrine, before heading out with the rest of an official delegation in their zealous search for the next Argentine frontier.[1]

Peru had long known about liberation by Argentine generals. Indeed, its first president, the "Protector of Peru," was the Argentine general José de San Martín, who in 1821 supported an uprising of Spanish-American landowners, defeated the royalist forces, and proclaimed Peruvian independence. The official mission traveling through the country in 1947 meticulously registered every statue and portrait of San Martín. In the outskirts of Huacho, ninety miles from Lima, they found a bust of the Argentine leader abandoned in a storage facility close to where he had given the memorable "Balcón de Huaura" speech, which declared Peru's independence, in 1820. The ambassador immediately made "all the necessary efforts," with "dignifying patriotic fervor," to build a cement base where the bronze effigy could stand on display. Argentina's redemptive presence in Peru was aimed both to forge an association with the country's struggles and to preserve an aura, evident in statues of San Martín as much as in pictures of Perón.[2]

The scene depicted at the grocery store suggests Peruvians already had an idea of what Peronism meant before the delegation's arrival. Articles in the local media and intense Argentine propaganda efforts provided information about Perón and the Argentine working class. As in most of the region, the attachés landed in Peru at a time when labor movements demanded, through various political projects, broader participation in politics and the redistribution of wealth, when new nationalist movements were replacing the narrower patriotism of local elites, and when widespread anti-U.S. sentiment was melding the two goals.[3]

Nobody condensed the threatening implications of Peronist ambitions for the region better than the Chilean ambassador to Argentina. In 1945, he shared his somber premonitions with his U.S. colleague in Buenos Aires, "fear[ing] that the dictatorial regime here is endeavoring to spread its ideologies and methods elsewhere." The Chilean diplomat built his case against Argentina around an eloquent, if unexpected, metaphor: he described Perón's advance in the region as "similar to the winning of the independence of South America, which began in Argentina, spread to Chile, thence to Bolivia and Peru, etc."[4] Embellished as it sounded, the notion that Perón's project was possibly the heir of an epic mission was an impression that hypnotized followers and detractors alike.

This chapter analyzes the attachés' actions in Latin America from 1947 to 1949. In a period of rising activism that demanded social and political rights for peasants and the working classes, the attachés solidified the ties of Peronism with progressive groups and labor organizations throughout the region. The chapter starts chronologically with the hopeful "democratic spring" of the first postwar years during which organized labor flourished. It ends on a more tragic note, characterized by the fierce reaction that social change provoked among various elites and economic sectors. Against studies that characterize Peronism as an exception in the early democratic wave across Latin America, the study of the attachés' work reveals the crucial place of Peronism in conceptualizing a powerful form of nationalism tied to the idea of "social justice" and reveals the enormous ambitions of Peronism and the potential of those aspirations in the region during those years.

This vitality resignifies the tone of alarm palpable in the Chilean official's metaphor about San Martín and situates that anxiety as part of the tide of reaction that put an end to the democratic spring and set the tone for the Cold War in the region. Even though the movement of opening and closing and of strengthening and weakening the forces of expansion and reaction is fluid, there is an identifiable hinge between these two periods, which can be traced to April 1948, at the Ninth Pan-American Conference, in Bogotá. This conference gave birth to the Organization of American States (OAS), partly as a byproduct of the reaction against the democratic spring, and partly as an expression of the realignment of forces in the hemisphere.

The attachés' intervention in this process was substantial, as well as fragile, contingent. With a domestic front characterized by a growing economy, the expansion of the welfare system, and the consolidation of political power, Perón launched one of Argentina's most remarkable attempts at regional leadership. As part of a foreign policy grounded in "the prevalent feeling of an Argentina perceived as strong, flattered by Europe and, finally, accepted by the United States," Perón's assault on liberal claims of advancing democracy in Latin America merged with an attempt to expand Argentine regional influence. [5] The Argentine leader developed a threefold strategy: the pursuit of bilateral economic agreements with most countries in South America to dispute U.S. hemispheric leadership; the fostering of potential allies through intervention in the domestic affairs of other Latin American countries; and the adoption of an aggressive labor diplomacy aimed at creating a working-class regional movement inspired by (and subject to) the Peronist principles of the Third Position.[6]

The first part of this chapter describes the attachés' deployment and show the ways in which their everyday actions contributed to building Peronism as a movement and as a worldview. Whether or not Perón's ambitious projects were sustainable, they were fiercely resisted by the United States and elites throughout the region. Government, labor, and political sectors in the region reacted in widely different ways, but in almost all cases, they sought to take advantage of the opportunities that the eruption of Peronism presented. The incursion of these labor activists into international politics was aimed at altering traditional diplomacy and modern transnational politics in general. With the allure of Peronism at its peak, the attachés went out to promote its principles, portraying Latin America as a battlefield between Argentina and the United States for the conquest of the region's working class. And on that battlefield, they advanced ideas of common good and national sovereignty forged during the struggles for independence. A close study of their actions reveals the limitations of this approach and how it shaped the fate of Peronist ambitions.

The final part of this chapter focuses on the actions of the attachés toward the Ninth Pan-American Conference. Before and during the conference, which marked the beginning of the postwar inter-American system, Argentine activists put Peronism in contact with a wide range of democratic and progressive movements, many of which defined the fate of the region during the twentieth century. The episode serves as a case study of the opportunities explored by Peronism, the hopes it aroused, and the combination of contingencies, structural forces, local and global realignments, and unforced errors that determined the fate of the attachés' mission and of the Peronist regional project at large. The conference became a hinge between two very different periods in the attachés' mission and in the region's history.

Building Support for the Rising Tide

At the age of eighteen, Torcuato Di Tella was still some way from becoming the prominent sociologist who explained populism as being the result of a rapid and aggressive expansion of capitalist relations in Latin America.[7] His father, Torcuato Sr., born in Italy, had come to Argentina as a child. In 1910, Torcuato Sr., asked a friend if they could build a better bread-kneading machine than the imported ones. He went on to become a powerful industrialist with ambitions for social reform, a kind of "Argentine Ford" with regional and global aspirations.[8] The Di Tella family took customary summer trips abroad, and in early in 1948, they boarded a steamship to the United States. Torcuato Jr. would sit on the ship's veranda to enjoy the view from the gallery. His memories from those days were not only of the soothing sea but also of the bustling activity in the seaports they were visiting. One image in particular struck him: at a stop in Brazil, a group of worker attachés traveling to Europe was perched on the edge of the ship's common deck, throwing Perón and Evita pins and Declaration of the Rights of Workers brochures to the black stevedores working the docks of Santos. For the Di Tella family, relations with the attachés on board were uneasy throughout the journey. The family was staunchly anti-Peronist but considered it necessary to keep a low profile, so as to avoid creating any additional noise in their relation with the government. But the scene at the Brazilian port filled them with anxiety.[9]

It did not reflect the extremely "ambitious and well-funded propaganda apparatus" described by the labor expert Robert Alexander, but it did offer a glimpse of the fervor of Peronist international activists, the potential reach of their actions, the reactions they provoked.[10]

Officials, media, diplomats, and businessmen across the region showed a similar mix of perplexity and trepidation as the attachés started their new activities, turning Argentine embassies into a reference for domestic labor activism and Peronist publicity. But the worker attachés' methods, obstacles, and results varied greatly from one country to the next, for complex reasons, including local politics, social dynamics, the relationship of each country with Argentina, the personal disposition of the attachés, the history of the labor movement, global and domestic economic trends, and the specific role of the United States in each country.

The ideas that the attachés advanced in each country, though, did share a common interpretation of their mission abroad. They set forth a populist language that linked social justice to national dignity as a tenet of democratic politics and tried to organize rising labor movements in support of reforms inspired by Peronism. Their Third Position discourse initially attracted the interest of a broad range of groups who shared certain defined goals—industrialization and social inclusion in opposition to backwardness and poverty—and who perceived local elites, the U.S. presence in the region, and the prescriptions of liberal politics to be the main obstacles to this Latin American version of postwar modernization. The degree of the attachés' anticommunist rhetoric swayed the views of Peronist supporters and detractors in the region. Yet in many cases it did not preclude leftist movements from approaching Peronism, and it certainly did not stop U.S. officials and local elites from denouncing the attachés as agents of a communist specter haunting the region.

THE REFUGEES

In conjunction with the attachés' aim of building a new world under Perón's leadership, their long individual trajectories in union activism in Argentina shaped the initial steps they took in their new destinations. The attachés were a genuine representation of Perón's political base, yet that did not mean that their actions were absolutely congruent with their leader's wishes. They were in plain conflict with Perón's aims on more than one occasion. A clear example of this conflict is the attachés' relationship with political refugees in many countries. The immediate postwar years in Latin America were characterized by swift political changes as many leaders and dictators experimented with forms of political openness and democratic institutions.[11] Many of these experiences were short-lived, and their paths were not always linear. On the ground, these rapid shifts created precarious conditions for officials and activists involved in democratization processes, often at the very moment when Peronism was launching its original diplomatic program.

The attaché Saverio Ragno arrived in Bolivia in March 1947, a week before the conservative Enrique Hertzog took office and two years after the assassination of Perón's strongest ally in the region, President Gualberto Villarroel. Local elites had seen Villarroel's death as the beginning of democratic restoration. As the Hertzog administration turned increasingly repressive, Ragno personally helped to usher out of the country members of the Villarroel administration and the Movimiento Nacionalista Revolucionario (MNR), and served as courier between Bolivian activists and the exiled MNR leader Paz Estenssoro, much to the government's irritation.[12] For those who had been aided, the gesture more than made up for the irritating irony of Perón's appointment of a dock stevedore as worker attaché to landlocked Bolivia. It also helped consolidate a long period of collaboration between Peronism and the MNR and paved the way for further assistance by the attachés: Ragno's successor, Modesto Alvarez, personally smuggled the revolutionary and future president Hernán Siles Suazo across the border in the trunk of his car.[13]

In Nicaragua, the glassworker Cossimo Piva had been an Argentine attaché less than a month when, in May 1947, General Anastasio Somoza cut short his family's brief experiment with postwar liberal institutions and overthrew his own puppet president, Leonardo Argüello, who had initiated a set of moderate pro-labor policies. In coordination with the ambassador, Piva organized for members of Argüello's family, and for union activists who were targets of Somoza's National Guard, to be given asylum at the Argentine embassy after other countries avoided the task and the United States followed a "hands-off" approach that benefited Somoza's strategy. Some of these union leaders, as well as supporters of the Argüello regime, remained active and became members of the opposition. A month later, with the assistance of the worker attaché in Costa Rica, Segundino Yanzi, Piva was in charge of delivering all of their sent or received correspondence in and out of Nicaragua.[14] These actions ran against Perón's quickly forged alliance with Somoza, but were among Piva's most unyielding political moves in the region and cemented a relationship between unions in the two countries that would survive Perón's administration and that would become a component of the populist dynamic between unions and Somoza's dictatorship.[15]

León Segovia also arrived in Paraguay at a moment of political turmoil. He settled his family into a boarding house in Asunción just as the 1947 civil

FIGURE 5.1. The Peronist worker attaché León Segovia (sixth from left), visiting a textile factory in Asunción, Paraguay. Courtesy: Personal Papers of León Segovia.

war erupted. The dictator Higinio Morínigo, who Franklin Delano Roosevelt had supported during the war in hopes of counterbalancing the dominance of pro-Axis Argentina, led a project for political openness in 1946, creating a multiparty coalition, which ended when the ruling Colorado Party expelled and repressed its former coalition partners, the Febreristas and the Liberals.[16] In what might have been Segovia's first encounter with national authorities, he was arrested and his room searched by Guión Rojo, the paramilitary group of a government faction, looking for evidence of collaboration with Febreristas and communists.[17] Despite the strong anticommunist rhetoric and beliefs of Segovia and most attachés, this would not be the last time that they would be seen as a leftist threat, nor would it be the last time that they would actually cooperate with leftist activists. The Febrerista activists were indeed seeking asylum at the embassy. Like the attaché in Bolivia, Segovia also helped Febreristas and communists cross Paraguay's border in early 1947. Segovia, a local familiar with the region, set up a system to get the activists out of the country, using his car to drive them to a boat that reached the city of Clorinda, in Argentina.[18] But if in the Bolivian case Ragno helped a party allied with Perón but opposed to the local government, here Segovia was helping the opposition to the Colorado Party, which would be among Perón's strongest allies throughout his government and his years in exile. The kinds of tensions found within Peronism are a trademark of Argentine populism. It becomes apparent in the discord between labor activists and their leader's alliances, and between activists' engagement with social protest and conflict and the leader's strong calls to social discipline.

To look at Peronism and its role in the region during this period solely through the lens constituted by Argentine foreign policy, Perón's proclamations, and his unusual alliances misses other fundamental factors in the movement's political inception. As a movement that at that time was a work in progress (and for many an enigma), Peronism was also the product of its activists, who shaped Peronism through the particular ways in which they interpreted and spread the ideas of Perón and even through the affects they felt for the transformations occurring in Argentina, the changes in their own lives, and the figures who were at the forefront of those changes. Even if the activists' relationships with political refugees were mostly derived from their own political experiences prior to 1945, these contacts came to shape for many (most obviously for their opponents) their perception of Peronism.

THE REPORTS TO BUENOS AIRES

Deployed across the region, the attachés immediately reported to Buenos Aires about social and political realities that were new to them. Their dispatches offer vivid descriptions of Latin America during those years as much as they express the attachés' own perception of the region when contrasted with their view of Argentina. They abound in descriptions of situations of economic exploitation or political exclusion. They present social relations as primitive—almost as if these societies lacked a public sphere in which individual grievances could be expanded into a collective claim. To some extent in conflict with this perception, the reports simultaneously emphasized the existence of a rising organization of workers, the sometimes violent struggles against local elites, and the interest that Peronism ignited among activists and workers at large. These perceptions further validated the Peronist diplomats' beliefs that the expansion of Peronism as a political worldview and the promotion of incipient forms of the welfare state were necessary answers to social injustice.

Following the instructions imparted in Buenos Aires, many attachés immediately left their host countries' capitals and went to the provinces. They received a warm welcome everywhere. Unions, city councils, political parties, and media paid a great deal of attention to their presence, their discourse, and the information that they distributed about Argentina. Their arrival was often used to bolster domestic labor disputes. But at times it also complicated workers' struggles, as the attachés often intervened in local confrontations with their strong anticommunist rhetoric, only to be identified as potential or actual allies of communist activists. Overall, though, the reaction to the attachés' visits was enthusiastic, partly because no foreign visitor—let alone a union activist with diplomatic status representing a leader whose achievements were already known—had ever ventured into the municipal workers' union of Matanzas, Cuba, the mines of Corocoro, Bolivia, the Finca "Cocales" in Patulul, Guatemala, the city of Cusco, in Peru or visited the striking oil workers of Barrancabermeja, Colombia.[19] To Buenos Aires, they sent thousands of dispatches offering a detailed picture of labor conditions across Latin America. For the attachés who wrote the reports, the officials who received them, and the media that released them to massive audiences, it did not take a stretch of imagination to contrast the hardships found across the region with the relatively easy situation of Argentina. These dispatches differed from the usual diplomatic reports in their vivid language, the experiences they described, and the slang, misspellings, and grammatical errors that sometimes characterized them. Throughout the reports, the attachés described poor living conditions as "backward," assigned blame to the concentration of wealth and a weak government, put hope in industrialization, and advocated for workers' struggles to organize their demands through unions. All of these details portrayed the particular notion of modernization that Peronism embraced as its recipe for Latin America.

After meeting a hundred delegates from the Federación Sindical de Guatemala in Patulul, for example, the attaché Alberto Viale reported at length about his visit to the Finca Cocales, with its large production of coffee, bananas, panela, and cattle. He reported the .36 quetzal per day wages and the .50 quetzal that workers obtained for a cut of a hundred bananas. To put these numbers in perspective, he highlighted that the prices of "the most-needed products [are] as expensive as in the city": .10 quetzal per pound of beans, .09 quetzal per pound of rice. "Milk is not available, and meat has to be brought in from town, 9 kilometers away, and it costs Q. 0.18 per pound of bones for stew, while other cuts can reach up to Q. 0.60 per pound," he wrote. As for housing, workers lived in constructions of wood, straw, and leaves, where "the roof leak[ed] inside the house" and running water was "in awful condition, mostly contaminated, and it [came] from only one source at the finca's house, up to ten blocks away from some houses." Workers had no electricity, even though "the finca had its own generator that could provide electricity for all workers," which was one of the central demands of the union.[20]

The lives of peasants across Latin America presented important differences. Viale's portrayal of medieval living conditions in Guatemala contrasts with the paternalism that permeated the attaché Cirilo Liendo's 1947 description of the Peruvian economy following a visit to the Hacienda Casa Grande, one of the largest sugar mills, seventy-five kilometers from Trujillo. There the attaché found "a real city of 30,000 people, between employees, workers and their families." Workers earned between seven and twenty soles per day, whether they worked in the field or the factory, and generated "170,000 tons per year, one third of the entire country's sugar production." All workers had "government insurance, decent housing . . . and [were] organized in unions," the report added, in a reference to sugar unions, one of the key bases for the nationalist American Popular Revolutionary Alliance (APRA).[21] The hacienda had its own school system, "although it [was] controlled by the government," and also boasted three hospitals, "including the Worker Regional Hospital, a model of efficiency in surgery." Yet after concluding in the city of Lambayeque his three-week journey throughout what were considered to be the "most developed regions of Peru," Liendo immediately expressed his Peronist idea of modernity. Most social reformers in Peru (and the attachés themselves on several occasions) presented the indigenous peoples as obstacles to progress.[22] This time Liendo focused more on "latifundium" as "the primary cause of economic backwardness . . . since it halts the increase in productivity, destroys the principle that the land belongs to those who work it, and has a negative impact on the consolidation of regular families." In a general overview of the country's provinces, he described education as "poor, to say the least," and housing as dreadful, "with no running water or hygiene, and a shocking degree of promiscuity, in which people of different sex live in a single room."[23]

MISSIONARIES OF SOCIAL REVOLUTION

In addition to reporting about labor conditions in their host countries, the worker attachés spent most of their time explaining the transformations underway in Argentina and promoting Peronism among labor and political organizations. The scope of their actions was broad: they purchased slots and led programs on some of the main radio stations, distributed aid from the Fundación Eva Perón, brought hundreds of labor leaders and activists on fully paid visits to Argentina to show firsthand the experience of Peronism, spoke actively in the press, participated in small union meetings and big party conventions, reached out to hundreds of thousands of workers in each country with propaganda about Peronism, and met with national authorities, the diplomatic corps, and small-town officials.

What did they proclaim, and how was their material generated? The attachés arrived with thousands of brochures and pictures. Using the figures of Perón and Evita, the propaganda effort was organized almost entirely around three simple axes: the promotion of a moderate form of welfare state, the emphasizing of the large role that organized labor should play in a democratic society, and the denunciation of the U.S. presence in the region as the main obstacle to economic development. Although the Foreign Ministry prepared and distributed a wide array of magazines about Argentina and Argentine workers' living standards, the Cancillería was not their only source of material. The Undersecretariat of Press and Propaganda, for example, bought time on radio airwaves to broadcast the attachés' programs and Perón's speeches. The undersecretariat was headed by the all-powerful Raúl Apold, who was a close aide to Perón and who, among his many activities, kept an updated list of the attachés.[24] When the attachés did not obtain resources from Apold, they received them directly from Perón and Evita, avoiding diplomatic channels and the involvement of ambassadors. The attachés regularly received a short note signed by either of the two leaders, reminding them to contact the Casa Rosada or the Fundación Eva Perón for anything they needed. They consequently did so and immediately received containers with more materials than they had requested.[25]

These direct channels gave the attachés the standing they needed to work with labor leaders abroad as "Perón's personal representatives." At the same time, it heightened the attachés' importance vis-à-vis their diplomatic colleagues, who were relegated to bureaucratic—and extremely slow—communication with political power in Buenos Aires. But this differentiation also caused resentment among diplomatic officers who already despised Peronism as a movement and the attachés as *cabecitas negras*, the heavily charged characterization that, as Natalia Milanesio explains, urban middle and upper classes made of what "they perceived as a threat to urban lifestyle, class identity, and social status."[26] Perón's transformations in Cancillería had been incomplete, and as in other areas of the administration, policymaking was not the direct expression of a revolutionary force but the outcome of arduous negotiations with older traditions and interest groups that survived within the state. It was true that the attachés' presence in the state "reinforced the regime's anti-bureaucratic image," to borrow Eduardo Elena's expression.[27] And the fierce opposition the attachés generated among Argentine diplomats is in itself a factor that needs to be studied as part of a comprehensive understanding of Peronism. But far away from Buenos Aires and the Peronist euphoria, most ambassadors translated their resentment toward Peronism into making things as difficult as possible for the attachés, internally and in the diplomatic world. A worker attaché like Pedro Otero could bring Perón's personal representation to Colombia as a daring action, but the ambassador easily sabotaged his efforts by not transferring external calls addressed to the labor activist, effectively cutting off Otero's communications. Otero could write to Buenos Aires to get more propaganda material, but he could not bother Perón to complain about an ambassador who did not transfer phone calls from a potential ally.[28]

What was the propaganda material? The attaché in Peru described what he had in his car when the Peronist delegation arrived to Huacho. "We started here our work of disseminating our ideas," he said. "We carried: 'Declaration of the Rights of Workers,' 'A Message of Peace from President Perón,' 'Argentina at the 30th International Labor Conference,' 'Transparent Elections,' 'Magazine of Argentine Information,' 'Magazine of Argentine Industries,' pins, brochures, books, including 'Peronist Doctrine' and 'Annals of the University during the Intervention,' and 'Revolutionary Work to Reinstate the Constitutional Regime in the Country.'"[29] In a note sent to the attaché at the United Nations, apparently similar to others sent everywhere else, Eva Perón added that books and brochures provided "the description of some of our social and labor legislation so that the transformations occurring in our Motherland can be known abroad. I am sending you also pictures of you and El General."[30]

These materials were a means for agitprop and a source of indoctrination. But also, and perhaps more important, they offered a thorough presentation of the worldview forged in Argentina and a revelation of the connections this view generated with labor movements, political parties, and workers in the region. For all the Peronist criticism of the United States, the political vision they presented was not a frontal attack on liberal rights, but rather an inclusive understanding of liberalism with social rights as its cornerstone, which they considered to be a Latin American contribution. As Perón had done when launching the program, the attachés described the changes in Argentina in the same terms as the French Revolution. "Workers' rights," the attaché in Colombia said in a radio speech, "are to this age what citizen rights were to the century of the great revolution."[31] The unrelenting public expression of this new age was the Declaración de Derechos del Trabajador (Declaration of the Rights of Workers).[32] The proclamation began by stating that "those rights derived from working, like individual rights, are natural and unalterable attributes of the human condition." It then posited the government as the "interpreter of peoples' demands for social justice," preventing capital's disregard of those demands, which "is the cause of antagonisms, struggles, and social unrest." It enumerated ten broad social rights, stressing the state's duty to satisfy general well-being and check capital's abuses.[33]

Only in a few instances did the attachés talk about the democratization of gender relations and the role of women in Peronist Argentina as part of the transformations they embraced. Isidra Fernández, one of the few women attachés deployed abroad, offered a conference in Peru framing the rise of women within the larger world history of feminism. She also traced the origins of modern feminism to the French Revolution, "when humanity embraced equality and universal rights." As Fernández stressed the larger spaces that women had conquered in society, her take on feminism also reinforced traditional notions about what female activists could contribute by following men. The two together built a perfect whole: "Men, because they're plenitude, vigor, energy, sacrifice; women, because in the logical and undeniable complementarity of human roles, they are the spiritual and universal adjective of love, the lofty motive for all unrest." The attaché based her idea of women's role in public life on the image of Eva Perón's "unwavering support to our leader, General Perón." In politics, she said, women "have to provide the universal spirit of love, the human complement of men's energy and determination."[34]

REACTIONS

It was not so much the innovations that the Declaration of the Rights of Workers introduced as the historical conjuncture in which they were launched that made it relevant to international politics. As debates over the edification of the welfare state ran throughout the region, the carriers of the declaration immediately intervened in domestic arguments on behalf of a broad set of political groups, which was probably much wider than Perón had intended.[35] So when the attaché in Honduras distributed thousands of copies of the declaration, the pamphlet reached unions demanding a new labor code while pushing the dictatorship of Tiburcio Carías for political openness. Rights like those consecrated in Peronist Argentina became the basis for the Honduran welfare state, which started to emerge only a year later, with the end of Carías's regime, as other countries in Central America also debated modes of social reform.[36] The attaché made sure to meet with unions, such as the Sociedad Obrera Esfuerzo y Cultura, the Asociación de Motoristas, and other emerging political actors to distribute abundant material about Argentine politics and social reform.[37] In his meeting with the foreign minister of Honduras, the attaché in Tegucigalpa, Roberto Federico Ferrari, described his activities as part of the larger national effort to "explain the prosperity in our country" and "promote the improvement of our working classes."[38] But in the Latin America of 1947, local elites and U.S. foreign officials reinforced each other's concerns about social unrest. And in this context, nationalist agitprop was also a proxy for communist expansion, turning Peronist activism into an early factor in the Cold War and starting the repressive cycle in which elite groups assembled an answer at times more related to their growing fear than to the nature of the challenge they faced. Two weeks after the brochures started to circulate in Tegucigalpa, a close aide to the Honduran president characterized the attaché's activities as "communist propaganda." The aide instructed the allied press not to publish anything about the brochures and assured the U.S. embassy that "if such activities continue, the Honduran government will take appropriate measures."[39]

Throughout the region, the attachés confronted economic elites, conservative political leaders and media, and U.S. officials; however, in each case, this confrontation took on different particulars. The attaché Cipriano Barreiro, activist at the Union of Tailors and Garment Industries, arrived in Rio de Janeiro and presented Peronism as a model for fighting "against the poverty and malnutrition of workers in Brazil."[40] Barreiro arrived at a moment in which "the Brazilian worker" was a highly contested concept. Business, political, and labor sectors were producing competing images of the kind of worker who was to be a central player in modern Brazil. They conceived, even if problematically, the image of Brazilian workers as agents of a larger process of rational industrialization, not as the malnourished, exploited men that Barreiro wanted to redeem.[41] The attaché immediately—and clumsily—induced a nationalistic reaction against his efforts. The government and the national press denounced his characterization of the Brazilian working class as "unfair" and as provoking "the puzzlement and anger of Brazilian workers." The government formally asked Argentina to refrain from intervening in domestic matters at the very moment that local unions were being purged of thousands of activists in the name of fighting communist penetration, with the near total silence of the press and the support of the United States. In an expression of the limits imposed on the attachés' strategy, Barreiro went on to write about communist "penetration" in Brazil but did not approach the Partido Communista Brasiliero, which had adopted a flexible perspective on Peronism and even considered it a tactical ally.

Conflicting notions of the role of unions in politics and disputes over wealth distribution were evident in Brazil, and Barreiro's power lay in the resources deployed by Peronism as much as in the ideas they promoted. By mid-1947, Peronist publicity was available at unions in São Paulo and Río. Around three hundred Brazilian activists had already traveled to Argentina with funding from labor fellowships. These fellowships included courses at the General Confederation of Labour (CGT), visits to factories, meetings with labor leaders, and participation in massive rallies led by Perón and Evita. When a British labor attaché visited Minas Gerais in September, he found, not without trepidation, "the unions too busy selecting the people that they will send to Buenos Aires."[42]

Romualdi and other American officials countered the energy of the Argentine attachés in Brazil. They met with union leaders as well as with President Eurico Dutra. They raised their concern about Peronist activities and supported the purge of communist activists in exchange for the U.S. government's approval to send Brazilian union leaders to the labor meeting in Lima the following year.[43] The negotiations over the participation in regional labor organizations were, in part, an abstract fight over power structures, but the U.S. officials' actions exposed the ideological and political nature of the competition. While the Peronist attaché was working to guarantee that unions in São Paulo and Río de Janeiro had thousands of copies of the Portuguese translation of the declaration that established inalienable workers' rights, the U.S. labor attaché was sending the Brazilian government ten copies of the Taft-Hartley Act, which restricted those very same rights, along with the copies of debates in the U.S. Congress and President Truman's overridden veto. Inspired by the U.S. move toward more restrictive legislation, the Brazilian minister of labor and an allied congressman had requested from the U.S. embassy more information about the controversial legislation. American officials were eager to comply.[44]

The reach of Peronism was extensive but thin. For a few years, communists from Chile and Brazil were persuaded to overlook the strong anticommunist Peronist rhetoric and their own previously fierce anti-Peronism. Christian Democratic leaders in Costa Rica were willing to travel to Buenos Aires for a firsthand experience of the social reforms enacted by a regime that they had condemned. Union leaders working under U.S. patronage in Cuba and Nicaragua moved closer to the attachés' positions and showed their openness to what the attachés had to say (and offer).[45] The basic principles that had fortified the domestic consensus on the New Deal in the United States were now the source of inspiration to oppose U.S. influence in the region.[46]

By early 1948, the competing postwar projects of regional integration started to materialize into a new set of institutions, which were destined to shape hemispheric politics. In January, unions from the entire hemisphere met in Lima, Peru, to create a body from among the competing projects of com-

Time and Place

munists, Peronists, and U.S. labor diplomats to represent the labor movement. A March meeting in Havana, Cuba, gave birth to the General Agreement on Tariffs and Trade (GATT). In April, at the Ninth Pan-American Conference, in Bogotá, the governments of the entire Western Hemisphere created the Organization of American States (OAS), the most significant institution of the postwar inter-American system, in accordance with the resolutions approved a year earlier in Rio de Janeiro, Brazil.[47]

At this point, the attachés had spent one year in their respective destinations. They had established contact with most union leaders and built relationships with thousands of activists while hoping that the vast publicity they had brought would reach an even larger audience to their message. The meeting in Lima, sponsored and dominated by the United States, formalized the split of the labor movement and the confrontation between communist forces grouped in the Confederación de Trabajadores de América Latina (CTAL) and U.S.-allied unions gathered in what would later be called Organización Regional Interamericana de Trabajadores (ORIT.)[48] The exclusion of the Argentine delegation gave Perón the opportunity to accelerate the creation of the union-based Latin American organization, the Agrupación de Trabajadores Latinoamericanos Sindicalistas (ATLAS), the first inter-American institution to explicitly exclude the United States.[49] Between the January meeting in Lima and the Bogotá Conference in April, worker attachés and Argentine diplomats escalated their work, trying to gather support for the creation of a common anti-U.S. front.

Following Perón's instructions, the attachés started to invite delegates from all over Latin America to Argentina to participate in a new regional organization of uncertain shape and purpose. The diverse group of delegates that subsequently arrived in Buenos Aires ranged from recognized union leaders, such as Juan Lechín Oquendo from the Bolivian miners, to obscure former leaders of small unions in El Salvador who landed in Argentina with clearly scripted speeches about the hopes that Perón had opened for workers in Latin America. All in all, by March more than a hundred delegates were already in Argentina or were expected to arrive soon. While some delegations consisted of a single member, as was the case for El Salvador, the attachés in Bolivia, Brazil, Chile, and Paraguay assured the presence of more than twenty delegates from each country.[50] In March, more than thirty activists from Cuba and Mexico, as well as the attachés assigned to those countries, stayed in Argentina for twenty days, their expenses paid by the Peronist government. They not only met Perón, Evita, and CGT officials in Buenos Aires but they also visited the industrial suburbs in Córdoba and the sugar mills of Tucumán. The local press focused on presenting Peronism as a fair and effective means of fighting communism. The delegates from Latin America praised the country's public works and the living standards of the working class, and expressed their own ideas of freedom and equality. One testified to a freedom of expression "that cannot be observed in other countries, with more than 12 workers' periodicals and papers." At times, their choice of words revealed a particular feature of Peronism and its allure abroad. Referring more often to the discourse of the New Deal rather than to the rhetoric of class warfare, visitors praised unions for fulfilling and also controlling worker demands. They found signs of a modernized society that was galvanized by the same ambitions as the American dream. A Cuban delegate noted, "The living standards here are admirable. In Cuba, we just don't have a middle class."[51] In any case, as evidence of the guests' ideological versatility and of the fragility of their loyalty, many of the confidential reports to the U.S. State Department came from the same delegates who were praising Perón in the press.[52]

In the meantime, Perón had dispatched Senator Diego Luis Molinari on an urgent tour throughout the region, extending invitations to political leaders, student organizations, and unions to visit Buenos Aires.[53] Most of these efforts would converge in the Pan-American Conference in Bogotá. Perón expected that at the meeting, Argentina would play a crucial role by proposing a comprehensive plan of economic aid for the region and by presenting Peronism and its nationalist defense of social equality as a far more effective deterrent to leftist radicalism than the free-trade policies advocated by the United States.

Caudillos

Early in the evening of 31 December 1947, the attaché Pedro Otero's Argentine accent flooded the Colombian radio airwaves: "Those who have served the foreign master are against the State and *el pueblo* of Argentina. Our nation is sovereign because of the revolutionary action of those who take charge of the future . . . bringing happiness to the nation that is free . . . just as all the peoples of the earth desire, especially those from this struggling America."[54] Many in Colombia already knew who Pedro Otero was. He appeared regularly on the radio, and just one month prior, he had visited the country's main newspapers, lecturing about the social revolution led by Perón to journalists who were critical of Argentina. He had also secured Perón's support for the strike at the American Tropical Oil Company in Barrancabermeja and delivered five containers of food from the Fundación Eva Perón.[55] But more important, Otero met a few times with the Liberal caudillo Jorge Eliécer Gaitán, the most important figure in Colombian politics, who rallied crowds of workers and peasants with a populist program of social reform. The attaché reported to Buenos Aires about contacts with high officials from the Liberal Party, all devoted to the *Gaitanista* cause. Closely following Gaitán's contacts with other Latin American leaders, U.S officials had singled him out as "the most significant threat" to the region's stability. One American official went so far as to call him "the Colonel Perón of Colombia."[56]

The relation with Liberal leaders and activists was productive. On 3 November 1947, the council of the industrial city of Soacha, located south of Bogotá and controlled by Liberals, bestowed on the worker attaché a resolution supporting "the ideals of General Perón and the organization of a meeting of Spanish-American workers to endorse his policies that offer vast and universal benefits."[57] It was an auspicious sign for Otero, who immediately on arrival saw Colombia as a place with the right ingredients for supporting Perón's regional project. At that moment, Gaitán, like Perón two years earlier, was pushing in Congress for a broad set of social and economic reforms known as El Plan Gaitán. With Gaitanismo rapidly growing, the Argentines decided to intensify contacts and over the following year increased resources in publicity, political activity, and social work by the Fundación Eva Perón in Colombia. They were not the only ones interested in Colombia's fragile political moment. From what looked like a politically insurmountable distance, the Soviet Union also viewed the rise of communist forces in the labor movement and their deflection toward Gaitanismo with some interest, but didn't engage actively.[58]

The reports by Otero and by the Argentine embassy argued that the U.S. State Department backed conservative government factions in Colombia while providing massive assistance to military forces under a lend-lease agreement with the overarching goal of fighting communism.[59] The real actions of U.S. labor diplomats painted a different picture, though it was not entirely incompatible with the one suggested by the attaché.[60] Serafino Romualdi described the Colombian labor movement as "one of the best organized in Latin America." He prepared a visit to Washington and New York for some of the movement's leaders as a way of helping allied groups "expel . . . the communist faction" from the Confederación de Trabajadores Colombianos (CTC) and of promoting "the organization of an effective inter-American movement."[61] These tensions prefigured regional dynamics over the following decades, as international forces provided symbolic and material resources that emboldened contenders in domestic conflicts, hardening their stances and fostering radicalization. Armed with the belief that their political project was global in scope, Peronist activists like Otero or U.S. labor diplomats like

Romualdi sought (and to some extent achieved) the power to contribute to internal disputes that changed the lives of millions of Colombians, affecting their working conditions, cultural options, land ownership, safety, and income.

Otero found a welcoming environment in the labor movement in which the rank-and-file seemed to converge en masse toward the Liberal caudillo.[62] The Peronist attaché worked ceaselessly. In a few months, he gave more than twenty speeches on radio programs (most of them sponsored by the Argentine government), along with press interviews and donations. Otero participated in worker rallies from railway unions in Bogotá to the Andean mine in Medellín. The attaché did not stop at explaining the achievements of Peronism in Argentina but immediately became engaged in local disputes. In another strike of oil workers at a refinery in Medellín, the Peronist diplomat told workers "your fight is our fight." When invited to Popayán by the Federation of Highway Workers, he was so emphatic in his call to "fight against the oligarchs" (a word that at that time unmistakably belonged to Gaitanista jargon) that he had to clarify his words after a local newspaper mentioned his "unfair comparisons." The unions sided with the Argentine.[63] Excited by the prospect of his mission, Otero asked Buenos Aires for more propaganda material. He received not only the usual kit with Peronist brochures, but also copies of *Martín Fierro* (the epic poem, written by José Hernández in the 1870s, that became the narrative of a native identity) "so our culture can reach Colombian workers who are eager to learn more and more about Argentina." Soon, Colombian unions had hundreds of copies of *Martín Fierro*, as well as brochures about the Argentine social-security system illustrated with images of massive rallies in Plaza de Mayo full of banners with the face of Perón.[64]

Throughout his dispatches, Otero felt the need to clarify that the role of communism in Colombian social turmoil was not as important as the press suggested. Most likely, he wrote these reports as a preemptive effort to placate anxieties about communism among Peronist officials in Buenos Aires. Otero's description of Colombia echoed what observers of Argentina noted about the massive migration of leftist activists to Peronism after 1943: activists in Colombia realized that "the Liberal Party no longer represent[ed] their interests" and saw in Gaitán "a leader who finally talk[ed] to them in terms they [understood] and about the problems they had."[65] When the wave of strikes reached its peak, Otero reassured his superior in Buenos Aires that communist activists were not involved and that claims to the contrary were just "an invention of the conservative press." (Communists actually did lead some of the strikes and supported others organized by Liberal unions, though the press often exaggerated Gaitán's ties with the communist Partido Socialista Democrático (PSD).) In late 1947, in a lengthy document about the Left in Colombia, the attaché explained, "Communism does not represent a real threat in this country: The elements they used to recruit are joining Liberalism, today the most popular party."[66] In Otero's view, Gaitanismo "controlled at its pleasure the union movement through the Confederación de Trabajadores Colombianos [CTC]." It could be an overstatement, but Otero's view nonetheless gave an idea of the growing popularity of Gaitán, as well as the attaché's interest in drawing the attention of Buenos Aires toward the Liberal leader.[67]

The similarities between Gaitán and Perón's final steps to power were indeed remarkable. Gaitán's popularity among the poor was unprecedented and was rooted not only in his ideas of social reform but also in his rhetoric and public persona, which sharply contrasted with that of traditional politicians. He pressed the Ministry of Labor to speed up social reforms in 1943, the same year that Perón did so in Argentina. Less than a year later, Gaitán was expelled from his office as minister of labor, health, and social welfare by the most traditional sectors of the government coalition, only to be immediately elected "the people's candidate" by the Liberal Party in a massive rally in an open square, a setting unheard of at the time. The rally took place on 23 September 1945—only twenty-four days before 17 October, the mythical day on which Perón was hailed by a multitude of workers in the Plaza de Mayo in Buenos Aires, starting his political career.[68]

Otero met with Gaitán's closest men during his first days in Bogotá. The attaché was convinced of the need for a strategic meeting between the two leaders and for an endorsement to Perón's ATLAS from local unions. "They tell me that the boss of Colombian Liberalism fervently wants to visit our country, so they would like him to be invited by our government," he reported on 4 November 1947, after meeting the speaker of the house and several Liberal union leaders.[69] The attaché pressured the Foreign Ministry in Buenos Aires to ask Gaitán to come as the official guest of Perón and Evita. Days later, Otero received a letter from Hernando Restrepo Botero, deputy speaker of the House of Representatives in Colombia, supporting the creation of a Latin American alliance and suggesting that he would gladly travel to Buenos Aires to discuss it. In addition, Otero sensed that Gaitán was "the one with the most *argentinista* position [who] usually cites the revolutionary ideas of our leader, General Perón. In my work here, the unions from the Liberal Party also give me all their support."[70]

The domestic impact of the internationalization of labor politics attracted the attention of the Colombian government as well. From Buenos Aires, the

Colombian embassy provided the background that placed Otero's work in the context of a regional Peronist strategy. Colombian officials registered every reference to the expansion of Peronism. By January 1948, the Colombian embassy in Argentina described the massive rallies led by Perón and Evita, in which the special guests were union activists from all of Latin America, "including leaders from Cuba, Mexico, and Colombia." "The purpose of these meetings is to show the failure of the [U.S.-sponsored] Lima Conference . . . and to publicize the 'Third Position' across the labor movement, independently from the CTAL (which they [the Peronists] accused of being dominated by communists) and the AFL, which they consider a mouth piece of Yankee-imperialism," the embassy reported. Colombian diplomats stationed in Buenos Aires stressed that a multitude of workers welcomed the foreign activists, highlighting the meetings the activists later had with Perón, and the statements by the Mexican Luis Morones, former secretary general of the powerful Confederación Regional Obrera Mexicana (CROM) and the Cuban Angel Cofiño, of the Federation of Electrical Workers and future leader of the Confederación General del Trabajo (CGT) in order to give the sense that "America is getting ready, led by the Argentine CGT, not only because of the magnificent future of Argentina under Perón, but also for the admirable model for the modern woman that is the First Lady, Señora de Perón."[71]

From Colombia, Otero expanded the scope of his dispatches and activities in order to locate them within a regional dispute that went beyond the labor movement itself. He reported on Romualdi's actions in Colombia, noting that the U.S. labor diplomat had traveled across the country to meet "with the leaders of the Unión de Trabajadores de Colombia [UTC], a federation of religious background, . . . causing the anger of the CTC, which called him an 'internationalist maverick' in the service of the AFL."[72] After a dinner at his home with union leaders, diplomats, and high-ranking members of the local armed forces, the Peronist attaché described a country dragged into a confrontation between the Soviet Union and the United States, a picture that fit neatly with the idea of the Third Position. According to what a Colombian colonel said during that night, the government "had just bought 40,000 gas masks from the U.S.," to be used domestically. The Soviet Union could be fueling social unrest, but Colombia, he argued, "could not break with the U.S.S.R. without becoming enslaved to the U.S." According to Otero's guest, a U.S. special envoy was about "to meet Colombian President Ospina Pérez to try to postpone the Pan-American Conference" in view of the wave of strikes and political conflicts.[73]

Otero finally met Gaitán on 7 January 1948. The Liberal leader "manifest[ed] his wish to visit our nation and talk with our President, His Excellency Juan D. Perón, whose work Gaitán admires."[74] Otero became obsessed with setting up a meeting between Perón and Gaitán. But as 1948 began, the fate of a summit between the two leaders became intertwined with the spiral of violence engulfing Colombia. Facing massacres of peasants and Liberal caudillos, Gaitán led the massive Marcha del Silencio on 7 February. Four days later, a brief notice in the Peronist-friendly *Diario del Pacífico* in Colombia indicated that Evita might join the Argentine delegation to the Pan-American Conference in Bogotá but that these plans remained subject to the evolution of Colombian domestic politics.[75] The CGT finally invited Gaitán and several union leaders to visit Argentina on 15 February.[76] That same day, Gaitán arrived in the town of Manizales to pronounce his *Oración por los Humildes* in front of the graves of dozens of Liberal leaders who had been slaughtered by death squads. Pressured by the domestic turmoil, the Colombian delegation traveled to Buenos Aires without Gaitán on 27 February.[77]

The following day, the Conservative-led government confirmed Gaitán's exclusion from the Colombian delegation to the Pan-American Conference, which precipitated events and made his position as member of the government coalition untenable. At the convention of the Liberal Party, Gaitán broke with the official coalition. The Argentine ambassador and the attaché met with the "euphoric leader" right after the convention. "Gaitán doesn't care about the resolutions that Conservatives vote at the conference," Otero reported, "since whatever they agree will have to be ratified by Congress, which he controls completely." According to the Argentines, Gaitán did not expect that the president would exclude him from the Pan-American Conference, but thought that ultimately "this misstep reassures his rise to power." With growing social violence, massive popular support, and control of large sectors of Colombian institutions, Gaitán faced resistance from the entire political establishment. He had to choose either a democratic path through general elections or a violent route, alternatives which were separated by an ever-diminishing gap. According to the Argentines, "If Gaitán doesn't make a revolution, it is not because it is not possible, but because it would be a bad move for the Liberals now to lead a revolution without weapons and the army." Ultimately, Gaitán would mobilize the interior and the entire party by demanding the resignation of President Ospina. The ambassador concluded on a hopeful note: "Gaitán told me that after three more months of struggle, he will be able to visit America, including our country in particular."[78]

April in Bogotá

The work of the Argentines in Colombia was not an isolated initiative. In what emerged as a massive effort by Peronists to build a regional network of political organizations, the worker attachés and Perón's special representatives simultaneously established relations with an ideologically diverse range of leaders and activists throughout the hemisphere. This had been part of the duties of the Senator during his regional tour. Molinari had visited more than ten Latin American countries by the time he landed in Havana, Cuba, in February 1948, for the foundational meeting of the International Trade Organization (ITO), the immediate predecessor of the GATT.[79]

At that time, Peronism was making vast efforts to strengthen its relationship with the Cuban labor movement.[80] In 1944, Ramón Grau had won the elections against Fulgencio Batista's protégé. He started his term open to the demands of unions and students and, not surprisingly, suggesting an affinity with Peronist economic thought.[81] But with the Cuban economy tied to the United States through the Sugar Act, Batista quickly undermined Grau's legitimacy and broke their delicate political coalition. By 1948, Grau was finishing his presidency with fragile political and social support.

During his trip, Molinari relied on the worker attachés to initiate relations beyond diplomatic circles. In Cuba, he called on the attachés César Tronconi and Luis Priori. The two attachés organized a set of meetings with labor and student leaders for Molinari at his suite in the Hotel Nacional. Although the Argentine ambassador discouraged these contacts, which "undermine the country's respectability in Cuba," Molinari, with the help of the attachés, put together an intense parallel agenda to organize strong support for the creation of a new inter-American labor organization and regional student organization, the Centro de Estudiantes Latinoamericanos (CEL), which could be inspired (and funded) by Argentina.[82]

Over the course of just a year in Cuba, Tronconi had established contact with the major labor and student organizations. He arrived right after the major split in the CTC and the exclusion of the communist leader Lázaro Peña, the black tobacco worker who returned to the CTC as its leader only after the 1959 revolution. Tronconi worked mostly with the CTC and avoided contact with unions and leaders who claimed to be communist (though, as with the attachés in other countries, he embraced Perón's anticommunism as much as his movement's pragmatism, and he maintained contact with many communist activists and communist unions in the interior). The main focus of the Argentine actions was the promotion of the Peronist recipe throughout the Cuban labor movement. In early 1948, more than fifty Cuban activists had been invited to Buenos Aires. Among these activists were leaders like Angel Cofiño, of the Federation of Electrical Workers, which opposed the emergence of communist unions, and Juan Arévalo, a legendary leader who was also courted by the United States and who had been to Buenos Aires before, seen the social transformations and public works, and met with Perón and Evita. Tronconi was everywhere. Pictures of him appeared throughout the Cuban media during the swearing in of the new leadership of the Confederation of University Workers, at the Argentine Night at the Telephone Workers Union, and in the general assembly of the Woolworth Union of Cuba, the first union in the Woolworth empire located outside the United States, which was led by Raquel Valladares.[83] *Prensa Libre* announced that the CTC "has a good relationship with Peronist activists."[84] In a radio program in Havana, Tronconi explained to Cuban workers "the labor code . . . and social security that have given Argentine workers what can be considered, *without boasting*, the most advanced living standard in the world."[85] In a long and friendly interview in a weekly magazine, where he was presented as "a man from the Americas," Tronconi said "we have everything to be a fundamental part of the Marshall Plan, but there is one condition: that the funds also contribute to the industrialization of Latin America."[86] U.S. intelligence echoed the rumor that Argentina had bought one of the main newspapers, *La Marina*, for $50,000, to promote Peronism on the island, a unique example in the region.[87]

At Molinari's request, the attachés organized a meeting for him with Enrique Ovares, the president of the Cuban Student Federation (FEU), some of his rivals, and other students with "Peronist sympathies." During the talks, which took place at the Hotel Nacional, they discussed what could be shared grounds for a prospective student organization at a regional level. The platform was quite similar to the ideas put forward by the unions: the termination of colonialism in Latin America, the creation of a regional fund for a massive set of social policies, the independence of Puerto Rico, the Argentine claim over the Falkland Islands (Islas Malvinas), the overthrow of Rafael Trujillo in the Dominican Republic, and the U.S. relinquishment of naval bases in Guantánamo and the Panama Canal.[88] As at his other stops, Molinari put aside the anticommunist jargon that Peronism was offering to Bogotá and made a concrete offer. Inside the conference, Argentina would push for an economic recovery plan for Latin America and an inter-American security system loose enough that it would not weaken the authority of national states in the face of the power of the United States. Outside the conference, political and social organizations would repudiate the presence of U.S. Secretary of State George Marshall while gathering support for the creation of labor and political institutions that would exclude the United States.

The Cuban students were enthusiastic about the prospect of strengthening the regional side of a social movement that was growing in size and activism within a weakened political system.[89] Before the meeting with Molinari, the attachés were approached by another student who was already known in political circles for his charisma and radicalism. Someone had tipped him off about Molinari's mission, and he wanted to be invited as well. He explained that he was impressed by Perón's anti-imperialist message and wanted to help organize the students in Bogotá. Molinari told him that the Argentine students traveling to Colombia, in turn, had met Perón and obtained his blessing. If the protests at the conference were successful, they would call for a meeting in Buenos Aires. The newly arrived Cuban student was excited about the initiative and told Molinari that he could pull together students from other countries as well.

The Cuban student made a good impression on the attachés and Molinari. Perón's envoy immediately decided to sponsor the actions of his entire group. In accordance with a hurriedly designed plan, they were to be sent in groups to several different capitals, to gather support for the CEL before converging on Bogotá. Though Molinari was staying in Havana as a representative to the ITO, the organization that was supposed to promote free trade across the hemisphere, he had just set in motion another, quite different organization. The group had little funding of its own, but the newly involved member was enthusiastic. With logistical help from the attachés, Molinari funded everything else and then provided diplomatic support in order to discreetly send the Cubans out of the country and to organize their activities abroad.

The name of the charismatic student was Fidel Castro.[90] At twenty-one years old, Castro was a figure of growing stature in Cuba, even if he was far from dominant. It is likely that Peronist propaganda attracted his interests as part of the wide range of influences he was absorbing at the time. A few years earlier, Castro had started to read Marx and study the French Revolution and the relationship between democratic politics and violence. As a member of the nationalistic Partido Ortodoxo, his political ties were much broader than his party affiliation. His ambivalence about the use of political violence paralleled his interests in popular movements that, like Peronism, had reached power through mass mobilization.[91] Castro had already built a reputation as a captivating leader. In 1947, he had been a member of the expedition of Cubans and Dominicans who disembarked in the Dominican Republic seeking to overthrow Trujillo. The incursion had worried American intelligence officials who, incidentally, speculated that it had been undertaken with Argentine weapons.[92] The military operation failed, but it called attention to Castro and the other activists. In 1948, Castro led a public assault against the Cuban Student Federation authorities, accusing them of complicity with the government. In an obscure episode, the attack against the student leadership ended with the assassination of the federation president.[93]

Paid for by Peronist funds, the Cuban trip was a journey through Latin American postwar progressive politics. Accompanied by Ovares and Guevara, Castro first went to Venezuela, where the novelist Rómulo Gallegos had taken office three weeks prior their arrival. Castro missed him during the Easter holidays but met his family at the presidential palace. Gallegos was the first president elected under universal suffrage and was a hopeful reference point for progressive forces in the hemisphere. Castro did make contact with Rómulo Betancourt, the former president of Venezuela, who had taken power in 1945 and proclaimed the "50–50" tax reform, which secured substantial revenues from the oil industry for the first time in the country's history.[94] Betancourt did not trust Perón but felt comfortable with the idea of the rallies as it came through Castro. Betancourt told the Cuban that he would support the students in Bogotá, where he would lead the Venezuelan delegation.[95] Castro then traveled to Panama, where he contacted the students protesting against the U.S. base in the Canal, a movement that succeeded in forcing the Panamanian Congress to overturn its earlier approval of permanent U.S. troops. In both countries, Castro sought and obtained support for the creation of the CEL. By the time he arrived in Bogotá, he had already espoused the Peronist idea of an alliance of varied movements grouped under the umbrella of denouncing U.S. imperialism and advancing labor demands.[96]

Peronist funds were productively used in the hands of Castro. The Cuban students arrived in Bogotá, and Castro immediately met Argentine Canciller Bramuglia—the second most prominent figure at the conference after Secretary Marshall. They had a long conversation, after which the Argentine foreign minister apparently took one of his index cards and wrote three words and a question mark: "Intelligent. Brilliant. Communist?"[97] Castro then had a long conversation with Gaitán. The Cuban told him about the idea of CEL and the boost his endorsement would give it. Gaitán, who was at that moment the most popular leader in Colombia, showed his support and promised he would address the students during the conference.[98]

A few weeks later, an unusually extended, ten-page dispatch from the U.S. embassy in Havana analyzed in depth Castro's trip to Bogotá and the Argentine involvement in the operation. This Latin American "Long Telegram" left little doubt about the role of the Peronist activists. Its title was "Possible Perón-sponsored New Student Movement in Latin America, Cubans Suspected of Taking Part in Colombian Revolution."[99] U.S. officials confirmed that "certain officials of the Argentine government have been engaged in featuring a Latin American student movement in which Cuban Communists and 'fellow travelers' have participated, aimed at defeating United States policy at the Bogotá Conference and in Latin America." Through a network of informants, journalists, local officials, and reports from Buenos Aires and other capitals, Americans reconstructed the genesis and purpose of the group. The embassy's report specified that Perón's money had been handed to Castro and his two colleagues through Molinari's secretary. A journalist, apparently an informant to the embassy in Havana, gave details of the way in which the Argentine official distributed money. "In one case he [the secretary] had asked Castro for a receipt of $200 for only $100 of expense money," the report said, noting Peronism's colorful relationship with public funds. Even during Peronism's most epic moments, corruption would permeate U.S. descriptions of Argentine actions in the decade to come, often accurately so.[100]

But U.S. officials were mulling over a broader problem than the trip to the Bogotá Conference: they shared a marked concern about how Peronism was uniquely suited to bring together, on cultural and social grounds, forces that shared the idea that Latin America constituted an entity separate from the United States. The United States placed this attribute in line "with current Argentine international policy . . . clearly anti-American and anti-Pan-American." Their concern about the internationalism of Cuban activists was second to their anxiety about how Argentine influence could open a vast range of possibilities for a regional project competing with the United States. "That the Argentines have been making a terrific, and by no means unsuccessful, cultural effort in Cuba is recognized," the cable said. Going through the activities of the attachés, it described how "Cuban students, newspapermen, and other youth and labor representatives have been sent off in recent months to Buenos Aires," and how Cofiño and Arévalo "had been recipients of free and fancy trips to Argentina at Perón's expense." The U.S. diplomats framed this information in political terms by characterizing "this new student organization" as "an effort similar and parallel to the Perón Latin-American labor project."[101]

With centripetal force, these efforts converged at the conference. From the tarmac at the Buenos Aires airport, Perón gave a hero's farewell to the Argentine delegation. Once at the conference, the Peronist officials captured the region's attention with the announcement that Argentina had ten billion dollars for "a Marshall Plan for Latin America." In the Peronist view, the new organization would not have authority over national states and would keep U.S. dominance at bay while guaranteeing national autonomy (and repressive capabilities) for its members. And it would fight communism by attacking what Peronism saw as its causes, namely poverty and political exclusion.[102] Simultaneously, the aggressive regional strategy, of which the attachés were part, yielded fruit. Union leaders from several countries were in Buenos Aires, talking about a regional labor organization that would exclude the United States. Students traveled from more than ten countries to Bogotá to protest the presence of Secretary Marshall at the conference and to create CEL under a Peronist-inspired program. Gaitán was rightly convinced that his exclusion from the conference had bolstered his regional status, and he said enthusiastically that he would visit Buenos Aires to meet Perón after the Pan-American Conference. With Peronist sponsorship, Castro had established contacts throughout the continent—from presidential palaces to clandestine student shelters and union halls—and was ready to receive Gaitán's endorsement. On 4 April an ecstatic Castro wrote from his hotel in Bogotá to his father in Cuba, telling him he was happy about "an extraordinary success among students in Venezuela and Panama," for the "conference that I'm organizing here." He was pleased that "the Argentines had provided the largest possible support to our movement" and concluded with a hopeful note about his future after Bogotá: "After this, I might go to Argentina and spend three months there, with a fellowship from the Argentine government."[103]

Liberal Gaitán in Colombia during the 1930s and 1940s, nationalist Perón in Argentina during the 1940s and 1950s, and Marxist Castro in Cuba from the 1960s on—the three leaders who embodied the most powerful movements for social reform in twentieth-century Latin America and shared a marked anti-Americanism were being brought together through the work of the attachés, a group that nonetheless stood on shaky ground and was unaware of this historical sequence.

Yet the meeting never came to fruition. On 9 April 1948, half an hour before his scheduled second meeting with Castro, Gaitán was killed by a hired assassin, putting an end to the consolidation of his progressive alternative in Colombia. His killing sparked a massive riot, the Bogotazo, and was followed by ferocious repression, the violent dismantling of his Liberal faction, and the descent into the civil war known as La Violencia. Castro, who was smuggled out of the city with the help of the Argentine embassy, rapidly lost interest in a deeper relationship with Peronism and with reformist projects in general. Peronism's "tactical approach" had encouraged his exploration of a democratic path to power, which was in line with what he had witnessed in the region. But the fate of those projects quickly closed off that possibility. The stardom of Rómulo Gallegos collapsed under the pressure of the Venezuelan military, led by Marcos Pérez Jiménez. A few months after the Pan-American Conference, Jiménez overthrew the democratic government and sent Gallegos (and Betancourt) into exile. In Panama, just days after Castro's visit, students marching against the U.S. bases were violently repressed, and a few months later, a new president won office through fraudulent elections.[104]

In the days following Gaitán's assassination, Colombia and the United States blamed communism for the crime and the subsequent riots. Perón took a few days, but in the end, he also blamed communism for the violence.[105] Now an almost unified front gave birth to the OAS against the backdrop of a city literally in flames. Hardly any other event at any other moment could have so successfully channeled into this new body the elites' perception that the rapid incorporation of the masses into politics exposed the Americas and their liberal institutions to the danger of derailment. National politics in each Latin American country quickly coalesced into a wider turn to right-wing politics and social containment.

The Pan-American Conference resumed its sessions a week after Gaitán's assassination in the less glamorous setting of a small classroom and with the city of Bogotá still under siege and violent confrontations in the streets. Mostly on the defensive, Argentina insisted on the need for an organization that did not interfere with the domestic affairs of sovereign countries, immediately withering the original plan for the attachés. An article in the Peronist press titled "We Want Sovereignty, Not Superstates" summarized the ideas of the Argentine delegation during those days. "We don't want to form a group of nations that legally surrender themselves to a command's ferule that curtails the economic, political and military rights and the self-determination of each nation," the article said, stressing the Argentine opposition to any name like "union" or "association" that could suggest the relinquishing of national rights to a superior body.[106]

The OAS still carried the mark of regional concerns about national sovereignty and equality and the influence of these ideas. The stated mission to improve social conditions in order to avoid radicalism was a byproduct of the efforts of Mexico and Chile. The very name of the new body was a victory of Argentine diplomacy. It stressed a coordination of sovereign states rather than a stronger Pan-American federation with the potential for a regional military force dominated by the United States (which was what the United States wanted and Brazil had proposed).[107] Latin American countries succeeded in locating the fight against inequality as the best form to prevent extremism: The OAS chart declared "the elimination of extreme poverty, equitable distribution of wealth and income and the full participation of their peoples in decisions related to their own development" were the best ways preserve democracy.[108] But the conference's social agenda was inconclusive and did not translate into the actual steps assured by Argentina. Perón's promises evaporated with the Bogotazo. More important, the "anticommunist resolution," as Resolution XXXII became known, went even beyond what the United States had originally expected.[109] It left the door open for coordinated forces to intervene politically and militarily in countries facing instability so long as that instability could be presented as a communist threat—a prescriptive translation of what had just happened in Bogotá within and beyond the conference walls. Argentina criticized the United States and communism, but it went along with the resolution.[110]

The Peronist attachés' efforts to create a broad regional social movement of nationalistic and progressive forces reached its peak right before imploding in Bogotá in 1948. This was not an automatic conclusion of the new reality. Over the course of the following years, the worker attachés expanded their actions, doubling their presence and resources abroad while securing a more solid place within the foreign service. Yet Perón's priorities were changing, and this also defined their fate. He shifted his view about the attachés, no longer seeing them as a potential source of Peronist allies, but as a force that could easily escape the control he now tried to stress as a central component of the Argentine experiment. Perón read the violent answer of the Colombian government to the riots and the firm support it received from the United States as shaping a new regional dynamic in which the United States was more openly involved in assisting local elites with crushing any form of social unrest. At the same time, the United States made clear that there would be no economic recovery plan for Latin America and that it would not incorporate Argentina as a provider into the Marshall Plan.[111] Moreover, the United States would also reject Perón's secret but persistent requests to join the International Monetary Fund and the World Bank, which could have helped the country overcome its economic bottleneck.[112] The Argentine leader watched as the immediate prospects for his novel Third Position dimmed.

Conclusion

For a period of around two years after World War II, a loose convergence of Gaitán, Perón, and the young Fidel Castro on the basis of shared political grounds was more than a specter of the feverish imagination of U.S. officials. It was a real possibility, as real as Argentine labor activists' endeavors to forge the regional labor movement they had been told to build. The attachés were instrumental in trying to bring together aspiring and consolidated leaders from such different backgrounds. But equally important, they nurtured the network of an incipient social movement, organizing meetings across the region with leaders and activists from nationalist, Liberal, Christian, and communist organizations; spreading their version of Peronism via radio programs, brochures, and paper interviews; offering donations from the Fundación Eva Perón; visiting factories, sugar mills, and unions in remote provinces; and bringing thousands of activists and rank-and-file workers to Argentina to view up close the transformations effected under Perón.

The magnet meant to entice this vast array of groups was broad but precise. The attachés presented Argentine industrialization and the Peronist welfare state in the ideological form of the Third Position, an alternative to a form of liberalism equated with the U.S. presence in the region and its support of political and economic elites. Peronism and nationalist movements characterized this U.S. presence as the cause of economic exploitation, restrictions to social modernization, and radically unequal wealth distribution. Despite their sometimes atavistic and labor-obsessed flavor, the attachés and their allies envisioned goals similar to those of the modernizing ideals that shaped political projects across the region: the allure of industrialization and growing middle classes, a progressive and controlled integration into global trade, and the strengthening—however problematic—of democratic institutions.[113] As part of a movement previously viewed by many as a mere offspring of fascism, the attachés' role and the mission they embraced were critical in offering an alternative take on the changes occurring in Argentina. With the legitimacy that labor activism provided to diplomacy, they bridged the gap that estranged Perón from reformist and revolutionary groups in a way that few other Peronists and no Argentine diplomat could have done.

The attachés placed Peronism in conversation with movements that preceded and that would follow it, allowing a historical continuity of Latin American revolutionary processes throughout most of the twentieth century. Yet the bridge they built was fragile and easily damaged by competing forces. The events around the Pan-American Conference put an early end to the spectral image of a Gaitán-Perón-Castro axis before it became a reality. This end did not kill the project embraced by the attachés; they continued to expand their presence in significant ways. But it radically changed the context in which their actions took place. Perón became wary of the risks entailed in processes of social upheaval, such as the one he had led up until then, as well as of the violent and transnational reactions they could trigger. Peronism did not give up its regional ambitions, but it altered its components. This change affected Perón's plans for the attachés as much as it did the attachés' autonomy in relation to those plans.

The conference was one more episode in a string of international events in which Peronism exhibited its expanding force, and it was therefore avidly followed in Argentina. Canciller Bramuglia received thousands of letters about the conference. They were written by small Peronist organizations in Buenos Aires, a soccer team in Tucumán, even an individual who felt, for the first time, that he was being represented abroad.[114] Perón received Bramuglia in Buenos Aires with even more fervor than when Bramuglia had left for Colombia, treating him as a general who had survived the crossfire of social revolt and the U.S. reaction (discouraging for the moment those who, like Eva Perón, pushed for his removal).

Yet with the benefit of historical hindsight, it is possible to locate Bogotá 1948 as a turning point in the labor attachés' project and in Peronist labor diplomacy, as well as in the history of populism as a viable path for social change in Latin America. In many cases, the incipient alliances that the attachés had explored either lost importance or shifted emphasis. In some instances, nationalism became more a discourse of order than a vehicle for social demands. In other cases, the strategy remained intact, but domestic partners changed or the support the attachés received from Buenos Aires ebbed. Perón was not interested in getting rid of the attachés, and he showed more than one sign of hope for the project. Yet he became increasingly wary of the dangers the attachés' actions entailed, leaving the labor activists in a difficult position.

The focus on the Pan-American Conference as a significant landmark in the history of Peronism has at least two important analytical implications. First, it complicates traditional periodizations of the history of Peronism that emphasize a set of economic benchmarks or that describe its evolution as the inevitable unfolding of a conservative soul encrypted in the movement's origins. Both founding and recent studies signal the economic crisis of 1949 as the turning point after which Perón adopted a more conciliatory approach to the United States and became less interested in projects of social reform, domestically or abroad.[115] Another strand in the historiography of Peronism sees the same crisis simply as an opening to adopt with greater sincerity the proximity that Peronism, regardless of rhetoric, had ultimately always had for U.S. foreign policy.[116] This volume joins recent studies of other aspects of Peronist history that challenge both assumptions, as it aims to untangle the politics of social change during the postwar.[117] This is not to deny that the 1949 economic stall delivered a blow to Peronist regional ambitions. But the political turn started before the limits of the economic strategy became evident. It materialized as Perón reinforced his anticommunist stance and as his potential partners were assassinated or radicalized or when they yielded to heavy pressure from repressive forces. Likewise, this study recognizes the clear presence of conservative forces and ideas in Peronism from its inception. But nothing indicates that those forces were predestined to succeed. On the contrary, evidence shows that the Third Position, and Peronism in general, harbored many different notions of social change and that, in its newly acquired allegiance with leftist activists across the region, Peronism did not automatically dissolve previous beliefs.

Ultimately, the legacy of many former leftist activists shaped aspects of Peronism, becoming in some cases its face abroad. The attachés opened paths and forged alliances that were in tension with the ideas and interests of other sectors within Peronism and with Perón's own intentions. The evolution of those conflicts was far from the straightforward realization of Perón's wishes; rather, because the attachés continued to connect his movement with forces that would not have necessarily approached Peronism otherwise, the resolution of those tensions was a long process of negotiation with diverse legacies.

By analyzing the events around the Pan-American Conference as a watershed in the history of Peronism, this work also explores the mostly ignored implications of transnational politics in domestic developments in Argentina. This does not deny the local dynamics shaping Peronism; rather, it incorporates the international arena in which Peronism intervened as something more complex than diplomatic agreements. It shows the point of contact between the local and the external as something different than the perpetual and active impact of a foreign force (usually U.S. foreign policy) on a rather static domestic political fabric. The contacts established by the attachés, the efforts deployed by Perón's personal representative throughout the continent, the Argentine students sent to Bogotá after meeting their leader, the thousands of foreign activists brought to Buenos Aires by the attachés and Peronist diplomats—these actions were not merely an outgrowth of a domestic dynamic. They were an engagement with foreign affairs that was considered crucial for Peronism as a whole.

In Latin America at large, the space for fueling and satisfying demands for social inclusion shrunk in the face of a robust reaction. Like others in the region, Perón inaugurated a new period after the postwar spring. Few could have deciphered between 1946 and 1948 the signs of the world to come as clearly or as early as the Argentine ambassador in Colombia traveling through the country immediately after Gaitán's assassination. After reporting the killing of Liberal caudillos in the countryside, he told Perón he had seen newly arrived American weapons for the Colombian army, which was occupying the industrial area of Medellín, and wondered how the conflict had escalated in that way. The massacres, he concluded, were not merely the consequence of conflicts between a growing labor movement and a recalcitrant oligarchy, nor simply the result of the massive U.S. push to restore social order. "What is going on," he said, in a prophetic expression that would characterize the region in the decades to come, "is simply a Cold Civil War."[118]

CHAPTER SIX. **POLITICAL DECLENSION**

Colombia was one of the countries in which Peronist attachés worked most zealously. Beginning just weeks after the program was created, in 1947, they had christened a public school after Eva Perón and built a relationship with the country's main workers confederation. During a peasants' meeting in the countryside, one attaché was hailed as the representative of "the leader of Latin American workers." Another described the details of Argentina's successful social-security program to a packed auditorium in Bogotá. The general features of Peronism were widely known, so Colombia's decision to award Perón the Orden de Boyacá in the category of the Gran Cruz Extraordinaria was not surprising.[1] What was surprising was that the honor did not come from any Gaitanista leader or from the unions and peasant organizations with whom the attachés had worked for years. Rather, it was bestowed in 1950 by President Mariano Ospina Pérez, the face of the coffee oligarchy and the leader who had worked steadily first to isolate Gaitán and later to support the massacre of Gaitanistas following their leader's assassination.[2]

The decoration conferred by Colombian elites was one more sign of Perón's shift to the Right, a winding journey that began hours after Gaitán was assassinated. Perón's tenacious anticommunism had been relatively restrained since 1943. His relationship with the labor movement and its activists from leftist origins had informed many of his ideas about how social reform could prevent the rise of radicalism. The slogan "Ni Bolches ni Fascistas/Peronistas" synthesized the priorities during the rise of the new labor movement. As the years passed, workers consolidated their new political identity at home, as fascism and Nazism were fading from the horizon. By the time of the Bogotá Conference, in 1948, the Peronist slogan had begun to mutate into a slightly different version: "Ni Yanquis ni Marxistas/Peronistas."[3] The new jingle expressed (and produced) the unique climate for the inception of the Cold War in Latin America. It framed anti-Americanism as something broader than the geopolitical confrontation with the Soviet Union for this region. Max Friedman observes that conflicts with the U.S. presence in Latin America preceded and exceeded the confrontation with communism, in a region where "U.S. marines [had] been landing on Caribbean beaches since long before the Bolshevik Revolution of 1917."[4] In Latin America, the notion that U.S. economic control and repeated military interventions were responsible for the region's problems was the early core of nationalist and nativist, not Marxist, identities.[5] At the same time, nationalist anticommunism, like the one Perón and other leaders exhibited in Latin America, also merged with the United States's vitriolic anticommunism. While these expressions of anticommunism were rooted in different perspectives, U.S. officials and nationalist movements in the region generated a compatible rhetoric against the perceived potential sources of communism: the excesses in the struggle over wealth distribution and the activism that ignited these struggles within and beyond national borders.

This chapter examines the expansion of the worker-attaché program from 1949 to 1952 and the ambivalent context in relation to which it unfolded. Precisely when the attachés had more experience, know-how, and resources than ever, Perón became less interested in encouraging transnational labor activism and more concerned with adapting his movements to the conservative demands of the Cold War. This period saw the institutional and political consolidation of the attaché program, as well as the attachés' vigorous efforts to bring the Peronist gospel to the most remote places in Latin America through their work in Peru, Uruguay, and, most notably, Bolivia. These actions aimed to lay the groundwork for the creation of the Asociación de Trabajadores Latinoamericanos Sindicalistas (ATLAS), the labor-based inter-American organization that excluded the United States and was expected to coordinate labor activism across the region. However, Argentine labor activism experienced waning political vigor as it was undermined by their leader's shift toward a virulent brand of anticommunism. Until then, Peronism had justified the expansion of the welfare state as a true and effective form of anticommunism, a means of preventing the rise of extremism; now Peronism invoked anticommunism to seek a common ground with nationalistic dictatorships and the United States for social control and military containment.

This phase of international labor activism exposes a crucial feature of Peronism as a historical construct: its plasticity in adapting itself from a postwar spring to a Cold War winter. Nearly all the movements and leaders that had dominated the former period were in retreat in the latter, but Peronism was the exception. Forged in an initial moment of expansion of social rights and economic growth, Peronist identity was put to test under much less favorable circumstances. Perón's nationalism came to emphasize the subordination of workers' rights to the nation's interest. As the economy stalled, the aggressive dominance of the United States in the hemisphere offered a dose of realism about Argentina's possibilities as an international leader. Analyses of Peronism could take a cue from William Roseberry's discussion on the uses of Antonio Gramsci's notion of "hegemony"; Peronism should be analyzed as both different from a fixed ideology and beyond Perón's instrumental uses of class, national, or anti-imperialist claims. As representatives of Peronism, labor activists conceived their actions as part of a "field of contention" or a "field of possibilities." Within this conceived field, and in dialogue with Roseberry's discussion of "language of contention," the attachés thought that it was possible to advance workers' rights and call into question social hierarchies at any given historical moment by sharing and disputing the language, institutions, and resources deployed in this form of nationalism with greater chances of success than outside that field.

An ordered modernization of the region became the common ground for the confluence of both pro-U.S. and anti-U.S. anticommunism. The region's anti-Americanism was built on a robust ideological and legal apparatus that provided a framework for nationalist movements like Peronism to merge anti-imperialism with an agenda for social inclusion. As much as nationalism recovered atavistic notions of social (and in many cases racial) regeneration, nationalists' discourse was not always structured as a return to a glorious past; rather, their discourse suggested a way of including new social agents (industrial workers, above all) in modern forms of social organization. Odd Westad describes how, after 1917, communism became a "deadly rival of Americanism" because it "put forward an alternative modernity; a way poor and downtrodden peoples could challenge their conditions *without* replicating the American model."[6] In Latin America, that alternative was advanced under nationalist programs. In a region where the presence of the Soviet Union was weak, the Cold War initially became meaningful as a U.S. project against nationalism. The specificity of this period resides in how the overarching mantra of the Cold War provided local elites with symbolic, political, and material resources in their quest to reaccommodate their interests in order to contain and/or reverse the explosion of social demands that followed the end of World War II. Greg Grandin has rightly stated that "the Cold War in Latin America had less to do with geopolitical superpower conflict than it did with bitterly fought battles over citizenship rights, national inclusion, and economic justice."[7] Taking this characterization further, this book reframes Peronism not as an aberration from the Cold War framework which pitted communism against capitalism, but rather as a crucial protagonist of the Cold War in Latin America. What is singular about Peronism is the way in which it was able to embody both the most progressive and the most conservative moments of this chronological curve.

Cold War Abroad, Cold Weather at Home

Peronist attachés now operated in the shadows of the conservative haze, which the birth of the Organization of American States (OAS) had cast across the region and its international labor organizations. The novel inter-American system partly helped to reproduce the increasing confrontation between the United States and the Soviet Union worldwide. In fact, the OAS was launched at the Bogotá Conference, in 1948, in parallel with the April Crisis at a global level. During the April Crisis, Soviet authorities established traffic restrictions in Germany, which led to the Berlin Blockade, the first major confrontation of the Cold War handled by the nascent interstate system of the United Nations (UN).[8] Argentina acted very differently on the regional and global stages. This disparity revealed the limits of Perón's attempt to advance a Third Position independent of the two emerging superpowers. At the UN, during an emergency meeting called to deal with the situation in Germany, the United States declined the offer to preside over the Security Council because it was an interested party in the blockade. Argentine Foreign Minister Bramuglia sought and obtained the post, most likely against Perón's wishes.[9] During the crucial weeks of October and November, in what was Bramuglia's first trip overseas, Argentina presided over negotiations around the Berlin crisis. In a context in which all of the countries from the Western Hemisphere sided with the United States, and a belligerent spirit prevailed among diplomats, Bramuglia's position gave Argentina a unique opportunity to put the Third Position into practice. The diplomat sought, with some realism, a way for the United Nations to avoid "any resolution that openly condemns any of the superpowers involved in Berlin," a step many considered possible and which Perón thought "conspires against the very life of the UN and can be used to accelerate the beginning of a war."[10] As Bramuglia explained to Perón, the Third Position could play out at the UN in favor of a peaceful solution. Bramuglia offered a prophetic and realistic view of the narrow role of the interstate system during the Cold War: "In the end, in relation to this conflict, the United Nations is not the organization to trust, and it even seems that it is used not for solving but for creating atmospheres and environments."[11]

The Argentine press magnified Minister Bramuglia's role and embellished real stories about the union activist-turned-diplomat's meetings with Cold War leaders like Harry S. Truman or Andrey Yanuarevich Vyshinsky. The nationalist paper *La Fronda* exaggerated when it suggested that Perón was a serious candidate for the Nobel Peace Prize.[12] Argentina's role during the resolution of this conflict was mostly symbolic, as has been the case of the nonpermanent members of the UN Security Council since its creation. Yet over time, those symbolic efforts also have contributed to build the discursive and legal framework for international relations. For the first and probably only time in Peronist diplomacy, Bramuglia was able to apply the principles of international arbitration and peaceful conflict resolution which characterized Argentine and Latin American foreign relations. Argentina's role at the UN did in fact serve as an effective conduit for the peaceful solution that settled the conflict six months later, with the partition of Berlin.

But within Latin America, Argentina embraced anticommunism as the rationale of the OAS, and the Third Position dissolved. With increasing bluntness, Perón expressed the idea that communism was a threat to the region. U.S. officials and nationalistic dictatorships—the very same sectors that blamed the attachés of complicity with communism—could not agree more. Argentina quietly dropped proposals for the creation of financial institutions that would promote social policies in the region, as Minister Bramuglia had supported in Bogotá, in favor of an emphasis on social containment. Perón linked this change to the environment of the Cold War, and by 1950, he went so far as to suggest that Argentina would send troops to fight alongside the United States in Korea, something that only the Colombian government actually did. To borrow the wording of U.S. diplomatic officials, the "policy regarding anti-Communist measures which could be planned and carried out within the Inter-American System" set the parameters for the end of the democratic spring that had begun in 1945.[13]

The Bogotazo enabled Perón to revive his old notions of social order on a new basis: the retreat of most of the progressive potential allies in the region prompted him to explore a different understanding with the United States.

By the end of 1948, it was clear that the United States was outmaneuvering most Peronist efforts to use Argentina's economic power to influence political processes in the region. Perón adapted Argentina to this scenario. As he privately told his foreign minister in December, "There is little we can do in terms of sustainable economic cooperation with the U.S. since we have similar production and we compete in the global market. . . . But on the political stage, the U.S. might need Argentine cooperation in the event of a war, and we can offer more than they can imagine [in the fight against communism]. . . . We have the best good will as long as the U.S. offers us the same sincere and loyal good will."[14] With the OAS in place, the United States led the region toward a repressive phase, which directly influenced organized labor and its regional organizations.

Domestically, Perón also intervened in the contested realm of his movement. Some scholars argue that Perón started moving toward more authoritarian actions in 1948 in parallel with a shift in his political alliances from organized labor to the Church and the military.[15] Yet the evidence suggests the opposite. By the end of 1948, Peronism radicalized its conflicts with the Church and the military, in a struggle that would later intensify. Relations with organized labor remained solid. The economy was showing very early signs of distress, but consumption remained robust, as manufacturing activities had radically changed the relation between production and consumption for workers.[16] The exclusion of Argentina as a provider for the Marshall Plan greatly affected Perón's plans for economic development. Even if Argentina presented its exclusion from the International Monetary Fund (IMF) as a patriotic achievement, the fact remained that the government had been keen and made active efforts to join the IMF because the country needed a constant influx of capital to keep pace with the Peronist-generated industrialization.[17] With these and other sources of economic growth jeopardized, Perón put a brake on wage increases in order to contain inflation. But in spite of this moderate macroeconomic approach, the inclusive dynamics of social policies, public works, and social rights that had already been put in place remained the dominant feature of Argentine politics. The expansion of full voting rights to women, approved in 1947 but exercised for the first time in the 1951 presidential elections, made political inclusion an even more palpable reality. In this context, labor was still the most vital and loyal core of the movement, even as cracks and internal conflicts began to appear in the declarations of Peronist activists at home and abroad.

As a group, the attachés faced new challenges. Domestically, their own unions were confronting early constraints on workers' aspirations, which marked some limits on the long-term sustainability of the model they pro-claimed. At a regional level, the attachés were losing the other two pillars of the Peronist version of Argentine ambitions for regional leadership: bilateral economic agreements and diplomatic relations. In sum, by the time the atta-chés had consolidated their position in government and started working on making the dream of ATLAS a reality, the ground beneath them had shifted, and their political base, allies, and enemies were very different from only a few years earlier.

Institutional Consolidation

In many respects, however, 1949 was a year of celebration for the attachés. Over the previous two years, they had consolidated an extensive agenda across the hemisphere. By most indications, Argentina was still growing, and workers were increasing their share of the national wealth.[18] As unions in Argentina trumpeted their actions abroad, their activity produced what one Colombian official described, with more concern than sympathy, as "the spontaneous formation of political movements in other nations of the conti-nent analogous to the one that brought General Juan Perón to the Presidency of Argentina."[19]

This consolidation of the program paralleled a new moment in domestic class relations. Under Peronism, the subservience of workers' struggles to the national interest took the form of the incorporation of organized labor into the state. For the attachés, their role as labor activists grew in complex-ity as they took on diplomatic functions. In 1946, the eight-week training courses focused primarily on activism; by 1949, the courses had evolved into a complete two-year instruction program that covered all areas of foreign relations and diplomacy. At the request of the Ministry of Foreign Affairs, the Argentine Congress increased the program's budget for personnel and pro-paganda activity. Most important, in order to strengthen relationships with activists across the globe, participate in political and labor agitation in many countries, and create the new inter-American labor organization, the admin-istration doubled the number of attachés deployed abroad. By 1949, there were ninety-six attachés abroad, the largest number of attachés appointed in a single year. In addition, one hundred more completed the training courses and remained in Buenos Aires working for the Foreign Ministry, the General Confederation of Labour, or their respective unions.[20]

This institutional consolidation validated their actions but presented new challenges. Perón demanded they play a greater role as activists, but this goal clashed with the traditional role of foreign officers, one which the courses were now trying to inculcate. This institutional dysfunction was largely a consequence of the transformative process unleashed by Peronism, a process that regime officials sought to both promote and contain. This tension is a quintessential problem of the institutional consolidation of populist reforms, one that is unlikely to emerge from revolutionary movements. Even as these movements radically reform institutions and traditions of the previous order, they nonetheless preserve some basic roles and functions of those ancien régime institutions. This conflict cements the contradictory goals of the new stage, alternately agitating for and containing social change.[21] In this context, the most important news for the attachés arrived on 15 March 1949, when Perón signed Executive Order 6420. The order turned the position of worker attaché into part of the Foreign Office's diplomatic service. Until then, the attachés were outsiders, appointed by the government but not full members of the foreign service and with no opportunity to rise within the public administration. Now, instead of remaining dependent on Perón's support, the creation of the "Career of Worker Attachés" allowed them to rise through the Foreign Office ranks in six different steps subjected to the same evaluations as the rest of the diplomats. These former rank-and-file union members now had the opportunity to represent their constituencies and the nation beyond Peronism—and to enjoy the prestige and stability of the institution they had denounced in the past. From that moment on, these labor activists embodied a dual role as full members of the foreign service and as representatives of organized labor.[22]

The training courses also consolidated the program by creating more permanent institutions, developing its own bureaucracy, and defining a specific knowledge base. The few weeks of instruction in the borrowed premises of a public school in 1946 were replaced in 1947 by an intensive fifteen-month program. Originally, classes were held in the working-class suburb of Avellaneda, in a public school that had previously been the home of Alberto Barceló, the famously brutal and corrupt mayor who had been a Conservative powerbroker during the dark years before Perón's rise. By 1949, the courses were a part of a two-year program, taught at the School of Law at the University of Buenos Aires. [23]

Unlike those rushed early classes in which former leftist activists, Falangist intellectuals, and Perón himself debated what Peronism would be, these new courses took place when Peronism was fully deployed. The classes still included long sections on political doctrine and on the role of Perón and Evita in Argentine history, and the school still bore the name Juan Domingo

Perón Cultural Elevation Course. But those strictly Peronist components of the first courses were now part of a much larger program, which included classes on economics, international relations, international history, political economy, administrative and international law, geography, mathematics, the national and international labor movement, basic principles of sociology and political science, English, and French. In addition, starting in 1950, labor activists selected for the program had to complete a two-year program at the Union School of the General Confederation of Labour, which was supervised by the Ministry of Education.[24]

This new and comprehensive approach was also connected to a broader project which aimed to professionalize the foreign service beyond the realm of the attachés. This effort contradicts the familiar notion of Peronism as a plebeian force assaulting elite-dominated institutions, an image constructed by Peronist hagiographers who claimed it as a badge of honor, as well as by elites who emphasized the movement's barbaric origins and supposed anti-institutionalism. In 1949, Perón created the School of Diplomacy, the first government-led attempt to train diplomats in Argentine history.[25] The first cohorts included between forty and sixty union members each year, along with middle-rank members of the foreign service and officials from the army, navy, air force, and Ministry of Interior. The program offered a broad educational approach to international affairs, but the courses added more political content, including new topics of the postwar order, such as the relationship between the labor movement and international affairs. Most other courses were simply instructions in Peronist ideas, such as "General Elements of the Justicialista Doctrine," "International Outreach of the Justicialista Doctrine," and "Organized Labor and the Justicialista Doctrine." These courses were in line with larger Peronist efforts to massively expand education and increase professionalization, in parallel with the cult of the figures of Perón and Evita.[26]

On examination of materials from the later round of courses, three aspects stand out. First, the worker attachés had consolidated their position within Peronism and the Argentine government; the program was not going to be a brief episode, as the opposition had hoped. Second, the attachés were no longer the only bearers of Perón's message. Now the diplomats of the old guard, who had been initially shunted aside, were also taught the basics of Peronist doctrine. Finally, after initially defining itself in its frontal clash with the status quo, Peronism was now launching a strategy of slow penetration into the state apparatus, implicitly setting limits to the confrontation that it had unleashed.

The most unambiguous indication of the consolidation of the worker-attaché program was the 100 percent increase in the number of activists sent abroad in 1949. The ninety-three worker attachés appointed throughout the globe that year constituted the largest number yet.[27] They covered every Argentine diplomatic mission, although most of the attachés went to the Americas. Argentine embassies in Brazil, Chile, Bolivia, Cuba, and the United States had up to three worker attachés each. While some attachés focused exclusively on building ties with the local labor movement, others prepared extensive reports about social and political conditions in the host countries, and still others handled the more traditional diplomatic tasks of any embassy. From a Peronist perspective, an evaluation of the attachés' activities offered a hopeful perspective on how organized labor might transform the state. For the Ministry of Foreign Affairs, the attachés' performance validated this vast expansion and ad hoc budgetary increases, and it would continue to do so in the coming years.[28] The attachés' commitment and the quality of their work varied greatly. The diplomatic conflicts generated by their actions were, in most cases, the inevitable outcome of the perception that they were fomenting labor and social unrest in another nation while working under diplomatic status. But a large part of the attachés corps worked efficiently and creatively to forge new ties between Argentina and other countries and labor organizations and to increase awareness of the experience of the Argentine welfare state. At the same time, the attachés reported to Buenos Aires with a sharp eye that honed in on social developments in ways that surpassed conventional diplomats' dispatches. The volume of information and correspondence they exchanged is stunning. In 1949 alone, the attachés sent 2,850 reports to the Foreign Ministry. From Buenos Aires, the International Labour Organization division, which employed attachés stationed in Argentina, had produced 3,877 reports for other areas of government, for unions, and for private entities. Most of the traffic was to and from the Argentine embassies in Latin America, the likeliest locations for Peronist-style revolutions.[29]

Unexpected Offspring: Intersections of Class and Race Identity in Peronist Activism Across Latin America

On 10 May 1950, the Argentine worker attaché in Peru, Bengasi Salvador Di Pasquale, made a decision that he hoped would change the course of the Andean history. "I have decided to have translated into Quechua 'The Declaration of the Rights of Workers' and 'The Declaration of the Rights of Senior Citizens.'"

According to the Peronist labor diplomat, roughly 75 percent "of the country's population speaks Quechua, the dominant language among the indigenous element of Cusco, Arequipa, Puno and La Oroya." Along with the two proclamations, he also had other pamphlets about Argentine workers' achievements translated. Di Pasquale's conception of the labor question echoed domestic notions that extended among the Odría dictatorship and the previous democratic administrations in Peru: that the indigenous peoples needed non-indigenous (i.e., white) orientation in order to become a modern work force and improve their living conditions. But unlike most Peruvian reformers, he saw that this civilizing mission could be the core of a transnational effort led by Peronism. The need for translation was evident for him: "As of today, there are no social concepts translated into Quechua that can orient the peasants and mineworkers of this region."[30]

Broadly speaking, the actions of Di Pasquale and the rest of the attachés targeted three different audiences. They targeted the mass of workers and peasants to raise awareness of the experiences of Argentine workers, union organizations to coordinate local labor actions, and labor confederations to outmaneuver U.S. labor diplomats. In these three spheres, the attachés presented the specific features of Peronism in ways that should be analyzed separately. But it was in their interactions with workers and the population at large that the basics of the Peronist worldview and the sense of a civilizing mission for the movement were most clearly revealed.

Complying with the initial instructions that they had received from Evita and in the training courses in Buenos Aires, the attachés did not stay in the countries' capitals, but went to the most remote places in Latin America, preaching the gospel of a social revolution under capitalist relations of production that would bring prosperity to the vast majority while preventing the rise of radicalism. Di Pasquale was not the only one making these creative incursions onto a terrain rarely explored by non-Peronist labor activists or diplomats, Argentine or otherwise. Fellow attachés in Bolivia, Chile, Brazil, Guatemala, Cuba, and Paraguay reported on their travels throughout their host countries. Their visits to factories and haciendas and their conversations with workers offer vignettes of a vivid social history of the period. The regular presence of indigenous people during these visits immediately captured the attention of the attachés. Mixing the racial language of Argentine nationalism and Latin American social reformers, they elaborated on dreadful living conditions in the countryside, judging that indigenous people lacked the will and/or the tools for change. In the Peruvian countryside, Di Pasquale added, "workers preserve the impregnable indigenous feeling, they are insensitive, apathetic, with an indifference that turns into mistrust if one attempts to improve their lives."[31] Against that reality, the attachés seemed amazed by the achievements of the Argentine working class. In the egalitarian language of Peronism, this view exuded a sense of national superiority forged from the nation-state since the late nineteenth century. As the attaché in Honduras said in a letter to his former leader in the Socialist Party, "The economic and industrial progress of Argentina is such that it has become a beacon for Latin America." For the attaché, the racial dimension of this role was evident. A few lines below, he observed in relation to Honduran workers: "They would benefit so much from the immigration of some 5,000 Italian farmers. When we come to these countries, the different character of Argentine people, due to our great and beloved immigration, is evident."[32] The redemptive political mission of a civilizatory race was both a raison d'être for the nation and for the movement.

Racialized language and the "indigenous problem" played a central role in both Peronist transformations and the reactions against them. On the one hand, the very category of "cabecitas negras" used by the opposition to discredit Perón's followers ascribed racial features to the political choice of supporting Perón.[33] The attachés were themselves the objects of these racial representations. But on the other hand, Perón and his policymakers considered that part of Peronism's redemptive mission, domestically and in Latin America, was to expand rights to indigenous people as workers and to turn them into national political subjects as workers, without necessarily incorporating their claims *as* indigenous demands. In what the historian Diana Lenton calls "protected incorporation" of "indigenous descamisados," Peronism left unanswered most of the demands of these communities (portrayed in ritualistic "malones" that traveled the country to meet Perón in Buenos Aires), yet it also expanded economic and political rights to previously excluded indigenous populations. As ambivalent as it was, Peronism nonetheless occupies a prominent place in the collective memory of Argentine indigenous communities.[34]

Peronist activism abroad took this redemptive goal to an altogether different level, by tying this sense of a mission to an aspiration to reform entire nations. For Argentine attachés, building powerful labor movements was key to overcoming the obstacles nations might be facing on the path to becoming modern economies. But the need for such a mission was justified in what they perceived as an individual and collective incapacity to implement reforms. A year before requesting the translation of Perón's Declaration of the Rights of Workers into Quechua, Di Pasquale reported about another trip in a way that furthered his argument for Argentina's redemptive mission in the region. According to the attaché, "The reasons for the apathy of the Peruvian people . . . are their indigenous heritage and the later arrival of Asian immigrants, of naturally calm character, that degenerates into a venal, lazy, and alcoholic type, in the vast majority."[35]

Peronism's adoption and recasting of older undertones of Argentine exceptionalism was double-edged. It allowed Peronism to tap into deeper strands of national thought. But it blinded Peronist activists to many of the real possibilities of alliances and solidarity on the ground. The attachés made sense of Argentine prosperity and workers' advances with the discursive resources available to them, and this is especially evident in discussions of race. If—borrowing from Ernesto Laclau—emancipation implies a moment of departure from how preexisting language formally represents prior power relations, then the attachés were struggling very much within hegemonic ideas. Their struggles revealed an "uncomfortable familiarity" with notions of social order expressed through racialized language and representations. These discourses were constitutive of Argentine nationalism. Notably, the domestic target of these representations were workers themselves.[36]

Peronist activists often came to consider the rest of Latin America as economically underdeveloped, socially backward, and/or racially inferior in relation to Argentina. Unsurprisingly, these views were not always rejected by the host countries, where not only elites but also social reformers at large held similar views about the "indigenous problem" and about the role of Argentina. After a worker attaché visited Cuzco with other diplomats in order to distribute aid from the Fundación Eva Perón, a future member of the Central Committee of the Peruvian Communist Party and future director of the Training School for Labor Activists of the General Confederation of Peruvian Workers (CGTP) wrote an article praising the Argentine efforts. Responding almost directly to the attachés' concern about the role of Argentina and the relationship of the native population with organized labor, the article presented Peronism as a hinge between indigenous traditions and "the least American of the Republics of the Southern Cone."[37]

The actions of the attachés in the Peruvian countryside also had more unexpected and significant consequences. By 1952, in Tarata, six hundred miles southeast of Lima, Peronist propaganda had reached the hands of an indigenous community. A young Argentine backpacker along with his friend spent a night in an "inhabited wasteland" with no food and in extreme cold. At six in the morning, they finally saw two shacks by the roadside, where they were received and fed. "Never had a welcome been so friendly, the bread they sold us with a chunk of cheese never so delicious." It was not trivial that they were coming from Argentina. "For these simple people . . . we were like demigods, from Argentina no less, that wonderful country where Perón and his wife Evita lived, where the poor have as much as the rich and the Indian isn't exploited or treated callously as he is in this country."[38]

The backpacker was Ernesto Guevara. The encounter took place during the Peruvian part of his Latin American travel, the journey that *produced* Che. Guevara, in turn, immortalized his impressions in the travelogues that *produced* Latin America for the future revolutionary leader, as Paulo Drinot suggests in the study of *The Motorcycle Diaries*.[39] How did these people come to learn about Peronism? And exactly what did they tell Che Guevara about Argentina? Was the emphasis on the egalitarianism of Argentine society part of the original conversation, or was it Che's emphasis? The answers to these questions remain a mystery. But given the period, the kind of information or propaganda, and the circulation of information in the Peruvian countryside in the early 1950s, it is more than likely that the source of those claims was either one of the many activities of the worker attachés in the previous years or the articles written about them. Coming from a fervently anti-Peronist background, Guevara was developing a more ambivalent view at the time. He certainly expressed a more positive evaluation of Perón than of the Peruvian leader Víctor Raúl Haya de la Torre, arguing that the former had done something in favor of workers and against local elites and the United States, and remembering how the maids at his family house had always voted for Perón.[40] But until then, he had not been aware of the transnational dimension of Peronism. A few days later, in the remote mountains of Ilave, Guevara was astonished again when "an Indian timidly approached us with his son who spoke good Spanish, and began to ask us all about the wonderful 'land of Perón.'" We could assume from this cryptic passage that the father spoke little Spanish and read none. Guevara, who wrote liberally about the indigenous people during his trip, accepted shared notions of the "indigenous problem" that posed an obstacle to the development of a modern working class. In a fleeting moment that would start to change Guevara's view of Peronism, "the man asked us for a copy of the Argentine Constitution with its declaration of the rights of the elderly."[41] The chances that this very specific information about the "land of Perón" had reached indigenous people with limited Spanish through the actions of the attachés in the region are highlighted even more clearly than in the previous encounter. The ramifications of the attachés' activities not only reached remote areas of Latin America, but also helped to shape the ideas of the region's revolutionary leaders. In these ordinary episodes of the "Cold War from below," Guevara witnessed the extended social and transnational presence of Argentina, which in turn contributed to his more open understanding of Peronism.[42] More important, the episode was the first clear sign that he registered of the effects of transnational activism and of the *exporting* of social revolution to areas considered backward, two notions that Guevara would later symbolize as a crucial engine of the Cold War in Latin America.

ORGANIZED LABOR

The attachés' relation with labor organizations revealed a different facet of their work. While their actions varied greatly from country to country, they had a common denominator: the attachés always had to negotiate between contradictory orders from Buenos Aires, their own labor traditions, and the demands of local situations. This bundle of conflicting inputs evidenced the tension between the conservative order and labor struggle, both of which coexisted within Peronism. In each country, the Argentines established relationships with seasoned labor activists, figures who combined a deep involvement in domestic political movements with experience working with external organizations. And within this context, they entered in direct competition with U.S. labor diplomats.

Starting in 1949, the Foreign Ministry in Buenos Aires insistently requested reports about communist activities from all embassies.[43] The request immediately changed the work of some attachés. Some obeyed the instructions with zeal, most just went through the motions, and others continued to work with communist and other Marxist organizations. Paradoxically, the attachés almost never warned of impending communist-led revolutions—the original justification for Peronist reforms. Instead, they usually denounced communist complicity with the United States or, with brutal simplification, "with extreme rightist nationalists."[44]

Other reports resorted to the same ideas U.S. foreign officers had employed to explain the rise of Peronism in Argentina. One attaché in Peru described the strong presence of communism in Cuzco as a consequence of "the large proportion of illiterate people, mostly indigenous peasants, exploited by the *terratenientes*."[45] From Colombia, the attachés, who had worked closely with communist unions in 1947 and 1948, now denounced "communist cells that work secretly on propaganda." But even if they mentioned communist actions, the attachés never presented them as a threat.[46]

Yet, where tensions between organized labor and repressive political regimes were prevalent, Peronism and its symbology repeatedly stood on the workers' side as an ally of and an inspiration for the expansion of social rights and economic citizenship. The attachés' aggressive actions in Bolivia between 1949 and 1952 offer an example of this dynamic. The influence of Argentine nationalists in Bolivia predated Perón but had only intensified with his rise to power. Argentine activists were considered (with some justification and considerable paranoia) to be the main outside agitators among miners, peasants, and military men. In the years between Gualberto Villarroel's overthrow and the 1952 Bolivian National Revolution, the attachés worked with members of the Movimiento Nacionalista Revolucionario (MNR), including the future president Paz Estenssoro and the leader of the miners' union Juan Lechín. The tasks ranged from delicate matters, like secretly crossing the border between Bolivia and Argentina with the revolutionary and future president Siles Suazo, to bringing to Argentina a miner-activist from the country's south in order to get medical treatment. He was described as "a man of rooted Peronist faith," and his care was entirely financed by the Fundación Eva Perón.[47]

But most of their actions were direct expressions of the kind of labor activism that the United States feared and denounced. By the late 1940s, there were clear signals of the political dynamics that would shape the 1952 revolution in Bolivia and of the competition between indigenous, leftist, and nationalistic identities in formulating demands for changes to the political role of workers and peasants. Peronist ideas had an important role on the incorporation of labor-rights language into the inclusive form of nationalism that was coalescing around the MNR. The confrontation between Argentine activism and the Hertzog administration reached its climax in March 1949, when the worker attaché Eleuterio Cardozo was invited to two rallies organized by the Textile Workers Federation. One rally was held at the union office, the other at Lanificio Boliviano Soligno, one of the largest factories in Bolivia at the time. There, Cardozo encouraged the audience to "follow the Argentine example in which workers are part of the administration, the Congress, and the Foreign Service. That is the only way workers can fight against capitalists." The Argentine called workers out into the streets "to defend labor rights against Bolivian oligarchs."[48]

These words reached a space of political affinities and defined clear-cut enemies. Despite Perón's increasingly conservative inclinations, Cardozo (and Peronism) won praise from the most popular and radical workers' organizations in Bolivia: the Confederación Sindical de Trabajadores de Bolivia and the Federación de Trabajadores, both composed largely of MNR nationalists and Revolutionary Workers Party (POR) Trotskyists. Cardozo's comments were the latest in a two-year campaign of open and clandestine actions by the attachés in collaboration with leftist unions and the MNR. The immediate endorsement came from Lechín, the leader of Bolivian miners. In 1944, the Trotskyite activist had joined the ranks of the MNR and became the emerging leader of revolutionary activism among Bolivian workers. "We had the chance to talk with compañero Cardozo about the forms of organized labor in Argentina, the social state reached under the government of Colonel Perón, as well as the government institutions focused on the question of labor," he wrote in a letter to the Argentine ambassador, objecting to his own government's objections. "We agreed on the need to unite all workers, mostly in Latin America, a total and definite unity, as the only way of defending the proletariat against international capitalism."[49]

For terrified elites in Bolivia, everything was connected: labor agitation, social chaos, the swindle of uninformed workers, and the totalitarian threat. To the Hertzog administration, the words of the Peronist diplomat sounded like a call for a workers' soviet. The already weakened president instructed the foreign minister to present an official protest against the Argentine government, declare the attaché persona non grata, and expel him from the country. In a meeting with the Argentine ambassador, the Bolivian foreign minister, Fernando Guachalla, suggested that Cardozo's words were part of a larger Argentine plan to overthrow the government and take over Bolivia. He was not entirely wrong about the first part.[50] The conservative paper El Diario announced that after Cardozo's speech, workers at Soligno factory were planning a strike. The following day, the paper wondered whether Perón's Third Position didn't actually amount to a second position: communism. Populism, as a category used by U.S. foreign officials to warn about the dangers of modern mass movements, permeated narratives like El Diario's. The newspaper showed its alarm over allowing the "intromission in Bolivian factories of those who keep workers in deceit and thereby repay their moral and material debt to the totalitarians who manipulate them."[51]

This case offered a particularly good fit between the attachés' job description and Perón's ambitions for Bolivia. Perón, who followed Bolivia with attention, was personally interested in the incident, and in private, he showed sympathy toward the actions of his activist. Yet in public, the president accepted the protests of the Bolivian government, replaced the attaché, and ordered the foreign minister to issue a new set of instructions about the limits of attachés' actions abroad and about the need to not intervene in the domestic affairs of other nations.[52] There was wide publicity around the incident in Buenos Aires and abroad. Cables about the confrontation circulated within the Ministry of Foreign Affairs and were sent to all representations abroad; Perón's decisions could not have gone unnoticed by the rest of the attachés. The disciplinary effects of his reaction, reinforced with the new set of instructions, marked a turning point in the political and institutional environment in which the attachés worked, which came to function more as a conservative bureaucracy than as a revolutionary corps.

In fact, a study of the instructions Buenos Aires sent to the attachés offers a unique perspective on how the reconfiguration of the state apparatus overlapped with a process of identity formation among the Argentine working class and with the transformations in the region's labor movement. Before the incident in Bolivia, the attachés had taken part in similar actions and provoked similar reactions in (at the very least) Brazil, Chile, Uruguay, and Honduras. All of these governments officially protested while local media often criticized the attachés. Balancing his drive to support workers across the region with the national interest of signing economic and political agreements, Perón decided in late 1948 to restrain the attachés' actions, effectively prioritizing international economic cooperation over labor. He ordered the Foreign Ministry's Direction of International Labor Organization (DOIT) to prepare a classified executive order. Numbered, signed by Perón, and delivered in strict confidentiality to the ambassador and the worker attachés in each country, the order responded to protests from other governments by tying the hands of attachés and ordering them to comply with the general rules of the diplomatic world. It started by negating the attachés' core objective, declaring that the "actions of some attachés have provided grounds . . . for the propaganda against this government stating that the program is an attempt to establish the hegemony of Argentina over the Latin American labor movement or to intervene in the domestic matters of other countries."[53] Going against what Perón himself had proclaimed less than two years earlier, the new regulation required labor activists to explain the situation of workers in Argentina, "not with the purpose of agitating the masses or their spirits, but in order to belittle the systematic propaganda campaign . . . against us."[54] Furthermore, it highlighted the need to be "equidistant between pro-government and opposition labor groups." "If the case arises that they have to contact workers who are considered as being from the opposition, this will be done with special tact, not accepting any kind of intervention, participation or even knowledge of any kind of conspiracies against the established government," the order continued. The blunt instructions warned the attachés that "interference in other country's politics is against our spiritual formation and our doctrine."[55] Finally, it established a long list of reports that attachés had to send periodically to Buenos Aires about labor and social conditions in their assigned countries, along the lines of the dispatches produced by labor attachés from other countries.[56]

The new decree imposed a heavy workload on the attachés and constrained them to a more defined desk job with the kind of schedule that ambassadors would now try to force them to fulfill. But it would be a mistake to understand these orders and the emphasis on social peace strictly as a direct effort by Perón to discipline his corps of international labor activists within the more conservative parameters of the coming era. Against the conventional image that sees in Peronism a linear evolution toward an increasingly reactionary stance, the history of the attachés shows how that path was in fact full of contradictions. The regulations followed and produced those ambiguities. In December 1951, for example, the DOIT issued Directive No. 19, in direct opposition to the 1948 decree. Calling for a massive propaganda and agitation effort in all of Latin America, the directive was unambiguously titled "Action Plan for the International Justicialista Movement."[57] With the creation of ATLAS on the horizon, the text ordered the attachés to work in Latin America to "awaken a *justicialista* conscience among workers . . . fighting capitalism and communism."

Even as Perón sought various forms of economic and military aid from the United States, the text of the directive that provided the basis for ATLAS returned to the original Peronist rhetoric of a class-based anti-imperialism. Equally important, it left behind the anticommunist pledge and presented a realistic map of the adversaries of the Third Position as the international expression of the Peronist idea of social justice. It warned the attachés, "The fight is mainly against capitalism and, consequently, against the United States [because] capitalism is the real enemy of Latin American workers." The directive ordered the attachés to stress that "capitalism and the U.S. are supported [in Latin America] by the oligarchic governments." Directly contradicting the 1948 instructions, it also suggested that the attachés "work with the *pueblos* that are enemies of those governments."[58]

As in the Bolivia episode, attachés often managed to remain involved in actions with radical and nationalist unions that were protesting against their country's government and the United States—an association that infuriated local elites. Moreover, they continued to do so in Perón's name despite his clear and explicit orders to the contrary. In the space between the two sets of instructions, attachés found a way to proceed with some of their most radical actions. In Bolivia, in particular, as the revolutionary movement grew and Perón moved forward with the idea of ATLAS, the attachés duplicated and divided their actions. Overall, they assumed that sympathizing with a communist organization would hinder the construction of a regional organization led by Peronism. They continued to work closely with the MNR, the POR, and the political parties that made up the most radicalized sector of the labor movement. U.S. and Bolivian reports, as well as national media, made constant references to the actions of Peronist activists alongside the revolutionary forces. Yet, when analyzing the role of Lechín, then leader of the Mine Workers Unions Federation, the attaché Mario Torres Calleja (who had replaced Eleuterio Cardozo) reported, "He said he was with our Third Position 'as all Latin American workers should be.' However, . . . he talks like a leftist Marxist and has expressed at different moments the need to support [the communist-oriented] CTAL, with the consequent damage to our cause."[59] As the Soviet-aligned Bolivian Communist Party was founded only in 1950 and played a role in the wave of violent protests and strikes upsetting the Bolivian status quo, the attachés saw no problems in working with the other Marxist, leftist, and nationalist unions that were spearheading the first revolution in the Western Hemisphere since the end of World War II.

"IF IT WEREN'T FOR THE U.S."

By the early 1950s, American unions and U.S. labor diplomats became crucial participants in the early stage of the Cold War, advocating a political opening that quickly folded back onto itself. First, they identified the need for social change, then quickly highlighted the risks that justified the repression of the forces demanding that social change. It was a fight against communism, but it was also something else, as was made plain by another diplomatic skirmish about the future of Bolivia. In 1952, when the U.S. labor diplomat Serafino Romualdi asked the former (and future) president of Costa Rica, José Figueres, to rush to Bolivia to contain the risks entailed by the nascent revolution, he summarized the mission of the United States and its allies in an expression that embodied the spirit of the Cold War: "We are all in favor of the economic and social revolution now taking place there, but we cannot see how all this will succeed if the Bolivian regime ties itself with either the *Peronista* or the Communist totalitarian brand."[60] In a few words, the language Romualdi used exposed the productive common ground on which organized labor, political leaders, and social sciences equated communism and fascism during the postwar under the label of "totalitarian" movements.

However hard Peronism worked to present itself as anticommunist, the U.S. offensive against communism and any ideology that bore a resemblance to it left little room for those distinctions.[61] With the creation of the Organización Regional Interamericana de Trabajadores (ORIT, the CIA-funded branch of Confederación Internacional de Organizaciones Sindicales Libres [CIOSL] in the region), American unions now had a powerful tool to deploy against both nationalist and communist labor movements.[62] At times, as in the case of Bolivia, American Federation of Labor (AFL) labor diplomats outpaced official U.S. government advocacy in the containment and repression of communist and nationalist unions. They sabotaged union activism in Cuba and put enormous pressure on reformist activists there and in Ecuador to publicly reject any contact with communist or Peronist sympathizers.[63] As with Figueres in Costa Rica, they recruited the nationalist Alianza Popular Revolucionaria Americana (APRA), in Peru and reformist Acción Democrática, in Venezuela, parties with strong labor ties, to participate in Cold War efforts aimed at moderating worker demands. U.S. labor diplomats denounced Cheddi and Janet Jagan in British Guiana, starting a long sabotage and subversion campaign that first tried to block their rise and later succeeded in ousting them.[64] The diplomats counted on the support of the recently created CIA and convened the old guard of anticommunist democratic leaders who had been working with the United States since 1945.

In Argentina, changes on the domestic front in the 1950s altered how labor activists tried to build consensus for social reforms abroad. Once more, political and economic events in Peronist Argentina were neither part of a linear decline of Peronism, nor the product of a single factor, such as economic duress or Perón's conservative turn. But they do indicate that the mounting difficulties Perón faced at home forced changes in how the government related to organized labor. In that context, the government increasingly curtailed the attachés' activities that could be perceived as destabilizing in other countries.

These domestic tensions became evident in 1951 as the Peronist Party found it increasingly difficult to channel political conflict through democratic institutions. With lingering inflation eroding workers' purchasing power, the Railroad Workers Union declared the first massive strike against the Peronist government in January. As the strike did not end even when it was declared illegal, Perón mobilized the military to guarantee the resumption of public transportation, arresting more than a thousand workers. On 22 August, under pressures from right-wing conservative sectors in the army, Eva Perón, whose popularity rivaled that of her husband, announced that she would not serve as her husband's running mate in the coming presidential election. With support from major opposition leaders, a rightist army group launched an unsuccessful coup against Perón on 28 September. Yet in the presidential elections of 11 November, the first election in which women went to the polls, Perón won reelection with 63.5 percent of the votes, doubling the support received by the runner-up, one of the largest margins of victory in Argentine history.[65]

With victory in his pocket and the impending death of his sick wife, Perón attempted a political opening. Early in 1952, he met with a leader of the opposition Socialist Party, freed all socialist political prisoners, reopened their legendary publication, La Vanguardia, and promised a more open dialogue. But political tensions sharpened the confrontation between Perón and the opposition. Instead of accepting dialogue with Perón, Socialist Party leaders (some of whom had flirted with the 1951 military putsch) expelled the leader who had met "El Tirano" and hoped that the economic problems would bring Perón down.[66] The economy certainly did not recover to the level of vertiginous growth seen in 1945–1947, and Perón cut spending and the expansion of the monetary base. His conservative fiscal approach differs from the usual characterization of populist policy, which supposedly offers rapid gains that are not sustainable over time. In fact, this policy proved very efficient in preserving the gains workers had made in previous years.[67] But it had a different effect on the attempts to shore up support for a Peronist project across Latin America. Calls for restraint and frugality were not as appealing as calls to advance workers' rights. When newspapers that were friendly to Peronism, like the prorevolutionary La Nación in Bolivia, ran articles under headlines like "Once again, this will not be the year that abundance returns to Argentina, and it will be necessary to produce more and to consume less," Peronism's appeal to revolutionary workers began to fade.[68]

Even so, in many Latin American countries, the Cold War realigned domestic social relations into an apparently simple and dramatic opposition between liberal democracy and organized labor. Sometimes, this context enabled (or perhaps forced) activists from nationalist, communist, and progressive organizations to work together more closely than their interests or ideology would have otherwise suggested. At least on the surface, the borders of nationalist and leftist identities became fluid, dynamic, and overlapping. Conflicts in Uruguay in 1952 showed the reality of Cold War-driven social polarization and the challenges this presented for Peronist activists. Uruguay's small size relative to Brazil and Argentina and its economic reliance on the latter allowed fears of a class-based Argentine expansion to emerge in their crudest form. The crisis started on 10 September, when the Transportation Workers Union shut down the country (including its ports) to demand wage increases. Confrontations between business and unions had been increasing in previous years. A few months earlier, during a walkout by public workers, the Colorado government had passed the "Urgent Security Measures" (Medidas de Pronta Seguridad), a mild version of martial law that allowed massive arrests and military deployment.[69] The day after the transportation strike began, the Government National Council (CNG) met, and a few hours after midnight, it made the drastic decision to accuse the Argentine worker attaché, Alejandro Mignone, and his assistant, Ricardo Patolano, of having instigated the unrest. According to the Uruguayan government, the attachés had provided support, funding, and logistics for a larger plan that aimed at the takeover of national communications by communist and Peronist sympathizers and, eventually, at the overthrow of the administration with the help of Herreristas. (The Herreristas were the most powerful fraction of the Partido Nacional, led by Luis Alberto de Herrera, a popular leader who, incidentally, had joined Argentina's anti-U.S. stance at the 1933 Montevideo Pan-American Conference.) The government expelled the attaché and his assistant from the country, arrested hundreds of Uruguayan union activists, and deployed military forces at the main radio stations. The escalation reached its climax on 12 September, less than forty-eight hours after the strike began, when the U.S. ambassador in Uruguay sent an urgent telegram to the State Department. The cablegram informed Washington of Perón's attempt to overthrow the Uruguayan government and added a frantic plea "for weapons and ammunition."[70] All this had begun with the two Peronist attachés who were suspected of fomenting a bus strike.

Initially, U.S. officials read the cable as an overreaction to a strike and another attempt to gain economic or military benefits by playing to U.S. fears. Yet, as the hours passed, they came to consider the Peronist threat as real. They had historical reasons to believe the ambassador. Since 1945, Perón had worked with Herreristas, a moderate party with an emphasis on economic nationalism. In the 1946 presidential election, Argentina had pressured Uruguay economically in a failed attempt to damage the chances of the ruling Partido Colorado. And the worker attachés were very active among unions of all backgrounds that constituted a labor movement characterized since 1947 by its mobilized radicalism.[71]

When Perón learned of the expulsion of the attachés the following morning, he went into a rage against the Uruguayan government, against his Herrerista allies for not supporting Argentina publicly, and against the attachés for having been discovered. He gave orders to break diplomatic relations with Uruguay and to undertake economic retaliations. While these measures would have plunged the country into chaos, Perón's motivation at this point appeared to stem more from the immediate political dispute than from a desire to overthrow Uruguay's current government and replace it with a friendly one. Eventually, the moderate Foreign Minister Jerónimo Remorino (who succeeded Bramuglia in mid-1949) dissuaded Perón from both measures, and Argentina decided to intensify its campaign in Uruguay, though focusing it solely on support for the strike and making no reference to the government. Simultaneously, Perón agitated Argentine nationalism against Uruguay by suggesting the collaboration of the Herrerista government with the United Kingdom against Argentina in the dispute for the Falkland/Malvinas Islands.[72]

In general, descriptions of a regional landscape dominated by governments strongly aligned with Perón gave credence to Uruguay's claims about Argentine ambitions. By September, the Bolivian revolution had already triumphed. The MNR government declared its good will toward Argentina and launched a process of radical economic change, including, the following year, the second agrarian reform of the twentieth century in Latin America. In Chile, nationalist General Carlos Ibáñez del Campo assumed the presidency the following month, after a campaign that had benefited from Argentine funds and support. This support was given despite the fact that Ibáñez represented a conservative alliance that emphasized social order, an end to corruption, and the containment of unions and welfare-state advocates. (One of Ibañez' defeated rivals was the young socialist Salvador Allende.) In Brazil, the return of Getúlio Vargas a year earlier had spurred many (including Perón and Vargas) to imagine an alliance between the two countries. The previous administration had harshly repressed unions since 1946 with the support of the United States. Now U.S. officials viewed the country's main port of Santos, the very city in which the attachés had distributed pins with pictures of Perón and Evita at the docks, as "the 'lung' through which Brazil breathes," but where "65 percent is communist." Against this regional background, Uruguay's minister of foreign affairs, Alberto Domínguez Cámpora, told U.S. officials a few days after resigning that he knew of agreements between Peronists and communists and that Uruguay could not expect Brazil's support in the event of a Peronist-sponsored insurrection.[73]

This environment seemed to explain U.S. concerns about a minor strike in such a remote place. In a tragic tone, a prominent member of the official Colorado Party said, "If it weren't for the U.S., Argentina would have already absorbed Uruguay."[74] The United States reconsidered its initial skepticism about Uruguay's fear and concluded that "in its essential arguments, this story is probably true."[75] And if this were not enough to invoke the Cold War to justify U.S. support for repression of social protest in Uruguay, a U.S. official in Montevideo had earlier described Argentine trade barriers against Uruguay as simply "an economic Iron Curtain in miniature between the two countries."[76]

Conclusion

Even after the postwar spring of democratic movements and labor activism came to an end, worker attachés remained active across Latin America. The project remained the same: promoting massive government intervention in the economy, the aggressive redistribution of wealth, and the enactment of a vast array of new social and political rights, while emphasizing the central political role of organized labor. Yet, over time, Perón also became less demanding about the regimes and movements he supported. Paradoxically, worker attachés had more resources and better preparation for this second and different phase.

Yet the attachés' work also changed significantly as the onset of the dualistic Cold War narrowed the space for the project loosely referred to as the Third Position. While Argentina had to overcome economic obstacles and Perón faced domestic political turbulence, the United States explored possibilities for a closer alliance with local elites and any government, democratic or not, willing to fight the rise of organized labor in order to contain social unrest that the United States feared would slip into communism.

There are at least three important features of this process. One is the centrality of U.S. unions and labor diplomats in the containment efforts of U.S. foreign policy. Under the idea of preserving liberal democracy against the threat of communism, U.S. labor representatives actively helped build workers' organizations at a national and regional level with the explicit purpose of limiting the potential of workers' demands. The fact that they were defending rather illiberal and often undemocratic regimes was ruled immaterial in this crusade; Peronist activists would act under these equally blurred standards later. The second peculiarity is that, unlike in many other parts of the world, the Soviet Union had virtually no presence in the region. This meant that the United States's fight against communism was directed at repressing communist- and nationalist-tied activists and unions, which, paradoxically, had been central in expanding workers' rights and incorporating them into the region's capitalist economies.

This brings us to the third singular feature of the period: however hard populist and nationalist movements worked to distance themselves from communism, they were targeted by U.S. officials and labor diplomats as much as—or even more than—before. Situations in which different forms of nationalist, socialist, and communist labor movements acted together were precisely what concerned the United States. As many authors have shown, the anxiety of U.S. officials and labor diplomats in Latin America during the 1950s was not about communism in itself. They focused instead on what communism could have in common with these other political formations—the advance of "economic nationalism." This was a decades-old challenge in U.S.–Latin American relations.[77]

The combined U.S. focus on Latin American economic nationalism and organized labor had an impact on the actions of the Peronist attachés, on the process of the formation of Peronism, and on how labor activists negotiated their space within nationalism in general and within Peronism in particular. Despite all of Argentina's attempts to establish friendlier terms, seek financial assistance, and increase trade with the United States, the attachés remained a central source of U.S. anxiety. Even if Perón frequently shifted his alliances toward nationalist dictators or conservative governments, Peronist labor activists often continued to work with the progressive movements that had been their partners since 1946, when they perceived them as potential allies for their regional project. Often, they did a perfunctory job of filing reports about communist activity (and a less-than-perfunctory effort at traditional diplomatic tasks). In parallel, even if limited by Peronism's conservative shift, the attachés dedicated their efforts to publicizing the welfare-state policies developed by Perón (as in Peru), to forging alliances with labor-based revolutionary movements despite the strong presence of communist and leftist organizations (as in Bolivia), and to providing political and logistical support for aggressive labor actions against liberal governments and elites (as in Uruguay). Amid the growing dominance of the United States, the attachés kept Argentine projects for the region alive, fueling concerns about transnational labor activism and bringing Peronism back into the Cold War.

For the attachés and for Argentine labor activists in general, Peronism appeared to be a field of possibilities, and its nationalism a "language of contention" open to renegotiation rather than operating as a strict doctrine dictated from above. Facing the obstacles of the early 1950s, they did not adopt a different rhetoric, which might have opened space for a political alternative to Peronism. Nor did they migrate to other political formations, as the leftist and liberal sectors in Argentina were not in a position to credibly demand the expansion of workers' rights.

The study of this period casts the relation between Perón and labor activists in a singular light, challenging the generalized assumption that vertical subordination to the leader in the name of the nation left organized labor with no autonomy. The way in which this integration occurred and the historical conjuncture in which it took place granted labor activists some space to define their role in national politics, to assert the centrality of social rights in democracy, and to defend those rights already won. The attachés continued to act in the name of Perón; but rather than simply repeating Perón's changing interpretation of the national interest, their decisions defended Peronism as a legitimate site from which to question social order and inequality. In many instances, the attachés acted against Perón's wishes and against his conservative turn, albeit without ever rejecting his leadership or explicitly questioning his wisdom. This notable insistence on shaping the meanings of Peronism is central to understand the dislocated dynamic between Perón and the attachés in the last, declining phase of populism.

CHAPTER SEVEN. **A BITTER PILL**

When invited to talk to a vast audience of Brazilian steel workers in 1952, the Argentine attaché Vicente Diana decided to make the first move toward integrating national labor movements into a regional alliance. Perón was about to sign a bilateral agreement with Getúlio Vargas and planned to develop a common front with rightist Chile and revolutionary Bolivia despite their differences. Against this background, Diana reminded Brazilian workers that they "ha[d] to work harder in order to reach the continental unity of the labor movement." The proposal was not an easy one: they had to "fight against foreign enemies" and also "overcome the domestic obstacles that work against the goal of a continental workers' organization."[1]

The setting should have been an early indication of the magnitude of the obstacles facing Peronism's comprehensive project for hemispheric leadership. To make his appeal to regional unity, the Argentine attaché chose, of all places, the steel industrial complex of Volta Redonda, the largest steel producer in Brazil. The complex had been built in 1941 with massive U.S. financial and technical support. Nestled in a city that had been planned by American architects and engineers, Volta Redonda stood as a powerful symbol of the two countries' deep and lasting bond, which had been sealed during World War II, as well as of Brazil's second industrialization phase.[2] The modest repercussions of the attaché's call for action—a critical mention in an editorial note published in the *Jornal do Brasil*—and Brazilian unions' insistence on maintaining friendly terms with all regional labor organizations suggested the moderate success of Peronist inroads into Brazilian labor after six years of activism, which had started on a much more hopeful note.[3] Many unions were foiled by U.S. influence and by the repressive atmosphere; most others had developed their own long-term strategies.[4] Despite the attention many leaders and activists gave to Peronist ideas, by the mid-1950s it had become clear that organized labor in Brazil had little interest in a strategic alliance with Peronism.

This chapter situates the creation of Agrupación de Trabajadores Lationamericanos Sindicalistas (ATLAS), the labor-based Latin American regional union promoted by Peronist attachés, in the context of the retrenchment of Peronist social reforms and the full-scale reaction against the labor activism of the early postwar. To further dim the horizon of progressive forces, this reaction features Perón as one of its visible figures. The previous chapter analyzed a period of ambivalence and uncertainty; this one explores a more forcefully conservative moment in Perón's regional policy. By 1953, Perón's frank and consistent effort to dismantle all forms of labor activism abroad stood in direct conflict with the continuation of the attachés' mission. Yet many of the attachés continued to work to expand labor organizations and promote demands for social and economic rights in an increasingly conservative atmosphere. And they continued to do so in Perón's name. Since 1945, Argentine labor activists had forged Peronist rhetoric as their own "language of contention." The new era, which started in 1953, exposed how productive the symbolic economy of this renewed version of Argentine nationalism could be, as well as its limitations.

The creation of ATLAS confirmed the perceived importance of organized labor's role in defining the features of the inter-American system. The most evident confirmation of that importance is to be found in the wide-ranging efforts of U.S. labor diplomats to influence political processes in Latin America and to create a regional organization (Inter-American Regional Organization of Workers, ORIT), which competed with and eventually defeated the Peronist-led ATLAS and the communist-oriented Confederación de Trabajadores de América Latina (CTAL). Weak from the moment of its birth, ATLAS expressed in its ambivalences and limitations the shift toward a violently conservative Peronism. Yet Peronist activists stubbornly persisted as a source of progressive politics, either through inspiration, support, or reference. Labor activists in general and the worker attachés in particular continued to restrict Perón's freedom of movement. This particular function of Argentine labor contrasts with scholarly interpretations that emphasize the vertical organization of Peronism under its leader. The study of Peronism's relationship with the two revolutionary movements still in power during the 1950s in Guatemala and Bolivia reveals a complex picture and shows that, despite the collapse of populist projects, Perón remained at times a symbolic representation of their achievements and potentials.

This exhaustion of Latin American populism reached its nadir in 1955 when a military coup in Argentina overthrew Perón. Cornered by economic troubles and increasing political turmoil, Perón was unable or unwilling to defend himself by using the enormous support that he still had among workers. By that point, the attaché program had been decimated; the military dictatorship buried it for good as part of a vast (and illusory) attempt to de-Peronize Argentina. This strategy was heavily influenced by the discourses of both social sciences and foreign policy that revamped theories held by fascist movements in Europe and applied them to Cold War Latin America, considering Peronism to be a deviation from the path toward proper political development. The generals hoped that Peronism had not left a legacy or a social formation of its own, that the road could be rectified simply through erasure. The following years showed how the aftermath of the attachés' actions abroad and of their reputation at home acquired a life of their own, even after the attaché program was dismantled and most attachés had retired from public life. Despite Perón's orders and the expectations of the military dictatorship that overthrew him, labor activists still nurtured a sense of belonging to a collective worker identity across the region. In unexpected ways, they also provided the seeds for those who would replace Peronist and populist ideas with new, more radical projects.

Lifting the World

ATLAS was one of various efforts aimed at creating supranational labor organizations in parallel with the emergence of the postwar interstate system. After the war, almost all of these organizations, in Latin America and elsewhere, were intended to function as stalking horses for the United States or the world communist movement.[5] By contrast, ATLAS was supposed to be the institution that best expressed Peronist labor activism's defining features. As a regional tool to help organized labor advocate for the construction of welfare states and the redistribution of wealth, ATLAS would repudiate both radicalism and U.S.-sponsored liberalism. Lit by those ideas, the worker attachés marched across diverse geographies and political landscapes. But the distance between early 1947, when Peronism first considered this plan, and late 1952, when ATLAS was finally created, was far greater than what the calendar suggests. In those five years, the rise of organized labor had generated a conservative backlash, giving way to a new period in which the containment of social demands increasingly took the form of the violent suppression of social unrest. Even if Peronism was still an inspiring force among many labor activists, Peronists were no longer in a position to translate that regional sympathy into a program and an institution.

The postwar fracture of the international labor movement took place at the 1945 World Labor Congress in London. The division between communist and noncommunist unions was an early expression within the international labor movement of the parameters of the Cold War. The meeting was marked by the efforts of the American Federation of Labor (AFL) to exclude communist unions (particularly powerful in countries such as France or Italy), to gain support (if conflictive and conditional) for the exclusion of communism from European socialist, labor, and Christian unions, and to transfer to Europe the U.S. domestic dispute between the AFL and the Congress of Industrial Organizations (CIO). (Though both the AFL and the CIO enlisted in the Cold War and purged communism from the U.S. labor movement, the AFL showed a more marked hostility to anything that could be related to the Soviet Union.) Within this tension, the CIO participated in 1945 in the creation of the Federación Sindical Mundial (FSM), along with communist unions. The AFL started simultaneously to undermine the legitimacy of these organizations, last remnants of the popular fronts, eventually sponsoring the creation in 1949 of the strongly anticommunist Confederación Internacional de Organizaciones Sindicales Libres (CIOSL). Since at least 1948, these unions worked in open collaboration with the U.S. State Department and in covert collaboration with the CIA.[6] They were crucial players in trying to contain the wave of social protests led by communist forces that swept Western Europe in 1947 and 1948. Under the argument that the most effective way to combat communism was by raising workers' living standards, they became equally important in building transnational alliances—first in their support for the Marshall Plan after 1948 and later in the construction of the modern welfare state.[7]

In Latin America, CTAL, founded in 1938, brought together a broad arc of antifascist labor organizations (communist, socialist, reformist liberal, and, increasingly, nationalist) under the tutelage of the powerful Confederación de Trabajadores de México (CTM), led by the teachers union leader, Vicente Lombardo Toledano.[8] In Argentina, almost all the future Peronist attachés had been active CTAL members during the 1930s and early 1940s.[9] Just as the antifascist fronts did, CTAL imploded at the end of the war. As communist unions gained more control of the organization, U.S. officials and labor diplomats accused Toledano of being a "puppet" of the Soviet Union, and the AFL led a virulent anticommunist crusade across the region, replicating its European strategy and its domestic dispute with the CIO over the authority to direct the course of organized labor in the Cold War United States.[10] What was distinctive about U.S. labor diplomacy in Latin America was exactly what gave grounds to the creation of ATLAS: AFL representatives aligned with the U.S. State Department on the frontline of the Latin American theater of the Cold War. From this position, they warned about the threat that the "different totalitarian brands" mentioned by Serafino Romualdi posed for workers' rights and for democracy. From the outset, the AFL established as their targets both communist labor organizations and the international actions of the Argentine Confederación General del Trabajo (CGT).[11]

The postwar rise of labor activism and social demands was not directly linked to the emergence of the regional labor movement. On the contrary, in almost all cases, regional activism only took on an institutional form when a conservative backlash put workers' organizations on the defensive. This was also the case with ATLAS. Perón and the CGT originally planned to create a regional force *within* the existing system. But the exclusion of Argentina from the Lima conference of January 1948, just four months before the creation of the Organization of American States (OAS) in Bogotá, opened the possibility for Peronist activists to create their own organization. During the Lima meeting, the AFL broke away from the CTAL and created the Confederación Interamericana de Trabajadores (CIT). The new CIT included representatives from almost all Latin American countries.[12] With CTAL in retreat and the CIT on the march, Perón decided that, in the labor movement, the Third Position was going to have an institutional expression of its own.

Over the next three years, the creation of a labor-based Latin American organization to compete with U.S. plans for the region came to occupy ever more space in the attachés' daily schedules. The visits of labor leaders to Buenos Aires, the support for labor activities abroad, and the distribution of funds and logistical support were often executed with an eye to a future regional organization. But at a national level, many of these organizations underwent significant transformations after 1948 because of domestic dynamics and international movements that made anticommunism a regional priority. In Mexico, Lombardo Toledano was expelled from the CTM in 1947, and by 1950, Fidel Velázquez had started his forty-seven-year tenure as leader of the CTM. Faithfully, Velázquez followed the more conservative directions of the Mexican Government's Partido Revolucionario Institucional (PRI). In Brazil, the right-wing administration of Eurico Dutra had intensified since the 1947 repression of communist activists. The government's legally mandated control over unions made the attachés' work in Brazil more difficult. The AFL worked with local unions and the government under the mandate of fighting Peronism. By the time Vargas returned to power in 1951, ORIT was the only regional organization recognized in the country.[13] In Chile, the Confederación de Trabajadores was under control of Bernardo Ibáñez, a former CTAL vice-president and now a proper anticommunist and ally of the AFL who led the Chilean labor movement, for a short time, to an active alliance with ORIT.[14] In Peru, the nationalist movement Alianza Popular Revolucionaria Americana (APRA), which was in control of the Confederación de Trabajadores since its inception in 1944, clearly welcomed an anticommunist alliance with the United States.[15] In Cuba, the Confederación de Trabajadores expelled communists and those in contact with Argentine Peronism, including the former secretary general Angel Cofiño, who had a good working relationship with the attachés and had personally spoken with Perón about organizing the labor movement in the region.[16] In Colombia, the labor movement formerly controlled by Gaitanista forces split into three different organizations while Gaitanistas and communists were being repressed. One sided with ORIT, the Catholic-aligned one remained independent, and only the third, the small Confederación Nacional de Trabajadores, sided with ATLAS.[17]

If these changes were a victory for the AFL, they also came with concessions to Latin America. Unions from the region demanded (and initially obtained) that the organization stress labor rights and the attack on economic inequality in addition to its anticommunist mission. But these goals were further diluted in 1951, when the CIT was dissolved and the hemispheric activity of the unions that orbited around the AFL was rebaptized as ORIT, a regional branch of the recently created CIOSL.

In order to consolidate the support that populist activism could gain in the narrow space remaining, Perón decided to act quickly to create ATLAS. Under his instructions, the Ministry of Foreign Affairs sent the attachés a new set of directions with the mandate of accelerating the creation of an alternative regional organization. In February 1952, the Argentine CGT was finally able to bring delegates from fifteen countries to a public hospital in Paraguay to discuss the creation of a regional organization inspired by Peronist principles. The participants approved the creation of a committee, the embryonic version of the future organization, which reflected many of the tensions that marked

Peronism's institutional presence in the region. One of these tensions was the organization's overwhelming dependence on Argentine financial support—the meeting was entirely funded by the Argentine government. Like pilgrims, the delegates first stopped in Buenos Aires to meet Perón on their way to Asunción.[18] Another tension was the differing emphasis with which each national delegation understood the Third Position. The delegate from Chile argued in favor of an explicit condemnation of capitalism and communism, while Mexicans and Brazilians argued for a qualified condemnation: "It's exploitative capitalism we are against, not honest capitalism that generates the wealth without which workers could not live." Yet the delegate from Guatemala stressed that in his country "the anticommunist campaign is financed by the Yankee regime" and argued that the organization should plainly "fight against political and economic imperialism."[19] The final document, which was approved later that year as ATLAS's declaration of principles, included all these suggestions in very general terms, but made few specific recommendations for social legislation or political programs. The text also incorporated the nationalist and anticolonial demands that had been at the core of Peronist activism across the region: the independence of Puerto Rico, the release of Panama from its obligations to the United States regarding the Canal, the condemnation of Patiño Mines in Bolivia, and the censure of the policy of United Fruit in Guatemala.[20]

The delegates met again in November 1952, this time in Mexico, to formally create ATLAS. In the meantime, Romualdi crisscrossed the region denouncing "Perón's aims of continental domination."[21] In its early reports, ORIT singled out Peronism as a crucial foe and monitored Peronist presence in almost all Latin American countries. In coordination with the U.S. State Department, they also pressured unions with sanctions if they joined Peronism and promised incentives if they signed on with ORIT. By the time a hundred union activists from eighteen countries met to create ATLAS in November, U.S. efforts had succeeded at eroding most of its potential support. When the largest labor organizations from Brazil and Mexico opted not to join, thanks in part but not exclusively to the increasing lobby of the AFL, ATLAS became a mostly Argentine organization, with small delegations from relatively small countries.[22] In its actual incarnation, ATLAS was an expression of the limits of populist projects by the early 1950s. A number of factors constrained it: the growing U.S. influence, the appeal of liberalism among many democratic union leaders, the appeal of leftist activism, the reservations about Peronism, and Perón's own ambivalences about the project.

Four main obstacles arose in the construction of the new organization. First, while labor movements were deeply connected with regional and global debates, they fought their struggles on a national level, demanding national laws and disputing resources with national elites. This element created a major problem for ATLAS and ORIT. It was difficult for ATLAS to present itself as a regional organization attuned to every single domestic debate without losing much of its impact.[23] Second, unlike in Europe, nationalism became a fundamental weapon for labor movement demands in Latin America, particularly after World War II, because threats to labor rights usually came from the combination of elite interests and the United States's expanding power. This environment compounded the problems of explicitly international organizations. Even if all those nationalist movements shared an anti-imperialist agenda, most of those common interests and aims remained local rather than regional. Third, in historical terms, ATLAS arrived too late. By 1952, the tide of labor activism looking to regional organizations for support or inspiration was in clear retreat, and the progressive forces that could have used ATLAS support were either pulling back, alienated from Peronism, or in the early stages of exploring other means of political action. Fourth, even as the Cold War presented clear alignments with little space for dialogue between different sectors, Peronism created ATLAS as a separate organization rather than as a subprogram within a larger organization. This forced unions to define themselves politically in ways and to a degree that they not all were ready to do. Unions in Brazil or Chile were interested in being close to Peronism and shared common regional goals. But they were not eager to subordinate themselves under the Argentine CGT, and they were even less interested in explicitly confronting U.S. labor diplomats. The clearest example of this problem appeared in Bolivia. Under the direction of Juan Lechín Oquendo, the powerful Confederación de Obreros de Bolivia (COB) was as close to Peronism as any labor movement in the region and maybe even closer than some. But as the Bolivian National Revolution built a complex relationship with the United States, which included some forms of cooperation, Lechín decided to stay on good terms with all the regional organizations by not committing to any of them in particular.[24]

In this context, the dominance of Argentina also became a liability. ATLAS elected the Argentine José Espejo as its first secretary general and chose Buenos Aires as its official headquarters. Its leaders claimed to represent some 6 million workers from Latin America; later estimations put the number of workers represented by the unions that went to the meeting in Mexico at around 3 million. Out of that total, some 2.4 million were actually from the Argentine CGT.[25] In a gesture whose overtones revealed the weaknesses it tried to hide, the Argentine delegate José Alonso suggested the name ATLAS "because of its symbolic analogy" and proposed the figure of a gigantic worker carrying the world on his shoulders as the emblem of the organization.[26]

Dismantling Regional Activism

Domestically, the attachés also experienced a set of transformations that affected their work and the way they viewed ATLAS. When Juan Atilio Bramuglia left the Foreign Ministry in 1949, the attachés lost, if not an ally, then the person who had created the program. As a long-standing labor advocate, he had come to understand the potential of the attachés' work. Three years later, with the death of Eva Perón in 1952, the attaché program lost one of its strongest supporters. Around the same period, Perón pursued a friendlier relation with the United States, and this new strategy had an immediate impact on the attaché program. Once Jerónimo Remorino became minister of foreign affairs in 1951, the diplomatic leadership demonstrated no interest in international labor activism and redoubled efforts to discipline the attachés to conform to the narrow functions of the foreign service.

The ministry became very receptive to foreign governments' and Argentine diplomats' complaints about the attachés, and it used those protests to justify a stricter review of the attachés' functions. In 1948, the attaché in Cuba spent most of his time contacting activists like Castro and hosting conferences at the most important unions. Nobody in the Argentine government paid attention to his discretionary use of the funds at his disposal, his daily schedule, his administrative duties. Now, most of the communications that the attaché received from Buenos Aires referred to the need to comply with administrative procedures and made insistent references to his unclear handling of public funds. In a perplexing change, when César Tronconi paid a Cuban activist for an ATLAS-related activity, he was now severely reprimanded from Buenos Aires for mixing his duties as Argentine diplomat and as Peronist union activist.[27]

While it accelerated the pace of sanctions against the attachés, the ministry simultaneously began to reduce the number of attachés. The government stopped replacing the attachés who were tired, died, or were called back to Buenos Aires. From the ninety-three labor activists overseas in 1949, the numbers declined to eighty-three, seventy-nine, sixty-nine, fifty-five, and forty-seven in the following years. When Perón was ousted by a military coup in 1955, there were only forty-four attachés at Argentine embassies— fewer than half of the total number just six years earlier.[28] The new military government dismantled the program, yet it never formally eliminated the position of worker attaché.

Argentina's economic constraints were aggravated domestically by exceptional circumstances, changes in global markets, and the uneven fate of the bilateral agreements. A severe drought diminished agricultural output and spurred higher inflation, forcing a rearrangement of redistributive policies. After winning reelection in 1951, Perón implemented a rather orthodox adjustment plan that, among other things, slowed down wage increases and restricted domestic consumption. The plan was a political and economic success. The massive identification of workers with Peronism did not evaporate once the government stopped offering immediate benefits, as many had expected; on the contrary, worker support increased in the following elections. The economy responded quickly to the plan. Within a year, inflation was curbed, and by 1954, economic growth had reached 5 percent.[29] Yet social conflict and labor protests had started to crack the impressive Peronist apparatus. Social rights obtained during the first years remained intact, but the country was still unable to advance toward a more industrialized economy that would guarantee its international autonomy and long-term sustainability.

Argentina's bid for regional leadership had been built on the dual pillars of the worker attaché program and bilateral economic agreements. Those agreements were the first victims of economic setbacks and political ambivalence. The much sought-after trade agreement signed by Perón and Vargas in 1953 established that Argentina would sell Brazil 1.5 million tons of wheat (80 percent of Brazil's total wheat imports) in exchange for Brazilian wood, coffee, and fruit. Yet Argentina managed to fulfill its quota and obtain a surplus only in 1953. In 1954, the balance of trade was even, and by 1955, Argentina was in deficit to Brazil. The agreements with Chile, Bolivia, and Peru followed similar patterns, alienating partners and giving the domestic opposition reasons to object to any deal with Perón and succumb to U.S. pressures.[30] The United States's ability to outmaneuver Perón in most disputes and in the race to sign up regional allies was a sharp reminder of Argentina's real influence on the global scene. But in addition, the changes in the priorities of Argentine foreign policy rendered useless initiatives generated during more hopeful times, like ATLAS. By the time Peronism had created the instrument to forge the large regional labor movement of which Perón and the worker attachés had dreamt, the instrument had lost its meaning and purpose.

By 1953, Perón aligned himself unequivocally with the suppression of social conflict and ended his criticism of U.S. liberalism and U.S. foreign policy as obstacles for the region's development. This new alignment diminished the usefulness of the worker attachés. Only four months after the creation of ATLAS, Perón received U.S. Ambassador Albert Nufer at the government palace in Buenos Aires. Complaining about an "anti-U.S. campaign," Nufer showed Perón a *Look* magazine article from the previous January with "vicious anti-U.S. cartoons distributed throughout the Hemisphere by Argentine labor attachés." He stressed how close the cartoons were "to the communist line." Half for show and half in truth, Perón "reacted strongly" to this accusation. The president reaffirmed that "Argentina was strongly anti-Communist" and that communist activity was "under constant police surveillance." As for the attachés, Foreign Minister Remorino added that the activists appointed by Perón "were really 'laborers' with the mentality of 'laborers,' who had merely taken a course in a local school for labor attachés." According to the minister, "Most of them were not particularly bright." Perón interceded to note: "If his government had been responsible for the distribution of the propaganda, it would have used more subtle methods."[31]

Perón ordered an immediate stop to anti-U.S. activities. The Ministry of Foreign Affairs sent new orders further restricting attachés' activities. But for the United States, the containment of social conflict required suppressing any kind of social protest or regional activism that could ignite it. None of Perón's gestures deterred the United States in its pursuit of the definitive closure of the worker-attaché program. When White House staff requested information for President Eisenhower about the "current status of U.S.-Argentine relations" a month after the ambassador met with Perón, the State Department came back with a terse one-page summary: "We want from Argentina: cessation of the Communist-line propaganda which, until modified recently, was being propagated throughout the hemisphere by the Argentine Government and labor elements which it controls."[32]

The Guatemalan Test

By the early 1950s, the only democratic processes of radical social reform still thriving in Latin America were in Guatemala, Bolivia, and (to a lesser extent) Argentina. The vigor of the first two contrasted with the waning vitality of Argentina's movement. This disparity is evident not only in a comparison of domestic conditions but also in Peronism's shifting relationship with the other two revolutionary movements. The relation with them was an area that tested the potential and limits of Peronist labor activism and revealed the flaws of ATLAS.

The actions of Peronist attachés came into conflict with Perón's decisions in 1954 Guatemala. The significance of this conflict was such that it reverberated later, during the tragic decades of the Cold War. Even as Perón sought a rapprochement with the United States and aligned Argentina with anticommunist forces throughout the region, Argentine foreign policy remained a thorn in the United States's side. The principles of multilateralism and non-intervention, which had shaped Argentine foreign policy and its anti-Americanism since the nineteenth century, permeated even the belligerent environment of the Cold War. During 1953 and 1954, Argentina demanded that any actions related to the democratically elected government of Jacobo Arbenz, in Guatemala, be undertaken by the OAS and not unilaterally by the United States. So while the OAS held its tenth conference in Caracas in March 1954 and with U.S. covert operations in Guatemala fully underway, the Eisenhower administration insistently sought a regional "vote of confidence for the U.S.," a request that stemmed in part from Latin American emphasis on multilateralism. Eisenhower attempted to turn the coup into a "Pan-American consensus that Arbenz must be overthrown."[33] Argentina proved incapable of stopping the U.S.-sponsored resolution condemning Arbenz, which passed by a seventeen-to-one vote (Guatemala). It was a Pyrrhic victory for the United States though: the two largest countries in the region (Argentina and Mexico) abstained on the grounds of defending the sovereignty of member states, an argument that undoubtedly seemed like a useful defense against possible future actions undertaken against Perón himself. Brazil sided with the United States, underscoring the fragility of its alliance with Argentina, but half of the seventeen countries that voted with United States were dictatorships, a fact described by Secretary Dulles as embarrassing. For the other half to go along with the anticommunist resolution, the United States was forced to dole out generous funds for financial and infrastructure projects. This regional landscape forced many U.S. supporters, including Bolivia, Brazil, and Uruguay, to look for ways of arguing in favor of Guatemalan sovereignty as a main instrument of democratic consolidation in the region at large. In the end, the resolution was ambiguous about what amounted to a foreign intervention in a sovereign state. Most countries argued in favor of preserving democracy, rejecting military options. As Max Paul Friedman states in analyzing this period, the arguments against the U.S. position in Caracas "were made in favor of democratic principles, not against them," and they were not particularly anti-American.[34] At the end of the conference, the OAS unanimously passed another resolution, the Declaración de Caracas, in favor of the principles of self-determination and non-intervention in the domestic affairs of other states.

The CIA-orchestrated military coup began on 18 June 1954. The coup followed years of covert operations, which had solidified the Cold War alliance between local elites and U.S. military forces, intelligence agencies, policymakers, and economic corporations. Concluding on 27 June, the paramilitary invasion, codenamed Operation PBSUCCESS, brought down the democratic government of Jacobo Arbenz.[35] Not a day too late, on 27 June, Perón indicated the primacy of anticommunism in his brand of nationalism and made a consequently ineffectual or cynical attempt to promote non-intervention without condemning the U.S. actions that had just undermined that principle: he wrote to Milton Eisenhower, the president's brother, who had earlier visited Buenos Aires, suggesting that the best way to avoid the obstacle of non-intervention would be to launch massive and coordinated efforts between the United States and nationalistic leaders and dictators to remove communism from Latin America. Perón noted that the U.S. ambassador in Buenos Aires had "consulted [him] personally about the 'Guatelama case' and if Argentina would participate in a 'meeting of consultation.'" Coming full circle, Perón now invoked the thirty-ninth resolution of the OAS charter, which had been promoted by the United States and adopted in Bogotá in 1948, to justify a regional effort to remove a democratically elected president as part of a collective battle against a broader enemy. "Guatemala is only another incident; it is an effect. The cause lies in communism," he wrote.[36] Offering to host an OAS meeting in Buenos Aires, Perón declared, "We will be always ready and in the front line against communism." Narrowing the goals of non-interventionism to the point of making them meaningless, Perón seemed to advise the United States about how to avoid a confrontation with the rest of the region by expanding actions beyond the Guatemalan borders: he explained to Milton Eisenhower that in order to confront "the common enemy of Communism," the United States should avoid "mak[ing] a victim out of this country [Guatemala]." "You have surely been informed about the events in Brazil, Chile, Uruguay, Ecuador, Colombia, Honduras, Mexico, etc., where, among other things, flags of the United States have been burned in public squares," Perón wrote.[37] His words resounded in Washington. For Daniel James, an official at the U.S. State Department, the Guatemala coup had again aligned anti-Americanism, democratic principles, and national sovereignty. "No one could recall so intense and universal a wave of anti-U.S. sentiments in the entire history of Latin America," he wrote. Secretary Dulles confessed to his brother that U.S. officials were just "frightened by reactions all over . . . demonstrations are bad."[38] As if Perón were aware of the fear among

Perón holding onto power

U.S. diplomats, he tried to reassure the U.S. president's brother, and with only partial truth concluded by offering to relocate himself in a leading role in the hemispheric crusade against social unrest: "In Argentina, fortunately, apart from some unimportant and ineffective declarations and speeches, nothing has happened."[39]

As the copious historiography about the events of Guatemala in 1954 has established, the U.S. labor movement played a significant role in supporting the operations of the U.S. government, military, and intelligence agencies in the Central American country.[40] American labor diplomats were invested in the strategy of fighting communism. In an official statement, the AFL celebrated the overthrow of Arbenz in Guatemala. It "rejoiced over the downfall of the Communist-controlled regime," which had transformed the country "into a beachhead of Soviet Russia in the Western Hemisphere."[41] The coup in Guatemala provided an opportunity for the AFL to expand their presence in the country. As Romualdi said at a press conference in Guatemala, "With free trade unionism, the problem of communism will be reduced; without any unions, the problem will only grow."[42] The AFL "was very active in denouncing the government's character and its persecution against those who refused to accept Communist domination," he wrote to his boss, George Meany. When their rivals in the CIO denounced the role of United Fruit, Romualdi met with company executives to "offer the AFL's cooperation in rebuilding a free labor movement in Guatemala."[43] AFL leaders used the opportunity to differentiate themselves from their rivals, whom they suggested were communist-infiltrated. The two organizations merged in 1955.

For ATLAS and Peronist labor activists, Guatemala revealed the limits of Peronism as an emancipatory movement. The Argentine CGT sent ATLAS a proposal to discuss the situation in the country. Until 1953, ATLAS had publicly defended Arbenz's agrarian reform, stressing, as the organization had done earlier in Bolivia, how the "typically anti-feudal" laws recognized property rights but "guaranteed their social function." ATLAS claimed that "the massive concentration of land in a few hands alters the social function of property." Quoting the law signed by Arbenz, it advanced Comisión Económica Para América Latina (CEPAL)-like arguments that agrarian reform would foster the development of "capitalist methods of agricultural production, preparing the path for the industrialization of Guatemala."[44]

One year later, an ATLAS-approved document about the military coup showed how little room for maneuver the organization had by then. The text recalled that since 1944 "the governments in Guatemala have been of a revolutionary tendency that is in agreement with the people's interests" and insisted that "in our continent, there are no small or big countries, but free and sovereign ones that should be respected in order to avoid needless bloodshed." In a moderate tone that contrasted with the usual Peronist rhetoric, ATLAS said that it was "impossible for foreign spirits, coming from wherever they might, to impose domestic freedom in a country" and denounced United Fruit for conspiring against a government that "is not of communist tendency." Despite the claim of solidarity with the Guatemalan people, ATLAS did not explicitly condemn the invasion or the overthrow of Arbenz. Perón made his influence felt: even with U.S. flags being burned all over Latin America and with the U.S. role in the coup widely known, the resolution did not make a single reference to the United States.[45]

Yet, once again, the hardening of Argentina's foreign policy was neither linear nor uncomplicated. Acting from the fringes of politics, the attachés symbolized—to borrow Walter Benjamin's terms—"the street insurgence of the anecdote" against "the spirit of the period," expressed by Perón's diplomacy, in ways that would have a long-term impact in Latin America.[46] While Perón was privately throwing his full support behind the U.S. invasion and publicly accommodating the national principles of non-intervention to the rapprochement with the United States, the Argentine embassy in Guatemala became the second-largest asylum site in Guatemala, after the Mexican embassy, saving hundreds of activists and former members of the Arbenz administration from prison, torture, and death.

While the episode is well known, little has been written about how it happened.[47] The evidence illuminates the attachés' direct and indirect roles in it. Activists sought shelter en masse in "friendly" embassies in the days after the coup. The Mexican legation was preferred by many, because the Mexican government had been open to receiving them, and because the embassy was located in front of the seat of government. But once the Mexican embassy was packed with asylum seekers, other diplomatic representations from Latin America received an influx of political and social activists. The Chilean ambassador, Federico Klein Reidel, a cofounder of the Socialist Party with Salvador Allende, hosted seventy-two asylum seekers in his own residence. "The total population at the Embassy is 80 people. . . . The presence of men, women, and children from different walks of life, social origins and character has been, for me and my family, an experience that is as interesting as it is difficult," the ambassador dispatched to Santiago de Chile. He devised a rotation schedule to organize meals and bathroom use, helped the refugees start a daily humorous newspaper to keep up their spirits, and taught them to play hopscotch.[48]

Not far from the Chilean embassy, dozens of activists had already sought shelter inside the Argentine building in the days immediately after the coup. As part of his ambivalent take on the coup, Perón had instructed that the gates of the embassy be opened, but then he immediately ordered the legation to be shuttered. The ambassador (also worried about a humanitarian situation that could spin out of control) ordered gates, doors, and windows closed. By mid-July, most embassies from Latin America had done the same. Led by Mexico, Chile, and Argentina, they tried to coordinate a regional solution to the refugee crisis in a tense negotiation with the local military authorities and against the public and covert pressure of the United States in favor of handing the refugees to the military junta.[49] The activists' options were narrowing by the hour. But Alberto Viale, the worker attaché appointed by Perón, ignored orders from the ministry and the charge d'affaires (who might have turned a blind eye to his actions). The attaché, who had been in Guatemala since 1947, with a brief interruption of two years, had established a wide range of contacts with labor and political activists.[50] Through an intermediary, and with the collaboration of the charge d'affaires personally sent by Perón to Guatemala, he offered them entrance to the embassy despite the official prohibition.[51] By hiding activists from Guatemala and from the rest of Latin America in the trunk of a car, Viale secretly smuggled in more and more people; by the beginning of August, there were between 210 and 223 refugees on the premises of the Argentine embassy, more than three times the number of those hosted by the Chilean ambassador.[52] Accompanied by the worker attaché and other Argentine officials, the refugees stayed in the embassy for several weeks while the Guatemalan government threatened to bomb the building and the Argentine government sought a solution.[53]

The ways in which Viale managed to bring the activists into the embassy and the long-term reverberation of these simple actions deserve closer attention. His decisions reveal the process of political identity formation among Peronist activists, a process grounded in daily actions, ideas, contingent encounters, immediate interests, and the worldviews of those who claimed to be Peronist. In an email exchange with me, a surviving refugee, the sociologist Edelberto Torres Rivas, described Viale as "a very active attaché" who helped many of the labor activists, political leaders, and artists he had met over the previous years.[54] In those desperate hours, as the repressive apparatus was hunting activists down, there was little chance of finding other hiding places once the embassy closed. Word that "the worker attaché could smuggle us into the embassy in his car" reached activists through a notable messenger: Ernesto "Che" Guevara. Torres Rivas remembered,

A large number of us took shelter at the Argentine embassy. During the first days, the access was "free," but after a while the ambassador ordered gates and windows shut. Che had always been close to me, he had stayed at our place when he first arrived in Guatemala, so he looked for me and offered to help me to find asylum at the [Argentine] embassy. He told me that the worker attaché could do it in his [the attaché's] car. . . . He was a very active worker attaché. . . . Thanks to his offering, Ernesto [Che Guevara] was able to get me and many union leaders and activists through the gates, hidden in the trunk of the attaché's car.[55]

Guevara was a few months away from meeting Fidel Castro in Mexico, an encounter that shaped the hemisphere and the history of the Cold War. He was years away from becoming a leader of the Cuban Revolution and a worldwide symbol of transnational revolutionary activism. The young Argentine doctor, who during his previous trip across Latin America had met a Peruvian peasant who had asked him about Peronism after learning about it through a worker attaché, was now helping the Guatemalan activists through his relationship with another attaché.

Why did Argentina open the embassy to Guatemalan leftist activists when Perón was trying equilibrium between the principle of non-intervention and the support of the U.S.-sponsored anticommunist policies in the region? How did Guevara establish the contacts to do this when his relationship with the Argentine diplomats was, at best, perfunctory, and his position in Guatemala untenable? Understanding Viale's role helps to answer these questions. Guevara arrived in Guatemala in December 1953 and witnessed the final months of the Arbenz administration, a period that became fundamental to his political education. The events that led to the coup consolidated the anti-imperialism that his two trips throughout the region had instilled in him. More important, as some close to him have argued, Guatemala seemed to catalyze in Che's political life his transition from an interest in populist politics to Marxism.[56] During those months, he was a regular at the Argentine embassy. Although this routine seemed to many like concrete evidence that Guevara was a Peronist agent, he only visited the diplomatic representation to collect letters, occasional funds from his relatives, and a steady supply of yerba mate.[57] In those days, Guevara had been introduced to communist circles in the country through his girlfriend, the Peruvian *aprista* in exile Hilda Gadea. In these groups, he met the Nicaraguan exile Edelberto Torres Espinosa, whose son, Edelberto Torres Rivas, was two years younger than Guevara.[58]

Che himself and some of his biographers provide information about the life of Guevara in Guatemala before and during the coup.[59] In a letter to his mother from 20 June, Che mentions that "the Argentine embassy has not been functioning these days."[60] Later in his diaries, he describes spending the days of the coup "living in the house of two Salvadorean women who have sought asylum abroad—one in Chile, the other in Brazil"; he later moved to the embassy.[61] After that, Guevara mentions the arrival of "a new [Argentine] ambassador, Torres Gispena, a stocky little pedant from Córdoba"—he is referring to Carlos Torres Gijena, who was actually a counselor to Ambassador Julio Leguizamón—and adds some renowned descriptions of several of the activists sheltered in the embassy.[62]

The extent of Viale and Guevara's collaboration to turn the Argentine embassy into the second largest asylum site during the Guatemalan coup has not been revealed until now. Disclosed by Torres Rivas, a surviving beneficiary who was a firsthand witness of this relationship, the association shows how some significant historical episodes become more intelligible when reconstructed from the fringes of politics rather than from their center. Even in retreat and derided by Perón, the attachés were still able to work within what they had built as a Peronist tradition. In this sense, the episode also exposes how the tension between Perón and the labor activists became a politically productive space, domestically and regionally.

The ramifications of these actions made a sizable impact on Latin American history. In the previous years, Guatemala had become a laboratory for revolutionaries and expats from all over Latin America. The group at the Argentine embassy included poets, artists, intellectuals, leaders, and activists; their names dot the struggles that shaped the region during the twentieth century. Some were from Guatemala, like the prominent union leader Antonio Obando Sánchez, the well-known journalist Roberto Paz y Paz, the poet Gustavo Valdés, and Humberto Pineda, who had been incarcerated and tortured during the 1931–1944 Jorge Ubico dictatorship.[63] Raúl Sierra Franco, the minister of the Arbenz government, saved his own life by hiding in the Argentine embassy. Several members of the Urrutia family took asylum there, including Ester, of the Guatemalan Women's Alliance, who during the weeks at the embassy took charge of cooking boiled vegetables especially for Che Guevara.[64] Among the refugees there were the Honduran communist writer in exile Ramón Amaya Amador; the Puerto Rican nationalist Carlos Padilla, who had joined the nationalist revolt of 1950; Felix Sergio Ducoudray Mansfield, a Dominican communist from one of the wealthiest families in the country, who conspired against Rafael Leónidas Trujillo; Cubans who had participated in the 1953 attack on the Moncada Barracks, which started the revolutionary period on the island; peasant activists from Nicaragua who had fought with Augusto César Sandino.[65]

Retroactively, perhaps the most notable refugee was the young political leader Ricardo Ramirez de León. Later known as Comandante Rolando Morán, he would be a founding member of the Guatemalan Ejército Guerrillero de los Pobres (EGP), one of the four organizations comprising the Unidad Revolucionaria Nacional Guatemalteca (URNG), one of the largest guerrilla movements in Latin America.[66] During those days at the Argentine embassy, Guevara and Morán became friends.[67] When the EGP leadership adopted the image of Che Guevara as its main symbol years later, it was because Guevara's portrait conveyed the affective and ideological registers of identity formation.[68] The actions of the attaché were, literally, history in the making: by saving the life of a future Guatemalan guerrillero (Morán) through the contacts of a future Argentine guerrillero (Che), Viale became an invisible intermediary. Though a remnant of an era that placed its hopes in social reform, Viale had helped to bring to life a different and more violent period.

The fate of the refugees lays bare the contradictions inherent in Peronism's last years. With the embassy occupied by Guatemalan activists, Perón faced a de facto asylum. He granted the refugees political asylum and sent a government expert in international law to Guatemala. After three months, Perón accepted that the only available solution for the case was to evacuate many of the refugees to Argentina. They were flown to Buenos Aires in Argentine military planes and received as heroes not only by Peronists but also by communist, socialist, and other progressive forces. The refugees thanked the government and immediately contacted the Communist Party, whose activists had already been crushed by the government. Perón, who had reluctantly saved their lives, had them arrested.[69] They spent ten months in an Argentine prison, which may have seemed like a respite when compared to the situation in Guatemala. Some survivors claim that Perón's decision was simply a concession to mounting CIA pressures.[70] Peronist supporters in Argentina claimed that the defense of Guatemalan refugees was a Peronist policy, but that their arrest was not. Unaware of Perón's private support for the military coup, they chose to ignore Perón's repression of leftist and labor activism, which included the arrest of Viale on the attaché's return to Buenos Aires. The refugees became known as "Perón's secret prisoners." On 14 August 1955, one month and two days before the 1955 military coup that ousted Perón, the government that had saved them in Guatemala and sent them to jail in Buenos Aires released the refugees.[71]

FIGURE 7.1. Labor and political activists from all over Latin America, during their more than two-month asylum at the Argentine embassy in Guatemala, after the U.S.-sponsored military coup, July 1954. Many of the refugees gained access to the embassy with the help of the worker attaché Alberto Viale, who, with the help of Che Guevara, hid them in the trunk of his car. Courtesy of Sergio Valdés.

Back in Guatemala, Peronism continued to materialize under different guises. The 1954 coup put General Carlos Castillo Armas in power. As president, Castillo Armas was a puppet of the CIA. Under him, the undoing of the Arbenz democratic revolution started a long and tragic period. The United States had started its campaign against mobilized peasants and organized labor in the country almost a decade earlier, in 1947, when the CIA's precursor had set the goal of "monitoring Peronist and Communist activities."[72] By 1954, the work was done, but even at the dawn of this new era and after so much destruction, the spell of Peronism still held strong in Guatemala. To the frustration of CIA officers worried about Castillo Armas's "failure to articulate a political philosophy," he confessed in recorded conversations with his puppet masters in the months before the coup that he felt "attracted to 'Justicialismo,' a political program advocated by Juan Perón of Argentina."[73]

A Bitter Pill

Guatemala in 1954 not only exposed how limited Peronist labor activism had become and how ineffectual ATLAS was, but also showed the tremendous historical ramifications of the activists' individual actions. Labor activism was now motivated by personal commitment—not an overarching politics emanating from Buenos Aires. Even so, the attachés set in motion actions that would, over time, shape the construction of the political identity they represented. Despite Perón's shift toward political bigotry and the domestic challenges of the Argentine economy, Peronism remained a source of inspiration for labor organizations and revolutionary movements. These two opposing poles fueled an unresolved tension between reactionary and progressive forms of nationalism.

In Bolivia, ATLAS supported the revolution. ATLAS celebrated the agrarian reform of 2 August 1953, as "the backbone of the future happiness in Latin America."[74] With the accumulated effects of Peronist activism in the country since the 1940s, it was not surprising that when peasant organizations learned in 1955 that Perón was going to be the only foreign leader to join the Bolivian government in the massive celebrations for the third anniversary of the Movimiento Nacionalista Revolucionario (MNR) revolution, they immediately signed on for a leading role during the rallies. The peasants and agrarian regiments from the Irpa Grande community, which comprised a dozen estates, met in an assembly and sent a letter to the Ministry of Foreign Affairs to announce their "resolution to join the celebrations that the national government is expected to hold in relation to the visit" of Perón. "Under the ideas of the National Revolution," they offered to bestow on the Argentine president the "Insignia of the Incario or the 'Jachamallcu Decoration'" and to give him "the Baton of Kollasuyo." Defining themselves as the core of the "agrarian activism of the MNR, the Irpa-grande community would participate in the big patriotic parades" organized for the visit. The seals of twenty-eight peasant organizations under the rubric of "MNR Peasant Command" graced the letter.[75] The Bolivian government echoed the community-based organizations' display of admiration for Perón. In addition to the usual bilateral meetings with President Paz Estenssoro, officials also prepared a trip to Lake Titicaca and also a range of special events. Paz Estenssoro and Perón would appear jointly in the La Paz Stadium to speak to tens of thousands of MNR activists; activists would parade in front of the government palace; and there would be a visit to the streetlight pole from which, in 1946, protesters encouraged by the United States and the tin barons had hanged President Villarroel.[76]

None of this ended up taking place. Cornered by mounting domestic problems in Argentina and trying to gain economic aid from the United States, Perón was uninterested in celebrating revolution. On 18 March, just two weeks before the scheduled visit, Perón's ambassador wrote to the Bolivian foreign minister to cancel the trip. The official reason was "doctors' advice due to arterial spasms that had provoked circulatory problems in the right leg." "A bitter pill," as the Argentine ambassador said when he gave the news to Bolivian authorities. There would be no further reports of problems in Perón's circulatory system until his death almost two decades later.[77]

Demise

Perón's ousting was the ultimate demonstration of the exhaustion of the populist path toward social reform. A joint group from the Argentine army and navy led a three-day revolt that overthrew Perón on 16 September 1955. Perón was the leader of a movement that had been singled out by liberal forces for its alleged barbarity, that had encouraged political violence in recent years, and that had a labor base that called for the armed defense of its leader. Yet he left power without posing serious resistance. Three months earlier, navy jets had bombed the Plaza de Mayo on a weekday, killing hundreds of civilians. Even if this brutal display of the rebels' determination failed in the short term, it probably influenced Perón's decision to not fight back.[78]

The image of Perón escaping at dawn on a ragged Paraguayan gunboat provided by Alfredo Stroessner is still puzzling. One of the most popular leaders in modern Latin America abandoned power with the economy stable and massive support among the working-class masses. True, constant confrontation had produced material fatigue in the Peronist base. The government had been unable—and unwilling—to negotiate with the opposition and, when it attempted to do so, it did too little too late. As it became clear, the opposition's exasperation with the government's disregard for alternative voices was also easily reappropriated to justify a subsequent institutional collapse. This was explained less by the government's failure to ensure democracy and more by the conservative sectors' mighty reactions; they started the long process of rolling back the massive expansion of citizenship that had been built over the previous decade.

The international call to prevent the rise of extremism provided anti-Peronist reaction with rhetorical and material resources. The United States identified Peronism as a threat to regional stability, applied all forms of political and economic pressure against it, and ended up tolerating its existence but never supporting the democratization that Peronism was able to produce. Perón reacted by ultimately aligning the country with nationalistic dictatorships. This decision allowed him to incorporate anticommunism—though not without stirring tensions—in order to defend reforms against foreign forces. Those who were eager to restore the status quo by crushing labor quickly appropriated his call for social order.

Out of power, Perón obtained shelter and protection coming from a string of dictators: Stroessner in Paraguay, Marcos Pérez Jiménez in Venezuela, Trujillo in the Dominican Republic. But none of them could offer anything to prevent his demise; indeed, their support eroded the sympathy Peronism had enjoyed among labor movements across the region. Some nationalist movements even celebrated his fall. Víctor Raúl Haya de la Torre, exiled from Peru by the Odría dictatorship, denounced Peronism as a form of "political militarism" and called for a continental union and the creation of a "Bolivarian Army whose power would only come from popular sovereignty and from common American security."[79] Widely respected across the region by nationalists and liberals alike, Haya de la Torre offered a powerful contribution to rewriting the decade of Peronist politics as a reactionary experiment.

The coup against Perón found Juan Garone in Chile. Garone was then the secretary general of ATLAS. More than a decade earlier, in 1943, he had written to then Secretary of Labor Perón as an Argentine worker, to express his support for "your clear position in presenting Argentine social problems, for the benefit of the Motherland and its workers."[80] ATLAS did nothing about Perón's overthrow, nor did Perón ask it to. At that moment, the attachés' position was weaker than ever. The military government brought them home, one by one, over the following six months, until there were no worker attachés deployed at all. Yet the position of worker attaché was surprisingly never eliminated, and it formally exists even to this day. Perhaps in their awareness of the new reality that Peronism had created and the new players that had emerged, sectors of the new government studied (and later discarded) the idea of resuscitating the program along lines closer to the labor attachés of other countries and as a means to coopt labor activists.[81]

The attachés' answer to this new, post-Peronist Argentina varied greatly; they combined different doses of personal heroism, political pragmatism, and survival instinct. A few offered resistance; some went to prison. Tronconi, who had brought Fidel Castro to meet with Perón's envoy to Havana, immediately resigned from his post, denouncing the new government with a telegram in which he ratified his "affiliation to the Workers Confederation, to my union and to the Peronist Party" and declared his solidarity with "Perón, whose social, political and economic cause was and is my own."[82] In the following two years, he was arrested at least twice—first for giving logistical support to a failed uprising against the military government and later for organizing a union meeting.[83] Yet he was one of the few worker attachés to rejoin the foreign service while Peronism was still banned. While remaining a member of the banned Peronist Party, Tronconi joined the foreign service as a consul at the end of 1958.[84]

Other attachés were less staunch. With the already narrow space for labor activism shrinking even more, they tried to secure a future in which they would maintain the status they had enjoyed under Perón, which was far from luxurious but much better than their status before Perón. After the coup, Pedro Conde Magdaleno, the attaché who had gone to the Soviet Union and then to Peru, wrote to an official in the new Argentine administration. "I see in the papers that you are being mentioned as possible ambassador in Italy," the attaché said. "If that happens, I could join you. The position of worker attaché is empty in Italy, but if our government does not want to have worker attachés anymore, I am also Consul and 3rd Secretary."[85] Coming full circle, the attaché, who had declared that he had first become Peronist out of gratitude and then out of conviction, was now trying to discover a new object for his gratitude.

Cut off from their unions during their time abroad, rejected by a diplomatic corps that now sought revenge, and isolated from most potential allies in the region, the worker attachés found little space to continue their political careers or to channel their experience to contribute to future endeavors. Years of some of the most creative and daring efforts in international labor activism had left no political or institutional continuity on which to capitalize. Only a handful continued to work within Peronism, unions, or the foreign service; the vast majority returned to their earlier jobs, retired, or used the savings from a decade of good salaries to start small businesses. Their erasure from history was aided by rejection from both Perón and the Ministry of Foreign Affairs, the latter of which destroyed most of their reports.

ATLAS faced major challenges as it sought to survive without the political sponsorship of Peronism and the financial support of the Argentine government. The organization was unable to promote public policies in specific countries or to coordinate actions of labor movements at a regional level. It never achieved one of its main goals, the training of labor leaders. In the first years, ATLAS lost the membership of the few unions from outside Argentina that had joined, including organizations from Chile, Brazil, and Ecuador. The case of Colombia also revealed the complexity of the region's labor landscape and the contradictory influences of Peronism. In the country of Jorge Eliécer Gaitán, the main support for ATLAS was the Confederación Nacional de Trabajadores (CNT), the labor organization created under the influence of the dictator Gustavo Rojas Pinilla. But the CNT acquired more autonomy over time and confronted the government, following—according to its leaders— the model of the Argentine CGT. The CNT's final break with the government came when the Catholic Church blamed them for fostering conflicts and accused them of being "Peronist and Communist."[86]

In the beginning, ATLAS was instrumental to the victory of some local struggles: it successfully supported strikes of mine workers in Nicaragua, oil workers in Venezuela, and workers at the U.S.-owned plantations in Costa Rica. Aside from the logistical or financial help, the simple reference to Peronism was enough to give unions leverage and to trigger employer concern. Romualdi visited Nicaragua and, in describing the situation to Jay Lovestone, said that "the labor movement there is in an uproar on account of the situation in the gold mine fields where one American firm has fired all the Executive Board members of a newly organized union and a Canadian firm has fired close to three hundred workers." Romualdi admitted that "there is real starvation among these fired miners, most of them affected by silicosis or tuberculosis" and that his actions were limited because "Communists and Peronists are exploiting this situation to fan the flames of anti-Americanism."[87] These were all countries in which Peronism had established a fluid relationship with the government (Somoza in Nicaragua, Pérez Jiménez in Venezuela, and Blanco in Costa Rica), a fact that helps to explain ATLAS's effectiveness in reaching deals that favored unions.[88] In both Argentina and those countries, these deals were celebrated as early signs of ATLAS's potential.[89]

After Perón was ousted, the labor organization limited its actions to publishing a monthly bulletin with a panoramic view of the regional labor movement and expressing occasional support for strikes and workers' demands. But even these small-scale actions brought to life the complex tensions within Peronism and the space that labor activism tried to build within the movement. In a bulletin published in Lima in early 1957, ATLAS printed a strong document supporting the textile workers on strike in the Dominican Republic, denouncing the Trujillo dictatorship's repression and its curtailment of social rights. Exiled in Caracas under the protection of Pérez Jiménez, Perón reacted with fury against ATLAS's position. He scolded Garone in unambiguous terms: "What do we win by attacking anybody uselessly and brutally, let alone a person who likes us and one that enjoys the affection and support of workers in his country?" Perón lectured ATLAS on the new terms: "Our worst enemies are precisely those who now attack Trujillo . . . a campaign led by the Inter American Press Society, CIOSL and ORIT." He went even further and explained the regional implications: "I had already committed myself with Trujillo . . . in order to get help for ATLAS. How do I go now to brother García [minister of labor for Pérez Jiménez] to ask him for their support if he knows that any day we can publish slander against the President of Venezuela."[90] Perón did not stop there. Determined to fix the problem, he forced ATLAS to get in touch with the Dominican embassies in the region and explain to them that the article had been the product of communist sabotage that had infiltrated ATLAS.[91]

The movement that only a decade earlier had been attacked by the United States for helping to organize an armed insurrection against Trujillo from Cuba, was now told by its leader to heel to its former foe. The cycle of this specific form of labor activism had ended with a complete reversal.

CONCLUSION. **BRANDING MASS POLITICS IN THE AMERICAS**

Torcuato Di Tella Jr.'s meeting with his advisor at the beginning of the semester at Columbia University changed his life. The son of an Argentine industrialist, Di Tella had seen the worker attachés agitating the stevedores at the docks of Brazil while on their way to Europe in 1948. Now in 1951, as he started a master's degree in sociology, he confessed to his advisor that what he really wanted was to understand Peronism and "to learn how to get rid of it." "Have you read *The Eighteenth Brumaire*?" the advisor asked. Di Tella had not. "Then read it," the advisor replied. Di Tella bought the book right away. For years, the advisor remained close to Di Tella and to the leading Argentine sociologist Gino Germani. His name was Seymour "Marty" Lipset. In the early 1950s, Lipset was starting to draft his early ideas about the political behavior of individuals in democracy. On the basis of these ideas, he would produce some of the most influential works on theories of modernization and American exceptionalism, providing early and central arguments for the emergence of neoconservatism in the United States.[1]

In *The Eighteenth Brumaire of Louis Bonaparte*, Karl Marx analyzed how Napoleon's nephew combined personalism and state power as the head of a heterogeneous alliance of social sectors, whose only common ground was the hope that the leader would represent their conflicting interests. In the shadow of the demagogue, the revolutionary echoes of the 1848 revolutions faded away. Deprived of their capacity to rationally pursue their interests, unorganized workers and peasants lost their autonomy and became mere subjects of the ruler's ambitions. Marx's text informed among his readers (then and later) the notion of ideology as false consciousness. This notion grabbed the attention of Di Tella, who started to write some of the most relevant texts about nation, state, and politics in Latin America. Thus understood, "Bonapartism" became the standard paradigm by which to analyze Peronism. Its pervasive presence in studies of Latin American popular politics reveals its appeal.[2] Under the weight of the notion of Bonapartismo, modernizing discourses (Marxist and others) systematically neglected both the spaces of autonomy that workers built under this leadership and the way organized labor advanced its own project for modern democracy, two elements that could helped to explain the endurance of populist ideals in the region.

The meeting between Di Tella and Lipset occurred at a cultural crossroads that would profoundly shape the understanding of mass politics and social change in Latin America and the United States. It took place as part of a vast hemispheric exchange of theories, experiences, and recommendations. In an unprecedented migration, Latin American scholars began to arrive in large numbers at U.S. universities. For Lipset and for other scholars in the study of social conflict and democracy, the 1940s and 1950s were decades of transition from their Marxist training toward a new formulation of conservatism. In Marxist discussions of ideology and in its comprehensive understanding of social systems, Lipset found a useful form of structural functionalism. But the sociologist departed from any understanding of change and rupture that these views had opened; instead, he focused on rooting the exceptionalism of the American experience in the supposed self-regulatory capacity of modern democracy, which aimed for social inclusion but prevented a subjugation of the individual to the interests of the masses. Toward the end of World War II, reflections like those of Di Tella and Lipset helped to build a cultural realm that was defined by concern over the challenges that the participation of workers in politics and their pursuit of political rights posed to the transition to a modern industrialized world.

In these conversations, concerns about Peronism became a crucial component of Cold War conceptualizations of the threat faced by modern democracies and free societies. Serafino Romualdi's early description of communism and Peronism as "totalitarian brands" foreshadowed the terminology and conceptual frameworks of the decades to come. The study of Latin American nationalist movements was a crucial input to those debates. Anchored in theories of modernization like Lipset's and crowd psychology, scholars in Argentina and elsewhere developed a robust, original theoretical corpus about what would be later called Latin American populism. With a grim diagnosis of popular politics, sociologists worldwide understood strongmen in Latin America and postcolonial movements in Africa as forms of the oedipal insecurity of the masses, a malady that could be cured only after a painful process of growing up.[3] In the United States, these movements, and Peronism in particular, were more than a foreign example of the risks of mass politics; they offered an opportunity to compare Latin America with the United States's complex history of massive political participation and with domestic reflections about labor, individuals, and collective action, as well as with the challenges ahead.

Well-funded and legitimated in the public sphere by their scientific methods and institutions, Cold War social scientists provided central concepts for those discussions. Scholars applied the themes that characterized the fight against communism to the descriptions of Latin American nationalism. They were not alone in this exercise. In fact, the effort to compare and contrast the risks that demagogues posed for individual liberty was a hemispheric cultural endeavor. While Romualdi, Spruille Braden, and others brought their descriptions of Peronism to the United States, Latin American leaders also offered powerful insights. President Rómulo Betancourt, of Venezuela, an early, progressive ally of the United States, gave U.S. officials an appealing image of their common concerns, characterizing "Perón as a Latin Huey Long [the late governor of Louisiana] in his rousing abilities and fascistic tendencies, without the latter's saving grace of really having some interest in the common man."[4] Betancourt knew what parallels would catch the attention of his U.S. audience. Populism was in the air. With all the horrors of the war in Europe, the Pulitzer Committee awarded the 1946 prize for international reporting to Arnaldo Cortesi, for his faulty stories in the New York Times about the rise of Perón, told as tales of an impending inferno. The following year, the fiction Pulitzer went to Robert Penn Warren for All the King's Men, the novel loosely inspired by the political career of Huey Long ("the American Perón," if we reverse Betancourt's analogy). "Your need is my justice"—the desperate call of Willie Talos to the multitudes struck a powerful chord among early Cold Warriors and resonated as a threat that had to be addressed if the Cold War were to be won.[5]

In Argentina, the image of a strong labor movement coopted by the state, one which swept away established liberal forms of regulating conflicts in the name of the postponed rights of the majority, also provided a tempting interpretative framework. After Perón was ousted, in 1955, Germani founded the first modern sociology program in Argentina and translated into Spanish the work of Talcott Parsons and other studies from functionalist schools. He and Di Tella exchanged opinions and correspondence with Lipset and other scholars in the United States. They travelled to U.S. universities during the 1960s and presented the case that people of diverse political backgrounds but with a common concern about Latin America wanted to hear. With fascism as a template, Germani analyzed what was specific and different in Peronism— material transformations, social alignments, reactions of elites, and economic structures. In his correspondence with Lipset, who observed that fascism was supported by the upper classes and Perón by the proletariat, Germani went further and developed a prodigious theoretical edifice with the specificities of Peronism at its core. His groundbreaking work was the blueprint for the epistemological and institutional foundation of Argentine sociology, conceiving of Peronism as a unique political phenomenon: unlike fascism, which had exploited the uncertainty of the middle classes, Peronism had both recognized and fulfilled the basic rights of Argentine workers in an authoritarian fashion.[6] Yet as fascism faded and the Cold War settled in, concerns shifted toward the "extremist policies" that Peronism shared with communism.[7] In epistolary exchanges over decades, Lipset, Germani, and other social scientists began an ongoing set of periodic reclassifications of Peronism, which included (but was not limited to) "leftist extremism," "Fascism from the left," "working class authoritarianism," "lower class Fascism," and at its most comprehensive, "anti-capitalist populist nationalism that attracts the lower strata as well as the army."[8] As Lipset tried to clarify in the late 1960s, summing up the place of Peronism in the Cold War social sciences, "Working-class authoritarianism is Communism, and to a lesser extent Peronism."[9]

With the increasing political radicalization in Latin America during the 1950s and 1960s, charismatic leaders continued to challenge established social norms and entire political systems. Now that Jorge Eliécer Gaitán was dead and Perón gone, there was Fidel Castro. In the United States, the resilience of this experience south of the border triggered a renewed interest in the figure of the Latin American caudillo. In 1960, the Hafner Library of Classics published a new edition of *Facundo: Civilization and Barbarism* (1845), Domingo Faustino Sarmiento's monumental tale of big and small tyrants obstructing the consolidation of the national state. The new edition of this book, which had founded the narrative of the modern liberal state in Latin America, followed the original English translation of the book, a personal endeavor of Mary Peabody Mann, who had published it in 1868, in the aftermath of the Civil

War. The wife of Horace Mann, the progressive educational reformer from Massachusetts, Mary Mann befriended Sarmiento during his first visit to the United States in 1848. She became interested in the description of popular politics in the southern continent and tried to fathom how those caudillos had embraced a form of republicanism that offered a robust resistance to liberal reforms in Latin America. It was, and still is, a perplexing and circular social construct. By conceiving of *caudillismo* as an idealized form of bravery and political backwardness and obsessively focusing on the authoritarian personalism of caudillos, Sarmiento's narrative obscured the democratizing dynamics that underpinned the caudillos' leadership. So when popular support to a caudillo proved resilient and lasting, the answer could only be the assumed political backwardness of their followers.

The radicalization of Latin American politics in the 1960s and 1970s did not diminish the interest that in the United States had coalesced around personalism, caudillismo, and the forces mobilized around it. Even amid the rise of Marxist guerrilla groups and much more radical organizations in Argentina and the rest of the region, the Argentine labor movement and its engagement with democratic politics continued to inspire conservative reactions to the effects of mass mobilizations in democracy. By the late 1960s, Jeane Kirkpatrick, then a young political scientist at Columbia University, rehearsed arguments molded in the functionalist jargon. In her 1968 dissertation about Peronism, Kirkpatrick found that "for the student of non-democratic regimes, Latin America is an especially fruitful scene for research" in order to understand those "political systems that are neither democratic nor totalitarian." In line with the ideas with which Lipset had incorporated Peronism into his reflections about mass politics fifteen years earlier, Kirkpatrick described Peronism in new terms: "a contemporary Caesarist movement in a technologically advanced society." And in line with the concerns of U.S. social reformers, she warned that "the Peronist period [1945–1955] strengthened both egalitarian and autocratic trends in Argentine society."[10] Still a young scholar, she began at that time a political and intellectual transformation similar to the one Braden had undergone twenty years earlier, reflecting on the risks that mass politics presented for modern democracy. With Latin America and Peronism at the center of this reflection, Kirkpatrick undertook a slow shift from the fervent democratic liberalism of her youth to the no-less fervent neoconservative faith she would expound in the 1980s.

Braden, having become the single most important U.S. official voice against Peronism, turned his attention to domestic politics. Now cities and mobs within the United States expressed the threats to social peace that populism had sym-bolized in Latin America. He retired from the State Department in 1948, bit-terly angry at a foreign policy that he perceived as complacent about the real enemies of the United States.[11] By 1950, he had become the founder and chairman of the New York City Anti-Crime Committee, a conservative lobby group that sponsored anti-crime policies and denounced the supposed strong ties between organized crime and communism. Mafia power, with its foreign origins and grip on the poor in urban centers, emerged as an apparent enabler of communist infiltration. Frank Sinatra was, still, the deceptive beauty of the fifth column.[12] In a letter to Governor Thomas E. Dewey, of New York, Braden described longshoremen as "decent, God-fearing and patriotic citizens who have repeatedly demonstrated their abhorrence of Communism," hostages of the "mobsters who dominate the waterfront of the Port of New York [and who] are the underlying cause of the present strike." A central purpose of Braden's committee was to denounce the connection between the domestic deterioration of liberal democracy and the Cold War. "To permit the gang-sters and venal politicians who now infest the waterfront to continue their foul conspiracy is to help Stalin play his game," the letter added.[13] Two years before Elia Kazan released *On the Waterfront*, CBS Radio Network released *The Nation's Nightmare*, a two-part documentary produced and scripted mostly by Braden and the Anti-Crime Committee. Both parts, "The Narcotic Evil" and "Crime on the Waterfront," were successful, fueling (and fueled by) Cold War paranoia about domestic threats, seasoned with urban crime and Mafia my-thology. CBS rescheduled new broadcasts and released the two episodes as a long play, a conservative warning about urban decadence. As if Braden could not escape from the specters that followed him, the cover art of the long play was designed by a twenty-three-year-old, unknown Andy Warhol. The artist had won CBS's open contest for the cover (his first commercial appearance in print) with an entry of two drawings depicting a street fight and a young man injecting himself with a syringe. The design was selected because of "the gritty quality of the style."[14]

Abroad, the specter of popular politics in the form of a manipulated mob embodied in Peronism was presented in parallel with the role of U.S. free-dom fighters as liberators of the oppressed masses. By 1955, the *New York Times* journalist Herbert Matthews, a brand name in the United States, was the subject of *The Matthews Story*. Although it was never aired, the one-episode television show perfected all the commonplaces of Cold War cultural production in the fight against . . . Peronism. Scripted by the State Depart-ment, the show told the story of an American journalist who flew down to

Argentina in the 1940s and turned into a "freedom fighter" with the mission of releasing political activists from "Perón's catacombs' prisons." After the opening credits, the screen showed Perón speaking "impassionedly to a mob" while a voice off-screen recounted: "The Secret Police, the concentration camp, exile, a throttled press. For any and all against Perón—terror. But still, resistance."[15]

No matter how subtle Germani was in his studies, the anxieties generated by the threat of mass politics were laid bare at the center of his work—or so many understood. Perón was overthrown in September 1955—with no assistance from *New York Times* freedom fighters, but certainly with the aid of the U.S. press, under accepted pressure and surveillance by its own Cold War-obsessed government. The new dictatorship proclaimed itself liberal and called Germani to join a commission for the de-Peronization of Argentina.[16] Inspired by the models of de-Nazification in Europe, the military government assumed that Peronism had somehow brainwashed its followers, instilling adherence to a leader and to a form of mobilization on the bases of indoctrination, coercion, and the delivery of immediate benefits from the state. By this logic, expelling Perón from government, breaking the yokes that subjugated workers' minds, and erasing the leader's symbols from the earth's surface would awaken the nation from the collective nightmare of Peronism.

It did not. From 1955 onward, Peronism was banned, and Perón's name was prohibited from mention in the press and, at times, from even being spoken in public. Peronists could not participate in elections, so the weak governments that emerged from them did not last. On 23 September 1973, Argentina again held free democratic elections without proscriptions. After eighteen years that included executions, prohibition, censorship, exile, dissolution of political and labor organizations, and early rehearsals of U.S.-sponsored state terrorism, Perón returned to the presidency with 62 percent of the vote. It was not just a landslide—it was only one percentage point less than he had obtained twenty-one years earlier, in 1951, the last time that the country had (relatively) freely elected its president. The effects of two decades of de-Peronization inspired by the thinking of Cold War social sciences were, to put it mildly, as limited as they were tragic.

The Not-So-Cold War for Social Reform

Of course, neither the region nor the country to which Perón returned were the same as they had been in 1951. Perón's ouster marked the exhaustion of populist projects for social reform. He was one of the few leaders from the 1945–1948 democratic spring who survived into the cold winter that followed, but his survival came at the cost of an increasing conflict with the ideas and values that had made the movement that bore his name so powerful. In evident tension with the progress of Argentine labor, Perón had evolved into a caricature of the caricature that liberals made of Latin American authoritarian caudillos. The recalcitrant conservatism of his enemies helped save Perón from himself, but more generally, his act was just one more appalling evidence of the serious limitations faced by any strategy based on gradual change and the progressive redistribution of resources.

Almost everywhere else, reformist leaders had been eliminated on their way to power or ousted when elected to office. In all cases, elites led a conservative backlash that counted on U.S. support, either in the form of active military interventions and political pressure or tacit tolerance. The initial liberal instinct to support inclusive social changes and labor-based political movements waned. U.S. labor diplomats evolved from their ambivalence about the need for social reform in Argentina and Bolivia, as they became actively engaged with the U.S. government in sponsoring violent conservative backlashes against Perón in Argentina, Jacobo Arbenz in Guatemala, or Cheddi Jagan in British Guiana.

The dynamic of those years is crucial for understanding the violent history of the second half of the twentieth century. In 1948, the idea that the force required for drastic changes in social structures could be channeled through democratic systems—as the worker attachés argued—started a long but steady decline. And the most remarkable consequence of the declining hopes for democratic change was the growing drive to explore other means of political action. Over the years, the exhaustion of populist paths of social reform along with the eternal deferral of the liberal promises of inclusion left a space open for political radicalization. And nothing symbolized this change more clearly than Fidel Castro's and Ernesto Guevara's 1959 rise to power. The Cuban student and the Argentine doctor, whom the attachés had momentarily drawn close to Peronism, now led the revolution that drew entire generations into the political violence that came to engulf Latin America. The dialectics of history did not stop there. In exile in the Dominican Republic in January 1959, Perón was forced to share the favors of the dictator Rafael Trujillo with Fulgencio Batista, the Cuban dictator whom Castro, originally inspired by Peronism, had just deposed five hundred miles across the Caribbean.[17] The gap between the personal trajectory of the Argentine leader and the hopes he inspired in Latin America had never been wider.

By the time Peronism returned to power in 1973, leftist guerrillas inspired by the Cuban Revolution had tried to achieve more radical changes across the region. This time, they placed a stronger emphasis on aggressively redistributing resources, which included a more forceful and direct challenge to property rights than simply subordinating them to the general principles of common good. In a last, bitter twist, Perón managed to use the enormous power of his labor base and of the Peronist guerrillas to force the 1973 democratic elections and his consequent return to power only to, once in government, encourage the creation of paramilitary death squads to eliminate not only Cuban-style guerrillas but also the progressive political forces that had grown alongside them.

Other ideas of containment ended tragically as well. Attempts to erode the legitimacy of revolutionary strategies and to stymie the regional appeal of the Cuban Revolution by enabling moderate changes were brief and isolated (though not inconsequential). U.S. sponsorship of the Alliance for Progress proved weak and easily fragmented, although funds from the program financed relevant public policies, including aspects of the agrarian reform implemented in Chile. But the ambitious regional program never materialized the broad objectives of modernizing the region's economic and social infrastructure that President John Fitzgerald Kennedy promised when he launched it in 1961. The few housing projects, recreational centers, public buildings, and roads financed by the Alliance for Progress were scattered throughout Latin America and exhibited the limits of the initiative and the magnitude of the pending tasks. But the worst was yet to come. In parallel to the Alliance for Progress, the United States advocated for the National Security Doctrine, under which it offered protection against extrahemispheric communist influences and provided legitimacy, training, and resources to the military so they could repress social conflict within their national borders. Local elites embraced a reloaded conservative backlash in the form of U.S.-sponsored state terrorism, aimed at sweeping away the political violence that previous U.S. interventions had helped to generate. This dynamic ended up overshadowing the reformist aspirations that the Alliance for Progress expressed and set the tone of liberal involvement in Cold War in the region. In the end, if the history of U.S. actions in Latin America has taught us anything, it is that in most cases during this period, U.S. attempts to curb the authoritarian features of social reform ended up undermining social reform wholesale, creating instead conditions of possibility for far more tragically authoritarian options than those it had originally aimed to avoid.

The Afterlife of the Attachés

The outcome of the worker attaché program after 1959 and the trajectory of the activists who were part of it testify to the weaknesses of the initiative and the setbacks for populist labor activism. Even though the position of attaché was not formally terminated, the program was never reactivated. For the most part, the attachés themselves lost any chance of rising to power. As the sociologist José Luis de Imaz has stated, the program never drove the emergence of a new elite.[18] Many former attachés simply went back to the jobs they had held before Perón's rise to power; many others used the savings from their years in the foreign service to open small businesses and stores in their working-class suburbs.

Only one, Eleuterio Cardozo, became a significant labor activist. A member of the meatpacking union, Cardozo was present at the memorable events of 17 October 1945 that lifted Perón to power. Cardozo was instrumental in shaping Peronism's relationships with the Movimiento Nacionalista Revolucionario (MNR) in Bolivia and with Gaitanista forces in Colombia. In 1958, he joined the powerful "62 Organizations"—which, by coincidence, was founded in 1957 at a Buenos Aires restaurant called Les Ambassadeurs—the group of unions that led the labor movement in the negotiations with the state and the business sectors during the eighteen years in which Peronism was banned, while at the same time pushing for the leader's return.[19]

A few other former attachés found their place in the foreign service. César Tronconi, who had brought Fidel Castro close to Peronism, remained in the foreign service, representing Argentina abroad while maintaining contact with unions. In 1973, he talked with Perón about the chances of resuscitating the program of worker attachés, but the leader, who died months later, was in no position to start new initiatives. In 1977, the military dictatorship terminated Tronconi's tenure in the foreign service. Four years later, ill and depressed, Tronconi shot himself inside a telephone booth in front of the shuttered Congress building. It was 1981; for the previous five years, he had been unable to see the nephew who as a child had adored his embellished stories of diplomats and spies. Tronconi's nephew was a member of the leftist guerrilla Ejército Revolucionario del Pueblo and was serving jail time as a political prisoner for having overtaken a military barracks, just like his uncle had tried to do decades earlier.[20]

Others returned to local politics. Like almost all other attachés, León Segovia, the labor activist with whom this book started, was fired from the foreign service at the end of 1955. Segovia remained active within Peronist circles, and in the mid-1960s, he became the mayor of his native town in Las Palmas. But this did not happen through popular elections: The former welder at the sugar mill and representative of the working class abroad was chosen as executive director of the town by the local business chamber. But well after Segovia's death, the town kept providing examples of how Peronist identity served the purposes of grassroots demobilization. By 2013, Las Palmas was one of the thousands of towns benefiting from the soy boom in Argentina. On 23 May of that year, a leading scientist visiting the town was brutally beaten for denouncing the deadly effects of glyphosate, the Monsanto-produced agrochemical that enables the vast expansion of soy production. The thugs were later identified as members of the Peronist Party, which had led Argentina's remarkable economic recovery during the previous decade on the basis of the dramatic expansion of genetically modified soy production.[21]

The Tale of the Perpetual Decline

Over time, the captivating power of the images of populist decline has influenced our understanding of Peronism. In this narrative of declension, we have been eager to see a clear contrast between presumably more lasting policies anchored in institutions and those attached to personalist leaders, and between those policies set in universal values and those set in paternalistic relationships. In his insightful study about consumption under Perón, for example, Eduardo Elena reflected on today's Argentina and how some "landmark projects [from the Peronist era]—the vacation hotels, social assistance facilities, and union-run department stores—have fallen into ruin or been sold off to private investors." "These examples serve as reminders that Peronist-era reforms were mostly transitory and this moment in time was short-lived," he said in a narrative to which most of us could have subscribed.[22] Yet, the author was writing around 2010, between fifty-five and sixty-five years after these examples of Peronist transformations were erected. Whether in themselves or in comparative perspective, these reforms do not seem so short-lived. Give or take one decade, various products of the welfare state in Latin America and the United States, including those of the New Deal, have suffered transformations, a narrowing of their reach, a privatization of what was created as a common good, and the public deinvestment that precedes extinction. It is true that activists like Modesto Alvarez, the attaché in Bolivia who smuggled the MNR leader Silez Suazo in the trunk of his car, did not see in their lifetimes the egalitarian society for which they had fought under Perón's leadership. Alvarez died in 1977, days after his son-in-law, a member of a Peronist guerrilla group, was disappeared by the military dictatorship. He spent his last months at the Hospital Ferroviario, the union-run institution inaugurated by Perón in 1951. Functioning in one of the most imposing buildings of Peronist architecture, the Hospital Ferroviario provided free healthcare for hundreds of thousands of workers until 2000.[23]

Reflections about the intellectual and political contributions of the Peronist era present the same challenges in regard to their depth and scope. Scholars emphasize how universal entitlements and workers' rights largely rested on the personalistic, gift-giving mechanisms of assistance and clientelism. Reflections like these populate most of the historiography about populist politics. And there is a strong reason for that: Peronism emerged as a mighty political force grounded in the power of unions, their relation with the state, and the symbolic ties established with the images of Perón and Evita; in its latest incarnations, Peronism has largely operated on the basis of no less powerful clientelistic networks.[24] But in fundamental respects, this original sin did not erode the effectiveness of these policies and did not shorten their lives or affected the eagerness with which followers requested these services. Rather, what is remarkable about these transformations is how they became part of a deeply engrained idea of universal social rights. They had profound effects on notions of citizenship and civil society and extended well beyond the hierarchies established in the earlier gift-giving gestures and the narrow clientelistic perspective of the later years.[25] It is precisely this transformation that made a labor-based foreign policy suddenly imaginable and politically relevant. As part of his personal political project, Perón proclaimed annual bonus payments, severance payments, and paid vacations—to mention just a few relevant features of the early labor legislation—by executive order during the military government of 1943. These decisions were later turned into law by Congress and presented as a gift from the leader to the working classes. Yet the effects of the welfare state's tools on a more egalitarian distribution of wealth were more radical, extended, and permanent than those of most social reforms in the hemisphere, regardless of whether the reforms were implemented within fully functioning democratic institutions or as part of a liberal sense of universal citizenship. Rather than reaching into alternative temporalities in order to judge the resilience of populist reforms—in which nothing short of Egyptian times seems to offer evidence of an enduring life—the Peronist political experiment helps us to recast ideas of social citizenship, civil society, and government; it should move us to revise notions of popular politics and the extraordinary role of political activism (not only that of labor) in resignifying the sphere of rights.

Instilled at the center of Argentine political identities, social rights implemented under Perón survived more than two decades of political bans. Even the 1976–1983 military dictatorship, which provided one of the bloodiest examples of state terrorism in the region, was cautious when it came to curtailing basic worker benefits. When presented as an indissoluble part of a radical defense of human rights, the notion of social rights became a powerful tool against the dictatorship. After the military regime, the channeling of broader social expectations into political rights was the backbone of a kind of political liberalism. It was on the basis of this political liberalism that Raúl Alfonsín won the presidential elections that put an end to the dictatorship and defeated Peronism for the first time in the history of free democratic elections.[26] It took another Peronist president, in 1989, to lead a vast effort of structural reform that swept away the legacies of the welfare state. When Tulio Halperín Donghi, the leading historian of Argentina, made a powerful and concise description of this process, he insightfully called it "the Long Agony of Peronist Argentina." Clearly, it is the "long" dimension of the agony, rather than the agony itself, that deserves further attention.[27]

In the analysis of the life and actions of the worker attachés, we have seen labor activism's central place in turning populist politics into a strong (albeit problematic) democratic tradition in the Americas. The habits, choices, collective proclamations, and individual decisions of that time built populist worldviews on solid foundations. When the neoliberal reforms of the 1990s led to economic collapse in Argentina, yet another Peronist administration moved back toward earlier visions of populist politics. This return was part of a wave of Latin American governments that recast many of the populist political instruments in a new reality. Ideas that the attachés promoted seven decades ago which seemed forgotten, such as government control over agricultural exports or citizens' watch of domestic prices against business abuses, were revived with new vigor.

Even more remarkably, the highest moment of the attachés activism in Latin America had an unexpected and triumphal comeback. Since 1889, Argentina had used its ties to the British economy to lead a regional bloc against U.S.-led Pan-Americanism. By 1948, the attachés contributed to this aspect of Argentine foreign policy in one of the program's most memorable moments, a brief space in which the interests, ideas, and policies of Peronism aligned. With the inter-American system sponsored by the United States looming on the horizon, these activists from the working-class suburbs of Argentina went to the most remote corners of Latin America to build support for a regional bloc that would reject free-trade and social conservatism and to promote regional cooperation in a program for the industrialization of national economies and the expansion of the welfare state. They were instrumental in bringing together under these ideas the most important revolutionary and reformist movements of twentieth-century Latin America. It did not work. The Organization of American States, created that year, instead reflected and deepened most of the Cold War climate of social containment and conservative backlash.

It took another fifty-seven years for the chance to emerge again. In 2005, all the presidents of the Western Hemisphere met in Argentina in order to discuss the latest aggressive effort by U.S. President George W. Bush to create the Free Trade Area of the Americas (FTAA; in Spanish, Area de Libre Comercio de las Américas, ALCA). A new wave of progressive and populist presidents from Argentina, Bolivia, Brazil, Venezuela, Uruguay, and Ecuador, among other countries, revived almost verbatim the proclamations of 1948. This time, the diversification of global trade and the increasing importance of China gave them the confidence and material support to boldly reject Bush's proposal for the FTAA and discard future discussion of this plan. For the first time in the hemisphere's history, a common front had blocked a U.S. initiative in the strongest possible terms. It was a timely decision: when the financial cataclysm shattered the United States three years later, Latin America, for the first time, was the region least affected by its neighbor's collapse.

The scene of the events of the 2005 summit would not have been imaginable just a decade earlier. In Mar del Plata, a popular resort packed with union-run hotels that debunked the imaginary of the short-lived effects of Peronist welfare, just a few blocks from where Bush still plotted the last efforts to keep the initiative alive, the president of Venezuela, Hugo Chávez, appeared next to the Peronist Nestor Kirchner, of Argentina. His words "ALCA está muerto" were cheered by hundreds of thousands of people gathered in the city's downtown. Not surprisingly, the vast majority of the people, proudly identifying themselves as Peronist activists, were having their first taste of popular foreign policy in a Latin American spirit. Long after the attachés could have expected it, their actions continued to bear fruit with renewed strength and were celebrated by a multitude in the streets of Argentina.

INTRODUCTION

1 About the economy of the United States during the 2000s and the conceptual struggles to define the Great Recession, see Eichengreen, *Hall of Mirrors*.

2 *Rush Limbaugh Show*, radio program, 30 April 2009, 9:56 A.M.

3 John Paul Rathbone, "Donald Trump Evokes Latin America's Old Style Strongmen," *Financial Times*, 11 August 2016; Alejandro Corbacho and Jorge Streb, "Is Donald Trump a Peronist?," *Latin America Goes Global*, 3 November 2016; David Post, "On Donald Trump and the Rule of Law," *Washington Post*, 29 May 2016.

4 The term *criollo*, like *mestizos*, refers to those described as a mix of indigenous, Spanish, and, in some cases, African origins. In Latin America, *criollo* was the basis for *mestizaje* and the myth of a harmonic assimilation. In Argentina, the basic racial representation asserted that there were no ethnic or racial differences in the country and that Argentina's inhabitants were homogeneously white, laying the foundation for the "myth of the white nation." The rise of Peronism exposed the problems of this representation, giving visibility to a diverse population. See Oscar Chamosa's essay "Criollo and Peronist: The Argentine Folklore Movement during the First Peronism, 1943–1955," 113–14.

5 Interview with Irene and Elizabeth Segovia (daughters of León Segovia), Buenos Aires, 28 July 2012. Perón to León Segovia, 6 December 1946, scrapbook, personal papers of León Segovia.

6 "Perón to First Cohort of Worker Attachés: Speech," Teatro Colón, 19 December 1946, Perón, *Obras Completas*, book 10, vol. 2, 145.

7 As discussed later in this volume, the military dictatorship that ousted Perón in 1955 destroyed parts of the records about the worker attachés, including any systematic record of the labor activists who went through the program. Yet it is possible to establish a precise number by compiling and comparing five main records: the numbers provided in 1964 by the sociologist José Luis de Imaz in his book about Argentines elites (or lack of them), *Those Who Rule*; the lists of worker attachés stationed abroad confiscated at the Presidential Office after the

1955 military coup and available at the archives of the Ministry of Interior; the register of individual appointments and promotions in the yearly balance at the Ministry of Foreign Affairs, available at the Instituto del Servicio Exterior de la Nación (ISEN); the detailed record found among the personal papers of the worker attaché César Tronconi, with the attachés' respective addresses and telephone numbers; and the only article written about the attachés in an Argentine historical journal, written by the local historian Claudio Panella, "Los agregados obreros: Una experiencia inédita de la diplomacia argentina."

8 Chapter 3 discusses the characteristics of the program and of many other similar initiatives. But it is worth mentioning that during the 10 years in which the program existed, 506 labor activists received the diploma of worker attaché by the Argentine Ministry of Foreign Affairs. Some of them served abroad, while some others worked in Buenos Aires at the División Organización Internacional del Trabajo (DOIT) of the Ministry of Foreign Affairs.

9 There is a vast bibliography about the role of U.S. labor diplomats in gathering support for liberal democracy and supporting the noncommunist left across the region. Among others, see Waters and van Goethem, *American Labor's Global Ambassadors*; Kofas, *The Struggle for Legitimacy*; Scipes, *AFL-CIO Secret War against Developing Countries*; Wilford, *The Mighty Wurlitzer*, chap. 3; Busch, *The Political Role of International Trades Unions*; Iber, "Who Will Impose Democracy?" Several works focus on the role of U.S. labor diplomats in specific countries. They are analyzed in different chapters of this book.

10 For the larger transformations in postwar U.S. liberalism and the connections between domestic and foreign concerns, see Kleinman, *A World of Hope, a World of Fear*.

11 George Kennan, the Long Telegram, 22 February 1946, box 163, folder 45, Public Policy Papers, George F. Kennan Papers 1871–2005, Mudd Manuscript Library, Department of Rare Books and Special Collections, Princeton University (hereafter GKP). The Long Telegram, discussed later in the book, states that the "strong possibilities of opposition to Western centers of power" came from "such widely separated points as Germany, Argentina, Middle Eastern countries, etc." Kennan sent the telegram, a blueprint for Cold War Containment, from Moscow to Washington just two days before Perón won the presidential elections.

12 Dorn, *Peronist and New Dealers*, 113.

13 Alexander, "Labor and Inter-American Relations," 51.

14 Walcher, "Reforming Latin American Labor"; for a discussion of the historical evolution of Latin American notions of national sovereignty and social rights, Grandin, "The Liberal Traditions in the Americas."

15 There is abundant bibliography about the idea of Argentine exceptionality and its projection abroad. Lanús, *Aquel apogeo*; Escudé, *La Argentina vs. las grandes potencias*; Yankelevich, *La diplomacia imaginaria*.

16 Scholars have long discussed the material and symbolic exchanges among Perón, the state, and workers in order to explain the rise (and endurance) of

Peronism. Among the classic and more influential works discussed since the rise of Peronism, see Gino Germani, *Política y sociedad en una época de transición*; Portantiero and Murmis, *Estudios sobre los orígenes del peronismo*; Auyero, *Poor People's Politics*.

17 For a meticulous study of the Partido Peronista Femenino, see Barry, *Evita Capitana*. Bianchi and Sanchis offered a comprehensive selection of women's memories in their collection of oral interviews, *El Partido Peronista Femenino*.

18 Labor activism has been the center of several studies about Peronism, the most influential being Daniel James's classic history of activism after Perón's ousting. James, *Resistance and Integration*.

19 Though not focused exclusively on the relation between labor activism and foreign affairs, one central contribution to this mostly unexplored field is Raanan Rein's insightful biography of Juan Atilio Bramuglia, Perón's first foreign minister. Rein, *Juan Atilio Bramuglia*. See also Panella, "Los agregados obreros," 42; Zanatta, "Perón y el espejismo del bloque latino," 7.

20 Most of these studies on social history take up from E. P. Thompson's groundbreaking work *The Origins of the English Working Class*. Thompson and others wrote in the context of a post-Stalinist strong revision of approaches that emphasized the economic causes of class consciousness. His work and those of others at the time questioned a philosophy of history intrinsic to the process of class formation.

21 Montgomery, *The Fall of the House of Labor*, 7–9.

22 In the late 1980s, historian Barbara Weinstein discussed the transformations produced by the (then) "new Latin American labor history," arguing that rather than discarding structuralist approaches, what labor historians had done was "to make clear that 'structures' cannot be incorporated in any way that is autonomous from the realm of human experience." For Weinstein, "by privileging experience over structure, they are returning Latin American labor studies to the field of history." This book is greatly influenced by this shift in labor studies (and Weinstein's interpretation of it) produced by the works of, among others, Daniel James, Peter Winn, John French and Charles Bergquist. Weinstein, "The New Latin American Labor History," 26.

23 I follow here Karush and Chamosa's discussion about Peronism as an object of cultural inquiry, in the introduction of *The New Cultural History of Peronism*. For a general discussion of Gramsci's ideas and influence in Latin America, see Aricó, *La cola del diablo*. For Gramsci's legacy in Argentina, see Burgos, *Los Gramscianos argentinos*.

24 For an interesting discussion of the political, non-economic concerns of Friedrick Hayek's work, see Corey Robin, "Nietzsche's Marginal Children: On Friedrich Hayek," *Nation*, 13 May 2013.

25 The Tercera Posición, a key tenet of the Peronist idea of an alternative to communism and liberalism, both domestically and in Argentina, was officially announced in 1947. More than a geopolitical stance, the Tercera Posición recovered the social teachings of the Catholic Church from the encyclicals *Quadragesimo*

Anno and *Rerum Novarum*, calling for a regulation of the excesses of capital and labor in defense of the common good. The French religious philosopher Jacques Maritain used the expression "Third Position" in the 1920s. See Dunaway, *Jacques Maritain*.

26 James, *Resistance and Integration*, 34.

27 In the cases of Bolivia, Brazil, and Chile, for example, the competing alternatives for organized labor were always more diverse than in Argentina until 1955. For an overview, see Godio, *Historia del movimiento obrero latinoamericano*. In studying land demands by communal indigenous leaders to the 1952 Bolivian revolutionary government, Carmen Soliz persuasively argues that Bolivian nationalism, as embraced by the Movimiento Nacionalista Revolucionario (MNR) was also flexible enough as to contain and represent different agendas within its revolutionary rhetoric. Soliz, "'Land to Its Original Owners.'"

28 Mackinnon, *Los años formativos del Partido Peronista*.

29 I follow here, and develop later in this volume, William Roseberry's notion of "language of contention." Roseberry, "Hegemony and the Language of Contention."

30 Among the most significant contributions of these new studies are Healey, *The Ruins of the New Argentina*; Chamosa, *The Argentine Folklore Movement*; Salomón, *El Peronismo en clave rural y local*; Elena, *Dignifying Argentina*; Milanesio, *Workers Go Shopping in Argentina*; Pastoriza, *La conquista de las vacaciones*.

31 In addition to Auyero's *Poor People's Politics*, see also, more recently, Stokes, Dunning, Nazareno, and Brusco, *Brokers, Voters, and Clientelism*; Hilgers, *Clientelism in Everyday Latin American Politics*.

32 As an example of this historical approach during the twentieth century, see Chapman, "The Age of the Caudillos."

33 See de la Fuente, *Children of Facundo*; Chasteen, *Heroes on Horseback*.

34 From different fields and perspectives, Gino Germani, Ernesto Laclau, and Alan Knight, among others, have produced since the 1950s some of the most influential contributions to the debates about populism in Latin America, its conceptual framework as well as its historical experience. Germani, *Política y sociedad en una época de transición*; Laclau, *Politics and Ideology in Marxist Theory*; Knight, "Populism and Neo-Populism in Latin America, Especially Mexico." For a more recent discussion about the conceptual tensions between democracy, liberalism, and populism, see Gerardo Aboy, "Tensiones entre populismo y democracia liberal," presentation at the Eighth Latin American Congress on Political Science, organized by the Asociación Latinoamericana de Ciencia Política, Pontificia Universidad Católica del Perú, Lima, 22–24 July 2015. More recently, María Esperanza Casullo and Flavia Friedenberg have laid out a theoretical framework for understanding populism in Latin America, defining populist parties as "constructed around the authority and appeal of a charismatic leader, have a much weaker and fluctuating ideological program [than programmatic parties], use clientelism and patronage to obtain votes, and can rely on a personalized mechanism for recruitment that is largely based on the leader's vertical connec-

tions." Casullo and Friedenberg, "Populist and Programmatic Parties in Latin American Party Systems."

35 Knight, "Populism and Neo-Populism in Latin America, Especially Mexico."

36 Halperín Donghi, *La larga agonía de la Argentina peronista*, 26.

37 I acknowledge the influence of several recent works well beyond labor studies that, implicitly or explicitly, engage with transnational approaches to produce national and regional histories, some of them in relation to aspects of the Cold War in Latin America. Among the most important are Fink, *Workers across the Americas*; Tinsman, *Buying into the Regime*; Iber, *Neither Peace nor Freedom*.

38 Transnational history is (again) on the rise in studies about Latin America in general and labor history in particlar. We only need to see the list of the several panels about transnational history in the 2017 Annual Meeting of the American Historical Association (AHA) to confirm it. Some of them explored a point that is central to this book: a transnational understanding of Latin American nationalism and of left- and right-wing anti-Pan-Americanism. In particular, Herran Avila, "Nationalism, Hispanismo and Anti-Pan-Americanism in Colombia 1934–54," presentation to the panel "Transnational Perspectives on the Making of Twentieth-Century Latin American Nationalisms," American Historical Association, Denver, 6 January 2017.

39 Bender, *A Nation among Nations*, 7.

40 James, *Resistance and Integration*, 38–39.

41 See, for example, Rapoport and Spiguel, *Relaciones tumultuosas*, 287–93.

42 See, for example, Zanatta, *La internacional justicialista*, 179.

43 On the expression of anti-Pan-Americanism in Argentine foreign policy throughout history and its impact in the Western Hemisphere, see Morgenfeld, *Vecinos en conflicto*. For a study of anti-Americanism (in general and in Latin America), see Friedman, *Rethinking Anti-Americanism*, chap. 4.

44 "Un Plan Marshall para América Latina," *Democracia*, 20 February 1948, A1.

45 Adelman, *Sovereignty and Revolution in the Iberian Atlantic*; Grandin, "The Liberal Traditions in the Americas"; for an in-depth discussion about the origins of Latin America as a political identity created in confrontation against the expansion of the United States, see Gobat, "The Invention of Latin America."

46 Grandin, *Fordlandia*, 180.

47 Lipset, *Political Man*, 147–72. On modernization theories and the Cold War, see Gilman, *Mandarins of the Future*, particularly the relationship between modernization theories and U.S. foreign policy, 155–201.

48 Kenworthy, *The Function of the Little-Known Case in Theory Formation*.

49 Hayek, *The Road to Serfdom*, 194–200. Between 1973 and 1979, Hayek publishes the trilogy *Law, Legislation and Liberty*. The subtitle of the second volume is self-explanatory: *The Mirage of Social Justice*. Hayek argued that it was impossible to establish any rational criteria that would provide us with an idea of how much any individual should have of anything. He compared it, mockingly, with the notion of "just price" during the Middle Ages. For a study of Hayek's criticism to social justice, see Plant, "Hayek on Social Justice: A Critique"; Lukes, "Social

Justice: The Hayekian Challenge." For a discussion about the differences between the need of some "safety nets" in society and the notion of "social justice," see Caldwell, "Hayek and Socialism," 1870. Thanks to Sandra Peart for pointing me to sources and readings about Hayek.

50 Spruille Braden, letter to Roderic Crandal, 17 June 1947, box 22, Correspondence General, 1945–1947, Argentina, Spruille Braden Papers 1903–1977, Rare Book and Manuscript Library, Columbia University Library (hereafter sbp).

51 Benjamin, "Painting, Jugendstil, Novelty." Here Benjamin elaborates about Anatole France's criticism of historical discourses.

CHAPTER ONE. In Search of Social Reform

1 The term *oligarchy* has been widely used in politics not only by the Left but also by liberal groups and parties that present themselves as modernizing forces. The term connotes a classification of the dominant economic groups as almost unable to build a hegemonic political project in opposition to modern elites. For a recent discussion of the concept of "oligarchy" in political sciences and its difference from "elites" and its implications for democratic systems, see Winters, *Oligarchy*, 1–39 and 208–74. For an interesting reflection on uses of the word *oligarchy* during the emergence and consolidation of liberal republics in Latin America in the case of Brazil, see Woodard, *A Place in Politics*.

2 Torres, *La Década Infame*. Torres was an early acquaintance of Perón and helped him to write the GOU proclamation.

3 Alexander, *A History of Organized Labor in Argentina*, 19.

4 Gramsci, *Selection from the Prison Notebooks*, 12.

5 With different degrees and in very different political forms, a similar process of industrialization also took place in other countries in Latin America, including Brazil, Chile, Venezuela, Mexico, and Colombia. See Bethell and Roxborough, "The Postwar Conjuncture in Latin America."

6 Weinstein, *For Social Peace in Brazil*, 51.

7 Gerchunoff and Llach, *El ciclo de la ilusión y el desencanto*, 111, 114, and 119. Unless noted, the economic indicators about the 1930–1945 period are taken from this comprehensive study.

8 Rock, *Argentina*, 225. The agreement, of course, was also part of a larger dispute between the United Kingdom and the United States for foreign markets, and it aimed at limiting Argentina from spending the money obtained from British markets in U.S. goods. See Rapoport and Spiguel, *Historia política, económica y social de la Argentina 1880–2000*, chaps. 2 and 3. For a general context of the economic policies in the region during the period, see the introduction to Knight and Drinot, *The Great Depression in Latin America*.

9 The very representation of Roca for Argentina in the agreement did not help to gain domestic public support for it. His father, Julio Roca, was the general who led the Campaña del Desierto, the last and successful attempt to subdue through killing and forced displacements the mainly indigenous resistance to the

expansion of national borders and the incorporation of those lands to the market economy. Julio Roca was later president from 1880–1886 and 1898–1904. For a description of the pact and denunciations of it, see Drosdoff, *El Gobierno de las vacas*.

10 Gerchunoff and Llach, *El ciclo de la ilusión y el desencanto*, 142, 150.

11 Gerchunoff and Llach, *El ciclo de la ilusión y el desencanto*, 140.

12 Llach, "El plan pinedo de 1940."

13 Hora, "The Impact of the Depression on Argentine Society."

14 Tamarin, *The Argentine Labor Movement*, 26.

15 Cochran and Reina, *Entrepreneurship in Argentine Culture*.

16 Di Tella, *Torcuato Di Tella*, 109–11.

17 Pedro Otero, oral interview, 1981, file 1, p. 109, Archivo Histórico del Movimiento Obrero Argentino, Biblioteca Universidad Torcuato Di Tella (hereafter MOA).

18 "De Berisso, a Washington," PowerPoint file made by the Merlo family, personal papers of Oscar Merlo. Unless noted, all copies of Merlo personal papers in possession of the author.

19 Interview with Irene Segovia (daughter of León Segovia), Buenos Aires, 21 July 2012; Dante Fernández, "Las Palmas, Las Malvinas y Perón," *Diario Chaco*, 3 December 2009, 16. On the origins of Ingenio and the Hardy family, see "Las Palmas Sugar Plantation, Argentina," 45, http://www.archive.org/stream /louisianaplante01assogoog#page/n52/mode/2up.

20 Email correspondence with Silvia Maestro (granddaughter of Modesto Alvarez), 7–20 February 2010.

21 Interview with Jorge Tomasini (nephew of César Tronconi), Buenos Aires, 6 July 2012.

22 Tamarin, *The Argentine Labor Movement*, 32; Gerchunoff and Llach, *El ciclo de la ilusión y el desencanto*, 150.

23 Verbitsky, *Villa miseria también es América*.

24 In this section I review the ideas of Argentine nationalism in the 1930s, emphasizing the varieties of corporatist thought and the different articulation between ideas and political actions, and between the domestic debates and global conflicts of the time performed by members of Argentine nationalism. For a detailed study of nationalism in Argentine politics during the 1930s, see Halperín Donghi, *Historia contemporánea de América Latina*; Zanatta, *Del estado liberal a la nación católica*; Devoto, *Nacionalismo, fascismo y tradicionalismo en la Argentina moderna*; Finchelstein, *Fascismo, liturgia e imaginario*; Goldwert, *Democracy, Militarism and Nationalism in Argentina*.

25 Zanatta, *Perón y el mito de la nación católica*, 12–16.

26 The revival of the myth of the Hispanic race had various political and cultural expressions throughout Latin America around and after the time of the release of José Enrique Rodó's *Ariel*. Classic examples range from the philosophical essay *La evolución sociológica argentina: de la barbarie al imperialismo* (1910) by the Argentine intellectual José Ingenieros, to the quintessential Latin American novel *Doña Bárbara* (1929) by Rómulo Gallegos, the Venezuelan novelist who later

became president as part of the region's postwar democratic opening, as well as one of the first victims of the backlash that followed.

27 Zanatta, *Perón y el mito de la nación católica*, 197.

28 Zanatta, *Perón y el mito de la nación católica*, 212.

29 Zanatta, *Perón y el mito de la nación católica*, 212; Drinot, *The Allure of Labor*, 22.

30 Zanatta, *Perón y el mito de la nación católica*, 114.

31 Zanatta, *Perón y el Mito de la nación católica*, 210.

32 About the ideological and political domestic struggles reinforced by the Spanish Civil War, see Quijada, *Aires de república, aires de cruzada*. About the way in which these struggles took shape in the diplomatic sphere, see Figallo, *La Argentina ante la Guerra Civil Española*. For an analysis of the economic interests implicated in the Argentine position toward the conflict, see Muchnik, *Gallo rojo, gallo negro*. For an updated and useful overview of the entire process, see Casas, "La Guerra Civil Española y la sociedad política argentina en el marco de la ayuda a la república (1936–1941)."

33 Ochoa de Eguileor, *Memoria de un ciudadano ilustre*, 19.

34 Pedro Otero, oral interview, 1981, file 1, p. 101, MOA; Conde Magdaleno, *¿Por que huyen en baúles los asilados españoles en la U.R.S.S.?*, p 2; Godio, *El movimiento obrero argentino*.

35 Chávez, *Perón y el justicialismo*.

36 Fernández Bengoechea, *Carlos Saavedra Lamas*, 29.

37 Halperín Donghi, *Una nación para el desierto argentino*.

38 Rodó, *Ariel*.

39 Darío, *Prosa política (Las repúblicas americanas)*, 3, cited in Max Paul Friedman, "Argentina's Transnational Coalition-Building during the U.S. Rise to Empire: 'Soft Balancing' avant la Lettre," paper presented at *American (Inter) Dependencies: New Perspectives on Capitalism and Empire, 1898–1959*, New York University, 2 and 4 April 2014.

40 Ingenieros, *La evolución sociológica*; Ingenieros, *Las direcciones filosóficas de la cultura argentina*. Like many other intellectuals of the time, Ingenieros incorporated some ideas of European positivism as part of a complex background that influenced progressive and conservative projects alike. For an analysis of Ingenieros's work and its evolution, see Terán, "José Ingenieros o la voluntad de saber."

41 Lanús, *Aquel apogeo*, 194–96. The Argentine diplomat quoted by Lanús is Jorge Reyes, minister to Havana, Cuba.

42 On the mediation efforts, the connections between Argentine foreign officers and positivist thinking about Mexico, and the different evaluations of the ABC actions, see Yankelevich, *La diplomacia imaginaria*; Fernández Bengoechea, *Carlos Saavedra Lamas*; Lanús, *Aquel apogeo*, 194.

43 For a recent and comprehensive description of Argentine foreign policy and Pan-Americanism, see the introduction to Morgenfeld, *Vecinos en conflicto*.

44 For a description of the increasing economic presence of Argentina in Paraguay during the twentieth century, see Pereira Fiorilo, *Historia secreta de la Guerra del Chaco*.

45 About the region's embrace of arbitration and the role of Argentina in advancing this concept in the Western Hemisphere, see Max Paul Friedman, "Argentina's Transnational Coalition-Building during the U.S. Rise to Empire: 'Soft Balancing' Avant la Lettre," paper presented at American (Inter) Dependencies: New Perspectives on Capitalism and Empire, 1898–1959, New York University, 2 and 4 April 2014, pp. 8–9.

46 Fernández Bengoechea, *Carlos Saavedra Lamas*, 37–60.

47 Braden, *Diplomats and Demagogues*, 154. Braden was actually rephrasing an expression made by Brazilian diplomat José de Paula Rodrígues Alves, who had also clashed with Saavedra Lamas; the diplomat said that awarding the Nobel Prize to the Argentine was "actually an incentive to war: people were encouraged to promote hostilities in order to win the prize by making peace." "Un diplomático muy especial," ABC Color, Asunción, Paraguay, 6 January 2008. http://www.abc.com.py/edicion-impresa/suplementos/abc-revista/un-diplomatico-muy-especial-1035503.html.

48 Zanatta, *Del estado liberal a la nación católica*, 210–11.

49 About the place of Barrio Butteler in the origins of affordable housing in Argentina, see Dunowicz et al., *90 años de vivienda social en la ciudad de Buenos Aires*.

50 Fernández Bengoechea, *Carlos Saavedra Lamas*, 27–29. About Argentina at ILO, see Godio, *Historia del movimiento obrero latinoamericano*, vol. 2, *Nacionalismo y comunismo (1918–1930)*.

51 Fernández Bengochea, *Carlos Saavedra Lamas*, 66.

52 On the relation between organized labor and the state during and after the Porfiriato in Mexico, see Knight, *The Mexican Revolution*, vol. 1; Carr, *Organised Labour and the Mexican Revolution*. On Brazil, see Woodard, *A Place in Politics*.

53 Juan Carlos Torre, "¿Qué hubiera ocurrido si el 17 de octubre hubiese fracasado." In Torre's fictional essay, Perón retired until 1952, when he finally won the presidency, only to be ousted by a military coup in 1955.

54 This view of Perón as an aberration is later expressed more clearly in both Marxist and functionalist studies during the 1950s and 1960s, mostly but not only in the United States. For an influential example, see Lipset, *Political Man*.

55 Seymour Martin Lipset made an exhaustive categorization of the different forms in which mass politics could deviate from democratic paths and into totalitarian options, including Peronism among them. I will discuss the impact of his ideas later in this book. Lipset, *Political Man*, 173–76.

56 Nállim, *Transformations and Crisis of Liberalism in Argentina*, 160–65. Nállim makes a comprehensive analysis of the relation between World War II and the ideological and political development of Argentine liberalism and its dynamic relation with nationalism.

57 Juan Carlos Torre, "Sobre los orígenes del peronismo"; Luna, *El 45*.

58 The descriptions of this period are many and varied in their scope and focus. Among the most comprehensive and influential are Altamirano, *Bajo el signo de las masas*; Torre, *La vieja guardia sindical y Perón*; Zanatta, *Perón y el mito de la nación católica*; Luna, *El 45*.

59 This is what the scholar Juan Carlos Torre calls the "sobrerepresentación del movimiento obrero organizado," identifying it as an intrinsic characteristic of Peronism. I will discuss this category later in this book. Torre, *La vieja guardia sindical y Perón.*

60 Adelman, "State and Labour in Argentina."

61 Torre, *La vieja guardia syndical y Perón*, 27.

62 Healey, *The Ruins of the New Argentina*, 292.

63 Weinstein, *For Social Peace in Brazil*, 58.

64 Interview with Irene Segovia (daughter of León Segovia), Buenos Aires, 21 July 2012.

65 "Emotiva Despedida al Embajador Braden," in *La Prensa*, 29 August 1945. Saavedra Lamas had also defended Braden's wife during a public incident with Peronist supporters and had led the Marcha de la Constitución y la Libertad, a massive rally by liberal and socialist forces that had obtained Braden's support. Luna, *El 45*, 141, 338–39; Richard D. McKinzie, *Oral History Interview with John M. Cabot*, Massachusetts, 18 July 1973, Harry S. Truman Library and Museum website, http://www.trumanlibrary.org/oralhist/cabotjm.htm.

CHAPTER TWO. "The Argentine Problem"

1 Cable 9103, Policy Respecting Dictatorships and Disreputable Governments, Havana, 5 April 1945, p. 2, box 35, "Dictatorships and Disreputable Governments" folder, Spruille Braden Papers 1903–1977, Rare Book and Manuscript Library, Columbia University (hereafter SBP). About the importance of this document in U.S. policy toward Latin America, see Wood, *The Dismantling of the Good Neighbor Policy*, 155; Schmitz, *Thank God They're on Our Side*, 125–44.

2 State Department to Certain American Missions, Instructions Ref: Policy Respecting Dictatorships and Disreputable Governments, Washington, 28 May 1945, box 35, "Dictatorships and Disreputable Governments" folder, SBP.

3 Spruille Braden, Diplomats and Demagogues, pp. 1, 8 and 20, "Spruille Braden Bio.," box 7, "Diplomatic Correspondence, 1941" folder, SBP.

4 Spruille Braden to Woodin, 21 August 1933, box 35, "Ambassadorship 1933" folder, SBP; Woodin to Braden, 28 August 1933, box 35, "Ambassadorship 1933" folder, SBP.

5 Instructions to the Delegates to the Seventh International Conference of American States, Montevideo, Uruguay, pp. 122–24, box 32, SBP.

6 William Braden to Spruille Braden, 13 October, 1939, 28 May 1940, 4 December 1940, 11 March 1939, and 23 August 1939, box 8, "Correspondence, Personal" folder, SBP.

7 Blair Stewart to Braden, 29 July 1942, box 8, "Correspondence, Diplomatic 1942" folder, SBP.

8 Spruille Braden to Department, cable 984, Havana, 6 November 1944, box 35, "Argentina-General, 1944–1945" folder, SBP.

9 For an influential example contemporary to Braden's reflections during the 1930s and 1940s, see Chapman, "The Age of the Caudillos."

10 "Notes on Disreputable Government," notes for Cuba, January 1945, handwriting, box 36, "Cuba" folder, SBP.

11 Spruille Braden, Agenda for Washington, January 1945, box 14, "Correspondence, Diplomatic, 1945 (Cuba)" folder, SBP.

12 Spruille Braden to Ellis Briggs, Buenos Aires, 28 July 1945, no. 35, "Correspondence, Diplomatic, 1945, A-B" folder, SBP. Braden, like many other U.S. diplomats in the postwar period, tended to present his impressions about Latin America, and about populism in particular, within the long and wide intellectual tradition of the Black Legend, which cast a negative light on Spanish legacies in the United States. In some cases, as in George Kennan's writings during the 1950s, this backdrop became in turn the basis for a criticism of U.S. shortcomings, opposing the "savage" and "natural" condition of Latin America against a modern world submerged in consumerism. Latin America, for the U.S. diplomat, "may prove some day to be the last repository and custodian of humane Christian values that men in the European motherland and in North America—overfed, overorganized, and blinded by fear and ambition—have thrown away." Kennan, *Memoirs*, 484.

13 "The Argentine Problem: Memorandum: Statement of the Case, Exhibits I to VI," RG 43, Records of International Conferences, Commissions and Expositions, box 9, entry 696, National Archives and Records Administration of the United States (hereafter NARA).

14 Kleinman, *A World of Hope, a World of Fear*, 187.

15 For an overview, see Morgenfeld, *Vecinos en conflicto*, particularly parts B and C, 153–264.

16 See Sheinin, *Beyond the Ideal*, on the origins of Pan Americanism. Also see Castle, "Leo Stanton Rowe and the Meaning of Pan Americanism," 33–44.

17 Instructions to the delegates to the Seventh International Conference of American States, Montevideo, Uruguay, p. 22, box 32, SBP. For a description of the conflicts between the United States and Argentina during the conference, see Morgenfeld, *Vecinos en conflicto*, 242, 243.

18 For a detailed analysis of Mexico's active advocacy for establishing states' rights and duties in an international economic order that had to correct the unequal economic power and prosperity evidenced in the Western Hemisphere and globally, see Christy Thornton's article on Mexican diplomacy and the emergence of a New International Economic Order (NIEO). Theorizing about what would happen in the 1933 Montevideo Conference, a British diplomat expected (not entirely incorrectly) a competition for the defense of poor countries in which "Argentina has the resources, Mexico the theories." Thornton, "A Mexican International Economic Order?"

19 Instructions to the delegates to the Seventh International Conference of American States, Montevideo, Uruguay, p. 122–24, box 32, SBP.

20 Inman, "Lima Conference and the Totalitarian Issue."

21 Zanatta, "Auge y declinación de la Tercera Posición," 32.

22 Comparisons of Chávez to Perón abound. Though they are beyond the scope of this study, it is interesting to note how the historical conjunctures of both

leaderships, including international relations and the different role of government after World War II and in the twenty-first century, determined different
outcomes. Domestically, above all, Perón was able to produce social and economic transformations of a scale and depth that eluded Chavismo.

23 Even by 1949, International Monetary Fund officials confessed that, four years
after the end of the war, "the tie to bilateral commerce and to non-convertible
currencies is far higher than before the war." Richard Gardner, *Sterling-Dollar
Diplomacy*, 429–31.

24 Daniel James's brief description of this relationship between Peronism and the
New Deal is very clear: "Peronism aspired to be a viable hegemonic alternative for
Argentine capitalism, as promoter of economic development based on the social
and political integration of the working class. In this respect, comparisons of
Peronism with the New Deal policies of Roosevelt and the development of welfare state capitalism in Western Europe after 1945 clearly have merit, in that they
all to varying degrees marked the confirmation of the working class' 'economic
civil rights,' while at the same time confirming, and indeed strengthening, the
continued existence of capitalism." James, *Resistance and Integration*, 39.

25 Ruiz Jiménez, "Peronism and Anti-Imperialism in the Argentine Press," 560.

26 Torres, *La Década Infame*, 113.

27 Perón repeated verbatim the entire part of Roosevelt's Second Inaugural Address, of 20 January 1937, with one slight omission: where Perón quoted Roosevelt in reference to the autocrats, saying, "The legend that they were invincible
has been shattered," Roosevelt's original phrasing was "The legend that they
were invincible—above and beyond the processes of a democracy—has been
shattered." Perón's speech was delivered on 12 February 1946, a few days after it
became public that the U.S. State Department, where Braden was now assistant
secretary for the Western Hemisphere, had published the *Blue Book* denouncing
Perón's complicity with Nazism. Perón's speech was a particularly interesting and
an unusual episode in those intense days, and evidently a very special one for
Perón. Accustomed to improvising—he never read prepared speeches during the
campaign—the Argentine leader not only decided to read from a script, but also
to gather precise information in order to support his denunciation of Braden, who
is mentioned twenty-six times in the speech. For Roosevelt's speech, see *Inaugural
Addresses: From Washington to Obama* (Auckland, Floating Press, 2009), 464–73.
For Perón's discourse of 12 February 1946, see Carlos Altamirano, *Bajo el Signo de
las Masas*, 59–74.

   For the uses of Roosevelt in Perón's campaign, see Ruiz Jiménez, "Per-
onism and Anti-Imperialism in the Argentine Press," 551–71. Regarding how
Perón's speech was prepared and the quick use of the slogan "Braden or Perón,"
see Scenna, "Braden y Perón," 9–30. Scenna recalls how, "shyly, the Unión
Democrática tried another slogan with the name of its presidential candidate:
'Tamborini or Hitler,' forgetting that Hitler was dead and buried under his de-
stroyed Reichstag, whereas Braden was alive and awake at the State Department."
In 1959, with Perón already overthrown by a military coup, Braden admitted in

an interview, "The slogan 'Braden or Perón' was a brilliant maneuver of the ex-dictator." "¡Especial!," 3–8.

28 James, *Resistance and Integration*, 39.

29 Representative examples of these approaches include Rapoport and Spiguel, *Relaciones tumultuosas*; Tulchin and Garland, *Argentina*; Escudé and Cisneros, *Historia general de las relaciones exteriores de la República Argentina*; Dorn, *Peronistas and New Dealers*; Zanatta, "Perón y el espejismo del bloque latino."

30 Letter from Clara Applegate to her parents, 6 July 1943, n.p., personal diary of Clara Applegate. Copy of the diary in possession of the author.

31 Letter from Clara Applegate to her parents, 12 July 1943, p. 9, personal diary of Clara Applegate.

32 Wood, *The Dismantling of the Good Neighbor Policy*, 110. A good friend of Braden, Cabot became critical of the U.S. strategy against Perón, and was able see the strong class component of the anti-Peronist alliance and of U.S. foreign policy.

33 Cabot to Byrnes, 19 October 1945, in Stauffer and Wright, *Foreign Relations of the United States, 1945*, 286.

34 Report from Robert Alexander, Montevideo, 19 August 1946, box 1, folder 2, Serafino Romualdi Papers, Kheel Center for Labor-Management Documentation and Archives, Cornell University Library (hereafter SRP). See also the preface to Alexander, *A History of Organized Labor in Argentina*. There is an extensive correspondence between Alexander and Romualdi, Spruille Braden, and Jay Lovestone regarding this event. Alexander came to a different and more complex understanding of labor relations and economic modernization in Argentina during the 1930s.

35 Report of the U.S. Labor Delegation to Argentina, 10 March 1947, p. 6., box 32, SBP.

36 Walcher, "Reforming Latin American Labor," 127.

37 John Herling to Serafino Romualdi, Coordinator of Inter American Affairs, 3 April 1944, box 9, folder 7, SRP.

38 Vincent H. Scamporino to Director OSS, 1 August 1945, box 9, folder 7, SRP. There is abundant bibliography about Romualdi, his work with the OSS, and his role in establishing a relation between the U.S. and Latin American labor movements. For a good overview of the main arguments, see the articles in "Part 3: American Labor's Ambassadors in Latin America and the Caribbean," in Waters and van Goethem, *American Labor's Global Ambassadors*, 123–215.

39 On the U.S. labor claim for "democratic consciousness" as a pillar for the social democratic model during the postwar, see Patrick J. Iber's detailed account of U.S. actions in Latin America in general and in the Dominican Republic in particular after the assassination of Rafael Leónidas Trujillo in 1961. Iber, "'Who Will Impose Democracy?'"

40 Serafino Romualdi, "Appendix 1, Genesis of the Trip," in Statement by the Committee on International Labor Relations of the American Federation of Labor, March 1947, box 32, "Argentina-Memorandum to President Truman" folder, SBP.

41 Serafino Romualdi, "Appendix 1, Genesis of the Trip," in Statement by the Committee on International Labor Relations of the American Federation of Labor, March 1947, box 32, "Argentina-Memorandum to President Truman" folder, SBP.

42 Serafino Romualdi to Matthew Woll, "Development in the Labor Movement in Argentina," 19 January 1946, box 1, folder 1, SRP.

43 Braden to Kellogg, 6 March 1946, and "Plan to Invite Latin American Labor Representatives to the Chicago AFL Convention," 12 September 1946, box 9, folder 7, SRP.

44 Braden, *Diplomats and Demagogues*, 340. On the significance of the General Motors strike in U.S. history and in the evolution of political struggle within the labor movement between the AFL and the CIO, see among others Boyle, *The UAW and the Heyday of American Liberalism*, 30.

45 Lichtenstein, "From Corporatism to Collective Bargaining," 122–23.

46 Serafino Romualdi, "Appendix 1, Genesis of the Trip," in Statement by the Committee on International Labor Relations of the American Federation of Labor, March 1947, box 35, "Argentina-Memorandum to President Truman" folder, SBP.

47 Serafino Romualdi to Matthew Woll, "Development in the Labor Movements of Brazil, Argentina, and Ecuador," 4 December 1946, box 1, folder 1, SRP.

48 Serafino Romualdi to Matthew Woll, "Development in the Labor Movements of Brazil, Argentina, and Ecuador," 4 December 1946, box 1, folder 1, SRP.

49 Serafino Romualdi, "Appendix D," "Genesis of the Trip," in Statement by the Committee on International Labor Relations of the American Federation of Labor, March 1947, box 35, "Argentina-Memorandum to President Truman" folder, SBP.

50 Serafino Romualdi, "Appendix D," "Genesis of the Trip," in Statement by the Committee on International Labor Relations of the American Federation of Labor, March 1947, box 35, "Argentina-Memorandum to President Truman" folder, SBP.

51 O. D. Ivanissevich to William Green, Washington, 26 August 1946, 1946 Informes, Correspondencia, Archivo de Cancillería, Ministerio de Relaciones Exteriores y Culto, República Argentina (hereafter AC). The invitation was also extended to members of the CIO and the Railway Workers Union.

52 Perón used the affair to diffuse domestic tensions. Many activists, including members of the CGT, had created the Partido Laborista as an organization à la labor party that represented the labor movement *and* supported Perón as part of a larger coalition. Perón, instead, envisioned a party fused with the labor movement under his leadership, with little room for contesting his authority. With Romualdi still in Buenos Aires, Perón accused the *laborista* head of the CGT, Luis Gay, of complicity with the enemy. Within days, Perón had largely purged the leadership of the workers confederation, leaving loyal new members in place. For a detailed account of the Luis Gay episode and the use of the U.S. visit to purge the CGT, see Torre, "La caída de Luis Gay," 80–92.

53 Romualdi, "Labor and Democracy in Latin America."

54 Romualdi, "Labor and Democracy in Latin America," 480.

55 Romualdi, "Labor and Democracy in Latin America," 481.

56 Romualdi, "Labor and Democracy in Latin America," 481.

57 Romualdi, "Labor and Democracy in Latin America," 482.

58 "Perón Stifles Argentine Labor Movement: Regime Resembles Early Stages of Fascism under Mussolini," *Call*, 26 March 1947, 2; "Inside Labor," *New York Post*, 6 October 1947; "AFL Committee Says Perón Controls Argentine Labor," *Chicago Tribune*, 1 June 1947; "Perón Still Riding High: Rebuffed Braden to Quit," *Chicago Daily News*, 4 June 1947, A1; Stanley Ross, "Perón: South American Hitler," Buenos Aires, Associated Press, 14 May 1947.

59 Serafino Romualdi, "Excerpts from Address at Rutgers Labor Institute," 9 June 1947, 2 p.m., box 1, folder 6, SRP.

60 Boyle, *The UAW and the Heyday of American Liberalism*, 32.

61 *America's Town Meeting of the Air*, transcripts, Records of Town Hall, series 3, box 3, Tamiment Library and Robert F. Wagner Labor Archives, New York University Libraries (hereafter TL).

62 Convery Egan, State Department to All Embassies, 16 December 1946; Edward Rowell, *Monthly Labor Report*, no. 22, p. 10, folder RG84 850.4, box 370, NARA; Afonso, "Para Norte-Americano Ver," 165.

63 Juan de Zengotita to the Secretary of State, México, D.F., 30 June 1947, Subject: British Labor Attaché's Views on Activities of Argentine Labor Attachés and on Lombardo Toledano, box 5553, folder 835.5043/6–3047, NARA. Diplomats and English-language media used many different labels to refer to the attachés, including "labor," "union," or simply "*obrero*." For this book, I take from de Zengotita's cable the English translation "worker attachés," as it conveys not only the meaning in Spanish and the Argentine government's intention, but also the apprehension it caused in the United States.

64 George Kennan, the Long Telegram, 22 February 1946, box 163, folder 45, Public Policy Papers, George F. Kennan Papers 1871–2005, Mudd Manuscript Library, Department of Rare Books and Special Collections, Princeton University (hereafter GKP); Kennan, *Memoirs*, 294.

65 The mention of Argentina disappears in the later, polished text published in *Foreign Affairs* under the pseudonym "X." To my knowledge, Kennan's reference to Argentina in this document has not previously been analyzed by scholars working on U.S.-Argentine bilateral relations, the Cold War, or the role of George Kennan. See two of the most comprehensive books about the late diplomat published after his death: Gaddis, *George F. Kennan*; Costigliola, *The Kennan Diaries*.

66 Kennan traveled to Latin America in 1950 and developed an interest in the region. See note 12 in this chapter.

67 Ellis Briggs to George Kennan, Washington, 15 February 1946, box 140, folder 4, GKP. The suggestion is made by an unknown officer, who is referred to in the letter: "One of the officers of this shop sent [the Long Telegram] to me with the attached chit."

68 George Kennan to Ellis Briggs, Moscow, 11 March 1946, box 140, folder 4, GKP.

69 Memorandum from the ambassador to Mr. Berger, 29 June 1945, box 45, SBP.

70　Herbert Matthews, draft of memoirs, pp. 116–18, box 41, "Book: Manuscript—
'A World in Revolution'" folder, Herbert L. Matthews Papers 1909–2002, Rare
Books and Manuscript Library, Columbia University (hereafter HMP).

71　Victor Riesel, "Inside Labor," *New York Post*, 6 October 1947.

72　Serafino Romualdi to Alfredo Fidanza, New York, 29 October 1951, box 6, folder
10, SRP.

73　"Public Attitudes Toward Argentina," memorandum from Paul B. Sheatsley to
Shepard Jones, 17 October 1946, box 35, "A-Argentina" file, "Argentina-General"
folder, 1945, SBP. This was followed by two successive reports about specific cuts
of the national sample. After World War II, social sciences, polls, and statistics
became increasingly important to the decision-making process in the United
States. More than ever before, U.S. foreign officials relied on collecting a wide
range of data and information as means to know other societies and predict
social patterns, cultural preferences, and political orientations. Scholars provided
such information, producing a theoretical corpus that reimagined theories of
modernization and, with a particular focus on Latin America, discussed the
risks that the transition from traditional to modern social relations entail. For
a discussion about modernization theories and their relation with postwar U.S.
foreign policy, see Gilman, *Mandarins of the Future*.

CHAPTER THREE. **Apostles of Social Revolution**

1　Curriculum, Manuel Lobato, Washington, 28 August 1947, RG59, folder
701.5311/8–2847, National Archives and Records, United States (hereafter NARA).
Perón's cards confirming the appointments of the attachés and their destinations
were all identical. I found them among the personal papers of León Segovia
(in the possession of his daughter, Irene Segovia), Eduardo de Antueno (in the
possession of his son, Eduardo de Antueno), and Pedro Conde Magdaleno (in
the possession of his son, Pedro Conde Magdaleno). "Carta a los agregados
obreros," in Pedro Otero, oral interview, file 1, p. 101, Archivo Histórico del
Movimiento Obrero Argentino, Biblioteca Universidad Torcuato Di Tella (hereafter MOA).

2　Mackinnon, *Los años formativos del Partido Peronista*, chap. 2.

3　One of the founding studies of Argentine sociology is José Luis De Imaz's *Los
que mandan*. A main point of de Imaz's work is that Argentina does not have,
properly speaking, elites in terms of a group with some degree of coordination
and shared interests. Therefore the title, *Los que mandan* (*Those Who Rule*), as
distinct from simply "elites." The author follows the trajectory over two decades
of different groups in power, including the worker attachés.

4　There is abundant bibliography about Argentine foreign policy under Peronism.
For the most part, historians have stressed the oscillations between confrontation
and dialogue in relation to the United States as well as the efforts to consolidate
a leadership in Latin America, and they have recently integrated the domestic
dynamic of Peronism into the picture. The fate of the Argentine economy, the

United States's own vacillation between hostilities and appeasement, and the consolidation of the logic of the Cold War in the region are the overarching arguments in these studies. See, among others, Paradiso, *Debates y trayectoria de la política exterior argentina*; Peterson, *Argentina and the United States*.

5 Bethell and Roxborough, "The Postwar Conjuncture in Latin America," 1–32.

6 In *Perón y el mito de la nación católica*, Loris Zanatta analyzes the merging of Argentine Catholicism, military nationalism, and Europan fascism in the origins of Peronism (1943–1946), and interprets the rise of Perón as an "unwanted" effect of these groups' advance over liberal institutions. In *Fascismo, liturgia e imaginario*, Federico Finchelstein traces the long-term history of nationalist ideology and the relation between fascism, Catholicism, and political violence. Regarding the "convivencia" of leftist activists in the origins of Peronism, see Torre, *La vieja guardia syndical y Perón*; Mackinnon, *Los años formativos del Partido Peronista*.

7 Paradiso, *Debates y trayectoria de la política exterior argentina*, 119.

8 Juan Perón to Juan Atilio Bramuglia, Buenos Aires, 25 August 1947, box 30, correspondence with President Perón, Juan Atilio Bramuglia Papers, Hoover Institution Archives, Stanford University (hereafter JABP).

9 Roseberry, "Hegemony and the Language of Contention," 362–63.

10 Appleman Williams, *The Tragedy of American Diplomacy*, 106–18.

11 Lloyd C. Gardner, *Economic Aspects of New Deal Diplomacy*, 190–94.

12 Out of this group, Ricardo Labougle was one of the most prominent names, primarily because of his famous meeting with Adolf Hitler and Hermann Göring in 1939. The Argentine diplomat later reproduced the interview in a twenty-one-page report where he praised different aspects of the Nazi regime, commented at length on his friendship with the higher ranks of the SS, and discussed Hitler's racial ideas. Labougle defended Argentina's decision to distance itself from his hosts and stressed the ideas of miscegenation dominant among Argentine liberals: "I told Himmler that we disagreed with the German policy of maintaining the 'German' nationality by blood. Himmler said: 'All right, but [that is because] the Argentines are not a race; they're a mixture, a nationality.'" Labougle retorted: "Right, we're very satisfied with our mixture.... We're building a strong, defined type, with great conditions and . . . if we were to allow in our country that the sons of German people were educated as Germans and that they kept thinking as such, it would go against our own principles. . . . To clarify Göring's confusion about our country, I reminded him that we were all of European origin. Knowing his admiration for Sweden, I told him: 'We have as many Indians as Sweden has Lapons.'" As did other diplomats with nationalistic backgrounds, Labougle eventually developed a good relationship with the Peronist administration. Ricardo Labougle to Señor Ministro Don José María Cantilo, Buenos Aires, 23 July 1939, box 4254, División Política, Alemania 1939, Archivo de Cancillería, Ministerio de Relaciones Exteriores y Culto, República Argentina (hereafter AC).

13 Luna, *Perón y su tiempo*, 245.

14 Pedro Otero, oral interview, file 1, p. 181, MOA.

15 Pedro Otero, oral interview, file 1, p. 189, MOA. About the relation between Morones and the program of Mexican worker attachés in the 1920s, see Yankelevich, "Imitemos a México," 10.

16 Fascism, important for Perón and for some of his closest advisors, had had a fleeting engagement with a global agenda during the time of the 1933–1935 Fascist International. But the organization was an exclusively Italian project, and mostly directed toward disputing the spiritual authority of German National Socialism. It was organized by a large group of fascist intellectuals, but had no connection with the labor movement in Italy or abroad. The culmination of the project was the Fascist International Conference, organized in 1935 in a luxury hotel in Montreaux, an inconsequential meeting that Michael Arthur Ledeen, a leading historian of fascism, calls "a gigantic hoax." Ledeen, *Universal Fascism*. On the early relation between fascism and unions, see Reonello Rimbotti, *Il fascism di sinistra*. About Peronist international ambitions at large, see Zanatta, *La internacional justicialista*.

17 The anarchist Argentine Regional Workers' Federation had pushed for not participating in hemispheric initiatives that diluted the international dimensions of social conflict. See Godio, *Historia del movimiento obrero latinoamericano*, vol. 1.

18 Conde Magdaleno, *¿Por que huyen en baúles los asilados españoles en la U.R.S.S.?*, "Presentación," 2nd page (unnumbered).

19 Probably one of the earliest cases of a worker's access to power in his capacity *as worker* is that of Alexandre Martin (better known as Alexandre l'Ouvrier, Alexander the Worker), the socialist machinist appointed secretary of Louis Blanc's provisional government after the 1848 revolution. See Merriman, *A History of Modern Europe*, 671–84. For a study of the relation between organized labor and politics in the United States and Europe, see Montgomery, *Citizen Worker*. One core strategy of socialist worker organizations during the nineteenth century was to focus almost exclusively on urban politics. See Stromquist, "Claiming Political Space."

20 Report on the Consular Service by Lord Curzon, Secret, 8 May 1919, CAB 24/5, Dept: Records of the Cabinet Office Series War Cabinet and Cabinet: Memoranda (GT, CP and G War Series), Piece Paper nos. 201–66, pp. 12–13, Foreign Office Papers, National Archives, London (hereafter NA).

21 "The American Federation of Labor Delegation to the Congress," resolution no. 24, 18 January 1921. Informe del Tercer Congreso de la Confederación Obrera Pan Americana. Celebrado en la ciudad de México, del 10 al 18 inclusive, Enero de 1921. In *Reports on the Proceedings of the Congress of the Pan-American Federation of Labor*, p. 170, Littauer Center, Industrial Relations Library, Harvard University. "De Roberto Haberman a General Plutarco Elías Calles, Washington, D.C., Julio 30 de 1921," in Calles, *Correspondencia Personal*, 37–39.

22 Plutarco Elias Calles, "Discurso de apertura de sesiones del Congreso, el 1 de septiembre de 1925, in Yankelevich, "Imitemos a México," 2–3; and Estrada, *Un siglo de relaciones internacionales de México (a través de los mensajes presidenciales)*, 397.

23 Yankelevich, "Imitemos a México," 8.

24 Yankelevich, "Imitemos a México," 14–15.

25 There is an extensive bibliography about the U.S. State Department program of labor attachés, and about AFL and CIO labor diplomats, concerning the projects in general and their specific interventions in Latin America. The studies coincide in describing the program's inception not as an answer to U.S. unions' demands or the government's wish to incorporate them, but as a State Department concern over how to obtain, within the political sphere, more detailed information about (and more capacity to influence) the labor movement abroad. For a detailed study of the labor attaché program, see Fiszman, "The U.S. Labor Attachés." Also useful are the oral interviews with some of the program's early members. See, among others, oral interviews with the first labor attaché Daniel Horowitz (27 May 1994) and with Roger Schrader and Herbert Weiner (18 June 1991), The Foreign Affairs Oral History Collection of the Association for Diplomatic Studies and Training, Call Number: Labor Series, Library of Congress (hereafter LOC).

26 Barnes and Morgan, *The Foreign Service of the United States*, 245.

27 John T. Fishburn, Labor Attaché in Buenos Aires (1943–1944), oral interview by James Shea, July 1991, transcript published by the Association for Diplomatic Studies and Training in *Argentina: Country Reader*, p. 7, http://adst.org/wp-content/uploads/2012/09/Argentina.pdf.

28 Evidence suggests that the role of the attaché was not clearly understood at first within the U.S. State Department. Horowitz mentions how he was treated awkwardly by his colleagues at the U.S. embassy in Chile, only to learn, from the ambassador's mouth, that diplomatic officials had not known what to expect from a labor attaché. What ended up surprising them was that he was a Jew: "It was not part of the culture of that elite organization to accept Jews as normal colleagues." Daniel Horowitz, oral interview, 27 May 1994, p. 7 (LOC).

29 An updated and comprehensive study of U.S. labor diplomacy is the volume edited by Waters and van Goethem, *American Labor's Global Ambassadors*. Its articles cover the deployment of labor diplomats in all regions of the world, using a wide rage of recently open archives and primary sources. The book denounces previous studies about U.S. labor diplomacy: in the introduction, the editors argue that "the combination of anticommunism and CIA ties has produced a literature on the AFL-CIO Cold War foreign policy that has been overwhelmingly Leftist in political orientation and tending toward journalistic exposé rather than scholarly analysis." Yet the book reveals also the limitations of its revisionist efforts: the same volume concludes, particularly in relation to the role of U.S. labor diplomats in Latin America, that "given the close ties—at least in foreign affairs—between labor, business and the state, the charges [of depicting labor diplomats as agents of U.S. empire] were difficult to refute." "By adopting an uncompromising with-us-or-against-us approach," the author argues, "American labor contributed to the hemisphere's political and ideological polarization, and inadvertently reinforced the imperialist critique of the United States." Waters and Van Goethem, *American Labor's Global Ambassadors*, 3, 132. See also Scipes, *AFL-CIO Secret War against Developing Countries*, 31–38; Radosh, *American*

Labor and United States Foreign Policy; Alexander, "Labor and Inter-American Relations," 51; MacShane, International Labour and the Origins of the Cold War; Morris, CIA and American Labor.

30 Fiszman, "The U.S. Labor Attaches," 413.

31 For an eloquent discussion of this specific feature of Latin American populism, see Angela de Castro Gomes's study of the case of Varguismo in Brazil. Castro Gomes, A invencao do trabalhismo.

32 "Discurso del Presidente Perón," La Prensa, 3 September 1946, 12. The first two executive orders creating the program are nos. 7976 and 8890, issued on 23 and 30 August 1946, respectively, with notification appearing in the Boletín Oficial de la República Argentina. They established the creation of the position of attaché and the training courses, under the jurisdiction of the Legal Secretary of the Presidency and in coordination with the Consejo Superior. They refer to the future officials as "Delegados Obreros" (worker delegates). Executive Orders 23.579 and 23.581 appointed the first attachés to their new posts abroad. Boletín Oficial de la República Argentina, 9 December 1946. See also Bottarini, "Estrategias político-educativas peronistas," 416–17.

33 Executive Order 33.302, 20 December 1945, Boletín Oficial de la República Argentina. Turner and Miguens, Juan Perón and the Reshaping of Argentina, 201.

34 Chamosa, The Argentine Folklore Movement, 175–82. On the extent and implications of these changes, see Karush and Chamosa, The New Cultural History of Peronism.

35 James, "October 17th and 18th, 1945," 454.

36 Ferrer, La economía argentina.

37 Auyero, Poor People's Politics, 188.

38 The infamous phrase was first pronounced by the radical representative Ernesto Sanmartino during a congressional debate on 7 August 1947. It became, over time, a symbol of racialized confrontations over the economic and social changes enacted by the arrival of Peronism. See Gambini, Historia del peronismo.

39 "Trabajo y diplomacia," Asociación Bancaria flyer, 1948, personal collection of the family of Eduardo de Antueno.

40 La Prensa and La Nación challenged censorship during the early days of the administration and gave full voice to diplomats' complaints (see editions of both papers for 2–6 September 1946). To the extent that it was possible, they maintained similar coverage about the Cancillería in the following years.

41 "El servicio exterior," editorial, La Nación (Buenos Aires), 15 October 1949, 4.

42 "Trabajo y diplomacia," Asociación Bancaria flyer, 1948, personal collection of the family of Eduardo de Antueno.

43 "La verdadera democracia: Los trabajadores argentinos participan de la función pública," poster, box 12, misc., JABP. For a recent general examination of the varied artistic influences in Peronist propaganda, see González, López, Santoro, and Indi, Perón mediante.

44 Though the Teatro Colón came to symbolize the status of local porteño elites and their attachment to European values, opera fans were actually a heterogeneous mix

that included immigrants (mostly but not only Italians) and workers. Peronism's use of the premises was viewed as a challenge by those same elites, though Perón was more inclined to the idea of popularizing classical music rather than combating it. See Benzecry, *The Opera Fanatic*, chaps. 1, 2, and 6.

45 "Presidió el General Perón el acto de entrega de diplomas a los agregados obreros," *El Laborista*, 15 December 1946, 1–2; "Magnífico fue el acto de entrega de los diplomas," *Democracia*, 15 December 1946, 2–3.

46 Picture of León Segovia, 1947, Segovia scrapbook, personal collection of Irene Segovia.

47 Picture of César Tronconi at the Retiro railway station, personal papers of César Tronconi.

48 "Auténticos obreros argentinos llevan al extranjero la representación de nuestra patria," "UOM," magazine of the UOM (Buenos Aires), December 1946, 7–11.

49 "Iniciáronse los cursos para los obreros que irán a las embajadas," *La Nación*, Buenos Aires, 3 September 1946, 4.

50 "Discurso del Presidente Perón," *La Prensa* (Buenos Aires), 3 September 1946, 12.

51 Executive Order 37.788, Secret and Confidential, "Instrucciones a que deberán ajustar su cometido los señores agregados obreros," *Boletín Oficial de la República Argentina*, 6 December 1948, numbered copy 12, uncatalogued, premises of the embassy of Argentina in Peru.

52 Executive Order 5182, "Reglamentación de la dirección Organización Internacional del Trabajo," *Boletín Oficial de la República Argentina*, 24 February 1948.

53 For a meticulous study of the contradictions in the Partido Peronist Femenino, see Barry, *Evita Capitana*.

54 There are no official records about women worker attachés in particular. I arrived at the numbers provided here by combining two different sources: the lists of attaché appointments, transfers, and cessations published by the Ministry of Foreign Affairs, Biblioteca del Instituto del Servicio Exterior de la Nación, Buenos Aires (hereafter ISEN), and the list of attachés that Tronconi typed personally in 1954, presumably with the purpose of establishing contact with the rest of his colleagues, and that include the attachés' destinations as well as their addresses and telephone numbers in Argentina.

55 About the gender dynamics within Peronism, see also Lobato, Damilakou, and Tornay, "Working-Class Beauty Queens under Peronism," 176.

56 "Notas/Agregados obreros," scrapbook, personal papers of Agustín Merlo.

57 Ochoa de Eguileor, *Memorias de un ciudadano ilustre*, 14–16; Eleuterio Cardozo, oral interview, in Bottarini, "Estrategias político-educativas peronistas," 418.

58 Details taken from a picture of worker attachés in class during the first year of the training courses, scrapbook, personal papers of César Tronconi.

59 Bottarini, "Estrategias político-educativas peronistas," 417.

60 Bottarini, "Estrategias politico-educativas peronistas," 410. On education, indoctrination, and Peronism, see Plotkin, *Mañana es San Perón*. On education and organized labor in Argentina, see Belloni Ravest, *Educación sindical en la Argentina*, 3.

61 In 1939, the socialist-led CGT began the provisions for a "Worker University," in part to train a professional cadre of technical experts drawn from the working class. See Belloni Ravest, *Educación sindical en la Argentina*, 3, 4.

62 The professionalization of the foreign service also took place during Peronism. In 1949, the Ministry of Foreign Affairs created the Instituto del Servicio Exterior de la Nación (ISEN). The new government agency required a degree for all candidates, and it was a two-year school. Although the initial program included classes that could be considered part of the larger indoctrination efforts of Peronism ("The Idea of Social Justice in Perón's Thought," "Economic Justice: An Argentine Goal for All," "The Social Work of Eva Perón"), the bulk of the courses were about political science, economics, international relations, and Argentine and Latin American history.

63 "Los cursos de capacitación para agregados obreros a las embajadas," *Progreso* (magazine of the Tailors Union), December 1946, 11.

64 Pedro Otero, oral interview, file 1, p. 109, MOA; Panella, "Los agregados obreros," 42; Bottarini, "Estrategias politico-educativas peronistas," 407.

65 Bottarini, "Estrategias político-educativas peronistas," 443.

66 I arrived at this number, compiling and comparing (1) de Imaz's reference in *Those Who Rule*, (2) the list in Bottarini's article from Archivo de Cancillería, Bottarini, p. 432, (3) the list from compiled by the office of Perón's Chief Propaganda, Raúl Apold, available in Archivo Intermedio, Ministerio del Interior y Transporte, Buenos Aires (hereafter AI), (4) the number provided in the CGT magazine, October 1946, and (5) the list in *Progreso* (magazine of the Tailors Union), December 1946.

67 About the competing views of gender roles under Peronism, see Lobato, Damilakou, and Tornay, "Working-Class Beauty Queens under Peronism." On women's participation in politics, see Barry, *Evita Capitana*. Bianchi and Sanchis offer a comprehensive collection of women's memories in their oral interviews, *El Partido Peronista Femenino (1949–1955)*.

68 Gerchunoff and Llach, *El ciclo de la ilusión y el desencanto*, 90–119.

69 "Auténticos obreros argentinos llevan al extrangero la representación de nuestra patria," "UOM," magazine of the UOM (Buenos Aires), December 1946, 7–11.

70 Tamarin, *The Argentine Labor Movement*, 184–90.

71 Tamarin, *The Argentine Labor Movement*, 193–94.

72 Luna, *El 45*, 42. In November 1944, less than a year before his proclamation as the leader of the Argentine working class, Perón organized his first political rally to celebrate the creation of the Secretariat of Labor, which was providing all these benefits. Attendance was so small that one adviser said that if they had paid a large amount of money to each participant, they would have wasted fewer funds than they had spent in publicity.

73 Email correspondence with Silvia Maestro (granddaughter of Modesto Alvarez), 7–20 February 2010.

74 Oral interview with Pedro Conde Magdaleno Jr. (son of Pedro Conde Magdaleno), Buenos Aires, 21–25 July 2012.

75 Roberto Federico Ferrari to Nicolás Repetto, Tegucigalpa, 14 May 1947, Fondo Nicolás Repetto, ND 839. Ref. FR. 18. 43, Centro de Documentación e Investigación de la Cultura de Izquierdas en la Argentina, Buenos Aires, (hereafter CeDInCI).

76 Tamarin, *The Argentine Labor Movement*, 47–76.

77 Adelman, "State and Labour in Argentina," 73–102.

78 Zanatta, *Perón y el mito de la nación católica*, chap. 2.

79 As it happened, many of Perón's early allies from Catholic nationalism abandoned him before 1946, and many more followed them in the years after. For a concise and precise reflection on the ideological conflicts between Perón and Catholic intellectuals, see Terán, "Rasgos de la cultura durante el primer peronismo."

80 Rein, "Los hombres detrás del hombre"; González Bollo, "José Francisco Figuerola."

81 Page, *Perón*, 86–87; Tamarin, *The Argentine Labor Movement*, 182.

82 Ochoa de Eguileor, *Memorias de un ciudadano ilustre*, 26.

83 Ochoa de Eguileor, *Memorias de un ciudadano ilustre*, 32, 33; Cerrutti Costa, *El sindicalismo, las masas, el poder.*

84 Juárez, *Los trabajadores en función social*, 202.

85 Ochoa de Eguileor, *Memorias de un ciudadano ilustre*, 23.

86 Cerrutti Costa, *El sindicalismo, las masas, el poder.*

87 Ochoa de Eguileor, *Memorias de un ciudadano ilustre*, 19. On the 1944 earthquake and its place in the origins of Peronism, see Healey, *The Ruins of the New Argentina.*

88 See Cerrutti Costa's introduction to Juárez, *Los trabajadores en función social.*

89 Ochoa de Eguileor, *Memorias de un ciudadano ilustre*, 24.

90 Email correspondence with Eduardo de Antueno (son of Eduardo de Antueno), 9 December 2011.

91 "Los cursos de capacitación para agregados obreros a las embajadas," *Progreso* (magazine of the Tailors Union), December 1946, 7.

92 Ochoa de Eguileor, *Memorias de un ciudadano ilustre*, 34.

93 Email correspondence with Eduardo de Antueno (son of Eduardo de Antueno), 9 December 2011.

94 "Los cursos de capacitación para agregados obreros a las embajadas," *Progreso* (magazine of the Tailors Union), December 1946, 7.

95 Ochoa de Eguileor, *Memorias de un ciudadano ilustre*, 21.

96 Ochoa de Eguileor, *Memorias de un ciudadano ilustre*, 40–41.

97 "Renovación fundamental," Mercado de la Sociedad Cooperativa de Floricultores de Buenos Aires, November 1946, unnumbered.

98 Elementos de una nueva energía," Mercado de la Sociedad Cooperativa de Floricultores de Buenos Aires, November 1946, unnumbered.

99 Pedro Otero, oral interview, file 1, p. 208, MOA.

100 Ochoa de Eguileor, *Memorias de un ciudadano ilustre*, 26.

101 For a comparison with the views advanced by the Christian democratic parties, see Dunaway, *Jacques Maritain.*

102 Schivelbusch, *Three New Deals*, 15.

103 Ochoa de Eguileor, *Memorias de un ciudadano ilustre*, 19.

104 Military leaders close to Perón have emphasized their pride at having seen for the first time after 1943 that workers celebrated May 1st with Argentine flags instead of red ones and with the national anthem instead of *The International*. The recollection proved to be fake, as socialist and leftist organizations had debated "the national question" decades earlier, and in their rallies the national anthem was sung and Argentine flags abounded. Mariano Plotkin, *Mañana es San Perón*, 75–140.

105 For a comprehensive approach to many of the debates about Peronist ideology, see Piñeiro Iñiguez, *Perón*; Chávez, *Perón y el Justicialismo*, 16.

106 There is a vast body of work about this process, which took place between 1943 and 1945. See, above all, the essay "Encrucijadas políticas y dicotomías ideológicas," in Altamirano, *Bajo el signo de las masas*.

107 The prefix *over-* in Torre's assessment does not imply a hypothetically ideal "even" representation, but is used in order to stress the impact that the conjunctural factors of the 1943–1946 period had in the final outcome. Torre, *La vieja guardia sindical y Perón*, 2.

108 Perón's letter to the attachés appears in many of the attachés' personal papers. Personal papers of Eduardo de Antueno. I have reviewed the letters to another twelve attachés, they are all identical.

109 Weffort, *Los orígenes del sindicalismo populista en Brasil*; Torcuata S. Di Tella, *Argentina*.

110 "Reunión del presidente de la nación con delegados obreros latinoamericanos," 6 April 1948, typed speech, "Apold" folder, AI.

111 See, for example, Zanatta, *Del estado liberal a la nación católica*, 10–11.

112 Torre, *La vieja guardia sindical y Perón*; Plotkin, *Mañana es San Perón*, part IV.

CHAPTER FOUR. **From the Belly of the Beasts**

1 "Auténticos obreros argentinos llevan al extranjero la representación de nuestra patria," *Unión Obrera Metalúrgica* (weekly magazine), 1946, 5–9, personal papers of César Tronconi.

2 Even though organized labor had developed international actions in the past, the massive involvement in global affairs, and the perception among activists and workers that their fate was playing out both locally and globally, intensified during and after World War II. Luna, *Perón y su tiempo*, chaps. 1 and 4.

3 "Lista de agregados obreros en el exterior," "Comisión Investigadora: 'Documentación relacionada con la C.G.T.'" folder, Ministerio del Interior y Transporte, Archivo Intermedio Buenos Aires (hereafter AI).

4 "Declaración de los derechos de la ancianidad," brochure from the Argentine government translated into Greek and French, distributed by the worker attachés, and presented at the Argentine embassy in Athens on 10 September 1948

by Ambassador Dardo Corvalán Mendilaharsu, box 26, Juan Atilio Bramuglia Papers, Hoover Institution Archives, Stanford University (hereafter JABP).

5 Walker, *The Cold War*, 48; Truman, *Memoirs*, 98.

6 Embajador to Señor Canciller, "Cena y reporte," 12 September 1948, "Reportes: Grecia, 1947–1950" box, Archivo de Cancillería, Ministerio de Relaciones Exteriores y Culto, República Argentina (hereafter AC).

7 *El Laborista*, 15 January 1949, 24.

8 Panella, "Los agregados obreros," 43.

9 Panella, "Los agregados obreros," 43.

10 Panella, "Los agregados obreros," 40.

11 Merlo to Señor Embajador, 21 March 1947, pp. 2–3; "Informes del agregado obrero: Desde el 1 y hasta el 22 inclusive, y notas del 1 al 23 Incl." folder, p. 3, personal papers of Agustín Merlo. "La Cucaracha" is a popular Mexican tune, and the Argentine opposition to Perón widely used an alliterated rhyme of it during 1945: "Perón y Farrell / Perón y Farrell / ya no pueden caminar / porque les falta / porque no tienen / el apoyo popular."

12 Agustín Merlo to Señor Embajador, Dr. Oscar Ivanissevich, Washington, 21 March 1947, p. 4, personal papers of Agustín Merlo.

13 Dr. Oscar Ivanissevich, Washington, 23 March 1947, memo, box 5548, AC.

14 Luna, *Perón y su tiempo*, 223.

15 For a debate on the configuration of the ideological field of the Cold War and the specificity of the conflict in Latin America, see Grandin, "Off the Beach"; Agnew and Rosenzweig, *A Companion to Post-1945 America*, 426.

16 As scholars have convincingly argued, the particular opposition to Peronism by Serafino Romualdi added a specific dimension to the idea of Peronism as a threat, but this does not preclude the fact that the rest of them saw Peronism as a threat. See Walcher, "Reforming Latin American Labor."

17 Email correspondence with Eduardo de Antueno (son of Eduardo de Antueno), 9 December 2011.

18 Romualdi to Matthew Woll, Chairman, 10 July 1947, interview with the Argentine labor attachés, pp. 1–2, box 9, folder 2, Serafino Romualdi Papers, Kheel Center for Labor-Management Documentation and Archives, Cornell University Library (hereafter SRP).

19 "Report on Fascist Beachhead in Latin America Trotskyists and Communist Press," Counter Attack, box 9, Tamiment Library and Robert F. Wagner Labor Archives, New York University Libraries (hereafter TL).

20 Far from what the attachés expected, only the Republican representative from Wisconsin, Alvin O'Konski, was receptive to Peronism. O'Konski traveled to Argentina and met Perón. After that, interestingly, he described Perón as the strongest ally the United States could have in the fight against communism and denounced President Truman's policy toward Perón as the product of a "campaign developed by communist forces and their sympathizers in the United States." "O'Konski visita la Argentina," *La Prensa*, 10 April 1947.

21 Virgil Pinkley, "Perón, Propaganda—and Postage," *Mirror* (Los Angeles), 28 August 1951, box 2, Hipólito Jesús Paz, JABP.

22 On this approach to Latin America in the U.S. media, see Gerassi, *Great Fear in Latin America.*

23 Merlo al Señor Embajador, report, 19 June 1947, personal papers of Agustín Merlo.

24 "Eva Perón Clothing Gift to U.S. Children Accepted at State Department's Behest," *New York Times,* 18 January 1949.

25 "Eva Perón Clothing Gift to U.S. Children Accepted at State Department's Behest," *New York Times,* 18 January 1949.

26 Scrapbook, personal papers of Agustín Merlo.

27 Virginia Lee Warren, "Some Argentines Titter at Eva Perón Fight: U.S. Incident Held Lend-Lease in Reverse," *New York Times,* 19 January 1949.

28 John Dos Passos, "Lo que vi," undated brochure, box 35, "Misc." folder, Spruille Braden Papers, 1903–1977, Rare Book and Manuscript Library, Columbia University (hereafter SBP).

29 "Did You Know?," *International News Bulletin,* Confederación General del Trabajo, Buenos Aires, Volume II, undated.

30 Juan Perón to Juan Bramuglia, Buenos Aires, 23 August 1947, box 30, JABP.

31 Note from Eva Perón to Merlo, 19 February 1948, personal papers of Agustín Merlo. The same wording, encouraging worker attachés to demand more funds and resources if necessary, can be found in similar letters and cards signed by Eva Perón and sent to different attachés in Latin America.

32 "Informes y notas del agregado obrero, desde Marzo 19 hasta Abril 15 de 1947," personal papers of Agustín Merlo. Merlo's family kept letters, pictures, and reports of Agustín Merlo, from 1947 to 1949. In this case, the folder with these reports seems to belong to the Dirección de International Labor Organization (DOIT) at the Ministry of Foreign Affairs. The military government that ousted Perón in 1955 ordered the destruction of the reports at the DOIT. The folder appeared to have been removed from the ministry by Merlo himself, most likely during Perón's administration.

33 "Conflicto Brooklyn-Battery," 1 April, "Informes del agregado obrero" folder, personal papers of Agustín Merlo.

34 "Informe sobre el conflicto telefónico," 11 April, and "Informe sobre actividades diversas," 10 April, p. 1, "Informes del agregado obrero" folder, personal papers of Agustín Merlo.

35 Osvaldo Nani, Informe número 85/48, New York, 20 Mayo 1948, "Estadísticas de Pérdidas en el Trabajo y Empleamiento General," "United Nations 1948" box, folder 6, AC.

36 Speech by the worker attaché Eduardo de Antueno at the Pan-American Union general assembly, Washington, 7 October 1947, p. 4, personal papers of Eduardo de Antueno.

37 Speech by the worker attaché Eduardo de Antueno at the Pan-American Union general assembly, Washington, 7 October 1947, p. 4, personal papers of Eduardo de Antueno.

38 "Informe sobre nueva regulación de precios," 30 March, "Informes del agregado obrero" folder, personal papers of Agustín Merlo. Earlier than Merlo, the Puerto Rican poet Julia de Burgos, in a letter to her sister Consuelo, also commented: "Este es un pueblo verdaderamente organizado. En las esquinas, en vez de policías, hay luces rojas y verdes, que automáticamente indican a los carros y al público el momento de pasar." The two references are revealing of the vast set of technological advances that had been changing not only the economic performance of the United States but also the daily life of Americans since the early 1940s. New York, the prototype of the futuristic metropolis, exhibited the gap that was rapidly separating the United States from the rest of the world. Visitors from places less remote than Argentina were surprised by the technological innovations and rationalization of modern life in the city. Julia de Burgos to Consuelo, New York, 30 January 1940, in de Burgos, *Cartas a consuelo*, 9.

39 "De Berisso a Washington," Merlo family PowerPoint presentation, comprising first-person recollections, pictures, clips, and official reports, in personal papers of Agustín Merlo. Anecdotal evidence suggests that other attachés appointed in the U.S. and Latin American countries (including Osvaldo Nani, Eduardo de Antueno, Julio Caprara, and César Tronconi) also brought back to Buenos Aires their own brand-new cars, an unequivocal emblem of status among workers in the region. El Justicialista, along with the plane Pulqui, was a symbol of national industrialization. On the modernizing imaginaries associated with the automobile in twentieth-century Latin America, see Wolfe, *Autos and Progress*, particularly chap. 2, "The Coming of Tropical Modernity," 61–90.

40 "Informe: Truman pide a los patrones que bajen los precios," 12 April, "Informes del agregado obrero" folder, personal papers of Agustín Merlo.

41 "Tiempo perdido por huelgas en 1946," 2 April, p. 2, "Informes del agregado obrero" folder, personal papers of Agustín Merlo.

42 Castro Gomes, *A invenção do trabalhismo*, 296. See an extended discussion of this topic in chapter 1 of this book.

43 Emil Rieve, General President, Textile Workers Union of America, CIO, "International Labor Standards: A Key to World Security," New York, 1945, in Records Relating to International Labor Organizations 1932–1951, box 14, National Archives and Records Administration, United States (hereafter NARA); "Do You Know," undated AFL pamphlet, probably from 1945, comparing the work time required for U.S. and Soviet workers to buy some goods and services, Collection American Federation of Labor, box 1, AFL ephemera, undated (1935–1952), TL.

44 Agustín Merlo, "Objetivos perseguidos por la política de justicia social del gobierno de la Revolución Argentina," paper presented at a conference offered at the North American–Argentine Cultural Institute, Washington, 29 January 1948, p. 6, clips, personal papers of Agustín Merlo.

45 "Lecture by Admiral Swanson at Argentine Embassy: Few Latin Americans Turn Out," 19 December 1947, RG59, folder 701.3511/12–1947, NARA.

46 Agustín Merlo, "Objetivos perseguidos por la política de justicia social del gobierno de la Revolución Argentina," conference offered at the North

American–Argentine Cultural Institute, Washington, 29 January 1948, p. 4, clips, personal papers of Agustín Merlo. For a discussion about the place of food and nutrition in fashioning Peronist identity, see Elena, *Dignifying Argentina*, 88.

47 Agustín Merlo, "Objetivos perseguidos por la política de justicia social del gobierno de la Revolución Argentina," conference offered at the North American–Argentine Cultural Institute, Washington, 29 January 1948, p. 6, clips, personal papers of Agustín Merlo.

48 Agustín Merlo, "Objetivos perseguidos por la política de justicia social del gobierno de la Revolución Argentina," conference offered at the North American–Argentine Cultural Institute, Washington, 29 January 1948, p. 9, clips, personal papers of Agustín Merlo.

49 Eduardo de Antueno at the Pan-American Union, p. 8, personal papers of Eduardo de Antueno.

50 Charter of the Organization of American States, chap. 2, art. 3g: "The American States condemn war of aggression: victory does not give rights." In "The Liberal Traditions in the Americas," Greg Grandin traces the origins of this regional interpretation of liberal institutions to the end of the wars of independence and the political reconceptualization of the territory.

51 Alicia Masini, 27 August 1947, personal diary, personal papers of Pedro Conde Magdaleno (son of Pedro Conde Magdaleno). The quotes are part of a longer letter written for Masini's brother "Pepe," in the form of a diary kept during most of 1947 and delivered in person when they family reunited in Buenos Aires the following year.

52 More than two thousand cases of cannibalism were documented during the 1932–1933 famine in Ukraine. And cases of cannibalism have been also described during the 1941–1944 Siege of Leningrad. Rumors about cannibalism spread widely, and sporadic incidents of cannibalism might have continued to occur in Odessa and the rest of Ukraine after the famine. See Snyder, *Bloodlands*, 21–59.

53 Conde Magdaleno, *¿Por que huyen en baúles los asilados españoles en la U.R.S.S.?*, 16 and 32. The book was a manifesto denouncing life under Stalinism. Examining Alicia Masini's unpublished personal diary and correspondence, written in 1947 and kept within the family until now, I noticed that, in many instances, Conde Magdaleno wrote as his own stories that had actually happened to his wife. Familial plagiarism aside, what is telling in this case is not only Conde Magdaleno's view, but also how he wanted to be seen in relation to these events. For this study, I have relied more on Masini's personal papers, except for the cases in which Conde Magdaleno's book provides additional information (official documents, speeches, and decisions made by Conde Magdaleno in his official capacity).

54 About the impact in Argentina of the "popular fronts" and the later confluence of their activists with Perón, see Tamarin, *The Argentine Labor Movement*, chaps. 6–7.

55 "Un homenaje a los fundadores del 4 de agosto de 1887," *Unión de Personal de Establecimientos Panificadores* (magazine, Buenos Aires), August 1974, 2–3.

56 For an overview of this aspect of the bilateral relations between Argentina and the Soviet Union, see Gilbert, *El oro de Moscú*.

57 Conde Magdaleno *¿Por qué huyen en baúles los asilados españoles en la U.R.S.S.?*, 185. On Cantoni and his confluence with Perón as part of the broader relation of Peronism with provincial leaders, see Healey, *The Ruins of the New Argentina*, 40–41.

58 Alicia Masini to Pepe, Santos, 23 February 1947, personal papers of Pedro Conde Magdaleno; Conde Magdaleno, *¿Por qué huyen en baúles los asilados españoles en la U.R.S.S.?*, 185; picture of Pedro Conde Magdaleno with relatives, scrapbook, personal papers of Pedro Conde Magdaleno.

59 Conde Magdaleno, *¿Por qué huyen en baúles los asilados españoles en la U.R.S.S.?*, 56, 67.

60 Alicia Masini to her brother, Moscow, 29 April 1947, personal papers of Pedro Conde Magdaleno.

61 Conde Magdaleno, *¿Por qué huyen en baúles los asilados españoles en la U.R.S.S.?*, 32–65.

62 George Kennan, the Long Telegram, 22 February 1946, box 163, folder 45, Public Policy Papers, George F. Kennan Papers 1871–2005, Mudd Manuscript Library, Department of Rare Books and Special Collections, Princeton University; Kennan (hereafter GKP), *Memoirs*, 188, 250.

63 Conde Magdaleno, *¿Por qué huyen en baúles los asilados españoles en la U.R.S.S.?*, 58–59.

64 Conde Magdaleno, *¿Porqué huyen en baúles los asilados españoles en la U.R.S.S.?*, 67.

65 Alicia Masini's diary, 3 August 1947, personal papers of Pedro Conde Magdaleno.

66 Alicia Masini's diary, 10 and 25 August 1947, personal papers of Pedro Conde Magdaleno.

67 Conde Magdaleno, *¿Por qué huyen en baúles los asilados españoles en la U.R.S.S.?*, 95.

68 Conde Magdaleno, *¿Por qué huyen en baúles los asilados españoles en la U.R.S.S.?*, 46. The end of rationing cards in December of that year only worsened the situation.

69 Alicia Masini's diary, 2 May 1947, personal papers of Pedro Conde Magdaleno.

70 About the social and political connotations of "pan negro" in Argentina, see Elena, *Dignifying Argentina*, 228.

71 Alicia Masini's diary, 27 April 1947, personal papers of Pedro Conde Magdaleno.

72 Lobato, Damilakou, and Tornay, "Working-Class Beauty Queens under Peronism," 191.

73 Alicia Masini's diary, 13 May 1947, personal papers of Pedro Conde Magdaleno.

74 Alicia Masini's diary, 15 June 1947, personal papers of Pedro Conde Magdaleno.

75 Conde Magdaleno, *¿Por qué huyen en baúles los asilados españoles en la U.R.S.S.?*, 12.

76 See the introduction to Milanesio, *Workers Go Shopping in Argentina*.

77 Ana Cepeda Étkina, *Harina de otro costal*, 142.

78 There are many accounts of the incident, most of them from Conde Magdaleno, *¿Por qué huyen en baúles los asilados españoles en la U.R.S.S.?*, 272–77. An incident at the airport, where they were not allowed to pay with dollars for the

extra luggage, forced Conde Magdaleno to leave the other refugee, Pedro Cepeda Sánchez, in Moscow. When Tuñón was captured, he might have confessed to the incident and revealed his accomplices, presumably under torture, and three days later, Cepeda was arrested as he was leaving the Argentine embassy. On 1 January 1948, Alicia Masini recorded in her diary her husband's intention of bringing Tuñón as a case to the United Nations. See also Conde Magdaleno, *¿Por qué huyen en baúles los asilados españoles en la U.R.S.S.?*, 288. On the attaché's contact with Tuñón's brother, see Conde Magdaleno to Mateo Tuñón Albertos, Buenos Aires, 24 February 1948, in Conde Magdaleno, *¿Por qué huyen en baúles los asilados españoles en la U.R.S.S.?*, 281. Ana Cepeda Étkina, *Harina de otro costal*, 184, 307.

79 Alicia Masini's diary, 19 January 1948, personal papers of Pedro Conde Magdaleno.

80 "Russians Announce 2 Argentines Ouster," *New York Times*, 22 January 1948, A10; Conde Magdaleno, *¿Por qué huyen en bahúles los asilados españoles en la U.R.S.S.?*, 180–88.

81 Conde Magdaleno, *¿Por qué huyen en baúles los asilados españoles en la U.R.S.S.?*, 167.

82 "Do You Know?," AFL brochure, 1948, p. 2, "Official Figures from the U.S. Bureau of Labor Statistics," Collection PE 014, American Federation of Labor, box 1, "Fliers and Ephemera, undated, 1935–1950–1952" folder, TL.

83 Gambini, *Historia del peronismo*, 115.

84 "Do You Know?," AFL brochure, 1948, p. 2, "Official Figures from the U.S. Bureau of Labor Statistics," Collection PE 014, American Federation of Labor, box 1, "Fliers and Ephemera, undated, 1935–1950–1952" folder, TL.

85 On the international projection of the conflict between the AFL and the CIO, mostly in Latin America, see Kofas, *The Struggle for Legitimacy*, 347–52; Waters and Van Goethem, *American Labor's Global Ambassadors*, 123–215.

CHAPTER FIVE. **At the Turn of the Tide**

Epigraph from Spruille Braden, "The Inter-American Scene Today," unpublished essay, 28 March 1947, box 22, "Correspondence General: Statements and Articles" folder, Spruille Braden Papers 1903–1977, Rare Book and Manuscript Library, Columbia University (hereafter SBP).

1 Cirilo Liendo, trip to Peru, Ambassador to Señor Ministro, no. 632, Lima, 10 September 1947, uncatalogued papers, Embassy of Argentina, Lima, Peru. Unless noted, this and all the other files cited as "uncatalogued papers, Embassy of Argentina, Lima, Peru," were found in the basement of the embassy premises during the moving of the diplomatic representation to a new building in August 2011.

2 Cirilo Liendo, trip to Peru, Ambassador to Señor Ministro, no. 632, Lima, 10 September 1947, uncatalogued papers, Embassy of Argentina, Lima, Peru.

3 Bethell and Roxborough, *Latin America between the Second World War and the Cold War*, introduction.

4 Spruille Braden, memorandum, 14 July 1945, box 18: "Correspondence, Diplomatic, 1945," "Correspondence Diplomatic 1945 (Argentina) m-p" folder, SBP. In fact, it was Peronism that placed its regional project in a historical narrative that associated it with the nineteenth-century independence period and San Martín's role during it. During a talk with Latin American labor leaders in Buenos Aires, Perón called the role of the attachés "una epopeya Sanmartiniana." Juan Domingo Perón, "Reunión del Señor Presidente de la Nación con Delegados Obreros Latinoamericanos," 6 April 1948, Archivo Intermedio, Ministerio del Interior y Transporte, Buenos Aires (hereafter AI).

5 Luna, *Perón y su tiempo*, 1:213.

6 Zanatta and Aguas, "Auge y declinación de la Tercera Posición," 32; Alexander, "Labor and Inter-American Relations," 45.

7 Germani, "Democracia representativa y clases populares."

8 Cochran and Reina, *Entrepreneurship in Argentine Culture*, 45–49.

9 Oral interview with Torcuato di Tella, New York, 27 August 2012.

10 Alexander, "Labor and Inter-American Relations," 51.

11 Bethell and Roxborough, *Latin America between the Second World War and the Cold War*, introduction; Kofas, *The Struggle for Legitimacy*, 15–21.

12 Email correspondence with Silvia Maestro (granddaughter of Modesto Alvarez), 2 March 2009; "Incidentes en la embajada de Argentina," La Paz, 30 June 1947, box 5554, Bolivia, Archivo de Cancillería, Ministerio de Relaciones Exteriores y Culto, Argentina (hereafter AC).

13 Email correspondence with Silvia Maestro (granddaughter of Modesto Alvarez), 2–17 March 2009.

14 "Disgnación de Agregado Obrero Cosimo Francisco Piva," Managua, 31 May 1947, "Design de Diplomáticos Argentinos" folder, AC; Francisco Javier Canosa to Señor Ministro, Managua, 27 May 1947, "Nicaragua, Anexo II" folder, AC; Jorge Sánchez to Señor Ministro, San José de Costa Rica, 29 August 1947, "Nicaragua, Anexo II" folder, AC; "Departamento de Política: Nicaragua-Honduras-Haití, 1947" box, folder 7, AC. The asylum of union leaders in the Argentine legation was reported in Nicaraguan press as well. See, for example, "Líderes socialistas detenidos ayer: Armando Amador se refugió en la Embajada Argentina," *La Prensa* (Managua), 25 June 1947.

15 For an analysis of Somocismo as a form of populism that made consistent efforts to build support beyond the Guardia Nacional and among unions, see Gould, *To Lead as Equals*.

16 Mora, "The Forgotten Relationship: United States-Paraguay Relations, 1937–89," 454. For a general overview about Paraguay as a regional battlefield after the Chaco War but before Peronism, see Mora, *Struggle for Hegemony*.

17 Interview with Irene Segovia (daughter of León Segovia), Buenos Aires, 21 July 2012.

18 Interview with Irene Segovia (daughter of León Segovia), Buenos Aires, 21 July 2012.

19 Ambassador to Señor Ministro, "Discurso de César Tronconi del 23 de febrero en la Federación Provincial de Trabajadores de Matanzas," Havana, 9 March 1948,

box 8: "Ecuador-Cuba," "Copias de notas de la Embajada Argentina en Cuba" folder, AC; Pedro Otero to Señor Jefe, note 41, Viaje a Barrancabermeja, 6 October 1947, "Agregado Obrero 1948" folder, AC; Modesto Alvarez, note to Asiento Minero de Corocoro, 20 June 1951, white folder, uncatalogued papers found at the Embassy of Argentina, La Paz, Bolivia; Alberto Viale, report no. 14: "Asamblea de Gremios realizada en la finca Cocales," Guatemala, 29 April 1949, box 21, AC; "Gabinete Político Jurídico: Guatemala, Honduras, Haití, 1949," "Guatemala, Expediente 8" folder, AC; Cirilio Liendo to Señor Ministro, Nota Reservada 632, Lima, 10 September 1947, uncatalogued papers, Embassy of Argentina, Lima, Peru.

20 Alberto Viale, report no. 14, "Asamblea de Gremios realizada en la finca Cocales." Guatemala, 29 April 1949, box 21: "Gabinete Político Jurídico: Guatemala, Honduras, Haití, 1949," "Guatemala, Expediente 8" folder, AC.

21 On the role of sugar workers in the emergence of APRA, see the studies about the origins of the party in Ayacucho and Cajamarca: Heilman, "We Will No Longer Be Servile"; Taylor, "The Origins of APRA in Cajamarca, 1928–1935."

22 Drinot, *The Allure of Labor*, 18–20. With very different emphasis, the identification of indigenous, black, or ethnic minorities as an obstacle to modernity that could be overcome by either excluding the indigenous or by turning them into (implicitly or explicitly white) "workers" is prevalent in Latin America and the United States. See Roediger, *The Wage of Whiteness*.

23 Cirilio Liendo to Señor Ministro, Nota Reservada 632, Lima, 10 September 1947, uncatalogued papers Embassy of Argentins, Lima, Peru.

24 Lista de agregados obreros en el exterior, "Comisión Investigadora: Documentación relacionada con la C.G.T." binder, AI.

25 The attachés seem to have received similar (though not identical) notes from Eva Perón, always specifying the material that the foundation was sending and how it could be used in their destination. It appears that no note from Eva Perón survived in the Cancillería archives after 1955, but they are among the personal papers of León Segovia, Pedro Conde Magdaleno, Eduardo de Antueno, and César Tronconi.

26 Milanesio, "Peronist and *Cabecitas*," 55.

27 Elena, *Dignifying Argentina*, 250.

28 Otero to Señor Embajador, Reclamo, Bogotá, 18 February 1948, "Embajador Ramón del Río, Resoluciones Entradas, Agregado Obrero, 1947–1948" folder, AC. The worker attaché made clear that key contacts from the Colombian labor movement had been unable to reach him because the embassy personnel did not transfer the calls. The ambassador, in a note written the following day, told Otero that he had opened an investigation, but urged him to have a more specific workday schedule at his office "so the calls can be transferred." Embajdor to Señor Agregado Obrero, 19 February 1948, "Embajador Ramón del Río, Resoluciones Entradas, Agregado Obrero, 1947–1948" folder, AC.

29 Cirilio Liendo to Señor Ministro, Nota Reservada 632, Lima, 10 September 1947, uncatalogued papers, Embassy of Argentina, Lima, Peru.

30 Notes of Eva Perón, 13 January and 18 March 1948, personal papers of Eduardo
    Antueno.

31 Pedro Otero, transcript, program 18 December 1947, Radio Caracol, "Embajador
    Ramón del Río, Resoluciones Entradas, Agregado Obrero, 1947–1948" folder, AC.

32 Derechos del Trabajador, Boletín Oficial de la República Argentina, BORA,
    Executive Order 4865, 7 March 1947. The proclamation was first announced by
    Perón on 24 February, during a rally with CGT leaders in Buenos Aires. The
    ceremony, in turn, was broadcast to the rest of the country and abroad, including
    most of Latin America, Europe, and the United States.

33 Derechos del Trabajador, BORA, preamble.

34 Isidra Fernández, speech, Lima, Peru, 15 August 1949, uncatalogued papers,
    Embassy of Argentina, Lima, Peru. On Eva Perón as a model for women's role in
    politics, see Barry, *Evita Capitana*.

35 For a classic comparative study with a periodization of the welfare state in Latin
    America, see Mesa-Lago and Sociedad Interamericana de Planificación, *Modelos
    de seguridad social en América Latina*.

36 On the welfare state in Honduras and the relation with other experiences in
    Central America, see Euraque, *Reinterpreting the Banana Republic*, 62–65.

37 Panella, "Los agregados obreros," 47.

38 José Luis Gimenez to Señor Ministro, no. 23, Reservada: Audiencia con Señor
    Ministro de Relaciones Exteriores Doctor Silverio Laínez y Agregado Obrero
    a esta legación, Antonio Mariano Ferrari, Tegucigalpa, 21 February 1947, box 7:
    "Departamento de Política, Nicaragua, Honduras, Haití," folder 1: "Honduras,
    Política Interna," AC.

39 John B. Faust to the Secretary of State, Subject: Transmitting Pamphlet Distrib-
    uted by Argentine Legation in Tegucigalpa, 4 March 1947, folder 701.3515/3–447,
    National Archives and Records Administration, United States (hereafter NARA).

40 Flores, "El rol de la prensa," 46.

41 Weinstein, *For Social Peace in Brazil*, 277. For a study of U.S. efforts to "Ameri-
    canize" unions in Brazil, see Welch, "Labor Internationalism."

42 British Labor Attaché Clifford German to Ministry of Labour, Monthly Labour
    Report no. 26, 10 September 1947, LAB 13/498, Public Record Office, National
    Archives, London, cited in Afonso, "Para Norte Americano Ver. Adidos Trabal-
    histas e operários brasileiros (1943/1952)," 174–75.

43 The Brazilian law established that government approval was needed to represent
    unions abroad.

44 Clarence C. Brooks to State Department, Dispatch no. 3011, confidential, 11
    May 1947, box 394-PF-DS/USNA, folder RG 84-800 60/850.4, NARA, cited in
    Afonso, "Para Norte Americano Ver. Adidos Trabalhistas e operários brasileiros
    (1943/1952)," 176.

45 As I show in chapter 2 of this volume, the U.S. embassy in Buenos Aires followed
    as closely as possible the actions of most prominent union leaders visiting Argen-
    tina from Latin America, and tried to contact them in order to gauge the degree
    of their allegiance to Peronism.

46 On the influence of the New Deal in Peronism, James, *Resistance and Integration*, 39; Rapoport and Spiguel, *Relaciones tumultuosas*, 168–70.

47 Morgenfeld, *Vecinos en conflicto*, 365–92.

48 For an analysis of the confrontation in Mexico, Bolivia, Cuba, and Colombia between AFL-CIO labor diplomats and the Lombardistas of Latin America that converged into CTAL, see Kofas, *The Struggle for Legitimacy*, 284–307.

49 Alba, *Politics and the Labor Movement in Latin America*, 322–35.

50 A report from U.S. officials warning about the presence in Buenos Aires of activists from many Latin American countries was sent to Washington on 8 April 1948, the same day of the Bogotazo. Dearborn, Subject: Argentine Labor Organization Invites Labor Delegates from Other Latin American Countries to Visit Argentina, 8 April 1948, box 5553, folder RG 84 835.5043/4–148, NARA.

51 Luis Azurduy, "Aquí se lo combate con realidades dando al obrero un mejor 'standard' de vida," *Ahora*, 25 March 1948.

52 The general cable reporting the arrival of U.S. allies in Buenos Aires comments: "The Embassy has been waiting for one of the visitors to voluntarily call and discuss this subject. This was perhaps an optimistic hope but not a false one, because Juan Arévalo, a prominent Cuban labor leader, visited the Embassy yesterday on his own initiative." According to the U.S. official, Arévalo described in detail the meaning of the Third Position and what was attractive about it. Henry L. Pitts Jr., Subject: "Visit to Argentina of Delegates from Latin American Labor Organizations . . . ," Buenos Aires, 1 April 1948, box 5553, folder RG 84 835.5043/4–148, NARA.

53 Molinari was a nationalist member of the Radical Party who joined Peronism toward the end of 1945 and established a very close relation with Perón. See Luna, *Perón y su tiempo*, 177.

54 Pedro Otero, "Mensaje de fin de año" [transcript], letter to Ambassador Ramón del Río, 1 January 1948, "Embajador Ramón del Río, Reservado, 1948–1949" binder, AC.

55 Pedro Otero, letters to Ambassador Ramón del Rio, 29 September and 14 October 1947, note 147, "Agregado Obrero, 1947–1948" folder, AC; Favio Vazquez Botero, letter to the Minister of Foreign Relations, Consulate General of Colombia in Buenos Aires, 20 December 1947, fondo 155, binder 132, Archivo General de la Nación, Bogotá, Colombia (hereafter AGN).

56 John C. Wiley to State Department, 9 May 1946, dispatch 1669, in Galvis, "Así veían a Gaitán en Washington," 152. For a study of the social origins of Gaitanismo, see W. John Green, "'Vibrations of the Collective.'"

57 Otero to Señor Jefe, Bogotá, 3 November 1947, Referencia: Visita al Municipio de Soacha, "Agregado Obrero 1947–1948" box, AC.

58 W. John Green, "'Vibrations of the Collective,'" 286–90.

59 Pedro Otero to Señor Jefe, "Reunión en mi casa," 31 October 1947, "Agregado Obrero, 1947–1948" box folder, AC.

60 Bergquist, "The Labor Movement and the Origins of the Violence"; Kofas, "Containment and Class Conflict."

61 Memorandum from Serafino Romualdi to Matthew Well, 3 October 1947, Subject: Request for Financial Assistance from Colombia, box 2, folder 14, Serafino Romualdi Papers, Kheel Center for Labor-Management Documentation and Archives, Cornell University Library (hereafter SRP).

62 W. John Green, "Sibling Rivalry on the Left and Labor Struggles in Colombia during the 1940s," 90–92. Green contest the ideas of Herbert Braun and others who argue that Gaitanismo was not particularly strong among workers; Green contends, instead, that support for Gaitanismo was constantly growing after 1945 both among activists and ordinary workers.

63 Pedro Otero to Señor Jefe, Bogotá, 9 November 1947, Referencia: Huelga Petrolera, "Agregado Obrero 1948" folder, AC; Otero to Máximo Monzón, note 58, 17 October 1945, Referencia: Movimiento Obrero, "Agregado Obrero 1948" folder, AC; Otero to Máximo D. Monzón, note 51, 15 October 1947, Referencia: Reportaje de los diarios El Tiempo-Jornada-Siglo, "Agregado Obrero 1948" folder, AC.

64 Brochure: "Informaciones Argentinas: Bogotá-Colombia, Noviembre 1948, Publicación de la Embajada Argentina," "Embajador Ramón del Río, Salidas, 1948" folder, AC; Otero to Señor Jefe, Bogotá, 30 October 1947, Referencia: Solicitud de Material de lectura y propaganda, "Embajador Ramón del Río, Resoluciones Entradas Agregado Obrero 1948" folder, AC.

65 Otero to Señor Jefe, Bogotá, 8 November 1947, Referencia: Huelgas en sector farmacia y petroleros," "Agregado Obrero 1947–1948" folder, AC.

66 Otero to Señor Jefe, Bogotá, 1 November 1947 Referencia: Síntesis del movimiento político comunista y de izquierda, "Agregado Obrero 1948" folder, AC.

67 Agregado Obrero a Embajador, note 68, Bogotá, 27 February 1948. Asunto: Invitación de CGT de Argentina, "Embajada Argentina, Secretaría General, Bogotá, informes y notas D.O.I.T., 1948" folder, AC.

68 For a detailed political biography of Gaitán, see Sharpless, *Gaitán of Colombia*; Braun, *The Assassination of Gaitán*.

69 Agregado Obrero a Embajador, note 68, Bogotá, 27 February 1948, Asunto: Invitación de CGT de Argentina, "Embajada Argentina, Secretaría General, Bogotá, informes y notas D.O.I.T., 1948" folder, AC.

70 Agregado Obrero a Embajador, note 68, Bogotá, 27 February 1948, Asunto: Invitación de CGT de Argentina, "Embajada Argentina, Secretaría General, Bogotá, informes y notas D.O.I.T., 1948" folder, AC. Gaitán made some positive public references to Peronism after 1946, and his position seemed to be shifting from an initially cautious approach to a more enthusiastic appreciation. But these comments were not necessarily central to his political career, and at times the attaché might have felt too passionate about interpreting them as "inspiring" Gaitanismo.

71 Antonio Oviedo, Encargado de Negocios, a Señor Ministro, note A.2044, Asunto: Hacia una nueva organización obrera continental, 26 January 1948, Bogotá, Colombia, fondo 155, box 46, binder 136, AGN.

72 Pedro Otero to Señor Jefe, note 3, Referencia: "Señor Camacho; Serafino Romualdi; Congreso Ferroviario," 5 September 1947, "Agregado Obrero, 1947–1948"
box, AC.

73 Pedro Otero to Señor Jefe, Referencia: Reunión en mi casa, 31 October 1947,
"Agregado Obrero, 1947–1948" box, AC.

74 Pedro Otero to Señor Jefe, note 6, Entrevista al Dr. Gaitán Jorge E., 7 January 1948, "Embajador del Río, Resoluciones, 1948" box, AC. The letter's date
appears as "January 7, 1947," but both the note number, the events in which it is
inscribed, and the fact that the attaché had not arrived in Bogotá at that time
indicate that it is typographical error.

75 Agregado Obrero a Embajador, note 69, Encargado de Negocios to Viceconsul, 11
February 1948, Asunto: Recorte periodístico sobre la noticia de probable visita de
Evita, "Embajador del Río, Resoluciones, 1948" box, AC.

76 Pedro Otero to Señor Jefe, 27 February 1948, note 68, Invitación de la CGT, "Embajador del Río Reservado, 1948–1950" folder, AC.

77 Embajador a Señor Ministro, note 116, 2 March 1948, "La Situación Política,"
"Embajador del Río Reservado, 1948–1950" folder, AC.

78 Bogotá, 2 March 1948, Asunto: Situación Política, "Embajada Argentina, Secretaría General, Bogotá, informes y notas D.O.I.T." folder, AC.

79 A cable from the U.S. State Department warned about the "large Argentine delegation to the ITO" meeting led by Molinari and their "effort in Cuba to organize
student opinion against Bogotá Conference." Norwen, from Havana to Bogotá,
confidential, 8 April 1948, folder RG 84 800 B 8c (a handwritten note adds, "misc.
187"), NARA. See also Cafiero, *Desde que grité*, 40, who specifically mentions the
efforts of the attaché for working with Molinari.

80 Alexander, *A History of Organized Labor in Cuba*, 105–31.

81 Lester D. Mallory to Secretary of State, confidential, 26 April 1948, Subject:
"Possible Peron-sponsored New Student Movement in Latin America; Cubans
Concerned Suspected of Taking Part in Colombian Revolution," Havana, Cuba,
folder RG 84 800 Col. Revolution 8c, NARA.

82 Cafiero and others mention the role of the worker attaché in helping Molinari in
Cuba. Cafiero, *Desde que grité*, 40–43. José Pardo Llada provides a more detailed
description of the incidents around Molinari's visit, mentioning the role of the
worker attaché but mistaking his name for the one of the general secretary of
the Argentine embassy. Pardo Llada, *Fidel y el "Che,"* 44–45.

83 "Toma de posesión, directiva de graduados universitarios," *Pases de Primera*,
undated; "Noche Argentina en el sindicato telefónico de la Habana," *Unidad*, 15
February 1948; "Toma de posesión del ejecutivo de la U.S.W. de Cuba, *Paralelos*,
n.d., 12–14, personal papers of César Tronconi.

84 "Mantienen buenas relaciones la CTC y los 'peronistas,'" *Prensa Libre*, 27
May 1948, personal papers of César Tronconi.

85 "Argentina," Conferencia Radial Pronunciada por el Agregado Obrero el 21 December 1947 en "Radio Salas" de la Habana, transcript, personal papers of César
Tronconi.

86 "César Tronconi: La posición argentina es poder garantizar la libertad del movimiento obrero continental," interview with César Tronconi, *La Marina*, 28 August 1948, box 8: "Departamento de Política, Ecuador-Cuba," folder 1: Política interna, AC.

87 Allan Stewart to Bartlett Wells, dispatch 4165, memorandum: "Newspaper Situation in General," 10 July 1947, folder RG 84 837.91/7–1147, NARA. The cable specified that "according to information in journalistic circles, 'Diario de la Marina' is being paid by Perón to beat the drum for the Argentine cause. The amount allegedly being paid is said to be $50,000."

88 Several sources coincide in the same description: Lester D. Mallory to the Secretary of State, Havana, Cuba, 26 April 1948, no. 336, Subject: "Possible Perón-sponsored New Student Movement in Latin America; Cubans Concerned Suspected of Taking Part in Colombian Revolution," folder RG 59 737.39, NARA; Cafiero, *Desde que grité*, 35–50; Alape, *El Bogotazo*.

89 Henry L. Pitts Jr. to Secretary of State, Buenos Aires, 1 April 1948, Subject: Visit to Argentina of Delegates from Latin America Labor Organizations at Invitation of the Argentine Confederación General del Trabajo, box 5553, folder 810.5043, NARA; Alexander, *A History of Organized Labor in Cuba*, 122–30. Argentina was not the only country active in Cuba. U.S. labor diplomats counted as a cornerstone of their success in Latin America the support obtained by the CTC. The CTC belonged to CTAL, but withdrew from it in 1947, when it became dominated by communist forces. Cuban unions then flirted with Perón, and CTC Secretary General Angel Cofiño's visit to Buenos Aires generated hopes among the Argentines and concern among the Americans.

90 The Argentine ambassador made a critical description of Molinari and Tronconi's involvement in the organization of the trip (against the embassy's advice), adding that it hurt "the prestige built by this representation in Cuba and the United States." Embajador Carlos Riarte Ibazeta to Señor Ministro, confidential, 21 April 1948, "Departamento de Política, Ecuador-Cuba" box, "Copia de Notas de la Embajada Argentina en Cuba" folder, AC; Alape, *El Bogotazo*; de la Cova, *The Moncada Attack*, 18–19; Pardo Llada, *Fidel y el "Che,"* 44–46.

91 Alape, *El Bogotazo*, 640.

92 That was an object of internal dispute within the U.S. State Department. After revising the information provided by the embassy in Havana, an official in Washington found it "disquieting . . . to find the Embassy concluding . . . that there is a 'reasonable amount of evidence' to support the conclusion that a larger part of the arms used was manufactured in Argentina." Mackay to State Department, 12 January 1948, confidential, Subject: "Frustrated Plot to Invade Dominican Republic, Summer 1947; Embassy Habana's Recapitulation of Information," folder RG 84 737.39/1–1248, NARA. The doubts of Washington in this case might have been right, since Argentina had sold arms to Guatemala (a commercial transaction) but did not seem to have the capacity to provide weapons in the Caribbean for a military incursion.

93 Mackay to Walker, 12 January 1948, Subject: "Frustrated Plot to Invade Dominican Republic, Summer 1947," folder RG 59 737.39/1–1248, NARA; de la Cova, *The
Moncada Attack*, 18–19.

94 Many studies have argued that the reform was less radical than proclaimed at the
time, even if it added reasons for a confrontation with the oil industry. For a context and an appreciation of the impact of Betancourt reform on oil revenue, see
Ellner, "Venezuela"; Bethell and Roxborough, *Latin America between the Second
World War and the Cold War*, 150.

95 Venezuela is an interesting example of the kind of contradictory impression that
Peronism awoke abroad during its first years. Unlike Perón, both Betancourt and
Gallegos had deep political roots in the student movement, and they explicitly
identified the Peruvian party APRA as the model for Acción Democrática. Betancourt identified Perón as a kind of fascist caudillo, the kind that had become a
target of the Caribbean Legion, which the Venezuelan leader headed. But Perón
was equally disliked by Marcos Pérez Jiménez, the Venezuelan military strongman who overthrew Gallegos in 1948. He did not trust the activism of the labor
movement, and after meeting Perón in Buenos Aires in 1948, he described him as
"a Betancourt with military beret" (and he would offer asylum to Perón after he
was overthrown in 1955). See Alexander, *Romulo Betancourt and the Transformation of Venezuela*, 298–99.

96 Alape, *El Bogotazo*, 640–50, Pardo Llada, *Fidel y el "Che,"* 45–51.

97 Lanús, *De Chapultepec al Beagle*, 239. There is no other record of the content of
the conversation.

98 Blanco and Criado, *Todo el tiempo de los cedros*, 247–51.

99 Lester D. Mallory to the Secretary of State, Havana, Cuba, 26 April 1948,
no. 336, Subject: "Possible Perón-sponsored New Student Movement in Latin
America; Cubans Suspected of Taking Part in Colombian Revolution," folder
RG 59 737.39, NARA.

100 The amount contributed by the Argentines to Castro's expedition can be only
a general estimate. U.S. and Argentine reports mention that Molinari and his
secretary gave "several times" sums of $100, whereas the director of the Liberal
paper *La Marina* made a single contribution of $200. The significance of such
amounts can be deduced from the larger economic context. The equivalent of
one dollar in 1948 was $9.33 in September 2011, so each of Molinari's donations
was the equivalent to a little less than a thousand dollars in current value (the
Cuban peso was pegged to the dollar 1:1). Anecdotal evidence also suggests that
the purchasing power of that sum was bigger in 1948 than in 2011, mostly in Colombia and other Latin American countries whose currencies were devalued for
several years after the war. In one of his letters, Castro mentions that the Claridge
Hotel in Bogotá charged him 9.50 Colombian pesos daily, roughly $4 in 1948
currency, or $39 in 2015 currency.

101 Lester D. Mallory to Secretary of State, Havana, Cuba, 26 April 1948, confidential,
Subject: "Possible Peron-sponsored New Student Movement in Latin America;

Cubans Suspected of Taking Part in Colombian Revolution," folder RG 84 800, Col. Revolution 8c, p. 9, NARA.

102 Argentina and the United States had clashed during the Pan-American meeting of Rio 1947. Both parties argued strongly in favor of strengthening military capacities to fight communism (the Argentine case at that meeting was just slightly nuanced with references to social equality). But the United States proposed an inter-American defense council that would coordinate military spending and action, whereas Perón insisted that the money and decisions be managed by individual governments. Lanús, *De Chapultepec al Beagle*, 159–66.

103 Fidel Castro to his father, Bogotá, 3 October 1948, in Blanco and Criado, *Todo el tiempo de los cedros*, 250.

104 For Venezuela, see *El golpe contra el Presidente Gallegos*, Documentos para la historia: Gestores, animadores, colaboradores, Caracas, Ediciones Centauro, 1983. For Panama, see Bethell and Roxborough, *Latin America between the Second World War and The Cold War*, 17.

105 "Responsabiliza a Moscú por el levantamiento," *Noticias Gráficas*, 13 April 1948.

106 "Queremos soberanía, no superestados," editorial, *La Epoca* (Buenos Aires), 16 April 1948, 12.

107 Lanús, *De Chapultepec al Beagle*, 185.

108 Charter of Organization of American States, art. 34, quoted in "Text of Charter of Organization of American States Adopted in Bogotá to Form Legal Entity," *New York Times*, 1 May 1948, 17.

109 In the previous negotiations, U.S. officials had proposed very vague language in relation to the use of force against communism, because they thought it would be impossible to pass, but also because it opened a window that "dictatorial governments in other countries" would use as "a means of attacking all opposition." PPS-26, paper prepared by the Policy Planning Staff, enclosure no. 2, Washington, 22 March 1948, "Problem to Establish U.S. Policy Regarding Anti-Communist Measures which Could Be Planned and Carried Out Within the Inter-American System," in Wright, Cassidy, and Stauffer, *Foreign Relations of the United States, 1948*. About the OAS "anticommunist resolution," see Trask, "The Impact of the Cold War on U.S.-Latin American Relations, 1945–1949," pp. 113–22. Morgenfeld, *Vecinos en conflicto*, 386–89.

110 Morgenfeld, *Vecinos en conflicto*, chap. 13.

111 Although negotiations continued during 1947 and 1948, President Truman had made clear the U.S. position about this point. In April 1947, he publicly stated, "There has been a Marshall Plan for the Western Hemisphere for a century and a half, known as the Monroe Doctrine"—a parallelism that said as much about the relation with Latin America as it said about U.S. ambitions for Europe with the Recovery Program. *New York Times*, 15 August 1947, 8. In Bethell and Roxoborough, *Latin America between Second World War and the Cold War*, 22.

112 Rumors at that moment suggested it was Perón who wanted to postpone the conference from January to April, in order to wait a final decision from

the United States about the extent and participants of the Marshall Plan. For the efforts made by Argentina to join the International Monetary Fund and, particularly, the World Bank, see Kedar, "Chronicle of an Inconclusive Negotiation."

113 For a specific focus on the intellectual continuities of modernization discourses, see Kahl, *Modernization, Exploitation and Dependency in Latin America.*

114 The letters collected in the Bramuglia Papers reveal a wide support from a variety of social and political sectors, most of them for what seem to be social organizations sympathizing with Peronism but well removed from the center of power, small organizations formally unconnected with political parties (from soccer teams to small public-library branches to neighborhood associations), and individuals. They all stress the vindication of Argentine nationalism and its demands about the Falkland Islands (Malvinas Islas) as part of a Latin American common front opposing the United States. Box 30: "Letters, Correspondence," Juan Atilio Bramuglia Papers, Hoover Institution Archives, Stanford University (hereafter JABP).

115 A classic work studying the impact of the economic crisis of 1949 as a turning point is Gerchunoff, "Peronist Economic Policies, 1946, 1955." For a more recent study placing the economic crisis of 1949 as a turning point in Argentina, see Kedar, "Chronicle of an Inconclusive Negotiation."

116 This view underlines large parts of Tulio Halperín Donghi's work, in which he describes Perón's discourse on foreign policy as almost an artifact for deceit, hiding a more permanent pro-U.S. stance of Peronism. The author calls the Third Position a tool that "had to simultaneously help [Perón] gain the sympathy of the masses of Hispanic America hostile to the United States, and allow for the constant negotiation for the support of U.S. foreign policy, which most of the time he adopted as his own." Halperín Donghi, *Argentina en el callejón*, 67–68.

117 In his study about Peronism and domestic consumption, Eduardo Elena indicates that the 1949 crisis obviously had an impact on workers' purchasing power, but that it was different from what has been usually said, since Peronism worked, with more success than is usually admitted, toward a "soft landing" of the Argentine economy, avoiding both the risks of a heated economy and of a recession. Elena, *Dignifying Argentina*, 223–30. Mark Healey, in his analysis of the reconstruction of the city of San Juan after the 1944 earthquake, also noted that the 1949 crisis and its impact on the national economic team affected the reconstruction plans and the already delayed timeline. But the author stresses instead the social struggles in the province and the political confrontation at the provincial and national level to note that by 1947, some of the most daring reconstruction projects were already defunct. Healey, *The Ruins of the New Argentina*, 238–55.

118 Embajador a Señor Ministro, Bogotá, 30 April 1948, note 202, Asunto: "La situación política, propósitos; una carta del Embajador Urrutia," "Embajador del Río, Reservado 1948–1950" folder, p. 7, AC.

CHAPTER SIX. **Political Declension**

1 Secretario General to Embajador de la República Argentina, Bogotá, 11 August 1950, note 1195, Asunto: "Orden de Boyacá. Bogotá, Colombia," fondo 135, binder 99, Archivo General de la Nación, Bogotá, Colombia (hereafter AGN).

2 On the role of Ospina Pérez in Colombia during and immediately after Gaitán's assassination, see Pécaut, *L'ordre et la violence*.

3 Apparently, the new version of the old slogan was sung for the first time during the 1946 presidential campaign, but did not become central until a year later. Some authors argue that the first slogan was also "Ni Nazis ni Fascistas: Peronistas." See Luna, *El 45*, 550–51.

4 Friedman, *Rethinking Anti-Americanism*, 123.

5 Westad, *The Global Cold War*, 79–86.

6 Westad, *The Global Cold War*, 17.

7 Greg Grandin, "Off the Beach," 426.

8 For a reflection about the importance of this incident in the early years of the United Nations (and of the Cold War), and the role of Bramuglia, see Jessup, "The Berlin Blockade and the use of the United Nations," 172.

9 On 2 October 1948, Perón wrote to his foreign minister: "I suggested you not accept the Presidency of the Security Council . . . since we were informed . . . that there was a plan to descredit Argentina going on in the UN against us." Telegrama Cifrado Perón to Bramuglia, Buenos Aires, 2 October 1948, box 30, "Carpeta de Cables Enviados a S.E. El Doctor Bramuglia por el Excmo. Señor Presidente de la Nación y Señora de Perón, Año 1948" folder, Juan Atilio Bramuglia Papers, Hoover Institution Archives, Stanford University (hereafter JABP).

10 Telegrama Cifrado Remitido por el Excelentísimo Señor Presidente al Doctor Bramuglia, Buenos Aires, 7 November 1948, box 30, "Carpeta de Cables Enviados a S.E. El Doctor Bramuglia por el Excmo. Señor Presidente de la Nación y Señora de Perón, Año 1948" folder, JABP.

11 Bramuglia to Perón, 10 September 1948, sent from the steamboat *Los Andes* en route to Paris, box 30, "Carpeta de Cables Enviados por S.E. El Doctor Bramuglia al Excmo. Señor Presidente de la Nación, Año 1948, folder, JABP.

12 "La conciliación de Berlín da resonancia universal a la diplomacia argentina," *La Fronda*, Buenos Aires, 12 May 1949, 2.

13 The Secretary of State to Diplomatic Representatives in the American Republics, "Policy of the United States Regarding Anti-Communist Measures within the Inter-American System," Washington, 21 June 1948, 810.0013/6–2148, in Wright, Cassidy, and Stauffer, *Foreign Relations of the United States, 1948*.

14 President Juan Perón to Minister Bramuglia, encrypted telegram, Buenos Aires, 10 December 1948, box 30, "Carpetas de Cables Enviados a S.E. El Doctor Bramuglia por el Excmo. Señor Presidente de la Nación y Señora de Perón" folder, JABP.

15 See, for example, Zanatta, *La internacional justicialista*.

16 Milanesio, *Workers Go Shopping in Argentina*, 23–28.

17 Kedar, "Chronicle of an Inconclusive Negotiation," 637–68.
18 Gerchunoff and Llach, *El ciclo de la ilusión y el desencanto*, 181–82, particularly the graph captioned "Real Salary Expansion, 1945–1949."
19 Luis N. Nieto Arteta, Encargado de Negocios, to Señor Ministro, 22 October 1949, Embassy of Colombia, Buenos Aires; "Embajada de Colombia en Argentina," folio 215, AGN.
20 Bottarini, "Estrategias político-educativas peronistas," 420–22.
21 On populist movements and institutional consolidation, see Laclau, *On Populist Reason*, 14. Gerardo Aboy Carlés discusses some of Laclau's main arguments in "Populismo, regeneracionismo y democracia."
22 "Crease la Carrera de Agregados Obreros," Executive Order 6420, 15 March 1949, *Boletín Oficial de la República Argentina*.
23 Bottarini, "Estrategias político-educativas peronistas," 430.
24 Bottarini, "Estrategias político-educativas peronistas," 419. Although there is not enough information available, an interesting question here is whether the social profile of worker attachés changed. Daniel James and others suggest there was a change in Peronist Party recruitment around this time, as more lower-middle-class groups became prominent with institutionalization.
25 Bottarini, "Estrategias político-educativas peronistas," 433, fn. 43. Expectedly, the relation between the foreign service and Peronism remained complicated, and diplomats never fully recognized the role of Peronism (let alone the role of the union lawyer Bramuglia) in the professionalization of the foreign service. Even in 2014, a well-informed op-ed by an Argentine diplomat about the history of the Argentine foreign service "erased" its origins and locates the first attempts at professionalization a decade later. Maximiliano Gregorio Cernadas, "Medio siglo de diplomacia profesional," *La Nación*, 15 January 2014, 8.
26 "Cursos de formación para los miembros del Servicio Exterior," *Anuario del Instituto del Servicio Exterior de la Nación, 1949–1950*, Instituto del Servicio Exterior de la Nación (hereafter ISEN), 48.
27 Bottarini, "Estrategias político-educativas peronistas," 430 (the original number was 99, but six attachés from the previous cohort returned to Buenos Aires during the first months of the year).
28 "Decisión Presupuestaria," *Balance Anual, 1949–1950*, ISEN.
29 Memoria del Ministerio de Relaciones Exteriores y Culto. 1949–1950. Section, División Organización Internacional del Trabajo, ISEN.
30 Bengasi Salvador Di Pasquale to Anselmo Malvicini, Lima, 10 May 1950, "Subject: Remisión de iniciativas," note 37, uncatalogued papers, Embassy of Argentina, Lima, Peru. Unless noted, this and all the other files cited as "uncatalogued papers, Embassy of Argentina, Lima, Peru," were found in the basement of the embassy premises during the moving of the diplomatic representation to a new building in August 2011.
31 Bengasi Di Pasquale to Señor Embajador, "Visita a la zona petrolera y observaciones efectuadas durante mi permanencia en dicho centro de trabajo," Lima, 25 April 1950, note 21, uncatalogued papers, Embassy of Argentina, Lima, Peru.

32 Roberto Ferrari to Nicolás Repetto, Tegucigalpa, 14 May 1947, Centro de Documentación e Investigación de la Cultura de Izquierdas en la Argentina, Buenos Aires (hereafter, CeDInCI).

33 Milanesio, "Peronist and *Cabecitas*," 57–59.

34 Lenton, "The Malón de la Paz of 1946," 85, 89.

35 Bengasi Salvador di Pasquale to Ambassador, Lima, 21 July 1949, A.O. Report no. 19, uncatalogued papers, Embassy of Argentina, Lima, Peru.

36 Laclau, *Emancipación y diferencia*, 62.

37 Jorge Aliaga Merino, "Figuras de actualidad: General Don Juan Domingo Perón," *Diario El Sol de Cuzco*, 27 July 1950. The article came out a week after the visit of one of the worker attachés to Cuzco, during which they met with workers and officials in preparation for the arrival of aid from the Fundación Eva Perón. Arturo Sacomani to Señor Embajador, Agregado Obrero, note 26/50, Objeto: "Viaje al Cuzco en Julio," Lima, 22 August 1950, uncatalogued papers, Embassy of Argentina, Lima, Peru.

38 Guevara, *The Motorcycle Diaries*, 74.

39 See the introduction to Drinot, *Che's Travels*.

40 Drinot and Knight, "'Awaiting the Blood of a Truly Emancipating Revolution,'" 97, Elena, "Point of Departure," 35.

41 Guevara, *The Motorcycle Diaries*, 79.

42 Drinot, *Che's Travels*, 3.

43 Intelligence also provided the larger picture about communist in the Latin American labor movement at large. "Informe de Inteligencia sobre el accionar del comunismo en América Latina," March 1953, box 30, JABP.

44 Di Pasquale to Embajador, "Report on Social Conditions in the Republic of Peru." note 19, Lima, 21 July 1949, uncatalogued papers, Embassy of Argentina, Lima, Peru.

45 Di Pasquale to Embajador, "Activity of the Communist Party in Peru," note 8, Lima, 25 January 1950, uncatalogued papers, Embassy of Argentina, Lima, Peru.

46 Juan Durso to Señor Embajador, note 50, Bogotá, 19 April 1950, "Embajador Ramon del Rio 1948–1950" folder, AC.

47 Email correspondence with Silvia Maestro, 2 March 2009. The transit of the Bolivian leader to and from Argentina was reported in several embassy cables. Modesto Alvarez to Armando Bulacia: DOIT, note 51, Objeto: "Acompañar solicitud del dirigente minero Juan Iñiguez Ibañez," La Paz, 7 January 1951, uncatalogued file, found on the premises of the Embassy of Argentina in Bolivia.

48 Encargado de Negocios to Señor Ministro, Objetivo: "Ampliar Información," La Paz, 2 April 1949, "3 Gabinete Político Jurídico, Bolivia Año 1949" box, AC; "El Agregado Obrero de la Embajada Argentina Pronunció Dos Discursos Inamistosos en los Sindicatos 'Unión de Fabriles' y 'Soligno,'" *La Razón* (La Paz, Bolivia), 1 April 1949, A14, AC; "Diplomático Extranjero en La Paz Olvida su Deber de Neutralidad." *El Diario* (La Paz, Bolivia), 1 April 1949, 3, AC.

49 Lechín to Carlos Mármol, Encargado de Negocios de la Embajada Argentina. La Paz, Bolivia, 6 April 1949, "3 Gabinete Político Jurídico, Bolivia Año 1949" box,

attachment 1, AC. The attachés in Brazil, Chile, Honduras, Paraguay and Guatemala, among others, were involved in similar incidents.

50 Carlos Ríos Marmol to Canciller Bramuglia, La Paz, 2 April 1949, "3 Gabinete Político Jurídico, Bolivia Año 1949" box, attachment 1, AC.

51 "Falsa Tercera Posición," editorial, *El Diario* (La Paz, Bolivia), 13 April 1949, A1.

52 "Será Reemplazado el Agregado Obrero de la Embajada Argentina," *Ultima Hora* (La Paz, Bolivia), 4 April 1949.

53 Executive Order 37.788, secret and confidential "Instrucciones a que Deberán Ajustar su Cometido los Señores Agregados Obreros," 6 December 1948, numbered copy 12, uncatalogued papers Embassy of Argentina, Lima, Peru.

54 Executive Order 37.788, secret and confidential "Instrucciones a que Deberán Ajustar su Cometido los Señores Agregados Obreros," 6 December 1948, numbered copy 12, p. 3, uncatalogued papers, Embassy of Argentina, Lima, Peru.

55 Executive Order 37.788, secret and confidential "Instrucciones a que Deberán Ajustar su Cometido los Señores Agregados Obreros," 6 December 1948, numbered copy 12, pp. 4–5, uncatalogued papers, Embassy of Argentina, Lima, Peru.

56 Executive Order 37.788, secret and confidential "Instrucciones a que Deberán Ajustar su Cometido los Señores Agregados Obreros," 6 December 1948, numbered copy 12, pp. 8–10, uncatalogued papers, Embassy of Argentina, Lima, Peru.

57 "Plan de Acción para el Movimiento Justicialista Internacional," DOIT circular 19, box 1, AC; Bottarini, "Estrategias político-educativas peronistas," 427.

58 "Plan de Acción para el Movimiento Justicialista Internacional," DOIT circular 19, box 1, AC.

59 Modesto Alvarez to Señor Embajador, note 94/52, 24 November 1952, uncatalogued papers, Embassy of Argentina, La Paz, Bolivia.

60 Serafino Romualdi to José Figueres, New York, 6 November 1952, box 2, folder 2, Serafino Romualdi Papers, Kheel Center for Labor-Management Documentation and Archives, Cornell University Library (hereafter SRP). On the actions of the U.S. government, the CIA, and the U.S. labor movement particularly in relation with the Lombardistas in Latin America, see Kofas, *The Struggle for Legitimacy*, especially 289–324. On the relation of U.S. labor with the noncommunist Left in Latin America, see Patrick J. Iber's work about the Dominican Republic, "'Who Will Impose Democracy?'"

61 Kofas, *The Struggle for Legitimacy*, 7. Kofas's work focuses almost exclusively on the power struggle between the Lombardista camp and the AFL-State Department in Latin America. As such, it analyzes the countries where this struggle was relevant (Mexico, Chile, Cuba, Guatemala, and Bolivia) and leaves aside countries like Brazil and Argentina.

62 About the relation of the CIA with CIOSL, see Wilford, *The Mighty Wurlitzer*, chap. 3.

63 Serafino Romualdi to Juan Arévalo (Cuba), New York, 21 April 1951, and Serafino Romualdi to Sergio Barba Romero (Ecuador), New York, 2 February 1951, box 3, folder 10, SRP. See Walcher, "Reforming Latin American Labor"; Waters and van Goethem, *American Labor's Global Ambassadors*, 132–33.

64 "ORIT Affiliate Battles Communism in British Guiana," *Inter-American Labor Bulletin* (official organ of ORIT), May 1952. A report from January 1951 also stated that "several wildcat strikes in British Guiana have lately been led by elements of the so-called People's Progressive Party, the Communist Party of the Colony." See also Rabe, *U.S. Intervention in British Guiana*. Robert Waters Jr. presents a different version of the role of the AFL in British Guiana and British Honduras and criticizes Rabe. Waters stresses the differentiations that the AFL made between communist unions (that they condemned) and nationalist ones, as well as AFL comments in favor of the need for social reform. Yet his work leaves intact the evidence provided by Rabe about the AFL role in undermining labor in the British Caribbean. Waters, "More Subtle Than We Knew."

65 Luna, *Perón y su tiempo*, vol. 2, chap. 11.

66 About the significance of this episode and Perón's attempts to contact the opposition in 1952, see Bejar, "La entrevista Dickmann-Perón."

67 Eduardo Elena analyzes the impact on consumption of the government fiscal and monetary policies and how they affected Peronist discourse, investing in it a rhetorical (and practical) emphasis on austerity. Elena, *Dignifying Argentina*, 154–86.

68 "Afírmase que este año no será de retorno a la abundancia en la Argentina sino que habrá que producir más y consumir menos," *La Nación* (La Paz), 6 January 1953.

69 On social unrest in postwar Uruguay, see French, "Uruguay since 1930"; Leslie Bethell, *The Cambridge History of Latin America, Vol. VIII*.

70 Wallace Stuart to the State Department, note 247, Montevideo, 29 September 1952, 633.35/9–2952, NARA, in Oddone, *Vecinos en discordia*, 229–31.

71 Oddone, *Vecinos en discordia*, 3.

72 The full description of Perón's reaction was provided to the U.S. government by Fernán Cisneros, an official of the Peruvian embassy in Montevideo, who talked extensively with the Argentine authorities and reported to the American embassy. Wallace Stuart to the State Department, note 247, Montevideo, 29 September 1952, 633.35/9–2952, NARA, in Oddone, *Vecinos en discordia*, 229–31. During the bilateral conflict, activists used to sing rhymes at Peronist rallies in which they portrayed Uruguay as a collaborator of United Kingdom against Argentina, such as "Quieran o no los ingleses, quieralo o no el Uruguay, las Malvinas argentinas, patrimonio nacional." Thanks to Guillermo Bodner for providing me with this historical recollection.

73 Wallace Stuart to the State Department, note No 936 and annex 1, Montevideo, 17 April 1952, 633.00/4–1752, NARA, in Oddone, *Vecinos en discordia*, 223–28.

74 Wallace Stuart to the State Department, note 247, Montevideo, 29 September 1952, 633.35/10–952 XR 733.00 XR 833.062, NARA, in Oddone, *Vecinos en discordia*, 235–36.

75 Wallace Stuart to the State Department, note 936 and annex 1, Montevideo, 17 April 1952, 633.00/4–1752, NARA, in Oddone, *Vecinos en discordia*, 223–28.

76 Frank Devine to the State Department, note 635, Montevideo, 10 January 1952, 633.35/1–1052 XR 611.20 XR 935.5301, NARA, in Oddone, *Vecinos en discordia*, 217–20.

77 See among others James Siekmeier, "Latin American Economic Nationalism and United States–Latin American Relations," 59–76; Loayza, "An 'Aladdin's Lamp' for Free Enterprise," 83–105; Rabe, *Eisenhower and Latin America*.

CHAPTER SEVEN. **A Bitter Pill**

1 "Obrero Argentino Llama en Brasil a Unidad Regional," *La Prensa*, Buenos Aires, 15 October 1952, 5.

2 On Volta Redonda, see Dinius, *Brazil's Steel City*, particularly chaps. 2 and 3. For a perspective on its general impact in development projects, see the introduction to Ioris, *Transforming Brazil*.

3 Editorial, *Jornal do Brasil*, 12 October 1952, editorial page.

4 French, *The Brazilian Workers' ABC*, particularly part 3, "The Promise and Pitfalls of Democracy, 1947–1953."

5 Kofas, *The Struggle for Legitimacy*, particularly 289–94, in chap. 7, "The AFL-OIAA Initiative to Divide the CTAL."

6 For an overview of the creation of the WFTU and the ICFTU, see MacShane, *International Labour and Origins of the Cold War*. For CIA collaboration with American unions abroad in general, see Wilford, *The Mighty Wurlizer*, 51–69; Weiner, *Legacy of Ashes*.

7 Brogi, "The AFL and CIO between 'Crusade' and Pluralism in Italy."

8 Although Toledano was never a member of the Communist Party, both the CTM and the CTAL received strong support from the Soviet Union. This was part of the reason why the AFL tried, through different means, to undermine CTAL's influence in Latin America. See Levenstein, *Las Organizaciones Obreras en Estados Unidos y México*; Carr, "Vicente Lombardo Toledano."

9 Godio, *Historia del movimiento obrero latinoamericano*, 9–29.

10 There is abundant bibliography about the relation between the AFL and the CIO and their respective relations with unions abroad. For an overview of this process, see MacShane, *International Labour and Origins of the Cold War*.

11 The reports from all countries paid attention to the attachés' activities. The first one, besides, remarked that "immediately after our founding Congress, there was unleashed, principally by the followers of Perón, a violent campaign throughout the entire continent for the purpose of discrediting the new organization and making the workers of America lose faith in the possibilities which it offers for their defense." Report of the Regional Secretary of the ORIT, 17 December 1951–24 January 1952, box 4, folder 7, Serafino Romualdi Papers, Kheel Center for Labor-Management Documentation and Archives, Cornell University Library (hereafter SRP).

12 Panella, *Perón y ATLAS*, 22. There's an extensive body of work about labor regional organizations and the role of Argentina in the 1945–1955 period. See also Urquiza,

CGT y ATLAS; Teodoro Blanco, "ATLAS, la proyección sindical peronista en América Latina," 60–73; Alba, *Historia del Movimiento Obrero en América Latina.*

13 Afonso, "Para Norte-Americano Ver. Adidos Trabalhistas e operários brasileiros," 225–27.

14 Vergara, *Copper Workers, International Business, and Domestic Politics in Cold War Chile*, 83–84. In 1953, the reunification of the Chilean labor movement under the strong leadership of the Left was a hard blow to the ORIT, but not an endorsement to Peronism. See also Vergara, *Chilean Workers and US Labor*, 201–14.

15 Teodoro Blanco, "ATLAS, la proyección sindical peronista en América Latina," 62.

16 Alexander, *A History of Organized Labor in Cuba*, 188.

17 Panella, *Perón y ATLAS*, 41.

18 Urquiza, *CGT y ATLAS*, 43–49.

19 Teodoro Blanco, "ATLAS, la proyección sindical peronista en América Latina," 68.

20 Teodoro Blanco, "ATLAS, la proyección sindical peronista en América Latina," 68.

21 "On the Labor Front," *Hemispherica* (monthly bulletin of the U.S. Committee of the Inter-American Association for Democracy and Freedom) 1, no. 4, (April 1951): 4, box 10, folder 5, SRP.

22 Panella, *Perón y ATLAS*, 43–45.

23 Godio describes how labor movements in Latin America were conceived regionally but acted nationally. Godio, *Historia del Movimiento Obrero*, introduction.

24 Panella, *Perón y ATLAS*, 43.

25 Alba, *Historia del movimiento obrero en América Latina*, 190–92.

26 Teodoro Blanco, "ATLAS, la proyección sindical peronista en América Latina," 68.

27 Gartner to Tronconi, subject: "Work Planning," Buenos Aires, 12 February 1954, Dirección Organización Internacional del Trabajo (DOIT), uncatalogued papers, Embassy of Argentina, Havana, Cuba. There are at least a dozen more memorandums with similar content for 1954.

28 Memorias del Instituto del Servicio Exterior de la Nación, 1954. Biblioteca del Instituto del Servicio Exterior de la Nación (hereafter ISEN), 56; Bottarini, "Estrategias político; educativas peronistas," 410–19.

29 On the economic policies during this period, see Gerchunoff and Llach, *El ciclo de la ilusión y el desencanto*, 201–31. An analysis of the rearrangement of the political and symbolic relations between the Peronist base and the government during this period, Elena, *Dignifying Argentina*, 221–29.

30 Escudé and Cisneros, *Historia general de las relaciones exteriores de la República Argentina*, 164. The chapter "La Política Regional del Peronismo" offers an overview of all the bilateral agreements signed by Argentina under Perón.

31 The Ambassador in Argentina (Nufer) to the State Department. Subject: "Conversation with President Perón," Buenos Aires, 5 February 1953, 611.35/2–553. Kane and Sanford, *Foreign Relations of the United States, 1952–1954*, doc. 114.

32 Walter B. Smith, memorandum for the President. Subject: "Current Status of U.S.-Argentine Relations," Department of State, Washington, 5 March 1953, Dwight D. Eisenhower Presidential Library and Museum, Abilene, Kansas (hereafter DEPL).

33 Friedman, *Rethinking Anti-Americanism*, 135.

34 Friedman, *Rethinking Anti-Americanism*, 136–38.

35 There are several studies about the 1954 coup in Guatemala. The most comprehensive study of it and of the international involvement in the overthrew of president Jacobo Arbenz is Gleijeses, *Shattered Hope*.

36 Juan Perón to Milton Eisenhower, Buenos Aires, 27 June 1954, box 30, "Hipólito Paz-Juan Perón" folder, Juan Atilio Bramuglia Papers, Hoover Institution Archives, Stanford University (hereafter JABP).

37 Juan Perón to Milton Eisenhower, Buenos Aires, 27 June 1954, box 30, "Hipólito Paz-Juan Perón" folder, JABP.

38 Friedman, *Rethinking Anti-Americanism*, 144.

39 Juan Perón to Milton Eisenhower, Buenos Aires, 27 June 1954, box 30, "Hipólito Paz-Juan Perón" folder, JABP.

40 There is extensive bibliography about this episode of American unions and their relation with the U.S. foreign policy. In addition to Gleijeses's *Shattered Hope*, see Bergquist, *Labor and the Course of American Democracy*; Levenson-Estrada, *Trade against Terror*.

41 "AFL Statement on Guatemala," box 3, folder 16, SRP.

42 Levenson-Estrada, *Trade Unionism against Terror*, 30.

43 Romualdi to Schnitzler, confidential memorandum, "United Fruit Company," 21 March 1955, box 3, folder 11, SRP.

44 ATLAS, *Boletín Informativo*, no. 11, December 1953, 11.

45 "Adhesión al Pueblo de Guatemala," *Boletín de la CGT*, CGT, Buenos Aires, 17 July 1954, 12.

46 Benjamin, "Painting, Jugendstil, Novelty," 543–45.

47 There are very interesting, informed, and insightful works about this episode. In relation to the refugees at the Argentine embassy in Guatemala in particular, González Galeotti, *El exilio Guatemalteco en Argentina*, manuscript; Enriquez, *Guatemala: No más exilio*. An article by the Argentine journalist Rogelio García Lupo in the newspaper *Clarín* describes the events around the relation between the Argentine embassy and Che Guevara and the Guatemalan refugees. Rogelio García Lupo, "Perón, el Che y el derrumbe de Guatemala," *Clarín*, 17 January 1999. García Lupo attributes Che a much larger role in the asylum of the refugees than do most accounts. Ricardo Rojo, an acquaintance of Che Guevara, includes a somewhat embellished version of the events in his biography, *Mi amigo el Che*. For good and brief analysis of those days and their influence in Che's transition from populist to Marxist thinking, see Marco Vinicio Mejía, *La importancia de llamarse Che*, particularly 41–53. Other works locate it within the larger experience of the Guatemalan exile after the 1954 military coup, and especially in relation to the evolution of organized labor. See, for example, Obando Sánchez, *Memorias*.

Obando's book also offers a firsthand narrative of the refugees' journey from the time they left the Argentine embassy and during their time in Argentina. Several other studies about the Left in Latin America make reference to the episode; they are mentioned in the following pages.

48 "Sobre la situación de asilados en la Embajada. Oficio Confidencial 47/15," Guatemala, 21 July 1954. Document no. 19, Fondo: "Embajada de Chile en Guatemala," Archivo General Histórico del Ministerio de Relaciones Exteriores de Chile, Santiago de Chile. I am deeply grateful to Max Paul Friedman for having given me access to the embassy correspondence, part of a larger work he is preparing with Roberto García Ferreira about Klein's time in Guatemala.

49 The Chilean Ambassador Federico Klein Reidel described in detail the negotiations of the Latin American embassies with the local authorities. Oficio Confidencial 47/14, 21 July 1954; Oficio Confidencial 49/15, 31 July 1954; Oficio Confidencial 55/17, 19 August 1954; and Oficio Confidencial 56/18, 17 September 1954, Fondo: "Embajada de Chile en Guatemala," Archivo General Histórico del Ministerio de Relaciones Exteriores de Chile, Santiago de Chile.

50 Legajo de Alberto Viale, Appointment to Guatemala: Ministry Resolution 18, 11 January 1947; Transfer to Buenos Aires: Ministry Decree 11.953, 1951; Reappointment in Guatemala: Ministry Decree 924, 20 January 1953. All Viale's appointments and later expulsion from the foreign service are described in the Ministry Decree 369, 5 October 1955, and in the Boletín Informativo de la Dirección de Personal no. 20, 30 January 1956, uncatalogued, Archivo de Cancillería, Ministerio de Relaciones Exteriores y Culto, Argentina (hereafter AC).

51 The charge d'affair was Nicasio Sánchez Toranzo, who established contact with Che Guevara during those days and forged a relationship with him. On the role of Sánchez Toranzo (many times embellished by his own narrative), and on his relation with Che and with Perón, see Rogelio García Lupo, "Perón, el Che y el derrumbe de Guatemala," Clarín, 17 January 1999; Ricardo Rojo, Mi amigo el Che.

52 Email correspondence with Edelberto Torres Rivas, 12–15 June 2012. On both the asylum of some of the activists and their later fate in Argentina, email correspondence with Sergio Valdés Pedroni (son of the refugee Fernando Valdés Díaz), 2 June–10 July 2012. For the names of those who found asylum at the Argentine embassy, see "Personas asiladas en la embajada de la República Argentina," La Hora (Guatemala), 31 July 1954. The article listed 198 refugees. More refugees joined the group during the following weeks. See also, González Galeotti, El exilio Guatemalteco en Argentina. A subsequent, more limited list of the refugees that were still at the embassy by September is available in "Sólo 120 asilados podrán llevar aviones argentinos," Prensa Libre (Guatemala), 9 September 1954.

53 Nicasio Sánchez Toranzo, the charge d'affair who was sent by Perón to Guatemala and who developed a relationship with Che Guevara, remembered that he organized the logistics of daily life at the embassy in coordination with the workers and military attachés. González Galeotti, El exilio guatemalteco en Argentina, 18.

54 Email correspondence with Edelberto Torres Rivas, 12–15 June 2012.

55 Email correspondence with Edelberto Torres Rivas, 12–15 June 2012. Edelberto Torres Rivas was a twenty-four-year old communist activist, two years younger than Guevara at the time of the coup. He was the son of the renowned Nicaraguan activist in exile Edelberto Torres Espinosa, for whom Guevara did, during his time in Guatemala, a few translations of Karl Marx into Spanish. Guevara also established a close relationship with Myrna Torres, sister of Torres Espinosa, who remembers the conversations about politics with him in the days around the coup. About his relationship with Torres family, in addition to Guevara's diaries and Anderson's biography, see also Myrna Torres's testimony in Coco López, *Mate y Ron*, p. 91. About both the asylum and the later fate of the refugees in Argentina, email correspondence with Sergio Valdés Pedroni (son of the refugee Fernando Valdés Díaz), 2 June–10 July 2012. By Sergio Valdés Pedroni, see the documentary *Exilio de una Promesa* (Artenativas, 2010).

56 Among the several meetings and late-night conversations about politics were two that are remembered as important in his reflections about how Guatemala showed the limits of populist and nationalistic movements and about the appeal of political violence: one with his friends Ricardo Rojo and Eduardo García, and the other with Rojo and Alfonso Bauer Paiz, member of the Arévalo and Arbenz administrations. The two conversations took place in Guatemala between December 1953 and May 1954. Guevara, *Back on the Road*, 46–49; Mejía, *La importancia de llamarse Che*, 45; "Interview with Alfonso Bauer Paiz"; Coco López, *Mate y Ron*, p. 91. For a different perspective about the role of the Guatemalan period in Che's political education, see Jorge G. Castañeda, who does not give particular relevance to the events of those years in the future guerrillero's life. Castañeda, *La vida en rojo*, 101–5.

57 Guevara, *Back on the Road*, 60; Forster, "Not in All of America Can There Be Found a Country as Democratic as This One," 214.

58 Forster, "Not in All of America Can There Be Found a Country as Democratic as This One," 215.

59 Guevara, *Back on the Road*, 62; Anderson, *Che Guevara*.

60 Guevara, *Back on the Road*, 64.

61 Guevara, *Back on the Road*, 66,

62 Guevara, *Back on the Road*, 69.

63 Anderson, *Che Guevara*, 442.

64 Dan Saxon, *To Save Her Life*, 16. See Saxon's wonderful work for a full comprehensive history of the Urrutia family and their fate during and after the coup.

65 For the complete list of those under asylum at the Argentine embassy, see "Personas Asiladas en la Embajada de la República Argentina," *La Hora*, 31 July 1954.

66 In addition to several oral testimonies, Ricardo Ramirez de León's name appeared at the time in "Personas asiladas en la embajada de la República Argentina," *La Hora*, 11 July 1954. He also appears in some of the pictures taken by the

refugees at the embassy. In one of them, he poses with only ten of the refugees, who later became members of the Guatemalan resistence. Ariel Batres Villagrán, *Sabor de Guatemala en Gustavo Valdés de León: Homenaje in Memorian*, unpublished manuscript, Guatemala, 2015, 203.

67 Forster, "Not in All of America Can There Be Found a Country as Democratic as This One," 224.

68 About the role of "affective register" in the construction of political hegemony, see Beasley-Murray, *Posthegemony*.

69 On their complicated trip to Buenos Aires and the fate of the refugees in Argentina, see Obando Sánchez, *Memorias*, 143–50; Rogelio García Lupo, "Perón, el Che y el derrumbe de Guatemala," *Clarín*, 17 January 1999. According to Obando Sánchez, Perón offered him and the other refugees the opportunity to go from Buenos Aires to Czechoslovakia as political prisoners, a proposal that they rejected.

70 Obando Sánchez recalled being questioned by Argentine officers who showed him his file at the U.S. State Department, including all his trips abroad and his political activity, including a report by the FBI about his trip to the Soviet Union in 1930. According to Obando Sánchez, the Argentine police officer simply told him: "You are a communist. If you are going to become a resident here, you need to behave." Obando Sánchez, *Memorias*, 140.

71 Obando Sánchez, *Memorias*, 143.

72 Cullather, *Secret History*, 15.

73 Cullather, *Secret History*, 50, 51.

74 "ATLAS y la Reforma Agraria Boliviana," *Unidad Sindical* (Lima), no. 14, 1 September 1953, 5.

75 Miguel Sanjunez to Excelentísimo Jefe de Protocolo del Ministerio de Relaciones Exteriores, César Lafey Borda, Vischa, Capital de la Pronvia de Ingavi, 25 February 1955, file 31, Walter Guevara Arce Collection, Archivo y Bibliotecas Nacionales de Bolivia, Sucre, Bolivia (hereafter WGA).

76 Anteproyecto del Programa de Recepción al Excelentísimo Señor General Juan D. Perón, Presidente de la República Argentina, La Paz, 15 March 1955, file 31, WGA.

77 Cable from Bolivian Embassy in Buenos Aires to Ministry of Foreign Affairs in Bolivia, classified, 18 March 1955, file 31, WGA.

78 Felix Luna offers a broad description of Perón's downfall. Luna, *Perón y su tiempo*, vol. 3, 235–28.

79 Víctor Raúl Haya de la Torre, Crisis del Peronismo y del Militarismo en Iberoamérica, Copenhague, July 1955, manuscript, box 6, folder 1, pp. 9–10, SRP.

80 Garone to Perón, Buenos Aires, 26 November 1943, included as an annex in Panella, *Perón y ATLAS*, document 1, 111.

81 División Organización Internacional del Trabajo, Observations Regarding Its Structure, 1956 (no specific date), unnumbered box, Estructura, División Organización Internacional del Trabajo, AC.

82 Tronconi to Jefe Gartner, telegram, 9 October 1955, personal papers of César Tronconi.

83 "Fueron detenidos por causas políticas dirigentes gremiales," *El Diario* (Paraná), 19 February 1958, 4.

84 Interview with Jorge Tomasini, Buenos Aires, 6 July 2012.

85 Pedro Conde Magdaleno to General Dalmiro Videla Balaguer, Interventor in the Province of Córdoba, Lima, 11 November 1955, personal papers of Pedro Conde Magdaleno.

86 Godio, *Historia del movimiento obrero latinoamericano*, 157; Panella, *Perón y ATLAS*, 42.

87 Romualdi to Jay Lovestone, Costa Rica, 10 November 1953, box 5, folder 14, SRP.

88 Panella, *Perón y ATLAS*, 33.

89 *CGT Bulletin* (Buenos Aires), 16 October 1953, 5. Even with less impact, its leaders went as far as to support and campaign in favor of the Egyptian revolution that put an end to King Farouk's rule.

90 Perón to Garone, Caracas, 17 April 1957, included as an annex in Panella, *Perón y ATLAS*, document 21, 140–41.

91 Perón to Garone, 3 May 1957, included as an annex in Panella, *Perón y ATLAS*, document 24, 144–46.

CONCLUSION

1 Personal interview with Torcuato Di Tella, New York, 27 August 2012; email correspondence, 29 October 2012.

2 For a classical analysis of Bonapartism in Marxist theory as a departure from more economicist arguments, see Hobsbawm, *Marxism in Marx's Day*. In his writing, Antonio Gramsci refers to the same political process, but mostly calls it "Caesarism," a reference to Mussolini, who called himself "The New Caesar."

3 Gilman, *Mandarins of the Future*, 170. For an interesting contribution to the same perspective, see Latham, *The Right Kind of Revolution*.

4 Allan Dawson to the Secretary of State, Caracas, 8 February 1946, box 20, "Correspondence, Diplomatic 1946–7 A-D" folder, Spruille Braden Papers 1903–1977, Rare Book and Manuscript Library, Columbia University (hereafter SBP).

5 Penn Warren, *All the King's Men*, 366.

6 Germani, "La integración de las masas a la vida política y el totalitarismo," 153–76. For the most comprehensive study of Germani's contribution to social studies in Argentina, see Alejandro Blanco, *Razón y modernidad*. Blanco highlights how the fine distinctions in Germani's work laid the grounds for a second generation that produced some of the most original works about Peronism. For a different take about the constraints that Germani's legacy and his notion of modernization imposed on Argentine sociology, see Adamovsky, *Historia de la clase media argentina*, introducción.

7 Lipset, *Political Man*, 171.

8 For a detailed analysis of these exchanges, see Amaral, *Del fascismo al Movimiento Nacional Popular.*

9 Lipset, "Working-Class Authoritarianism," 380.

10 Jeane Kirkpatrick, "Peronist Politics in Argentina," iii, 23. Kirkpatrick did not do research in Argentina, but based her dissertation on a national opinion survey carried out in 1965 by International Research Associates among 2,014 people in cities of more than 2,000 inhabitants.

11 Braden to Ellis Briggs, 12 February 1949, box 33, "State Department" folder, SBP.

12 Jacobson, Frye, and Gonzalez, *What Have They Built You to Do?,* 12–20.

13 Braden to the Honorable Thomas E. Dewey, 29 October 1951, box 31, misc., SBP.

14 Braden, Report on "Crime on the Waterfront." "Re-Broadcast of Documentary Program 'The Nation's Nightmare.' Tuesday, September 27th, 9:30 PM over CBS Radio Network." Box 31, misc. (SBP). On Warhol's early work, see Meggs and Purvis, *Meggs' History of Graphic Design,* 20–28.

15 "The Matthews Story (Part One), directed by Leonard Valenta," re-revised draft, box 40, "Writings: 'The Matthews Story,' 1950s" folder, Herbert L. Matthews Papers 1909–2002, Rare Book and Manuscript Library, Columbia University (hereafter HMP). The correspondence in this folder indicates the back and forth between Matthews, the TV authorities and the State Department.

16 Amaral, *El líder y las masas*; Germani, *Autoritarismo, fascismo y populismo nacional,* 254. The U.S. State Department not only explicitly demanded loyalty from the U.S. correspondents abroad; it also regularly requested that the FBI prepare reports about their backgrounds, political preferences, and activities. Braden to Washington, Subject: "Information on Poland and Argentina," 25 February 1946, box 35, "Correspondence, Assistant Secretary, 1945–1946" folder, SBP.

17 Despite the coincidence and shared interests, the relation between the three men was never cordial. A few months after the arrival of Batista, Perón left his hotel in Ciudad Trujillo to visit a house in the suburbs, and later made a few statements sympathetic with the Cuban Revolution. "Dominican Republic: Three Men in a Funk," *Time,* 9 February 1959, 26.

18 De Imaz, *Los que mandan,* 98.

19 Eleuterio Cardozo, oral interview, p. 108, Archivo Histórico del Movimiento Obrero Argentino, Biblioteca Universidad Torcuato Di Tella.

20 Interview with Hugo Soriani (nephew of César Tronconi), Buenos Aires, 2 July 2012.

21 "Atacan a un científico que denunció graves efectos del glifosato en Chaco," *Salta Confidencial,* 23 May 2013.

22 Elena, *Dignifying Argentina,* 251.

23 Email correspondence with Silvia Maestro (granddaughter of Modesto Alvarez), 7–20 February 2010.

24 See also Elena, *Dignifying Argentina,* 256.

25 On the reinvention of Peronist clientelist networks, see Auyero, *Poor People's Politics.*

26 For an analysis of the confluence of social and human rights in the discourse of Raúl Alfonsín and its impact in his administration, see Jennifer Adair, *In Search of the "Lost Decade,"* PhD dissertation, New York University, History of Latin America and the Caribbean, manuscript, 2012.

27 Halperín Donghi, *La larga agonía de la Argentina peronista.*

Beyond the formally catalogued sources from different archives, this study also draws on miscellaneous uncatalogued files, usually the reports and correspondence of the worker attachés, as well as brochure and propaganda material, discovered in the basements or storage facilities of present-day Argentine embassies during the research of this book. These sources appear as such in the notes. Copies of all documents used are in the author's possession.

Archives and Collections

ARGENTINA

Archivo de Cancillería, Ministerio de Relaciones Exteriores y Culto, Buenos Aires (AC)
Biblioteca del Congreso de la Nación, Buenos Aires (BCN)
Archivo Intermedio, Ministerio del Interior y Transporte, Buenos Aires (AI)
Biblioteca del Instituto del Servicio Exterior de la Nación, Buenos Aires (ISEN)
Fondo Nicolás Repetto, Centro de Documentación e Investigación de la Cultura de Izquierdas en la Argentina, Buenos Aires (CeDInCI)
Biblioteca Museo Evita, Buenos Aires (BME)
Archivo Histórico del Movimiento Obrero Argentino, Biblioteca Universidad Torcuato Di Tella, Buenos Aires (MOA)

OTHER LATIN AMERICAN COUNTRIES

Biblioteca Nacional de Chile, Santiago de Chile, Chile (BNCH)
Walter Guevara Arce Collection, Archivo y Bibliotecas Nacionales de Bolivia, Sucre, Bolivia (WGA)
Archivo General de la Nación, Bogotá, Colombia (AGN)

UNITED STATES

National Archives and Records Administration, College Park, Maryland (NARA)

The Foreign Affairs Oral History Collection of the Association for Diplomatic Studies and Training, Library of Congress (LOC)

Juan Atilio Bramuglia Papers, Hoover Institution Archives, Stanford University, Stanford, California (JABP)

George F. Kennan Papers 1871–1875, Mudd Manuscript Library, Department of Rare Books and Special Collections, Princeton University, Princeton, New Jersey (GKP)

Robert Jackson Alexander Papers, Special Collections and University Archives, Rutgers University, New Brunswick, New Jersey (RAP)

Serafino Romualdi Papers, Kheel Center for Labor-Management Documentation and Archives, Cornell University Library, Ithaca, New York, United States (SRP)

Spruille Braden Papers 1903–1977, Rare Book and Manuscript Library, Columbia University, New York (SBP)

Dwight D. Eisenhower Presidential Library and Museum, Abilene, Texas (DEPL)

Herbert L. Matthews Papers 1909–2002, Rare Book and Manuscript Library, Columbia University, New York (HMP)

Tamiment Library and Robert F. Wagner Labor Archives, New York University Libraries, New York (TL)

OTHERS

Foreign Office Papers, National Archives, London, United Kingdom (NA)

Uncatalogued Papers

Embassy of Argentina, Lima, Perú
Embassy of Argentina, La Paz, Bolivia
Embassy of Argentina, Havana, Cuba

Personal Papers

WORKER ATTACHÉS

Pedro Conde Magdaleno
León Segovia
Agustín Merlo
Eduardo de Antueno
Jaime César Tronconi

OTHERS

Clara Applegate

Personal Interviews and Email Correspondence

RELATIVES OF WORKER ATTACHÉS

Irene Segovia (daughter of worker attaché León Segovia), Buenos Aires
Pedro Conde Magdaleno (son of worker attaché Pedro Conde Magdaleno), Buenos Aires

Eduardo de Antueno (son of worker attaché Eduardo de Antueno), Buenos Aires
Silvia Maestro (granddaughter of worker attaché Modesto Alvarez), Buenos Aires
Jorge Tomasini (nephew of Jaime César Tronconi), Buenos Aires
Hugo Soriani (nephew of Jaime César Tronconi), Buenos Aires
Oscar Merlo (son of Agustín Merlo), Buenos Aires

OTHERS

Torcuato Di Tella Jr., New York
Edelberto Torres Rivas, Guatemala

Secondary Sources

Aboy Carlés, Gerardo. *Populismo y democracia en la Argentina contemporánea: Entre el hegemonismo y la refundación.* Buenos Aires: Mimeo, 2009.

———. "Populismo, regeneracionismo y democracia." *Postdata* 15, no 1 (April 2010): 11–30.

Adair, Jennifer. *In Search of the "Lost Decade": The Politics of Rights and Welfare during the Argentine Transition to Democracy, 1982–1990.* PhD diss., New York University, 2012.

Adamovsky, Ezequiel. *Historia de la clase media argentina.* Buenos Aires: Planeta, 2015.

———. *Populismo, regeneracionismo y democracia.* Grupo Interuniversitario Postdata, 2010.

Adelman, Jeremy. *Sovereignty and Revolution in the Iberian Atlantic.* Princeton: Princeton University Press, 2007.

———. "State and Labour in Argentina: The Portworkers of Buenos Aires, 1910–21." *Journal of Latin American Studies* 25, no. 1 (February 1993): 73–102.

Afonso, Eduardo José. "Para Norte Americano Ver. Adidos Trabalhistas e operários brasileiros (1943/1952)." PhD diss., History, Universidade de São Paulo, 2011.

Agee, Philip. *Inside the Company: CIA Diary.* New York: Stonehill, 1975.

Agnew, Jean-Christophe, and Roy Rosenzweig. *A Companion to Post-1945 America.* Malden, MA: Blackwell, 2002.

Alape, Arturo. *El Bogotazo: Memorias del olvido.* Havana: Casa de las Américas, 1983.

Alba, Victor. *Politics and the Labor Movement in Latin America.* Stanford: Stanford University Press, 1968.

———. *Historia del Movimiento Obrero en América Latina.* Mexico: Libreros Mexicanos Unidos, 1964.

Alexander, Robert J. *A History of Organized Labor in Argentina.* Westport, CT: Praeger, 2003.

———. *A History of Organized Labor in Cuba.* Westport, CT: Praeger, 2002.

———. "Labor and Inter-American Relations." "Latin America's Nationalistic Revolutions," special issue, *Annals of the American Academy of Political and Social Science* 334, (March 1961): 41–53.

————. *Organized Labor in Latin America*. New York: Free Press, 1965.

————. *The Venezuelan Democratic Revolution: A Profile of the Regime of Rómulo Betancourt*. New Brunswick, NJ: Rutgers University Press, 1964.

————. *Romulo Betancourt and the Transformation of Venezuela*. New Brunswick: Transactions Books, 1992.

Alexander, Robert J, and Eldon M Parker. *A History of Organized Labor in Bolivia*. Westport, CT: Praeger, 2005.

————. *International Labor Organizations and Organized Labor in Latin America and the Caribbean a History*. Santa Barbara, CA: Praeger / ABC-CLIO, 2009.

Almeida, B. Hamilton. *Sob os olhos de Perón: O Brasil de Vargas e as relações com a Argentina*. Rio de Janeiro: Editora Record, 2005.

Altamirano, Carlos. *Bajo el signo de las masas*. Buenos Aires: Ariel, 2001.

Amaral, Samuel. *Del fascismo al Movimiento Nacional Popular: El peronismo y el Intercambio Germani-Lipset, 1956–1961*. Work Document 402. Buenos Aires: Universidad del CEMA, 2009.

————. *El líder y las masas: Fascismo y peronismo en Gino Germani*. Work Document 371. Bueno Aires: Universidad del CEMA, Area Ciencia Política, 2008.

Anderson, Jon Lee. *Che Guevara: A Revolutionary Life*. New York: Grove Press, 2010.

Aricó, José. *La cola del diablo: Itinerario de Gramsci en América Latina*. Buenos Aires: Puntosur Editores, 1988.

————. *Mariátegui y los orígenes del marxismo latinoamericano*. Mexico City: Ediciones Pasado y Presente / Siglo XXI, 1978.

Auyero, Javier. *Poor People's Politics: Peronist Survival Networks and the Legacy of Evita*. Durham: Duke University Press, 2001.

Bandeira, Moniz. *Brasil, Argentina e Estados Unidos: Conflito e integração na América do Sul: Da Tríplice Aliança ao Mercosul, 1870–2001*. Rio de Janeiro: Editora Revan, 2003.

————. *De Martí a Fidel: A Revolução Cubana e a América Latina*. Rio de Janeiro: Civilização Brasileira, 1998.

Bandeira, Moniz, and Instituto Latino-Americano de Desenvolvimento Econômico e Social. *O eixo Argentina-Brasil: O processo de integração da América Latina*. Brasília: Editora Universidade de Brasília, 1987.

Barnes, William, and John Heath Morgan. *The Foreign Service of the United States: Origins, Development, and Functions*. Washington: Historical Office, Bureau of Public Affairs, Department of State, 1961.

Barry, Carolina. *Evita Capitana: El Partido Peronista Femenino, 1949–1955*. Buenos Aires: Provincia de Buenos Aires: Untref, 2009.

Beasley-Murray, Jon. *Posthegemony: Political Theory and Latin America*. Minneapolis: University of Minnesota Press, 2010.

Béjar, María Dolores. "La entrevista Dickmann-Perón." *Todo es Historia*, no. 143 (April 1979): 83–93.

Belloni Ravest, Hugo. *Educación sindical en la Argentina: Experiencias sobre la capacitación obrera en España y Francia*. Buenos Aires: Arauco, 1973.

Bender, Thomas. *A Nation among Nations: America's Place in World History*. New York: Hill and Wang, 2006.

Benjamin, Walter. "Painting, Jugendstil, Novelty." In *The Arcades Project*, 543–45. Harvard University Press: Belknap, 2002.

Benzecry, Claudio E. *The Opera Fanatic: Ethnography of an Obsession*. Chicago: University of Chicago Press, 2011.

Bergquist, Charles W. *Labor and the Course of American Democracy: U.S. History in Latin American Perspective*. London: Verso, 1996.

———. *Labor in Latin America: Comparative Essays on Chile, Argentina, Venezuela, and Colombia*. Stanford: Stanford University Press, 1985.

———. "The Labor Movement and the Origins of the Violence." In *Violence in Colombia, 1990–2000: Waging War and Negotiating Peace*, edited by Charles Bergquist, Ricardo Penaranda and Gonzalo Sánchez, 51–72. Wilmington, DE: Scholarly Resources, 2001.

Bethell, Leslie, ed. *The Cambridge History of Latin America*. Cambridge: Cambridge University Press, 1984.

Bethell, Leslie, and Ian Roxborough. *Latin America between the Second World War and the Cold War, 1944–1948*. Cambridge: Cambridge University Press, 1992.

———"The Postwar Conjuncture in Latin America: Democracy, Labor, and the Left." In *Latin America between the Second World War and the Cold War, 1944–1948*, edited by Leslie Bethell and Ian Roxborough, 1–32. Cambridge: Cambridge University Press, 1992.

Bianchi, Susana, and Norma Sanchis. *El Partido Peronista Femenino (1949–1955)*. Buenos Aires: Centro Editor de América Latina, 1998.

Blanco, Alejandro. *Razón y modernidad: Gino Germani y la sociología en la Argentina*. Buenos Aires: Siglo Veintiuno Editores, 2006.

Blanco, Katiuska, and Jacqueline Teillagorry Criado. *Todo el tiempo de los cedros: Paisaje familiar de Fidel Castro Ruz*. Havana: Casa Editora Abril, 2003.

Blanco, Teodoro. "ATLAS, la proyección sindical peronista en América Latina." *Todo es Historia* 199–200 (December 1993): 40–53.

Blanco, Hugo. *Land or Death: The Peasant Struggle in Peru*. New York: Pathfinder Press, 1972.

Bobbio, Norberto. *Liberalismo y democracia*. Mexico City: Fondo de Cultura Económica, 1986.

Bottarini, Roberto. "Estrategias político-educativas peronistas: El caso de los agregados obreros." In *Estudios históricos de la educación durante el primer Peronismo, 1943–1955*, comp. Hector Rubén Cucuzza, 401–45. Luján: Editorial los libros del riel, 1997.

Boyer, Richard Owen, and Herbert M Morais. *Labor's Untold Story*. New York: United Electrical, Radio and Machine Workers of America, 1975.

Boyle, Kevin. *The UAW and the Heyday of American Liberalism, 1945–1968*. Ithaca: Cornell University Press, 1995.

Braden, Spruille. *Diplomats and Demagogues: The Memoirs of Spruille Braden*. New Rochelle, NY: Arlington House, 1971.

Braun, Herbert. *The Assassination of Gaitán: Public Life and Urban Violence in Colombia*. Madison: University of Wisconsin Press, 1985.

Brogi, Alessandro. "The AFL and the CIO between 'Crusade' and Pluralism in Italy, 1944–1963." In *American Labor's Global Ambassadors: The International History of* the AFL-CIO *during the Cold War*, edited by Robert Anthony Waters and Geert Van Goethem, 59–84. New York: Palgrave Macmillan, 2013.

Burgos, Raúl. *Los Gramscianos argentinos: Cultura y política en la experiencia de Pasado y Presente*. Buenos Aires: Siglo XXI, 2004.

Busch, Gary. *The Political Role of International Trade Unions*. New York: Palgrave Macmillan, 1985.

Cafiero, Antonio F. *Desde que grité: ¡Viva Perón!* Buenos Aires: Pequén Ediciones, 1983.

Caldwell, Bruce. "Hayek and Socialism." *Journal of Economic Literature* 35, no. 4 (December 1997): 1856–90.

Calles, Plutarco Elías. *Correspondencia Personal: 1919–1945*. Vol. 2. Sonora: Instituto Sonorense de Cultura / Fondo de Cultura Económica, 1991–1993.

Cambiasso, Norberto, and Alfredo Grieco y Bavio. *Días felices: Los usos del orden: De la Escuela de Chicago al funcionalismo*. Buenos Aires: EUDEBA, 1999.

Cardoso Dos Santos, Rodolpho Gauthier. "A construção da Ameaça justicialista: Antiperonismo, política e imprensa no Brasil (1945–1955)." PhD diss., Universidade de São Paulo, 2015.

Carr, Barry. *Organised Labour and the Mexican Revolution, 1915–1928*. Paper No 2. Oxford: Latin American Centre, St. Antony's College, Oxford University, 1972.

———. *Marxism and Communism in Twentieth-Century Mexico*. Lincoln: University of Nebraska Press, 1992.

———. "Vicente Lombardo Toledano." In *Encyclopedia of Mexico*. Vol. 1. Chicago: Fitzroy and Dearborn, 1997.

Casas, Saúl Luis. "La Guerra Civil Española y la sociedad política argentina en el marco de la ayuda a la república (1936–1941)." Master's thesis, Maestría en Ciencias Sociales, Facultad de Humanidades y Ciencias de la Educación, Universidad de La Plata, 2005.

Castañeda, Jorge G. *La vida en rojo: una biografía del Che*. Mexico: Alfaguara, 1997.

Castle, David Barton. "Leo Stanton Rowe and the meaning of Pan Americanism." In *Beyond the Ideal: Pan Americanism and Inter-American Affairs*, edited by David Sheinin, 33–44. Westport CT: Greenwood Press, 2000.

Castro Gomes, Angela María de. *A invenção do trabalhismo*. Rio de Janeiro: Instituto Universitario de Pesquisas do Rio de Janeiro, 1988.

Castro Gomes, Angela Maria de, and Maria Celina Soares d'Araújo. *Getulismo e trabalhismo*. São Paulo: Editora Atica, 1989.

Casullo, María Esperanza, and Flavia Freidenberg. "Populist and Programmatic Parties in Latin American Party Systems." In *Handbook of Political Populism*, edited by Christina Holtz-Bacha, Oscar Mazzoleni, and Reinhard Heinisch. Baden Baden, Germany: Nomos Verlagsgesellschaft, 2017.

Cepeda Étkina, Ana. *Harina de otro costal. Memorias de un niño de la guerra atrapado en el paraíso estalinista*. Madrid: Queimada Ediciones, 2014.

Cerrutti Costa, Luis. *El sindicalismo, las masas, el poder: Una historia del movimiento obrero argentino*. Buenos Aires: Trafac, 1957.

Chamosa, Oscar. *The Argentine Folklore Movement: Sugar Elites, Criollo Workers, and the Politics of Cultural Nationalism, 1900–1955*. Tucson: University of Arizona Press, 2010.

———. "Criollo and Peronist: The Argentine Folklore Movement during the First Peronism, 1943–1955." In *The New Cultural History of Peronism: Power and Identity in Mid-Twentieth-Century Argentina*, edited by Matthew B. Karush and Oscar Chamosa, 113–42. Durham: Duke University Press, 2010.

Chapman, Charles E. "The Age of the Caudillos: A Chapter in Hispanic American History." *Hispanic American Historical Review* 12, no. 3 (August 1932): 281–300.

Chasteen, John Charles. *Heroes on Horseback: A Life and Times of the Last Gaucho Caudillo*. Albuquerque: University of New Mexico Press, 1995.

Chávez, Fermín. *Perón y el justicialismo*. Buenos Aires: Centro Editor de America Latina, 1984.

———. *Peron y el peronismo en la historia contemporanea*. Buenos Aires: Editorial Oriente, 1975.

Chavez, Joaquin M. "The Pedagogy of Revolution: Popular Intellectuals and the Origins of the Salvadoran Insurgency, 1960—1980." PhD diss., New York University, 2010.

Clendinnen, Inga. *Ambivalent Conquests: Maya and Spaniard in Yucatan, 1517–1570*. Cambridge: Cambridge University Press, 1987.

Cochran, Thomas C., and Ruben E. Reina. *Entrepreneurship in Argentine Culture: Torcuato Di Tella and S.I.A.M.* Philadelphia: University of Pennsylvania Press, 1962.

Conde Magdaleno, Pedro. *¿Por qué huyen en baúles los asilados españoles en la U.R.S.S.?* Buenos Aires: Nandubay, 1951.

Conil Paz, Alberto A., and Gustavo Ferrari. *Argentina's Foreign Policy, 1930–1962*. Notre Dame: University of Notre Dame Press, 1966.

Costigliola, Frank, ed. *The Kennan Diaries*. New York: W. W. Norton, 2014.

Cullather, Nick. *Secret History: The CIA's Classified Account of Its Operations in Guatemala, 1952–1954*. Stanford: Stanford University Press, 2006.

Darío, Rubén. *Prosa política (Las repúblicas americanas)*. Madrid: Mundo Latino, 1911.

de Burgos, Julia. *Cartas a consuelo*. Prologue by Lena Burgos-Lafuente. San Juan, Puerto Rico: Folium, 2014.

de Imaz, José Luis. *Los que mandan*. Albany: State University of New York Press, 1970.

De Ipola, Emilio. *Ideología y discurso populista*. Mexico City: Folios Ediciones, 1982.

De Ipola, Emilio, and Institut de Ciències Polítiques i Socials. *Peronismo y populismo: Una nueva propuesta de interpretación*. Barcelona: Institut de Ciències Polítiques i Socials, 1991.

de la Cova, Antonio Rafael. *The Moncada Attack: Birth of the Cuban Revolution*. Columbia: University of South Carolina Press, 2007.

de la Fuente, Ariel. *Children of Facundo: Caudillo and Gaucho Insurgency during the Argentine State-Formation Process (La Rioja, 1853–1870)*. Durham: Duke University Press, 2000.

Devoto, Fernando. *Nacionalismo, fascismo y tradicionalismo en la Argentina moderna: Una historia*. Buenos Aires: Siglo XXI, 2002.

Dinius, Oliver J. *Brazil's Steel City: Developmentalism, Strategic Power and Industrial Relations in Volta Redonda, 1941–1964*. Stanford: Stanford University Press, 2010.

Di Tella, Guido, and Rudiger Dornbusch. *The Political Economy of Argentina, 1946–83*. Pittsburgh: University of Pittsburgh Press, 1989.

Di Tella, Torcuato S. *Argentina: Sociedad de masas*. Buenos Aires: Editorial Universitaria de Buenos Aires, 1965.

———. *Torcuato Di Tella: Industria y política*. Buenos Aires: Grupo Editorial Norma, 1993.

Dorn, Glenn J. *Peronistas and New Dealers: U.S.–Argentine Rivalry and the Western Hemisphere (1946–1950)*. New Orleans: University Press of the South, 2005.

Doyle, Don Harrison, and Marco Antonio Villela Pamplona. *Nationalism in the New World*. Athens: University of Georgia Press, 2006.

Drinot, Paulo. *The Allure of Labor: Workers, Race, and the Making of the Peruvian State*. Durham: Duke University Press, 2011.

———, ed. *Che's Travels: The Making of a Revolutionary in 1950s Latin America*. Durham: Duke University Press, 2010.

Drinot, Paulo, and Alan Knight, eds. *The Great Depression in Latin America*. Durham: Duke University Press, 2014.

———. "'Awaiting the Blood of a Truly Emancipating Revolution': Che Guevara in 1950s Peru." In *Che's Travels. The Making of a Revoluntionary in 1950s Latin America*, edited by Paulo Drinot, 88–126. Durham: Duke University Press, 2010.

Drosdoff, Daniel. *El gobierno de las vacas (1933–1956): Tratado Roca-Runciman*. Buenos Aires: Ediciones La Bastilla, 1972.

Dunaway, John M. *Jacques Maritain*. Boston: Twayne, 1978.

Dunkerley, James. *Rebellion in the Veins: Political Struggle in Bolivia, 1952–82*. London: Verso, 1984.

Dunkerley, James, University of London, and Institute of Latin American Studies. *Studies in the Formation of the Nation-State in Latin America*. London: Institute of Latin American Studies, 2002.

Dunowicz, Renée, et al. *90 años de vivienda social en la ciudad de Buenos Aires*. Buenos Aires: Programa de Mantenimiento Habitacional, Centro de Estudios del Hábitat y la Vivienda, Secretaría de Investigación en Ciencia y Técnica, Facultad de Arquitectura, Diseño y Urbanismo, Universidad de Buenos Aires, 2000.

Eichengreen, Barry. *Hall of Mirrors: The Great Depression, the Great Recession, and the Uses and Misuses of History*. Oxford: Oxford University Press, 2015.

Enriquez, Carlos Alberto. *Guatemala: No más exilio (estudio de casos de 1954 y 1978 en adelante)*. Guatemala: Coordinación de Organizaciones No Gubernamentales y Cooperativas para el Acompañamiento de la Población Damnificada por el Conflicto Armado Interno, 1995.

Elena, Eduardo. *Dignifying Argentina: Peronism, Citizenship, and Mass Consumption*. Pittsburgh: University of Pittsburgh Press, 2011.

———. "Point of Departure: Travel and Nationalism in Ernesto Guevara's Argentina." In *Che's Travels: The Making of a Revolutionary in 1950s Latin America*, edited by Paulo Drinot, 21–50. Durham: Duke University Press, 2010.

Eley, Geoff, and Ronald Grigor Suny. *Becoming National: A Reader*. New York: Oxford University Press, 1996.

Ellner, Steve. "Venezuela." In *Latin America between the Second World War and the Cold War, 1944–1948*, edited by Leslie Bethell and Ian Roxborough, 147–69. Cambridge: Cambridge University Press, 1992.

Escudé, Carlos. *La Argentina vs. las grandes potencias: El precio del desafío*. Buenos Aires: Editorial de Belgrano, 1986.

———. *Gran Bretaña, Estados Unidos y la declinación argentina, 1942–1949*. Buenos Aires: Editorial de Belgrano, 1983.

Escudé, Carlos, and Andrés Cisneros, eds. *Historia general de las relaciones exteriores de la República Argentina*. Vols. XI–XIV. Buenos Aires: Consejo Argentino para las Relaciones Internacionales / Centro de Estudios de Política Exterior / Grupo Editor Latinoamericano, 1998.

Estrada, Genaro. *Un siglo de relaciones internacionales de México (a través de los mensajes presidenciales)*. Mexico: Publicación de la Secretaría de Relaciones Exteriores, 1935.

Euraque, Darío A. *Reinterpreting the Banana Republic: Region and State in Honduras, 1870–1972*. Chapel Hill: University of North Carolina Press, 1996.

Farnsworth-Alvear, Ann. *Dulcinea in the Factory: Myths, Morals, Men, and Women in Colombia's Industrial Experiment, 1905–1960*. Durham: Duke University Press, 2000.

Fein, Seth. *The United States and the Mexican Film Industry after World War II*. Austin: Mexican Center, Institute of Latin American Studies, University of Texas at Austin, 1993.

Fernández Bengoechea, Teresa. *Carlos Saavedra Lamas: Un obrero de la paz*. Buenos Aires: Editorial Dunken, 2007.

Ferrer, Aldo. *La economía argentina: Las etapas de su desarrollo y problemas actuales*. Buenos Aires: Fondo de Cultura Economica, 1968.

Figallo, Beatriz J. *La Argentina ante la Guerra Civil Española: El asilo diplomático y el asilo naval*. Rosario: Instituto de Historia, Facultad de Derecho y Ciencias Sociales, Pontificia Universidad Católica Argentina, 1996.

Finch, Henry. "Uruguay since 1930." In *The Cambridge History of Latin America*, vol. 8, *Latin America since 1930: Spanish South America*, edited by Leslie Bethell, 195–232. Cambridge: Cambridge University Press.

Finchelstein, Federico. *Fascismo, liturgia e imaginario: El mito del General Uriburu y la Argentina nacionalista*. Buenos Aires: Fondo de Cultura Económica, 2002.

Fink, Leon, ed. *Workers across the Americas: The Transnational Turn in Labor History*. Oxford: Oxford University Press, 2011.

Fiszman, Joseph R. "The U.S. Labor Attachés: Expectations and Reality." PhD diss., Michigan State University, Department of Political Science, 1964.

Flores, Roberto Dante. "El rol de la prensa en los procesos de integración regional: Argentina, Brasil, Chile (1946–1955)." Presentation to the "IX Congreso Argentino-Chileno de estudios históricos de integración cultural," San Carlos de Bariloche, 15–27 April 2011.

Foner, Philip Sheldon. *U.S. Labor Movement and Latin America: A History of Workers' Response to Intervention*. South Hadley, MA: Bergin and Garvey, 1988.

Forster, Cindy. "Not in All of America Can There Be Found a Country as Democratic as This One." In *Che's Travels. The Making of a Revolutionary in 1950s Latin America*, edited by Paulo Drinot, 201–44. Durham: Duke University Press, 2010.

Fraser, Steve, and Gary Gerstle. *The Rise and Fall of the New Deal Order, 1930–1980*. Princeton: Princeton University Press, 1989.

French, John D. *The Brazilian Workers' ABC: Class Conflict and Alliances in Modern São Paulo*. Chapel Hill: University of North Carolina Press, 1992.

French, John D., and Daniel James, eds. *The Gendered Worlds of Latin American Women Workers: From Household and Factory to the Union Hall and Ballot Box*. Durham: Duke University Press, 1997.

Friedman, Max Paul. *Rethinking Anti-Americanism: The History of an Exceptional Concept in American Foreign Relations*. Cambridge: Cambridge University Press, 2012.

Furtado, Celso. *Economic Development of Latin America; a Survey from Colonial Times to the Cuban Revolution*. Cambridge: Cambridge University Press, 1970.

Gaddis, John Lewis. *George F. Kennan: An American Life*. New York: Penguin, 2012.

Gallegos, Rómulo. *Dóna Bárbara*. Caracas: Ministerio de Educacion, Direccion de Cultura y Bellas Artes, 1964.

Galvis, Silvia. "Así veían a Gaitán en Washington." In *El Saqueo de Una Ilusión: El 9 de abril, 50 años después*, 29–48. Bogotá: Número Ediciones, 1997.

Gambini, Hugo. *Historia del peronismo: El poder total (1943–1951)*. Buenos Aires: Editorial Planeta / Vergara, Grupo Zeta, 1999.

Gardner, Lloyd C. *Economic Aspects of New Deal Diplomacy*. Madison: University of Wisconsin Press, 1964.

Gardner, Richard. *Sterling-Dollar Diplomacy: Anglo-American Collaboration in the Reconstruction of Multilateral Trade*. Oxford: Clarendon Press, 1956.

Garrard-Burnett, Virginia, Mark Atwood Lawrence, and Julio Moreno. *Beyond the Eagle's Shadow: New Histories of Latin America's Cold War*. Albuquerque: University of New Mexico Press, 2013.

Gerassi, John. *Great Fear in Latin America*. New York: Collier MacMillan, 1965.

Gerchunoff, Pablo. "Peronist Economic Policies, 1946–1955." In *The Political Economy of Argentina, 1946–83*, edited by Guido Di Tella and Rudiger Dornhusch, 59–85. Pittsburgh: University of Pittsburgh Press, 1989.

Gerchunoff, Pablo, and Lucas Llach. *El ciclo de la ilusión y el desencanto: Un siglo de políticas económicas argentinas*. Buenos Aires: Compañía Editora Espasa Calpe Argentina, 1998.

Germani, Gino. *Autoritarismo, fascismo y populismo nacional*. Buenos Aires: Temas Academia Nacional de la Historia-Instituto Torcuato Di Tella-Universidad Torcuato Di Tella, 2003.

———. "Democracia representativa y clases populares." In *Populismo y Contradicciones de Clase en Latinoamérica*, edited by Gino Germani, Torcuato Di Tella Jr., and Octavio Ianni, 24–48. México: Ediciones Era, 1973.

———. "La integración de las masas a la vida politica y el totalitarismo." *Cursos y Conferencias* 48, no. 273 (1956): 153–76.

———. *Política y sociedad en una época de transición, de la sociedad tradicional a la sociedad de masas*. Buenos Aires: Editorial Paidos, 1962.

Gilbert, Isidoro. *El oro de Moscú: La historia secreta de las relaciones argentino-soviéticas*. Buenos Aires: Planeta, 1994.

Gilman, Nils. *Mandarins of the Future: Modernization Theory in Cold War America*. Baltimore: John Hopkins University Press, 2003.

Gleijeses, Piero. *Shattered Hope: The Guatemalan Revolution and the United States, 1944–1954*. Princeton: Princeton University Press, 1991.

Gobat, Michel. "The Invention of Latin America: A Transnational History of Anti-Imperialism, Democracy, and Race." *American Historical Review* 118, no. 5 (December 2013): 1235–375.

Godio, Julio. *Historia del movimiento obrero latinoamericano*. Vols. 2–3. Caracas: Nueva Sociedad / Editorial Nueva Imagen, 1980.

———. *El movimiento obrero argentino, 1943–1955: Nacimiento y consolidación de una hegemonía nacionalista-laboralista*. Buenos Aires: Editorial Legasa, 1990.

Goldwert, Marvin. *Democracy, Militarism, and Nationalism in Argentina, 1930–1966: An Interpretation*. Austin: University of Texas Press, 1972.

González, Horacio, Eduardo López, Daniel Santoro, and Guido Indi. *Perón mediante: Gráfica peronista del periodo clásico*. Buenos Aires: La Marca Editora, 2007.

González Bollo, Hernán. "José Francisco Figuerola: De funcionario del estado interventor conservador a experto de la coalición peronista (1930–44)." Mimeo: Presentation to the "Primer Congreso de Estudios sobre el Peronismo: La primera década." Universidad Nacional de Mar del Plata, 6–7 November 2008.

González Galeotti, Rodolfo. *El exilio Guatemalteco en Argentina*. Guatemala: Facultad Latinoamericana de Ciencias Sociales, 2010.

González, Sady, and Antonio Caballero. *El saqueo de una ilusión: El 9 de abril, 50 años después*. Bogotá: Número Ediciones, 1998.

Gould, Jeffrey. *To Lead as Equals: Rural Protest and Political Consciousness in Chinandega, Nicaragua, 1912–1979*. Chapel Hill: University of North Carolina Press, 1990.

Gramsci, Antonio. *Selection from the Prison Notebooks*. Translated by Quentin Hoare and Geoffrey Nowell Smith. New York: New York International Publishers, 1971.

Gramsci, Antonio, and Valentino Gerratana. *Cuadernos de la cárcel: Edición crítica del Instituto Gramsci*. Mexico City: Ediciones Era, 1981.

Grandin, Greg. *Fordlandia: The Rise and Fall of Henry Ford's Forgotten Jungle City*. New York: Metropolitan Books, 2009.

———. *The Last Colonial Massacre: Latin America in the Cold War*. Chicago: University of Chicago Press, 2004.

———. "What Was Containment?: Short and Long Answers from the Americas." In *The Cold War in the Third World*, edited by Robert J. McMahon, 27–47. New York: Oxford University Press, 2013.

———. "Your Americanism and Mine: Americanism and Anti-Americanism in the Americas." *The American Historical Review* 111, no. 4 (2006): 1042–66.

———. "Off the Beach: The United States, Latin America and the Cold War." In *A Companion to Post-1945 America*, edited by Jean-Christophe Agnew and Roy Rosenzweig, 426–45. Malden, MA: Blackwell, 2002.

———. "The Liberal Traditions in the Americas: Rights, Sovereignty, and the Origins of Liberal Multilateralism." *American Historical Review* 117 (2012): 68–91.

Green, David. *The Containment of Latin America: A History of the Myths and Realities of the Good Neighbor Policy*. Chicago: Quadrangle, 1971.

Green, W. John. "Sibling Rivalry on the Left and Labor Struggles in Colombia during the 1940s." *Latin American Research Review.* 35, no. 1 (2000): 85–117.

———. "'Vibrations of the Collective': The Popular Ideology of Gaitanismo on Colombia's Atlantic Coast, 1944–1948." *Hispanic American Historical Review* 76, no. 2 (1996): 283–311.

Guevara, Ernesto Che. *Back on the Road (Otra Vez): A Journey through Latin America.* New York: Grove Press, 2000.

———. *The Motorcycle Diaries: Notes on a Latin American Journey.* Melbourne: Ocean Press / Centro de Estudios Che Guevara, 2003.

Halperín Donghi, Tulio. *Argentina: La democracia de masas.* Buenos Aires: Editorial Paidós, 1972.

———. *Argentina en el callejón.* Montevideo: ARCA, 1964.

———. *Historia contemporánea de América Latina.* Madrid: Alianza Editorial, 1970.

———. *La Argentina y la tormenta del mundo: Ideas e ideologías entre 1930 y 1945.* Buenos Aires: Siglo Veintiuno Editores Argentina, 2003.

———. *La larga agonía de la Argentina peronista.* Buenos Aires: Ariel, 1994.

———. *Son memorias.* Buenos Aires: Siglo Veintiuno Editores, 2008.

———. *Una nación para el desierto argentino.* Buenos Aires: Centro Editor de América Latina, 1982. Haya de la Torre, Víctor Raúl, and Robert J. Alexander. *Aprismo: The Ideas and Doctrines of Victor Raúl Haya de La Torre.* Kent, OH: Kent State University Press, 1973.

Hayek, Friedrich A. *The Road to Serfdom.* Chicago: University of Chicago Press, 1944.

Healey, Mark A. *The Ruins of the New Argentina: Peronism and the Remaking of San Juan after the 1944 Earthquake.* Durham: Duke University Press, 2011.

Heilman, Patricia Jaymie. "We Will No Longer Be Servile: 'Aprismo' in 1930s Ayacucho." *Journal of Latin American Studies* 38, no. 3 (August 2006): 491–519.

Herran Avila, Luis, "Nationalism, Hispanismo, and Anti-Pan-Americanism in Colombia, 1934–54." Presentation to the panel "Transnational Perspectives on the Making of Twentieth-Century Latin American Nationalisms," American Historical Association, Denver, 6 January 2017.

Hilgers, Tina, ed. *Clientelism in Everyday Latin American Politics.* London: Palgrave McMillan, 2012.

Hobsbawm, E. J. *Marxism in Marx's Day.* Bloomington: Indiana University Press, 1982.

Hora, Roy. "The Impact of the Depression on Argentine Society." In *The Great Depression in Latin America*, edited by Paulo Knight and Alan Drinot, 22–50. Durham: Duke University Press, 2014.

Huneeus, Carlos. *La guerra fría chilena: Gabriel González Videla y la Ley Maldita.* Santiago, Chile: Random House Mondadori, 2009.

Iber, Patrick J. *Neither Peace nor Freedom: The Cultural Cold War in Latin America.* Boston: Harvard University Press, 2015.

———. "'Who Will Impose Democracy?': Sacha Volman and the Contradictions of CIA Support for the Anticommunist Left in Latin America." *Diplomatic History* (24 April 2013): 995–1028.

Ingenieros, José. *Las direcciones filosóficas de la cultura argentina*. Buenos Aires: Universidad de Buenos Aires, 1914.

———. *La evolución sociológica argentina (de la barbarie al imperialismo)*. Buenos Aires: Librería J. Menéndez, 1910.

Inman, Samuel Guy. "Lima Conference and the Totalitarian Issue." "Democracy and the Americas," special issue, *Annals of the American Academy of Political and Social Science* 204 (July 1939): 9–16.

"Interview with Alfonso Bauer Paiz." *Revista Alero* (Universidad de San Carlos) 3, no. 23 (March–April 1977): 179–85.

Ioris, Rafael R. *Transforming Brazil: A History of National Development in the Postwar Era*. New York: Routledge, 2014.

Jacobson, Matthew Frye, and Gaspar González. *What Have They Built You to Do? The Manchurian Candidate and Cold War America*. Minneapolis: University of Minnesota Press, 2006.

James, Daniel. *Doña María's Story: Life History, Memory, and Political Identity*. Durham: Duke University Press, 2000.

———. "October 17th and 18th, 1945: Mass Protest, Peronism and the Argentine Working Class." *Journal of Social History*, no. 2 (Spring 1988): 441–61.

———. *Resistance and Integration: Peronism and the Argentine Working Class, 1946–1976*. Cambridge: Cambridge University Press, 1988.

Jessup, Philip C. "The Berlin Blockade and the Use of the United Nations." *Foreign Affairs* (October 1971): 163–73.

Joseph, Gilbert M., Catherine C. LeGrand, and Ricardo D. Salvatore, eds. *Close Encounters of Empire: Writing the Cultural History of U.S.–Latin American Relations*. Foreword by Fernando Coronil. Durham: Duke University Press, 1998.

Joseph, Gilbert M., and Daniel Nugent. *Everyday Forms of State Formation: Revolution and the Negotiation of Rule in Modern Mexico*. Durham: Duke University Press, 1994.

Joseph, Gilbert M., and Daniela Spenser. *In from the Cold: Latin America's New Encounter with the Cold War*. Durham: Duke University Press, 2008.

Juárez, Juan C. *Los trabajadores en función social*. Buenos Aires: Departamento de Estudios Sindicales del Ateneo de Estudios Sociales, 1947.

Kahl, Joseph A. *Modernization, Exploitation, and Dependency in Latin America: Germani, González Casanova, and Cardoso*. New Brunswick: Transaction, 1976.

Kane, N. Stephen, and William F. Sanford Jr. *Foreign Relations of the United States, 1952–1954: The American Republics*. Washington: U.S. Government Printing Office, 1983.

Karush, Matthew B., and Oscar Chamosa, eds. *The New Cultural History of Peronism: Power and Identity in Mid-Twentieth-Century Argentina*. Durham: Duke University Press, 2010.

Kedar, Claudia. "Chronicle of an Inconclusive Negotiation: Perón, the International Monetary Fund, and the World Bank (1946–1955)." *Hispanic American Historical Review* 92, no. 4 (2012): 637–68.

———. *The International Monetary Fund and Latin America: The Argentine Puzzle in Context*. Philadelphia: Temple University Press, 2013.

Kennan, George F. *American Diplomacy, 1900–1950*. Chicago: University of Chicago Press, 1951.

———. *Memoirs*. Boston: Little, Brown, 1967.

Kenworthy, Eldon. *America/Américas: Myth in the Making of U.S. Policy toward Latin America*. University Park: Pennsylvania State University Press, 1995.

———. *The Function of the Little-Known Case in Theory Formation: Or, What Peronism Wasn't*. Ithaca: Cornell University, Latin American Studies Program, 1974.

———. *Peronism: Argentina's Experiment with Populism*. Ithaca: Cornell University, Latin American Studies Program Reprint series, No. 45, 1973.

Knight, Alan. *The Mexican Revolution: Porfirians, Liberals and Peasants*. Vol. 1. Cambridge: Cambridge University Press, 1986.

———. "Populism and Neo-Populism in Latin America, Especially Mexico." *Journal of Latin American Studies* 30, no. 2 (May 1988): 223–48.

Kirkpatrick, Jeane. *Peronist Politics in Argentina: Composition, Expectations and Demands of the Mass Base*. PhD diss., Columbia University, 1968.

Klein, Herbert S. *A Concise History of Bolivia*. Cambridge: Cambridge University Press, 2003.

Kleinman, Mark L. *A World of Hope, a World of Fear: Henry A. Wallace, Reinhold Niebuhr, and American Liberalism*. Columbus: Ohio State University Press, 2000.

Kofas, Jon V. "Containment and Class Conflict: U.S. Intervention in the Colombian Labour Movement, 1950–1958." *Canadian Journal of Latin American and Caribbean Studies* 25, no. 50 (2000): 229–65.

———. *The Struggle for Legitimacy: Latin American Labor and the United States 1930–1960*. Tempe: Arizona State University, 1992.

Kott, Sandrine, and Joëlle Droux. *Globalizing Social Rights: The International Labour Organization and beyond*. 2013. http://site.ebrary.com/id/10822279.

Laclau, Ernesto. *Emancipación y diferencia*. Buenos Aires: Ariel, 1996.

———. *On Populist Reason*. London: Verso, 2005.

———. *Politics and Ideology in Marxist Theory: Capitalism, Fascism, Populism*. London: New Left Books, 1977.

Laclau, Ernesto, and Chantal Mouffe. *Hegemony and Socialist Strategy: Towards a Radical Democratic Politics*. London: Verso, 1985.

Lanús, Juan Archibaldo. *Aquel apogeo: Política internacional argentina, 1910–1939*. Buenos Aires: Emecé Editores, 2001.

———. *De Chapultepec al Beagle: Política exterior argentina, 1945–1980*. Buenos Aires: Emecé Editores, 1984.

"Las Palmas Sugar Plantation, Argentina." *Louisiana Planter and Sugar Manufacturer* 43, no. 3 (17 July 1909): 45–46.

Latham, Michael E. *The Right Kind of Revolution: Modernization, Development, and U.S. Foreign Policy from the Cold War to the Present*. Ithaca: Cornell University Press, 2011.

Lazarte, Jorge. *Movimiento obrero y procesos políticos en Bolivia: Historia de la C.O.B., 1952–1987*. La Paz: n.p., 1989.

Ledeen, Michael Arthur. *Universal Fascism: The Theory and Practice of the Fascist International, 1928–1936*. New York: Fertig, 1972.

Levenson-Estrada, Deborah. *Trade Unionists against Terror: Guatemala City, 1954–1985*. Chapel Hill: University of North Carolina Press, 1994.

Levenstein, Harvey A. *Las organizaciones obreras en Estados Unidos y México: Historia de sus relaciones*. Guadalajara: Universidad de Guadalajara, 1980.

Lichtenstein. "From Corporatism to Collective Bargaining: Organized Labor and the Eclipse of Social Democracy in the Postwar Era." In *The Rise and Fall of the New Deal Order, 1930–1980*, edited by Steve Fraser and Gary Gerstle, 122–52. Princeton: Princeton University Press, 1989.

Lipset, Seymour Martin. *Consensus and Conflict: Essays in Political Sociology*. New Brunswick, NJ: Transaction, 1985.

———. *Political Man: The Social Bases of Politics*. Garden City, NY: Doubleday, 1960.

———. "Working-Class Authoritarianism: 'A Reply to Miller and Riessman.'" *British Journal of Sociology* 12 (September 1961): 277–81.

Llach, Juan Jose. "El plan pinedo de 1940, su significado histórico y los orígenes de la economía política del peronismo." *Desarrollo Económico* 23, no. 92 (1984): 515–58.

Loayza, Matthew. "An 'Aladdin's Lamp' for Free Enterprise: Eisenhower, Fiscal Conservatism and Latin American Nationalism, 1953–1961." *Diplomacy and Statecraft* 14 (September 2003): 83–105.

Lobato, Mirta Zaida; Damilakou, María; and Tornay, Lizel. "Working-Class Beauty Queens under Peronism." In *The New Cultural History of Peronism: Power and Identity in Mid-Twentieth-Century Argentina*, edited by Matthew B. Karush and Oscar Chamosa, 171–207. Durham: Duke University Press, 2010.

Lockey, Joseph Byrne. "The Meaning of Pan-Americanism." *American Journal of International Law* 19 (1925): 104–17.

———. *Pan-Americanism: Its Beginnings*. New York: Macmillan, 1920.

López, Coco. *Mate y ron: de Rosario a La Habana*. Rosario: Ameghino, 1997.

Lukes, Steven. "Social Justice: The Hayekian Challenge." *Critical Review* 11, no. 1 (January 1997): 65–80.

Luna, Félix. *Los caudillos*. Buenos Aires: Editorial J. Alvarez, 1966.

———. *El 45*. Buenos Aires: Hyspamerica, 1984.

———. *Perón y su tiempo*. Buenos Aires: Editorial Sudamericana, 1984.

Mackinnon, Moira. *Los años formativos del Partido Peronista (1946–1950)*. Buenos Aires: Instituto Di Tella / Siglo XXI, 2002.

MacShane, Denis. *International Labour and the Origins of the Cold War*. Oxford: Clarendon, 1992.

Meggs, Philip B., and Alston W. Purvis. *Meggs' History of Graphic Design, Fifth Edition*. New York: Wiley, 2011.

Mariátegui, José Carlos. *Siete ensayos de interpretación de la realidad peruana*. Barcelona: Linkgua ediciones, 2009.

Mejía, Marco Vinicio. *La importancia de llamarse Che: La etapa guatemalteca de Ernesto Guevara de la Serna*. Guatemala: Editorial Guatemala, 2002.

Merleau-Ponty, Maurice. *Signs*. Evanston: Northwestern University Press, 1964.

Merriman, John. *A History of Modern Europe: From the Renaissance to the Present.* New York: W. W. Norton, 2010.

Mesa-Lago, Carmelo, and Sociedad Interamericana de Planificación. *Modelos de seguridad social en América Latina: Estudio comparativo.* Buenos Aires: Siap-Planteos, 1977.

Milanesio, Natalia. *Workers Go Shopping in Argentina: The Rise of Popular Consumer Culture.* Albuquerque: University of New Mexico Press, 2012.

———. "Peronist and *Cabecitas.*" In *The New Cultural History of Peronism: Power and Identity in Mid-Twentieth-Century Argentina,* edited by Matthew B. Karush and Oscar Chamosa, 53–84. Durham: Duke University Press, 2010.

McKinzie, Richard. *Oral History Interview with John M. Cabot.* Massachusetts: Harry S. Truman Library and Museum, 1978.

Montgomery, David. *Citizen Worker: The Experience of Workers in the United States with Democracy and the Free Market during the Nineteenth Century.* Cambridge: Cambridge University Press, 1993.

———. *The Fall of the House of Labor: The Workplace, the State, and American Labor Activism, 1865–1925.* Cambridge: Cambridge University Press / Editions de la Maison des Sciences de l'Homme, 1987.

Mora, Frank O. "The Forgotten Relationship: United States–Paraguay Relations, 1937–89." *Journal of Contemporary History* 33, no. 3 (July 1998): 451–53.

———. *Struggle for Hegemony: Argentina, Brazil and the United States during the Second World War.* Miami: Miami University Press, 1979.

More, Alberto. "¡Especial! Desde Nueva York, Spruille Braden en una entrevista exclusiva para *Leoplan.*" *Leoplan* (Buenos Aires) 25, no. 590 (March 1959): 3–8.

Morgenfeld, Leandro Ariel. *Vecinos en conflicto: Argentina y Estados Unidos en las conferencias panamericanas, 1880–1955.* Buenos Aires: Peña Lillo / Ediciones Continente, 2011.

Morris, George. *CIA and American Labor: The Subversion of the AFL-CIO's Foreign Policy.* New York: International Publishers, 1967.

Muchnik, Daniel. *Gallo rojo, gallo negro: Los intereses en juego en la Guerra Civil española.* Buenos Aires: Grupo Editorial Norma, 2004.

Nállim, Jorge. *Transformations and Crisis of Liberalism in Argentina, 1930–1955.* Pittsburgh: University of Pittsburgh Press, 2012.

Nun, José. *Latin America: The Hegemonic Crisis and the Military Coup.* Berkeley: Institute of International Studies, University of California, 1969.

———. *A situação da classe trabalhadora na América Latina.* Rio de Janeiro: Centro de Estudos de Cultura Contemporânea: Paz e Terra, 1978.

Obando Sánchez, Antonio. *Memorias: La historia del movimiento obrero en Guatemala en este siglo.* Guatemala: Editorial Universitaria, 1978.

Ochoa de Eguileor, Jorge. *Memorias de un ciudadano ilustre: Historia oral.* Buenos Aires: Instituto de Invetigaciones Históricas Eva Perón, 2007.

Oddone, Juan Antonio. *Vecinos en discordia: Argentina, Uruguay y la política hemisférica de los Estados Unidos: Selección de documentos, 1945–1955.* Montevideo, Uruguay: Universidad de la República, Facultad de Humanidades y Ciencias de la Educación, Departamento de Historia Americana, 2003.

Osegueda, Raúl. *Operación Guatemala $$OK$$*. Mexico City: Colección Autores Contemporáneos, 1955.

Page, Joseph A. *Perón: A Biography*. New York: Random House, 1983.

Panella, Claudio. "Los agregados obreros: Una experiencia inédita de la diplomacia argentina." *Todo es Historia* 28, no. 328 (1994): 34–60.

———. *Berisso: Escenas de su historia*. La Plata: Archivo Histórico de la Provincia de Buenos Aires "Dr. Ricardo Levene," 2003.

———. *Perón y ATLAS: Historia de una central latinoamericana de trabajadores*. Buenos Aires: Editorial Vinciguerra, 1996.

Paradiso, José. *Debates y trayectoria de la política exterior argentina*. Buenos Aires: Grupo Editor Latinoamericano, 1993.

Pardo Llada, José. *Fidel y el "Ché."* Esplugues de Llobregat, Barcelona: Plaza and Janés, 1988.

Parsons, Talcott. *The Social System*. Glencoe, IL: Free Press, 1951.

———. *Social Systems and the Evolution of Action Theory*. New York: Free Press, 1977.

Pastoriza, Elisa. *La conquista de las vacaciones: Breve historia del turismo en la Argentina*. Buenos Aires: Edhasa, 2011.

Payne, Stanley G. *A History of Fascism, 1914–1945*. Madison: University of Wisconsin Press, 1995.

Pécaut, Daniel. *L'ordre et la violence: Evolution socio politique de la Colombie entre 1930 et 1953*. Paris: École des Hautes Etudes en Sciences Sociales, 1987.

Pereira Fiorilo, Juan. *Historia secreta de la Guerra del Chaco: Bolivia frente al Paraguay y Argentina*. La Paz: Federación de Entidades Empresariales de Cochabamba, 1999.

Perón, Juan Domingo. *Obras completas*. Buenos Aires: Proyecto Hernandarias, 1900.

Peterson, Harold F. *Argentina and the United States (1810–1960)*. New York: State University of New York Press, 1964.

Piñciro Iñíguez, Carlos. *Perón: La construcción de un ideario*. Buenos Aires: Ciudad Autónoma de Buenos Aires / Federación Argentina de Trabajadores de Edificios de Renta y Horizontal (FATERYH) / Instituto di Tella / Caras y Caretas / Siglo XXI, 2010.

Plant, Raymnod. "Hayek on Social Justice: A Critique." In *Hayek, Co-ordination and Evolution: His Legacy. Philosophy, Politics, Economics and the History of Ideas*, edited by Jack Birner and Rudy van Zijp, 164–77. London: Routledge, 1994.

Plot, Martín. *Destino sudamericano: Ideas e imágenes políticas del segundo siglo argentino y americano*. Buenos Aires: Teseo / Universidad de Belgrano, 2010.

Plotkin, Mariano Ben. *Mañana es San Perón: A Cultural History of Peron's Argentina*. Wilmington, DE: Scholarly Resources, 2002.

Poblete Troncoso, Moisés, and Ben G Burnett. *The Rise of the Latin American Labor Movement*. New York: Bookman Associates, 1960.

Portantiero, Juan Carlos, and Miguel Murmis. *Estudios sobre los orígenes del peronismo*. Buenos Aires: Siglo Veintiuno Argentina Editores, 1971.

Potash, Robert A. *The Army and Politics in Argentina, 1945–1962: Perón to Frondizi*. Stanford.: Stanford University Press, 1980.

Prado, Maria Lígia Coelho. *O populismo na América Latina: Argentina e México.* São Paulo: Brasiliense, 1981.

Prebisch, Raul, United Nations Organization, and Economic Commission for Latin America and the Caribbean. "The Latin American Periphery in the Global Crisis of Capitalism." CEPAL *Review* (1985): 63–88.

Quijada, Mónica. *Aires de república, aires de cruzada: La guerra civil española en Argentina.* Barcelona: Sendai, 1991.

Rabe, Stephen G. *Eisenhower and Latin America: The Foreign Policy of Anticommunism.* Chapel Hill: University of North Carolina Press, 1988.

———. *The Killing Zone: The United States Wages Cold War in Latin America.* Oxford: Oxford University Press, 2011.

———. *U.S. Intervention in British Guiana: A Cold War Story.* Chapel Hill: University of North Carolina Press, 2005.

Radosh, Ronald. *American Labor and United States Foreign Policy.* New York: Random House, 1960.

Rapoport, Mario, and Alberto Sosa. *Argentina-Brasil-Chile (ABC). Peronismo y Unidad Latinoamericana.* Buenos Aires: Fundación Argentina para las Relaciones Internacionales, 1982.

Rapoport, Mario, and Claudio Spiguel. *Estados Unidos y el peronismo: La política norteamericana en la Argentina, 1949–1955.* Buenos Aires: Grupo Editor Latinoamericano, 1994.

———. *Relaciones tumultuosas: Estados Unidos y el primer peronismo.* Buenos Aires: Emecé, 2009.

———. *Historia política, económica y social de la Argentina 1880–2000.* Buenos Aires: Ediciones Macchi, 2000.

Rein, Raanan. *The Franco-Perón Alliance: Relations between Spain and Argentina, 1946–1955.* Pittsburgh: University of Pittsburgh Press, 1993.

———. *Juan Atilio Bramuglia. Bajo la sombra del líder. La segunda línea del liderazgo peronista.* Buenos Aires: Lumiere y Universidad de Tel Aviv, 2006.

———. "Los hombres detrás del hombre. La segunda línea del liderazgo peronista." *Araucaria: Revista Iberoamericana de Filosofía, Política y Humanidades,* vol. 10, núm 19, primer semester, pp. 78–92. Sevilla: Universidad de Sevilla, 2008.

Reonello Rimbotti, Luca. *Il fascismo di sinistra: Da Piazza San Sepolcro at Congresso di Verona.* Roma: Edizioni Sttimo Sigillo, 1989.

Roberts, Timothy Mason. *Distant Revolutions: 1848 and the Challenge to American Exceptionalism.* Charlottesville: University of Virginia Press, 2009.

Robin, Corey. *Fear: The History of a Political Idea.* Oxford: Oxford University Press, 2004.

Rock, David. *Argentina: 1516–1987: From Spanish Colonization to the Falklands War.* Berkeley: University of California Press, 1987.

———. *Latin America in the 1940s: War and Postwar Transitions.* Berkeley: University of California Press, 1994.

Rodgers, Daniel T. *Atlantic Crossings: Social Politics in a Progressive Age.* Harvard: Belknap, 2000.

Rodó, José Enrique. *Ariel.* Barcelona: Linkgua Ediciones, 2008.

Roediger, David. *The Wage of Whiteness: Race and the Making of the American Working Class*. New York: Verso, 1991.

Rojo, Ricardo. *Mi amigo el Che*. Buenos Aires: Debolsillo, 2006.

Romualdi, Serafino. "Labor and Democracy in Latin America." *Foreign Affairs* 25, no 3. (April 1947): 476–89.

———. *Presidents and Peons: Recollections of a Labor Ambassador in Latin America*. New York: Funk and Wagnalls, 1967.

Roseberry, William. *Anthropologies and Histories: Essays in Culture, History, and Political Economy*. New Brunswick: Rutgers University Press, 1989.

———. "Hegemony and the Language of Contention." In *Everyday Forms of State Formation: Revolution and the Negotiation of Rule in Modern Mexico*, edited by Gilbert M. Joseph and Daniel Nugent, 355–66. Durham: Duke University Press, 1994.

Ruiz Jiménez, Laura. "Peronism and Anti-Imperialism in the Argentine Press: 'Braden or Perón' Was Also 'Perón Is Roosevelt.'" *Journal of Latin American Studies* 30, no. 3 (October 1998): 551–71.

Salomón, Alejandro. *El Peronismo en clave rural y local: Buenos Aires, 1945–1955*. Quilmes, Argentina: Universidad Nacional de Quilmes, 2012.

Sarmiento, Domingo Faustino. *Life in the Argentine Republic in the Days of the Tyrants: Or, Civilization and Barbarism*. New York: Hafner, 1960.

Saxon, Dan. *To Save Her Life: Disappearance, Deliverance, and the United States in Guatemala*. Berkeley: University of California Press, 2007.

Scenna, Miguel Angel. "Braden y Perón." *Todo es Historia* 3, no. 30 (October 1969): 9–30.

Schivelbusch, Wolfgang. *Three New Deals: Reflections on Roosevelt's America, Mussolini's Italy, and Hitler's Germany, 1933–1939*. New York: Picador, 2006.

Schmitz, David F. *Thank God They're on Our Side: The United States and Right-Wing Dictatorships, 1921–1965*. Chapel Hill: University of North Carolina Press, 1999.

Scipes, Kim. *AFL-CIO Secret War against Developing Countries: Solidarity or Sabotage?* Lanham, MD: Lexington Books, 2010.

Sheinin, David, ed. *Beyond the Ideal: Pan Americanism and Inter-American Affairs*. Westport, CT: Praeger, 2000.

Sidicaro, Ricardo. *Los tres peronismos: Estado y poder económico 1946–1955, 1973–1976, 1989–1999*. Buenos Aires: Siglo Veintiuno Editores Argentina, 2002.

Siekmeier, James. "Latin American Economic Nationalism and United States–Latin American Relations, 1945–1961." *Latin Americanist* 52, no. 3 (October 2008): 59–76.

Silva Falla, Jorge. *El exilio*. Panama City Edicano, 1998.

Sharpless, Richard. *Gaitán of Colombia: A Political Biography*. Pittsburgh: Pittsburgh University Press, 1978.

Snyder, Timothy. *Bloodlands: Europe between Hitler and Stalin*. New York: Basic Books, 2012.

Soliz, Carmen. "'Land to Its Original Owners': Rethinking the Indigenous Politics of the Bolivian Agrarian Reform." *Hispanic American Historical Review*. Forthcoming.

Solovey, Mark, and Hamilton Cravens. *Cold War Social Science: Knowledge Production, Liberal Democracy, and Human Nature*. New York: Palgrave Macmillan, 2012.

Spalding, Hobart. *Organized Labor in Latin America: Historical Case Studies of Workers in Dependent Societies.* New York: New York University Press, 1977.

Stauffer, David H., and Almon E. Wright, eds. *Foreign Relations of the United States, 1945: The American Republics.* Washington: U.S. Government Printing Office, 1969.

Stokes, Susan Carl, Thad Dunning, Marcelo Nazareno, and Valeria Brusco. *Brokers, Voters, and Clientelism: The Puzzle of Distributive Politics.* Boston: Cambridge University Press, 2013.

Stromquist, Shelton. "Claiming Political Space: Workers, Municipal Socialism and the Reconstruction of Local Democracy in Transnational Perspective." In *Workers across the Americas: The Transnational Turn in Labor History,* edited by Leon Flink, 303–27. New York: Oxford University Press, 2011.

Tamarin, David. *The Argentine Labor Movement, 1930–1945: A Study in the Origins of Peronism.* Albuquerque: University of New Mexico Press, 1985.

Tapia Mealla, Luis. *La producción del conocimiento local: Historia y política en la obra de René Zavaleta.* La Paz, Bolivia: Muela del Diablo Editores / Ciencas del Desarrollo-Universidad Mayor de San Andrés (CIDES-UMSA), 2002.

Taylor, Lewis. "The Origins of APRA in Cajamarca, 1928–1935." *Bulletin of Latin American Research* 19, no. 4 (October 2000): 437–59.

Terán, Oscar. *Historia de las ideas en la Argentina: Diez lecciones iniciales, 1810–1980.* Buenos Aires: Siglo Veintiuno Editores, 2008.

———. "Rasgos de la cultura durante el primer peronismo." In *Historia de las ideas en la Argentina: Diez lecciones iniciales, 1810–1980,* edited by Oscar Terán, 257–80. Buenos Aires: Siglo Veintiuno Editores, 2008.

———. "José Ingenieros o la voluntad de saber." Introduction to *Antimperialismo y nación,* by José Ingenieros, 11–118. Mexico: Siglo XXI, 1979.

———. *Nuestros años sesentas: La formación de la nueva izquierda intelectual en la Argentina, 1956–1966.* Buenos Aires: Puntosur Editores, 1991.

Terán, Oscar, and José Ingenieros. *José Ingenieros: Pensar la nación.* Madrid: Alianza Editorial, 1986.

Thomas, Evan. *The Very Best Men: Four Who Dared: The Early Years of the CIA.* New York: Simon and Schuster, 1995.

Thornton, Christy. "A Mexican International Economic Order? Tracing the Hidden Roots of the Charter of Economic Rights and Duties of States." *Humanity: An International Journal of Human Rights, Humanitarianism, and Development.* Forthcoming.

Tinsman, Heidi. *Buying into the Regime: Grapes and Consumption in Cold War Chile and the United States.* Durham: Duke University Press, 2014.

Torre, Juan Carlos. "La caída de Luis Gay." *Todo es Historia* 8, no. 89 (October 1974): 89–100.

———. *Interpretando, una vez mas, los orígenes del peronismo.* Buenos Aires: Instituto Torcuato Di Tella, Centro de Investigaciones Sociales, 1989.

———. "Sobre los orígenes del peronismo." *La Ciudad Futura,* nos. 23–24 (June–September 1990): 10–13.

———. *La vieja guardia sindical y Perón: Sobre los orígenes del peronismo*. Buenos Aires: Editorial Sudamericana / Instituto Torcuato di Tella, 1990.

———. "¿Qué hubiera ocurrido si el 17 de octubre hubiese fracasado." In *17 de octubre de 1945: Antes, durante y después*, edited by Juan Carlos Torre, Santiago Senén González, and Gabriel D. Lerman. Buenos Aires: Lumiere, 2005.

Torre, Juan Carlos, and Corp E-libro. *1930: La vieja guardia sindical antes del peronismo*. Buenos Aires: Taurus, 1998.

Torre, Juan Carlos, Santiago Senén González, and Gabriel D. Lerman, eds. *17 de octubre de 1945: Antes, durante y después*. Buenos Aires: Lumiere, 2005.

Torres, José Luis. *La Década Infame*. Buenos Aires: Editorial de Formación "Patria," 1945.

Trask, Roger R. "The Impact of the Cold War on U.S.-Latin American Relations, 1945–1949." In *Neighborly Adversaries: Readings in U.S.-Latin American Relations*, edited by Michael LaRosa and Frank O. Mora, 129–43. Lanham, MD: Rowman and Littlefield.

Truman, Harry S. *Memoirs: 1945, year of decisions*. New York: New American Library, 1965.

Tulchin, Joseph S., and Allison M. Garland, eds. *Argentina: The Challenges of Modernization*. Wilmington, DE: Scholarly Resources, 1998.

Turner, Frederick C., and José Enrique Miguens. *Juan Perón and the reshaping of Argentina*. Pittsburgh: University of Pittsburgh Press, 1993.

United Nations and Economic Commission for Latin America. *The Economic Development of Latin America in the Post-War Period*. New York: United Nations, 1964.

Urquiza, Manuel. CGT y ATLAS: *Historia de una experiencia sindical lationamericana (década del '50–década del '60)*. Buenos Aires: Legasa, 1988.

Verbitsky, Bernardo. *Villa miseria también es América*. Buenos Aires: Paidos, 1967.

Vergara, Angela. *Copper Workers, International Business, and Domestic Politics in Cold War Chile*. University Park: Pennsylvania State University Press, 2007.

———. "Chilean Workers and the U.S. Labor Movement: From Solidarity to Intervention, 1950s–1970s." In *American Labor's Global Ambassadors: The International History of the AFL-CIO during the Cold War*, edited by Robert Anthony Waters and Geert Van Goethem, 201–15. New York: Palgrave Macmillan, 2013.

Walcher, Dustin. "Reforming Latin American Labor: The AFL-CIO and Latin America's Cold War." In *American Labor's Global Ambassadors: The International History of the AFL-CIO during the Cold War*, edited by Robert Anthony Waters and Geert Van Goethem, 123–35. New York: Palgrave Macmillan, 2013.

Walker, Martin. *The Cold War: A History*. New York: H. Holt, 1994.

Warren, Robert Penn. *All the King's Men*. Restored edn. New York: Harcourt, 1946.

Waters Jr., Robert Anthony, and Geert van Goethem, eds. *American Labor's Global Ambassadors: The International History of the AFL-CIO during the Cold War*. New York: Palgrave Macmillan, 2013.

Waters, Robert Anthony, Jr. "More Subtle Than We Knew: The AFL in the British Caribbean." In *American Labor's Global Ambassadors: The International History of the AFL-CIO during the Cold War*, edited by Robert Anthony Waters and Geert Van Goethem, 165–76. New York: Palgrave Macmillan, 2013.

Weffort, Francisco C. *Los orígenes del sindicalismo populista en Brasil: La coyuntura de la posguerra.* Lima: Taller de Estudios Políticos, Programa Académico de Ciencias Sociales, Universidad Católica del Perú, 1975.

———. *O populismo na política brasileira.* Rio de Janeiro: Paz e Terra, 1978.

Weiner, Tim. *Legacy of Ashes: The History of the CIA.* New York: Doubleday, 2007.

Weinstein, Barbara. *For Social Peace in Brazil: Industrialists and the Remaking of the Working Class in São Paulo, 1920–1964.* Chapel Hill: University of North Carolina Press, 1996.

———. *The Color of Modernity. São Paulo and the Making of Race and Nation in Brazil.* Durham: Duke University Press, 2015.

———. "The New Latin American Labor History." *International Labor and Working-Class History,* no. 36 (fall 1989): 25–30.

Welch, Cliff. "Labor Internationalism: U.S. Involvement in Brazilian Unions, 1945–1965." *Latin American Research Review* 30, no. 2 (1995): 61–90.

Westad, Arno. *The Global Cold War: Third World Interventions and the Making of Our Times.* New York: Cambridge University Press, 2005.

Wilford, Hugh. *The Mighty Wurlitzer: How the CIA Played America.* Boston: Harvard University Press, 2008.

Williams, William Appleman. *The Tragedy of American Diplomacy.* New York: Dell Pub, 1962.

Winters, Jeffrey A. *Oligarchy.* New York: Cambridge University Press, 2011.

Wolfe, Joel. *Autos and Progress: The Brazilian Search for Modernity.* Oxford: Oxford University Press, 2010.

Wood, Bryce. *The Dismantling of the Good Neighbor Policy.* Austin: University of Texas Press, 1985.

———. *The Making of the Good Neighbor Policy.* New York: Columbia University Press, 1961.

Woodard, James P. *A Place in Politics: São Paulo, Brazil, from Seigneurial Republicanism to Regionalist Revolt.* Durham: Duke University Press, 2009.

Wright, Almon R., Velma Hastings Cassidy, and David H. Stauffer, eds. *Foreign Relations of the United States, 1948: The Western Hemisphere.* Washington: U.S. Government Printing Office, 1972.

Yankelevich, Pablo. *La diplomacia imaginaria: Argentina y la Revolución Mexicana, 1910–1916.* Mexico City: Secretaría de Relaciones Exteriores, 1994.

———. "Imitemos a México: La experiencia de Carlos Gracidas en la diplomacia obrera mexicana (1925–1928). *Journal of Iberian and Latin American Research* 7, no. 1 (2001): 1–20.

Zanatta, Loris. "Auge y declinación de la Tercera Posición: Bolivia, Perón y la Guerra Fría, 1943–1954." *Desarrollo Económico* 4, no. 177 (2005): 25–53.

———. *Del estado liberal a la nación católica: Iglesia y ejército en los orígenes del peronismo, 1930–1943.* Buenos Aires: Universidad Nacional de Quilmes, 1996.

———. *La internacional justicialista: Auge y ocaso de los sueños imperiales de Perón.* Buenos Aires: Sudamericana, 2013.

———. "Perón y el espejismo del bloque latino." *Revista de Ciencia Política y Relaciones Internacionales de la Universidad de Palermo* 2, no. 2 (November 2005): 7–52.

———. *Perón y el mito de la nación católica: Iglesia y ejército en los orígenes del peronismo (1943–1946)*. Buenos Aires: Editorial Sudamericana, 1999.

Zavaleta Mercado, René. *Lo nacional-popular en Bolivia*. Mexico City: Siglo Veintiuno Editores, 1986.

Zavaleta Mercado, René, and Luis Tapia Mealla. *La autodeterminación de las masas*. Bogotá: Siglo del Hombre Editores / Consejo Latinoamericano de Ciencias Sociales (CLACSO), 2009.